Europe
Since 1945

Praise for previous editions of Europe Since 1945

"I consider this volume invaluable to any college class working on a national field in post–World War II Europe. Given its compactness, the book is remarkably rich in illustrative detail, as well as balanced in its judgments."
　　—Franklin L. Ford, *Harvard University*

"A well-written, lively, and up-to-date account that is particularly suited for American undergraduates."
　　—Barrie M. Ratcliffe, *Northern Arizona University*

"Balanced treatment, intelligently organized, of a perplexing, often unwieldy period."
　　—Paul Teverow, *Missouri Southern College*

"Our perspective on all of the postwar years will undoubtedly undergo rapid modifications ... This text, however, will put its readers in a good position to evaluate and understand those changes."
　　—Loyd E. Lee, *State University of New York, College at New Paltz*

FIFTH EDITION

Europe

Since 1945

A Concise History

J. Robert Wegs and Robert Ladrech

Fifth edition published in 2006 by
PALGRAVE MACMILLAN
Houndmills, Basingstoke, Hampshire RG21 6XS and
175 Fifth Avenue, New York, N.Y. 10010
Companies and representatives throughout the world.

PALGRAVE MACMILLAN is the global academic imprint of the Palgrave Macmillan division of St. Martin's Press, LLC and of Palgrave Macmillan Ltd. Macmillan® is a registered trademark in the United States, United Kingdom and other countries. Palgrave is a registered trademark in the European Union and other countries.

ISBN-13: 978–1–4039–1790–4
ISBN-10: 1–4039–1790–6

This book is printed on paper suitable for recycling and made from fully managed and sustained forest sources.

A catalogue record for this book is available from the British Library.

A catalog record for this book is available from the Library of Congress.

10 9 8 7 6 5 4 3 2 1
15 14 13 12 11 10 09 08 07 06

Printed in Great Britain by CPD (Wales) Ltd, Ebbw Vale

Contents

List of Maps   x

List of Tables   xi

List of Illustrations   xiii

Preface   xv

1 A Bipolar World   1

The Emergence of the Superpowers   1
The Soviet Union at War's End   3
East–West Relations During Second World War   5
Teheran, Yalta and Potsdam   6
The Occupation of Germany   11
The Iron Curtain Descends   12
The Rift Widens   15
The War Decade Ends   21
Further Reading   22

2 From Left to Right: European Politics, 1945–48   27

Great Britain: The Welfare-State Begins   28
France: The Fourth Republic   31
Italy: A Policy of Muddling Through   36
Spain: An End to Ostracism   39
Portugal: Uninterrupted Peace   40
The Small Countries: Restoring Order   41
Greece: From Occupation to Civil War   42
Popularity of the Left   42
Further Reading   43

3 Economic Recovery in Western Europe   **45**

Characteristics of European Economic Recovery   45
Marshall Plan Stimulus to Recovery   46
Trade Stimulus to Recovery   47
Demographic Stimulus to Recovery   48
The New Capitalism   49
Industrial Concentration and
  Nationalization   51
Agricultural Developments   52
France: Economic Development   54
West Germany: Economic Development   55
Britain: Economic Decline?   56
Italy: Economic Development   58
Post-war Development Patterns   58
Further Reading   59

4 Western European Politics, 1948–60s   **61**

Italian Political Affairs   61
West German Political Affairs   63
French Political Affairs   66
British Political Affairs   71
Nordic Political Affairs   73
Benelux Political Affairs   74
Austrian Political Affairs   75
Iberian Political Affairs   75
The Economy in Political Affairs   76
Further Reading   77

5 The End of European Empire   **80**

Stages on the Road to Independence   81
India's Independence Movement   82
China's Independence Movement   84
Indochina's Independence Movement   86
Indonesia's Independence Movement   88
Middle East Independence Movements   89
Africa's Independence Movements   93
Decolonization and Immigration in Britain and France   98
Further Reading   99

6 **The Soviet Union and Eastern Europe in the 1950s and 1960s: The New Course and Polycentrism** **102**

Post-war Society under Stalin 103
The Post-war Economy under Stalin 104
The Choice of Stalin's Successor 104
Khrushchev's Leadership 106
The Polish October 106
The Hungarian Revolution 108
Polycentrism 111
Khrushchev's Fall from Power 115
Further Reading 117

7 **European Unity** **120**

The Beginnings of Unity 121
The Council of Europe 122
The European Coal and Steel Community 123
The European Defense Community 124
The European Economic Community 125
The Re-launch of the European Union: From
  the Single Market to Maastricht and Beyond 132
Deepening, Widening or Both? 134
Further Reading 138

8 **Post-war European Society: A Consumer Society and Welfare State** **139**

Europe's Class Structure 140
Wages and Fringe Benefits 142
Status of Women 144
Status of Immigrant Labourers 148
The Standard of Living 150
The Work Week and Vacation 152
The Voices of Labour 154
Social Levelling 158
A Ruling Elite? 161
Composition of the Elite 161
Education of the Elite 164
The Plutocrats 167
Political Attitudes and Social Class 169
Further Reading 171

**9 Economics and Society in the
Communist World**   **173**

The Soviet Economy   174
Khrushchev's Decentralization   174
Economic Policy from Kosygin and
  Brezhnev to Gorbachev   175
East European Economic Modernization   177
Agricultural Problems   181
Eastern European Agriculture   182
Living Standards   184
Status   187
The Role of Women   187
Social Structure   188
Changes in Education   189
The Elite   190
The Beginnings of Pluralism?   191
Further Reading   193

10 1968: Year of Crisis and Its Legacies   **196**

Student Unrest in Italy and Germany   197
Protest in France   198
Unrest in Czechoslovakia: The Prague Spring   205
Legacies of 1968: Political Violence   209
Legacies of 1968: Growth of the
  Green Movement and Parties   211
Further Reading   213

**11 Eastern Europe and the Soviet Union
to the 1970s and Beyond: Decline,
Fall and Transition**   **216**

The Brezhnev Years, 1964–82   218
The Gorbachev Phenomenon   220
Poland: Solidarity and Beyond   224
Hungary   228
East Germany: From Communist
  Orthodoxy to 'Unification'   231
Czechoslovakia: From 'Velvet Revolution' to 'Velvet Divorce' 233
Bulgaria: The Dutiful Ally   236
Romania: The Collapse of the last Stalinist Bastian   239
Yugoslavia: From Tito to Turmoil
  and then Disintegration   241

The Transition   246
Further Reading   249

12 Political and Economic Trends Since the 1960s in Western Europe   252

End of Authoritarian Government in Southern Europe   253
Foreign Policy Independence   259
European Problems: The End of
  Rapid Economic Growth   262
Germany: From Western Ally to European Power   264
French Political Transition   272
Italian Political Transition   278
The Vatican   286
British Political Transition   288
The Conflict in Northern Ireland   297
Political Transition in the Smaller Countries   298
Further Reading   304

13 Thought and Culture Since 1945   309

Philosophy   310
Literature   314
Cinema   320
Art and Architecture   324
Music   327
Culture and the Popular Media   328
Summary   329
Further Reading   330

14 Europe Enters the Twenty-first Century   332

1989 and After   332
Nationalism   333
Loss of European Distinctiveness   334
Looking to the Future   336

Index   338

List of Maps

1   Soviet Territorial Gains, 1945   16
2   Post-war Germany 1945–1949   18
3   Political/Military alignments, 1950   20
4   The End of Empire in Africa 1956–1990   92
5   European Economic Community   130
6   Growth of the EU, 1990–2004   134
7   Eastern and Central Europe   217
8   Former boundary line between East and West Germany   269

List of Tables

1–1	Growth of industrial production in Western Europe and the United States, 1901–55	2
2–1	Seats won in French elections, 1945–46	34
3–1	Compound rate of growth of gross domestic product in selected countries, 1949–63 (percentages)	47
8–1	Percentage of the working population in three economic sectors	141
8–2	2005 (estimated) GDP per person in dollars	142
8–3	Average hourly wages in manufacturing (in current US dollars)	143
8–4	Labour force participation rates and female share of labour force	145
8–5	Women's earnings as a percentage of men's average hourly earnings	146
8–6	Percentage of legislative seats held by women, 2005	147
8–7	Ownership of consumer durables (number per 1,000 inhabitants)	151
8–8	Work time needed to buy commodities in Germany	151
8–9	Per-capita private expenditure (in current US dollars)	152
8–10	Private consumption per capita using current PPPs	153
8–11	Minimum paid vacation mandates for full time workers who have worked for one year (2003)	153
8–12	Working days lost to strikes and lockouts	156
8–13	Trade union membership as a percentage of wage earners	157
8–14	Social mobility of the population 35–64 years by father's socio-economic group	159
8–15	Portion of total income received by the top 10 per cent of families before taxes	168
8–16	The decline in class voting	170
9–1	Comparing purchasing power in East Germany (GDR) and West Germany (FRG), April 1, 1990 (in hours of work by an average industrial worker)	177
9–2	The estimated hard-currency debt of the Soviet Union and East European states, 1990	179
9–3	Per-capita GNP (in 1977 US dollars)	180

9–4 Basic wage differentials in the Soviet Union, 1963
     (in US dollars per year, before taxes)   185
9–5 Per-capita meat consumption in 1978 and 1989   189
9–6 Worker and peasant students at Czech, East German
     and Polish universities   191
11–1 Polish ownership of consumer durables (per 100 households) 227
12–1 Declining numbers in uniform   262
12–2 *Bundestag* seats and votes (in percentages)   265
12–3 Seats and votes (in percentages) in the National Assembly
     throughout the Fifth Republic   273
12–4 Seats and votes (in percentages) in the Italian
     Chamber of Deputies   280
12–5 Seats and votes (in percentages) in the House
     of Commons since 1945   291

List of Illustrations

1 During World War II, cities on both sides were ravaged
by bombing raids. However, Leningrad, which was under
siege for two years, suffered especially severe damage and
loss of life. (© Getty Images)   6

2 Winston Churchill, Harry Truman and Joseph Stalin shake
hands after a meeting at Potsdam in July 1945. (© Getty Images)   11

3 Charles de Gaulle's triumphal return to France in June 1944
is symbolized in this enthusiastic reception by the people of
Bayeux. (© Bettmann/Corbis)   32

4 Election campaign posters in Rome, 1948. (© Istituto Luce/
Gestione Archivi Alinari, Firenze)   38

5 This automobile plant in Birmingham, England, helped to
meet the growing demand for passenger cars in postwar Europe.
(© Getty Images)   49

6 Algerian independence rally. (© Getty Images)   70

7 Mahatma Gandhi (*on right*) chats with Jawaharlal Nehru at
a meeting of the All-India Congress in Bombay in July 1946.
These two men supplied the leadership in the Indian liberation
movement. (© Empics)   82

8 Nikita Khrushchev, Mao Zedong and Ho Chi Minh at a banquet
in Peking (Beijing) marking the tenth anniversary of the founding
of the People's Republic of China, September 30, 1959.
(© Underwood & Underwood/Corbis)   85

9 Housing projects with apartments affordable to the average
citizen sprang up in new Europe during the postwar economic
resurgence. This building, located in a suburb of Paris, France,
has 450 apartments and houses 1,500 tenants. In 1959, when it
was built, it was the longest building in France. (© Keystone/
Getty Images (UK) Ltd.)   160

10 Former British Prime Minister Margaret Thatcher (*left*) and
Norwegian Prime Minister Gro Harlem Brundtland converse
on the steps of 10 Downing Street, the British government
leader's residence. The two served as Prime Ministers longer
than any other women in postwar Europe. (© Empics)   163

11 Paris demonstration in support of French students, May 13,
1968. (© Topham Picturepoint)   201

12 Former Italian Prime Minister Aldo Moro, murdered by the
    Red Brigades, who were holding him captive. (© Mykola
    Lazarenko/Reuters/Corbis)   210
13 Mikhail S. Gorbachev, the last Soviet Communist Party
    General Secretary, served from 1985 to 1991. (© Empics)   221
14 The Berlin Wall served as a symbol of the Cold War and, later,
    of East German economic and political failure. It was opened in
    November 1989. (© Magnum Photos)   232
15 McDonald's in St Petersburg. (Photo: Dirk Ingo Franke. This image
    is licensed under the "http://www.gnu.org/copyleft/fdl.html"
    GNU Free Documentation License)   246
16 Orange revolution demonstration in Kiev, Ukraine. (© Mykola
    Lazarenko/Reuters/ Corbis)   247
17 German army jeeps participating in French national day
    parade in Paris. (© Corbis)   261
18 President Clinton points out people in the crowd to
    Pope John Paul II upon his arrival in Denver, Colorado,
    in August 1993. (© Empics)   287
19 British Prime Minister Tony Blair. (© Empics)   294
20 Sinn Fein leader Gerry Adams (*left*) attending a peace rally
    in Belfast, Northern Ireland, in September 1994. (© Empics)   296
21 Bridget Riley, *Current*, 1964. Synthetic polymer paint on
    composition board, 58⅜ × 58⅞ inches (148.1 × 149.3 cm).
    Collection, the museum of Modern Art, New York. Philip
    Johnson fund. (© 2005 Digital Image, the Museum of
    Modern Art, New York/ Scala, Florence)   326
22 The Guggenheim Museum, Bilbao. (Photo: Michael K. Reeve.
    This image is licensed under the "http://www.gnu.org/copyleft/
    fdl.html" GNU Free Documentation License. It uses material
    from the "http:// en.wikipedia.org/wiki/Image:Guggenheim-
    bilbao-jan05.jpg")   327
23 This McDonald's restaurant on the most famous boulevard in
    Paris, the Champs-Élysées, has aroused the ire of some French
    nationalists opposed to American influence in French life.
    (© Empics)   335

Preface

Although nothing as dramatic as the fall of the Soviet Union and the end of communism in Eastern Europe, which the 4th edition traced, has occurred recently, significant change has continued apace in Europe. This is reflected in both increased coverage of events since the last edition, published in 1996, and the addition of material to earlier chapters that we hope provides a better background, that is, historical context, to contemporary issues. To this end, the chapter on 1968: Year of Crisis, is expanded to include two very different types of 'spin-off' movements, the environmental movement eventually leading to the formation of Green parties, and political terrorism, particularly in West Germany and Italy in the 1970s. The chapter on The End of European Empire now includes attention to the immediate impact of decolonization on the domestic European scene, notably in France and Britain. One 'structural' change in this edition has been the elimination of the division between the 'managed' and the 'managers' into separate chapters. Instead, the up-dated material is presented in one chapter, covering socio-economic changes in Europe.

Europe Since 1945 continues to be organized both chronologically and thematically. While the chapters on politics provide the basic chronological structure, other chapters, primarily thematic, are located at points where they will enhance the understanding of the chapters that follow. For example, the first chapter (on a bipolar world and the Sovietization of Eastern Europe) is fundamental to an understanding of the second chapter (on European politics from 1945 to 1948). The chapters on politics are tied to the other chapters by an underlying socio-economic theme that is viewed as the major determinant of political change or continuity.

We view developments in post-war Europe as the culmination of chain of events stretching back to the turn of the 20th century. However, we have not overlooked the enormous impact of the Second World War in shaping the post-war would. For example, we explain the Cold War confrontation between the Soviet Union and the United States as resulting in part from the growth of non-European power centres, beginning with the emergence of Japan and the United States in the late nineteenth century, and from the struggle between communism and capitalism that had been at work in domestic and international politics since 1917. The incorporation of Europe within a bipolar world after 1945 is, according to this interpretation, primarily the result of the attainment of superpower status by the United States and the former USSR during the twentieth century. But we do not neglect the importance of the lessening of German power, which created a power vacuum in Central Europe that could only be filled by the two superpowers. The analysis of the end of European empire moves outside the European-centered interpretive framework to explain the emergence of independent Third World countries in the post-war period as a three-stage revolutionary pattern stretching over nearly a century.

In the newly revised chapter on economic and social developments, demographic and statistical data are interwoven with theories that have been advanced to explain post-war European society. Such phenomena as changing occupational structures, the spread of affluence, and the persistence of distinct social classes and governing elites are treated in depth. In dealing with these themes, we have given special attention to the smaller European states, as they have often been forerunners in the development of the post-war welfare state. It is, for example, to Scandinavia that one must look in order to understand the impact of socio-economic policies that have been pursued by most Western European states since the Second World War. We have also examined the effect of economic modernization and communism on former Soviet and Eastern European societies, as well as their subsequent development of market economics in the 1990s.

Throughout the study, we have favoured conciseness over excessive attention to detail in order to highlight significant patterns and theses. Much of the statistical material is incorporated in the many tables located throughout the book. An annotated list of selected readings at the end of each chapter guides students in research and further study.

We wish to thank Kyril Drezov and Bulent Gokay for helpful suggestions on the sections dealing with Eastern Europe; Brian Doherty for the new discussion on social movements; and Gemma Loomes for updating most of the statistical material. Finally, we want to express our thanks to Terka Acton and Sonya Barker of Palgrave for seeing the book through to its final form.

J. Robert Wegs
Robert Ladrech

1 A Bipolar World

There are on earth today two great peoples, who, from different points of departure seem to be advancing towards the same end. They are the Russians and the Anglo-Americans.

Alexis de Tocqueville, *Democracy in America,* 1835

Contemporary history tends to exaggerate the influence of recent events – the impact of Second World War on Europe's role in world affairs, for example. Long-term developments – the growing economic and political importance of the United States, Japan and the Soviet Union, or the demographic patterns that began to reduce Europe's proportion of the world's population after 1930 do not receive the attention given to a recent cataclysmic event such as the Second World War. Europe's weakened condition, especially the collapse of the German centre, made the US and USSR military might appear even more formidable. Much of the history of the post-war years will involve a European recapturing of the worldwide influence it had in 1900 but lost in 1945.

The Emergence of the Superpowers

This is not to minimize the enormous consequences of the Second World War. But it was only one of many influences that led to the polarization of world affairs around the activities of the United States and the Soviet Union, which emerged as superpowers after the war. The eclipse of the European balance of power system seems on the surface to be primarily a result of the war. But in fact the origin of that eclipse can be traced to the pre-war emergence of power centres outside Western Europe. Even before the war, the countries rimming the Pacific Ocean had begun to shift the power balance away from Europe and usher in an era of global politics.

The meeting of the American and Soviet armies on the Elbe River in 1945 merely symbolized the changes that had been going on in the world's power relationships for over half a century. In First World War, Great Britain and France already had to call on the United States to restore the power equilibrium in Europe. In the interwar period, the growing economic strength and political importance of the United States and the Soviet Union were for the most part

1

Table 1–1   Growth of industrial production in Western Europe and the United States, 1901–55

	Index of Industrial Production (volume) (W.E. 1938 = 100)		Index of Industrial Production (per capita) (W.E. 1955 = 100)	
	WESTERN EUROPE	UNITED STATES	WESTERN EUROPE	UNITED STATES
1901	44	35	37	74
1913	69	66	51	109
1929	86	124	60	165
1937	102	127	67	160
1955	177	291	100	285

Source: Carlo M. Cipolla, *The Economic History of World Population*, 3rd ed., (Baltimore: Penguin Books, 1965), p. 69. Reprinted by permission of Penguin Books, Ltd.

ignored because of the American policy of isolation from European affairs and the Soviet concentration on internal problems.

As indicated in Table 1–1, the United States had overtaken Western Europe in industrial production in the interwar years. By 1939 the United States was producing one-third of the world's most important metals, one-third of its coal and electrical energy, two-thirds of its oil, and three-quarters of its automobiles.

Despite this rapid growth, between 1929 and 1938 the US share of the world's industrial output had actually declined from 42.2 to 32.2 per cent. This decline resulted from the Great Depression of 1929 and the growth in the Soviet share of world production from 4.3 to 18.3 per cent during the same period.

That such accelerated growth would ultimately have a far-reaching impact on world affairs did not escape the attention of some Europeans. It apparently convinced Adolf Hitler that Germany had only a short time to secure the territorial basis for competing in a world of superpowers. In 1928 Hitler wrote, 'With the American Union a new power of such dimensions has come into being as threatens to upset the whole former power and order of rank of the states.' The defeat of Germany and Japan in 1945 and the switchover to the production of war material in the United States and the Soviet Union brought about the concentration of power in the hands of the superpowers that Hitler had feared.

Although many had predicted the awesome military power exercised by the Soviet Union and the United States in 1945, few foresaw the collapse of power in Europe that brought about the Soviet–American confrontation. The Allied power of unconditional surrender made it impossible for Germany or Japan to seek a compromise peace. Leaders in both countries realized what fate awaited them and therefore exhausted their countries' resources in the hope that a last-minute miracle might avert defeat. Hitler put his hopes in German rockets, jet planes, and the possibility that the United States and the Soviet Union might come to blows before the defeat of Germany. With German resistance continuing until the fall of Berlin in May 1945, Germany lay in ruins. France, weakened by defeat, occupation and internal divisions, was incapable of assuming leadership in Europe. Only Great Britain seemed to offer an alternative power centre.

But the Second World War had in an economic sense been a hollow victory for the British. The nation that had ruled a quarter of the human race in 1914 was no match for the superpowers in 1945. The second largest creditor nation in the world in 1939, Britain became the largest debtor as a result of the Second World War. While expenditures increased fivefold during the war, exports were reduced to only 60 per cent of the pre-war total. To meet its wartime obligations, Britain had to liquidate more than a billion pounds in foreign assets.

The relative decline of Britain had begun even before the war. Its territorial base shrank as its colonies and territories gained independence or became autonomous members of the empire. Nor could it any longer tap the resources of colonies as it had done in the nineteenth century. As the empire was transformed into a commonwealth of nations in the two decades after the war, Britain was reduced to a small island nation whose population and resources were inadequate to compete with the superpowers. Although recently declassified documents have shown that Britain played a major role in shaping Western policy immediately after the war, British foreign policy in the post-war years became increasingly dependent upon the US economic and military power and the American view of world affairs. When Britain tried to act independently, as it did at Suez in 1956, American disapproval and limited British resources thwarted the attempt.

With no possibility of restoring a European power equilibrium because of the military preponderance of the Soviet Union, Western leaders were fearful that all of Europe would be at the mercy of what they saw as Soviet expansionism. A prostrate Europe appeared to offer Soviet expansionists a tempting bait. Yet did Soviet leaders actually desire an extension of Soviet hegemony over all Europe? Or, as American radical revisionists such as Gabriel Kolko and William A. Williams believe, were Soviet actions a response to the United States' attempt to use its economic and military superiority as a basis for global hegemony? Or are these positions extremist and unsupported by the evidence? The answers to these questions are to be found in Soviet and American objectives and actions.

The Soviet Union at War's End

At the end of Second World War, the Soviet Union controlled most of Eastern Europe, Manchuria, northern Korea and northern Iran and threatened to expand into Turkey. Despite Soviet military preponderance in these areas, which was soon to be of fundamental importance in determining post-war spheres of influence, Josef Stalin, as leader of the victorious Soviet forces, was awed by the enormous economic and military might of the United States and anxious about his role at home.

Stalin's fears for Soviet security, bolstered by serious weaknesses in the Soviet economy and growing suspicion and hostility abroad, were not unfounded. Twice in the previous twenty-five years Russia had suffered extensively from foreign invasions. Nearly 20 million Soviet citizens died as a direct or indirect result of Second World War. Large sections of the country were laid waste by German and Soviet armies. Cities such as Kiev and Minsk had been devastated and had to be completely rebuilt; Leningrad suffered severe damage during 900 days of siege and bombardment, and 1 million of its inhabitants – one-third the city's population – starved to death during the siege. In many industries, production had been halved because of the shortage of manpower and raw materials and the war damage to factories.

On the other hand, Stalin was keenly aware of American economic strength because of the vast amounts of US material shipped to Europe and the Soviet Union during the war and used by US and allied forces, including his own, in both the Pacific and the European war zones. Equally disturbing to him was the size of American military forces at the end of the war, numbering 12 million men as compared to the Soviet Union's 11 million. Stalin was aware that in an economic sense his country was not a superpower in comparison to the United States. To restore its economic strength, he hoped to obtain American aid and expected to acquire indispensable industrial equipment and raw materials from Germany and the countries of Eastern Europe. The US opposition to these goals was to be one of the major causes of the Cold War between East and West.

Stalin's feelings of insecurity both at home and elsewhere in the Communist world had a direct impact on his foreign policy. His opposition to independent Communist-led revolutionary movements, such as those in China and Yugoslavia, revealed his fear of outside rivals. His opposition to the leftist forces in the Greek civil war and to Yugoslav support of the rebels reflected his fear that President Tito of Yugoslavia might establish a Balkan Communist confederation big enough to challenge Stalin's pre-eminence in Eastern Europe and his domination over the Eastern European Communist parties. It was his dislike of Tito's independent course that led to Yugoslavia's ostracism from the Soviet-dominated Communist bloc in 1948.

Within the Soviet Union, Stalin had been excessively concerned with the possible ideological contamination of Soviet citizens because of their contacts with Western Europe during the war. After the war, his desire to keep the West unaware of Soviet economic weakness and to avoid further 'contamination' from Western ideas led to the curtailment of contacts with the West for all but a few Soviet nationals. By preventing Western knowledge of Soviet domestic affairs, Stalin only increased the mystery concerning life in the Soviet Union and promoted Western abhorrence of what came to be known as Stalinism – the dictatorial exercise of state power by a small elite to bring about certain Marxist–Leninist objectives. Widespread fear among nations of the West that such a system might spread beyond the Soviet sphere of influence provided considerable support for the eventual United States policy of containment of communism.

In order to achieve national security against a resurgent Germany, which he felt the West was not willing to provide, Stalin tried during the war and after to gain control over Eastern Europe. He had become convinced of Western hostility towards the Soviet Union long before the Cold War. He well remembered the West's attempts to defeat bolshevism after the First World War, the sell-out of Czechoslovakia in 1938 at the Munich Conference, and the failure to side with the Soviet Union against Germany before the war. In order to avoid an immediate war with Germany and gain control of additional territory, Stalin felt it advantageous to sign the Nazi–Soviet Non-aggression Pact in 1939. The Pact restored territories lost as a result of the First World War, Bessarabia and White Russia, and permitted the annexation of the Baltic countries (Latvia, Lithuania and Estonia). While this pact gave the Soviet Union two more years to prepare its armies for the conflict with Hitler, Stalin apparently considered it to be a more permanent protection against Nazi attack. Both N. Khrushchev's unofficial memoirs and Marshal Zhukov's unedited memoirs contend that Stalin was so shocked by the invasion that he was unable to act for over a week.

East–West Relations During Second World War

Stalin's suspicions concerning Western intentions were not allayed by Western actions during the war. His actions were therefore determined by traditional balance of power considerations aimed at obtaining strategic and economic benefits for the Soviet Union after the war. As early as the Moscow Conference in December 1941, Stalin offered Great Britain whatever security arrangements it wanted in France, the Low Countries, Norway and Denmark if the Western Allies would grant the Soviet Union similar rights in Eastern Poland, Finland and Romania.

Anthony Eden, at that time British foreign minister, later wrote of that conference, 'Russian ideas were already starkly definite. They changed little during the next three years, for their purpose was to secure the most tangible physical guarantees for Russia's future safety.' Only because of President Franklin D. Roosevelt's objections – British Prime Minister Winston Churchill had already accepted – were these East European riders excluded from the subsequent Anglo-Soviet Treaty of Alliance of May 1942.

Serious rifts began to develop among the Allies in 1942. Since Stalin was bearing the brunt of the German attack, he wanted his Western allies to open a second front in Western Europe to divert some German forces from the Russian front. The inability of the West to launch the Normandy invasion until June 1944, fed Stalin's suspicion that the West hoped to weaken Soviet forces by prolonged conflict in order to reduce Soviet strength in the post-war period.

Stalin's suspicions of Western intentions were further borne out, in his mind, when the United States and Great Britain tried to exclude the Soviet Union from any control over liberated southern Italy. Stalin's demands to be given a voice in Italian affairs prompted the Western Allies to form an

Leningrad during World War II which was under siege for two years.
(© Getty Images)

Advisory Council for Italy with French as well as Soviet participation. However, this council proved to be powerless. Real jurisdiction in Italy was lodged in an Anglo-American Control Commission and the military forces on the scene. A noted American historian, W. H. McNeill, astutely observed, 'Having excluded Russia from any but nominal participation in Italian affairs, the Western Allies prepared the way for their own exclusion from any but a marginal share in the affairs of Eastern Europe.'

Teheran, Yalta and Potsdam

Since Soviet domination of Eastern Europe eventually became one of the major reasons for East–West hostility, an understanding of the wartime diplomacy that facilitated Soviet control sheds much light on later Soviet actions in the area. Even before the Big Three meetings of US, Soviet and British leaders at Yalta and Potsdam – often viewed as the meetings that led to Soviet control of Eastern Europe – three factors had led Stalin to believe he would have a free hand in that area: The first factor was the Soviet military occupation of Eastern Europe. The second was the Anglo-American decision not to invade Germany through the Balkans. This decision, reached by the Big Three at the Teheran Conference in November 1943, left only Soviet forces and troops from Balkan nations to clear Eastern Europe of Axis troops. Churchill wanted to invade Europe through Greece and the Balkans for political reasons: to prevent Soviet domination of Eastern Europe. But his proposal was considered militarily inappropriate by US military experts at Teheran, who felt that a single concerted attack across the English Channel would achieve much faster results. By recognizing Soviet supremacy in an eastern zone of operations, the

Teheran meeting limited the West's participation in the post-war political affairs in that area.

The third factor that convinced Stalin he would have a free hand in the Balkans were the October 1944 agreements he negotiated with Churchill. When Soviet troops liberated Romania and Bulgaria in August–September 1944, Churchill decided to head off further Soviet expansion into Greece and Yugoslavia by reaching a *modus vivendi* with Stalin. At this meeting Churchill and Stalin agreed that the Soviet Union should have 90 per cent control over Romania and 75 per cent control over Bulgaria. With Soviet armies firmly in control of both countries, Churchill felt he was sacrificing little. Yugoslavia and Hungary were to be controlled equally. In return, Churchill got what he wanted – 90 per cent Western jurisdiction over Greece. While these percentages were vague, each side understood that control belonged to whoever had over 50 per cent jurisdiction.

Although Churchill was later severely criticized for such horse-trading, the Western Allies could have expected little more in the Balkans. Even though President Roosevelt never approved these agreements, Churchill's acquiescence apparently convinced Stalin that the West would accept Soviet predominance in these areas. Moreover, Churchill believed Stalin had upheld the agreement when the latter permitted the British to defeat the Communist forces in Greece during the first stage of the Greek Civil War in 1944. But it is also true that Stalin realized that the power balance in Greece favoured Britain and the United States and that Greece was hardly essential to Soviet security. As the post-war Vice President of Yugoslavia, Milovan Djilas, related in *Conversations with Stalin*, Stalin told a Yugoslav delegation, 'What do you think, that Great Britain and the US – the US, the most powerful state in the world – will permit you to break their line of communication in the Mediterranean Sea! Nonsense. And we have no navy. The uprising in Greece must be stopped, and as quickly as possible.'

The Yalta Declaration and the United Nations During the Yalta Conference in February 1945, Stalin's *Realpolitik* confronted Roosevelt's utopian view of post-war politics across an unbridgeable gulf. Stalin wanted to resolve issues before the war ended, but Roosevelt wanted to put off making decisions in order to avoid East – West acrimony that might doom his pet scheme of a post-war worldwide organization. By postponing final decisions on such issues as German borders and reparations, and by making some concessions to Stalin over Eastern Europe, Roosevelt avoided a direct confrontation that might, in his opinion, have led to a Soviet refusal to join the United Nations.

Roosevelt was convinced that, having obtained Soviet approval for the formation of the United Nations at Yalta, he could assure the world's nations that they would have a forum for the resolution of all post-war problems. After returning from the Yalta Conference, he told a joint session of Congress that the agreements at Yalta

> ought to spell the end of the system of unilateral action, the exclusive alliances, the spheres of influence, the balances of power, and all the

expedients that have been tried for centuries and have always failed. We propose to substitute for all these, a universal organization in which all peace-loving nations will finally have a chance to join.

When Stalin agreed to the Yalta Declaration on Liberated Europe that would provide governments responsive to the will of the people, he thought it an American propaganda weapon for home use. The 1944 agreements with Churchill and the presence of Soviet armies in Eastern Europe reassured him that the declaration was only for public consumption. He believed foreign affairs should be settled in private among government leaders, not decided in open forum. One month after signing the declaration, Stalin forced Romania and Bulgaria to accept governments 'friendly' to the Soviet Union.

In retrospect, the Yalta Declaration must be seen as a rather naive document. To expect the Soviet Union to withdraw its troops from Eastern Europe and permit free elections was unrealistic. Yet perhaps Roosevelt expected that world opinion, centred in the United Nations, could actuate the Soviet Union to carry out the agreements reached in the declaration. Roosevelt was surely aware the West would have a majority in the UN Security Council (in which the five permanent members could exercise a veto) since Great Britain, France and China could at that time be expected to side more with the American viewpoint.

Stalin obviously viewed the United Nations with great suspicion. After having long been denied membership in a similar world organization, the League of Nations, and then having been expelled from it in 1939 for invading Finland, the Soviet Union could not be expected to view the United Nations, where the West would have a four-to-one majority in the Security Council, as a guarantor of Soviet security. So Stalin continued to strengthen Soviet control over Eastern Europe and at the same time reluctantly permitted his foreign minister, Vyacheslav Molotov, to sign the United Nations charter in April 1945. Although the USSR would be in the minority in the United Nations, its veto power in the Security Council could block any proposals that it considered detrimental to Soviet interests.

Germany: Reparations or Dismemberment? Disagreements among the Allies over Germany also originated before the wartime conferences at Yalta and Potsdam. Allied failure to reach firm commitments on post-war German reparations and boundaries before the end of the war, led to Germany's division and contributed mightily to the development of the Cold War. The Allies' inability to resolve the German problem had its immediate cause in differing Soviet and Western attitudes towards reparations. But the reparations question stemmed from the earlier disagreement over Germany's future. The Soviet Union and France desired not only the destruction of Germany's war-making potential but also its dismemberment. On the other hand, the United States and Great Britain wanted to destroy Germany's war-making potential but retreated from the idea of dismemberment when it was discussed at the Quebec Conference in September 1944.

At Quebec US Secretary of the Treasury, Henry Morgenthau, presented his plan to dismember Germany, to eliminate all heavy industry in the newly constituted areas, and to leave Germany under the occupation of the Soviet Union and France. The plan was the major topic of discussion. Stalin already suspected that the West's late opening of a second front against the Germans was a prelude to the establishment of a German bulwark against the Soviet Union. To reassure him that they were not going to adopt a lenient policy towards Germany, Roosevelt and Churchill did not reject the Morgenthau Plan outright.

Soon after the Quebec Conference, however, Western actions and statements indicated that the West was indeed going to adopt a policy of leniency. To avoid specific guarantees to the Soviet Union on the amount of reparations it would receive, the British and American leaders now sought to postpone any discussion of Germany's future until after the war.

Roosevelt seemed to repudiate the Morgenthau Plan completely in December 1944 when he told his new Secretary of State Edward Stettinius that Germany should be permitted to 'come back industrially to meet her own needs' after the war and that the United States would not allow the imposition of reparations. Roosevelt was apparently able to overcome his fear of a resurgent Germany when confronted by the spectre of an all-powerful Soviet Union. He also believed that support of the Morgenthau Plan would steel German resistance, lengthen the war and possibly cost him some support in the coming presidential elections.

At the Yalta Conference in February 1945, Stalin directly challenged Western attempts to avoid specific agreement over reparations or dismemberment. Stalin wanted to have a specific dismemberment clause in the German surrender terms. He was opposed by Churchill and circumvented by Roosevelt, who was against such a clause but wanted Soviet help against Japan after victory was achieved in Europe. The only agreement reached was that the Allies would undertake the 'complete disarmament, demilitarization and the dismemberment of Germany as they deem requisite for future peace and security.' In other words, each ally could interpret the clause as it wished once Germany was defeated. An Allied Control Council, agreed upon at Yalta to provide and implement uniform policies throughout the separate zones of occupation, proved to be ineffective.

When the topic of discussion at Yalta switched to reparations, the impasse between the Soviet and Anglo-American views was even more readily discernible. Stalin wanted to set specific reparation sums; Churchill and Roosevelt opposed the idea. Roosevelt maintained that no precise amounts could be agreed on until after the war, when it could be determined how much Germany could pay. Churchill agreed with Roosevelt that no specific sums could be decided and that no specific percentage of total reparations for the Soviet Union could be set. Ultimately, it was decided at Yalta to instruct a Reparations Commissions, to be set up in Moscow, that a total reparations bill of $20 billion – of which 50 per cent should go to the Soviet Union – should serve as a basis for discussion after the war. Underlying the practical obstacles to reaching specific reparations figures was the Anglo-American desire not to weaken Germany to the extent that central Europe would be easy prey to Soviet expansion into the heart of Europe. Immediately after the Yalta Conference

Churchill said he wanted to postpone the question of 'dismembering Germany until my doubts about Russian intentions have been cleared away.'

Equally indecisive were the discussions concerning Germany's post-war borders. At Moscow in October 1944, Churchill had acceded to the Soviet desire to internationalize the Saar and Ruhr areas. Now, more concerned about Moscow's intentions, he sought to delay any agreements that would be binding after the war. Concerning Germany's eastern borders, the most the conference could agree on was that Poland had the right to expand north and west but that the final borders should not be established until a post-war peace conference was held. Stalin was willing to accept postponement of the Polish–German border issue since he knew his armies would control that territory at the war's end. Moreover, the division of Germany into occupation zones, agreed to at Quebec by Churchill and Roosevelt and at Yalta by the Big Three, put eastern Germany and thus the Polish–German border area under Soviet jurisdiction.

Since no major post-war peace conference was held because of the animosity among the Allies, both Germany's borders and the reparations issue were finally determined by the occupation zones set up at Yalta and confirmed at the Potsdam Conference in July 1945. Fears that the United States would not keep its troops in Europe for long led Churchill to demand and obtain a zone of occupation for France in order to counter the Soviet presence in Europe. At Potsdam the Big Three agreed to permit each occupying power to remove German property from its own zone but not so much as to jeopardize a tolerable German standard of living. In addition, the Soviet Union was to get 25 per cent of the dismantled industrial equipment from the Western zones, since most German industry was located there, in exchange for food and raw materials from the Soviet zone. The conference participants also agreed to establish the Polish–German border along the Oder and western Neisse rivers, thus moving Poland 200 miles to the west, and permit the Soviet Union to retain the areas annexed in 1939. Little else was achieved at Potsdam, owing to the growing intransigence between Stalin and Western leaders.

President Harry Truman, who had replaced Roosevelt at the conference table, was emboldened by America's explosion of the first atomic bomb in July 1945 and angry at what he considered to be Soviet betrayal of the Yalta agreements over Eastern Europe. Churchill was equally convinced that this new atomic weapon gave the West irresistible power. But the bomb never became as significant a factor in East–West negotiations as Churchill or Truman expected. Stalin was well aware that the United States would have few atomic bombs and would permit their use against the Soviet Union only under the most extraordinary provocation. He told a United Press correspondent, 'Atom bombs are designed to scare those with weak nerves, but they cannot decide wars because there are not enough of them.' Although only the threat of the bomb was used in diplomatic negotiations, its existence did significantly inhibit the actions of both East and West because of its destructive potential. As we shall see, it was instrumental in restraining both the Soviet Union and the West during the Berlin crisis of 1948–49.

Despite these growing differences over Germany, Truman still hoped to resolve East–West differences by establishing a personal relationship with

Winston Churchill, Harry Truman and Joseph Stalin at Potsdam in July 1945.
(© Getty Images)

Stalin in late 1945. *The Long Peace* by John Gaddis has established that Britain and France were much more distrustful of Soviet actions than was the United States. Truman opposed setting-up an American sphere of influence in Europe before 1948 even though he was constantly pressed to do so by the Europeans. But the continued Soviet resort to unilateral actions gradually led Truman to a policy of confrontation and eventually 'containment of communism' by 1947–48.

The Occupation of Germany

At the war's end, France and the Soviet Union hoped to rebuild their own economies and destroy Germany's war-making potential. To do so they immediately began to strip their zones of industrial plants and material. But the exchange of industrial equipment for food and raw materials between the

Soviet and Western zones led to endless acrimony because the Soviet Union and the West put different values on those goods and arrived at different estimates of a minimum tolerable level of industrial capacity for Germany. The United States maintained that the permissible industrial capacity would have to be raised in the American zone because of the influx of refugees from the Soviet Union. The Soviets refused to ship stipulated quantities of food from their zone to the Western zones because, they maintained, insufficient industrial equipment was being sent from the Western zones. This led the Western Allies to refuse, in May 1946, to continue dismantling and shipping industrial material from their zones to the Soviet Union. Only if both sides had been completely trusting and cooperative could an amicable settlement have been reached over the exchange of goods. Great Britain and the United States, faced with severe food shortages and economic chaos in their zones, stopped sending reparations out and began bringing food in.

Soviet policy in the Soviet zone contributed to the political impasse. East German Communist party leader Walter Ulbricht, who had been in exile in Moscow since Hitler's destruction of the Communist party in Germany, returned to the Soviet zone even before the war ended. After the war the Soviet Union permitted other parties to exist, although the Communist party was clearly favoured. But when local elections went against the Communists in early 1946, the Soviet Union decided to eliminate all other political parties; even the Socialist party was forced to unite with the Communists in a new Socialist Unity party (Sozialistische Einheitspartei Deutschlands, or SED) in April 1946. Stalin's policy towards the Soviet zone was guided by his threefold desire to keep Germany weak, to use it to help rebuild Soviet industry and to prevent the emergence of any groups, political or otherwise, that might challenge Soviet jurisdiction.

It was Western distrust of Soviet intentions as well as the economic misery in the Western zones that prompted the United States and Britain to change their occupation policies. Secretary of State James Byrnes's call for a revival of the German economy in September 1946 was soon followed by the fusion of the American and British zones into a single economic and administrative unit called Bizonia. France refused to merge its zone with the British and American zones at this time, since it opposed any measures that might lead to a unitary and therefore more powerful German state. It was still possible in 1946, however, that some sort of amicable settlement would prevent the division of Germany. East–West opposition had not yet reached the fever pitch that marked the relationship after 1947 and prevented any diplomatic solution.

The Iron Curtain Descends

The announcement of the Truman Doctrine and the Marshall Plan, and Stalin's reactions to them, split the world into two hostile camps in 1947. Until then, several important issues had been resolved between the superpowers. The Soviet Union withdrew its support of the Iranian separatist movement in May 1946 when the issue was brought before the UN Security Council. Determined

Western opposition, epitomized in Churchill's denunciation described below, apparently convinced Stalin that the attempt to incorporate northern Iran into the Soviet Union would lead to a major East–West confrontation. Moreover, the Soviet Union accepted its failure to obtain an oil concession when the Iranian Parliament refused to ratify the withdrawal agreement. The Soviets also gave up their claim for a base in the straits connecting the Black Sea to the Mediterranean when the Turkish government, bolstered by the dispatch of an American naval contingent, rejected their demands.

While these issues were being resolved according to traditional power considerations, anti-Communism gained importance in the confrontations. Although Truman and his Secretary of State James Byrnes remained ambivalent in their attitudes towards the Soviet Union, the British moved earlier under the influence of Foreign Secretaries Anthony Eden and Ernest Bevin towards a policy of firm opposition to Soviet aspirations. Truman's shift towards confrontation was heavily influenced by foreign policy advisor George F. Kennan's famous telegram in February 1946 in which he first sketched out the theory of containment, that is, opposition to what he depicted as ideologically driven Soviet expansionism. Then, in March 1946, at Westminster College in Fulton, Missouri, Churchill delivered a stinging attack on the Soviet Union. With Truman at his side, Churchill declared:

> A shadow has fallen upon the scenes so lately lighted by the allied victory. Nobody knows what Soviet Russia and its Communist international organization intends to do in the immediate future, or what are the limits, if any, to their expansive and proselytizing tendencies. ... From Stettin in the Baltic to Trieste in the Adriatic, an iron curtain has descended across the continent.

He warned that many nations, including Italy and France, were imperiled by Communist parties or 'fifth columns' which constituted 'a growing challenge and peril to Christian civilization.'

Concern about a worldwide Communist peril increased in 1946 as the forces of Mao Zedong gained strength in China and economic conditions deteriorated in Europe. Communist parties in France and Italy were seen as fifth columns ready to seize power when the economic collapse came. The decisive events that propelled the United States into a worldwide struggle against communism in 1947 were Communist support for the leftists in Greece and the British announcement it could no longer afford to extend economic aid to Greece and Turkey. The fact that it was Yugoslavia that supported the Greek leftists against Stalin's wishes was either not known or was purposely misrepresented by the Truman administration, since it would be easier to secure congressional approval of aid to Greece and Turkey if Yugoslav aid to Greek rebels was depicted as an aspect of Communist expansionism.

Since the Truman administration had previously drawn up plans for economic and military aid to Greece, Truman in February 1947 asked Congress for $400 million in aid to Turkey and Greece 'to support free peoples who are resisting subjugation by armed minorities or by outside pressures.' Arthur Vandenberg, chairman of the Senate Foreign Relations Committee, advised Truman 'to scare the hell out of the country' if he wanted congressional approval for what later would become known as the Truman Doctrine. Truman therefore stressed in his message to Congress that the aid was necessary to maintain freedom throughout the world. He did not mention the more legitimate foreign policy goal of protecting Western interests in the Eastern Mediterranean because he realized that such an objective was unlikely to sway the public. Identifying as a Soviet aim the spread of communism, rather than traditional Russian imperialism, the Truman Doctrine committed the United States to a global crusade to stem that tide.

The military and economic might of the two superpowers and Truman's ideological campaign against 'totalitarian communism' forced many nations to line up with one superpower or the other. A nation's support for either side was now equated with ideological commitment to the American or Soviet world view, irrespective of its domestic politics. Congress, convinced even before Truman of the spectre of Communist subversion, overwhelmingly approved $400 million of US aid for Greece and Turkey. This was a turning point not only for the United States but also for Great Britain. A dominant power in 1939, Britain was now forced into dependence on the United States, for only through co-operation with the United States could Britain hope to obtain the financial aid needed to overcome its severe domestic problems and maintain its empire.

Even more alarming to Washington was what appeared to be the imminent economic and political collapse of Western Europe itself. The immediate goal was to provide for German economic recovery within a general European recovery programme so that it would be acceptable in Europe and the United States. Fear that Communist parties in Italy and France would gain power in the event of economic chaos was enough to convince Americans that massive aid was necessary. The US response to Europe's economic needs, unlike the Truman Doctrine, was not couched in ideological terms. As formulated by Secretary of State George Marshall and a policy planning staff directed by George F. Kennan, the Marshall Plan was, in Marshall's words, 'directed not against country or doctrine, but against hunger, poverty, desperation, and chaos.' But the Undersecretary of State Dean Acheson, arguing that the Marshall Plan was to provide aid to 'free people who are seeking to preserve their independence and democratic institutions and human freedoms against totalitarian pressures, either internal or external,' viewed it as another tool in the battle against Soviet totalitarianism.

This European Recovery Program, the official name of the Marshall Plan, was ostensibly formulated to help all European countries, including the Soviet Union and its so-called satellites in Eastern Europe. Marshall and Kennan had opposed the sharp ideological tone of the Truman Doctrine and did not want the United States to appear to be responsible for the final division of Europe between East and West. Still, it was extremely doubtful that Marshall Plan aid would have been extended to the USSR. If Stalin rejected the programme – as he did in July 1947 – the onus of Europe's division would be shifted to the Soviet Union.

Stalin rejected the Marshall Plan because he thought it would increase US influence in Europe, including Eastern Europe, and thereby threaten Soviet hegemony in those areas it considered essential to its own security. Whatever its needs, the Soviet Union would not accede to the requirement that participating countries reveal their financial needs to an all-European conference that would determine the total amount required from the United States. Furthermore, Stalin did not expect that Europe would recover and believed it better to have a weak Western Europe that posed no threat to Soviet security than a revitalized Europe under the influence of the United States. When Stalin forbade the Eastern European satellite countries to accept Marshall Plan help, he completed the division of Europe into two antagonistic parts.

The Rift Widens

Realizing that an accommodation with the United States was impossible after the Truman Doctrine and Marshall Plan, the Soviet Union launched an offensive in 1947 to bring territories it occupied more firmly under its control. Soviet leaders instructed Eastern European Communist parties to remove all non-communists from their governments and all national communists (those who would not follow Moscow's direction) from the Communist parties. Diversity within the Communist camp was no longer tolerated as it had been from 1945 to 1947 when Stalin thought there might be a resolution of East–West problems.

The Communist International (Comintern) had been set up by Lenin to promote Communist revolution throughout the world and had been disbanded during the Second World War to please Stalin's Western allies. In its place a new organization, the Cominform (Communist Information Bureau), was established in September 1947. The Cominform's principal aim was to pressure Communist countries into strict obedience to Moscow to prevent them from being seduced into cooperation with the West. Terming the Marshall Plan and Truman Doctrine 'an attack on the principle of national sovereignty,' Andrei A. Zhdanov, the major Soviet delegate to the Cominform conference, instructed Western European Communist parties to 'take up the standard of defense of the national independence and sovereignty of their countries'.

Between 1946 and 1948, Communist parties loyal to Stalin, in many cases supported by the fact that the Soviet Red Army was stationed on their soil, consolidated their grip on power in Poland, Romania, Bulgaria, Hungary and Czechoslovakia. The method by which Stalin orchestrated the takeovers was similar. At the end of hostilities, coalition governments were formed, which included Communist parties in varying degrees of influence, ranging from dominance to junior member. However, through a combination of forced mergers with other leftist parties, rigged parliamentary elections and sheer bullying and persecution of individual non-Communist politicians, many of whom fled their respective countries, Communist parties were able to eliminate formal and legal opposition to their rule.

In Yugoslavia, Tito had led the Communist Underground Resistance that helped defeat the Nazis before Soviet troops arrived. Stalin could not dominate

Tito as he did other Communist leaders. While Stalin had been engaged during and after the war in political horse-trading over Eastern Europe, Greece and Trieste, Tito had been busy promoting the international Communist movement by aiding leftist forces in Greece. Tito was unwilling to accept the United Front government in Yugoslavia desired by Stalin and the Western Allies. Not only did Tito establish a one-party dictatorship, but by prematurely proclaiming Yugoslavia a people's democratic, he appeared to place Yugoslavia ahead of the Soviet Union in the transition to a true Communist society.

Several events were to intervene before Europe was finally divided into two extremely hostile camps. The first was the Communist takeover in

Czechoslovakia in February 1948. The heated reaction in the West portrayed the Czech coup d'etat as merely another step in the worldwide expansion of communism rather than a Soviet move to strengthen its control over Eastern Europe. Although the Czech coup convinced the United States Congress to approve the Marshall Plan, it was hardly unexpected in Washington. George Kennan, the formulator of the US policy of containment of communism, has supported the revisionist historians who insist that the administration knew the coup was not an indication of new Soviet aggressiveness. He wrote in his memoirs that the coup 'had nothing to do with any Soviet decision to launch its military forces against the West,' and that Soviet action 'flowed logically from the inauguration of the Marshall Plan Program, and was confidently predicted by US government observers six months in advance of the event'.

Nevertheless, Truman said the Czech coup proved that the Soviet Union intended to expand Communism 'to the remaining free nations of Europe'. His response to the coup and the previously formed Cominform was to introduce a bill in Congress for universal military training and a return to conscription. Panicked British and French leaders pressed the United States for a military alliance, and the foreign ministers of Great Britain, France, Belgium, Holland and Luxembourg signed a treaty in March 1948 establishing the Western Union for collective defence against armed attack on any member nation. The West further held the London Six-Power Conference (excluding the Soviet Union) to discuss further integration of the Western occupation zones in Germany that led ultimately to the first major East–West confrontation in Berlin in June 1948.

London Conference representatives announced in a communiqué of 6 March 1948 that agreement had been reached on a plan for a federal form of government and the further economic integration of the Western zones. This provoked an angry reaction from the Soviet Union. Stalin realized that successful implementation of the London communiqué would end his hopes of keeping Germany neutralized and weak. Two weeks later Soviet Marshal Sokolovsky ended the charade of East–West co-operation concerning Germany by walking out of the Allied Control Council deliberations in Berlin. Next, Stalin ordered a meeting of the Second People's Congress in the Soviet zone of Germany in March to create a People's Council (later the People's Chamber of the German Democratic Republic) for the Soviet zone. He also began restricting access to Berlin on 31 March, apparently in the belief that this would divide the Western powers and force a retreat from their plans. But France, now receiving Marshall Plan aid, finding no support for the plan to keep Germany dismembered and weak, and confident that the United States and Britain were going to be in Germany indefinitely because of the Soviet threat, had less reason to fear the unification of the Western zones. On 18 June 1948, France agreed to fuse its zone with Bizonia, the Anglo-American zone. Now Stalin was presented with a solid Western front.

The Berlin Blockade   When the West decided to reform Germany's currency by introducing a new deutsche mark on 20 June 1948, Stalin realized that a strong German currency under Western sponsorship would destroy the weak

18

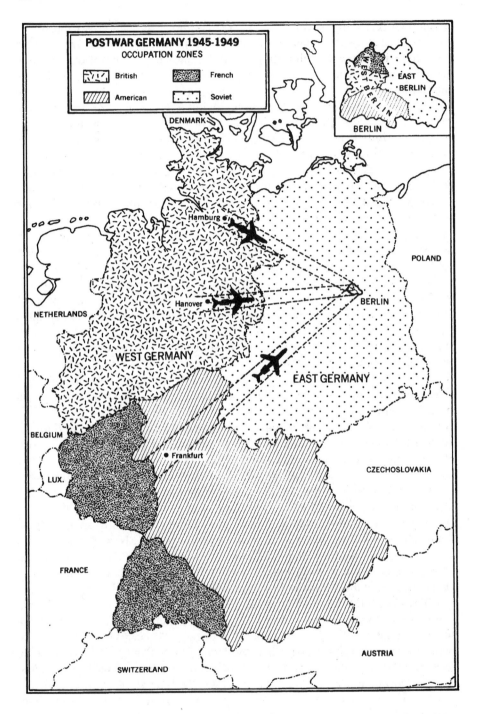

POSTWAR GERMANY 1945-1949
OCCUPATION ZONES

British   French
American   Soviet

DENMARK

NETHERLANDS

Hamburg

Hanover

WEST GERMANY

BELGIUM

LUX.

Frankfurt

FRANCE

SWITZERLAND

POLAND

BERLIN

EAST GERMANY

CZECHOSLOVAKIA

AUSTRIA

WEST
BERLIN

EAST
BERLIN

BERLIN

German currency in the Soviet zone. The Soviet Union therefore responded four days later by introducing a similar currency reform in its zone. At the same time it initiated a blockage of all land traffic into and out of Berlin, which was deep inside the Soviet zone. Stalin hoped the blockage would be a bargaining weapon to prevent the establishment of a strong German state under Western auspices since the French had not yet decided to merge its zone with the Anglo-American zones. But this plan was thwarted when the Western powers instituted an airlift that kept Berlin supplied with food, fuel and medicines for nearly a year.

Stalin knew he had lost. Recognizing that a Soviet attack on Western aircraft would mean war, denied the bargaining leverage he had sought, and fast losing face in what appeared to be an attempt to starve 2.25 million residents of Berlin into submission, Stalin had to call off the blockade in May 1949. This first major East-West confrontation made vividly apparent the limits of Soviet power when faced with the West's air superiority and nuclear monopoly. Stalin could not use his massive land superiority against Berlin to force the West to bargain because of the West's ability to destroy Russian cities with airpower and nuclear weapons.

The New West German State   The Berlin blockade speeded up the West's plans for the establishment of a separate German state comprising the three Western zones. After the West founded the German Federal Republic on 21 May 1949, the Soviet Union responded by establishing the German Democratic Republic in October of the same year. The first parliamentary elections in West Germany produced a Christian Democratic (CDU) majority with Konrad Adenauer as the chancellor. Having gained fame for his resistance to Nazism, Adenauer was a popular choice. He also represented almost everything the West desired in a German leader: cooperation with the West; rapprochement with Germany's traditional enemy, France; a federal structure rather than the highly centralized Nazi state; and, after 1948, an active anticommunist posture.

The United States distrusted the other major German party, the Social Democrats (SPD). SPD leader Kurt Schumacher's call for the nationalization of industry and banks, combined with the growing Western fear of the Soviet Union, had prompted active Western support for the CDU prior to the Berlin Crisis. Although the CDU had a slim seven-seat advantage over the SPD in the legislature, Adenauer put together a coalition with the Free Democratic Party (FDP) that excluded the SPD from any role in the government.

US Military Might in Europe   The Berlin crisis provided a powerful stimulus for the integration of Western Europe into a military alliance dominated by the United States. Negotiations began in July 1948 after the US Congress dropped the traditional American opposition to alliances with foreign powers. In April 1949 eleven European countries joined with the United States in forming the North Atlantic Treaty Organization (NATO). Thus began the return of American military might in Western Europe and the division of Europe into two armed camps.

20

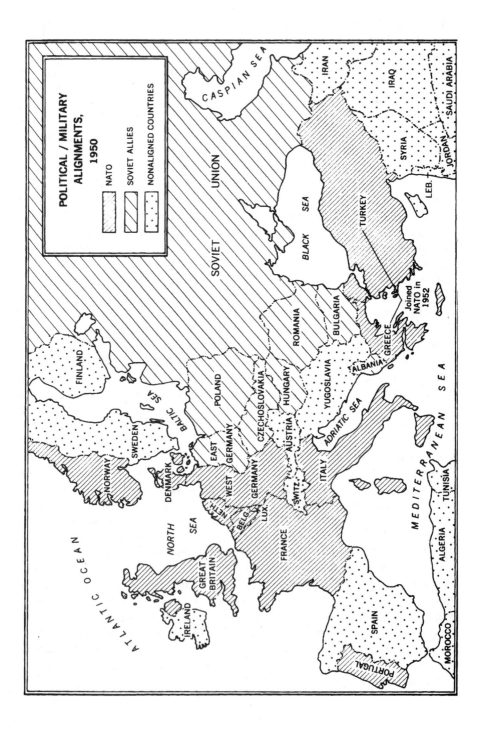

POLITICAL / MILITARY
ALIGNMENTS,
1950

NATO

SOVIET ALLIES

NONALIGNED COUNTRIES

CASPIAN SEA

IRAN

IRAQ

SAUDI ARABIA

SYRIA

JORDAN

LEB.

SOVIET UNION

BLACK SEA

TURKEY

Joined
NATO in
1952

FINLAND

ROMANIA

BULGARIA

GREECE

SWEDEN

BALTIC SEA

POLAND

CZECHOSLOVAKIA

HUNGARY

AUSTRIA

YUGOSLAVIA

ALBANIA

ADRIATIC SEA

MEDITERRANEAN SEA

NORWAY

DENMARK

EAST GERMANY

WEST GERMANY

NETH.

BELG.

LUX.

SWITZ.

ITALY

TUNISIA

NORTH SEA

FRANCE

ALGERIA

ATLANTIC OCEAN

GREAT BRITAIN

IRELAND

SPAIN

PORTUGAL

MOROCCO

Military co-operation among Western countries seemed even more imperative in 1949, when the Soviet Union developed its own nuclear capability. Western Europe was now more than ever economically and militarily dependent upon the United States. Economic aid from the United States was often tied to military and political co-operation (see Chapter 3). Western European nations were made aware that the reduction of Communist influence in their governments was necessary if they were to achieve economic recovery.

Western Europe now moved towards integration under the auspices and encouragement of the United States. Containment of the Soviet Union became the official US policy. One way to achieve this goal was to restore Europe's economic vitality and integrate it further in a Western economic and military bloc. Sixteen nations of Western Europe established the Organization for European Economic Co-operation (OEEC) to dispense American aid. At the same time, the United States allocated $5.3 billion to meet the needs of OEEC members in the first year of the Marshall Plan. These financial resources provided a strong boost to the economic recovery of Western Europe.

By 1949 the iron curtain that Churchill had described in 1946 had become a reality. With the build-up of American strength there, a power equilibrium had been restored in Europe that could not be disrupted short of all-out war. Since both sides now portrayed the East–West conflict as an ideological struggle, there was little possibility of resolving conflicts through normal diplomatic procedures. Each side was now in a struggle to protect freedom, either from 'Western imperialism' or from 'Soviet communism,' throughout the world.

The War Decade Ends

Although United States–Soviet predominance in the world continued in the 1950s, the early 1960s marked the beginning of the end of the bipolar world. A new power, the People's Republic of China, posed a threat to United States forces in Asia and, later in the decade, challenged Soviet domination of the Communist world. As the monolithic Communist world began to disintegrate, United States leadership in the Western world also began to come under pressure. United States leadership in the Western world was challenged by a resurgent Western Europe, led by Charles de Gaulle, which no longer shared the US fear of communism.

In retrospect, it is difficult to see how the outcome of the immediate post-war struggle between East and West could have been much different. The wartime policy of unconditional surrender had produced a power vacuum in Europe. Soviet–American hostility was inevitable, because neither side was willing to make a major concession to the other. Even revisionist historians William A. Williams and Lloyd Gardner admit that the early stages of the Cold War were perhaps unavoidable, although they maintain that the United States bore primary responsibility for the lengths to which the Cold War was carried. Some revisionists argue that the United States, because of its superior power, should have been willing to make concessions to the Soviet Union. In particular, they say, a concession of a sphere of influence for the Soviet Union in Eastern

Europe would have avoided conflict. Such concessions would have required magnanimity on the part of American leaders that they were far from possessing in the immediate post-war period and they would have been politically impossible in the face of ethnic, especially Polish voting blocs.

The revisionists have pointed out the importance of American economic objectives in the Cold War, and especially the US desire to keep all areas of the world open for its trade. This recognition is fundamental to the understanding of the broadening of the Cold War into a worldwide conflict. However, the revisionists tend to overlook the duplicity of Stalin's objectives and the fear and distrust they provoked in Washington. It now appears that Stalin may have wanted a sphere of influence only in Eastern Europe. However, Soviet actions in the post-war period in Iran, its demands for bases in Turkey and its support of the North Korean invasion of South Korea led many Western leaders to believe that the Soviet Union would not limit its expansion to Eastern Europe. Indeed, Western European leaders, fearing expansion into their territories, pressured the US to adopt an anti-Communist policy.

FURTHER READING

The following studies contend that the Soviet Union was primarily responsible for the Cold War: Winston S. Churchill, *The Second World War* (8 vols., 1948–1986); Herbert Feis, *Between War and Peace: The Potsdam Conference* (1960); *Churchill, Roosevelt, Stalin* (1951); and *From Trust to Terror: The Onset of the Cold War, 1945–1950* (1970). Although the last-named work was written as a refutation of the left-revisionist interpretation, it combines some revisionist arguments with earlier standard views of the Cold War. Adam Ulam, *Expansion and Coexistence: The History of Soviet Foreign Policy 1917–1967* (1968); *The Rivals: America and Russia Since World War 11 (1971)*; and Dangerous Relations, *The Soviet Union in World Politics, 1970–1982* (1983). Ulam's works contain keen insights concerning Stalin's motives. George Kennan's *American Diplomacy 1900–1950* (1951). and *Memoirs, 1950–1963* contain valuable information on his personal recollections of the diplomacy of the post-war period. His *Memoirs* contain information that tends to support the revisionist as well as the orthodox interpretations of the Cold War.

It is difficult to fit the following interpretations into any precise category since they take the position that the Soviet Union was primarily responsible for the Cold War but that the United States must share some of the blame: William McNeill, *America, Britain, and Russia: Their Co-operation and Conflict, 1941–1946* (1953); and John L. Gaddis, *The United States and the Origins of the Cold War, 1941–1947* (1972). Gaddis's study is a scholarly fusing of the orthodox and revisionist views that is critical of the extreme revisionist argument. Norman A. Graebner's *Cold War Diplomacy* (1962) is a brief but important critique of American foreign policy. Graebner finds an inconsistency between the broad nature of United States foreign policy goals and the limited means Americans were willing to use to carry out those goals. Louis J. Halle in *The Cold War as History* (1967) concludes that historical circumstance, such as the power vacuum in Europe at the end of Second

World War, propelled both the Soviet Union and the United States into a confrontation that neither desired. A recent account of the Cold War by Vojtech Mastny, *Russia's Road to the Cold War: Diplomacy, Warfare, and the Politics of Communism, 1941–1945* (1978), contends that primary responsibility rests with the Soviet Union because its post-war territorial demands were 'far in excess of its reasonable security requirements.' He maintains that the West shares some responsibility in that it failed to set limits on Soviet desires and make them clear to Stalin. Mastny's view that the Soviet 'system' compelled Stalin to seek to expand it resembles the revisionists claim that American 'capitalism' is intrinsically expansionistic by looking towards domestic causes for the source of expansionist desires. Another 1978 study, *Stalin Embattled, 1943–48* by William O. McCagg, Jr., agrees that Stalin's policies resulted from division within the Communist world. He contends that Stalin was placed on the defensive by those within the Communist movement who sought to revive Leninism – 'Party Revivalists' within the Soviet Union and 'insurrectionists' in the European Parties – and an international order defined by Western norms. By overcoming his wartime allies diplomatically, Stalin could achieve ascendancy over 'opponents' within the Communist world.

Although there are important differences in the interpretations of the revisionist studies of the Cold War, all agree the United States was primarily to blame for the global nature of the Cold War and that US diplomacy was guided by its economic imperialism. Gar Alperovitz in *Atomic Diplomacy* (1965) contends that Truman's policy of confrontation represented a dramatic shift from Roosevelt's policy of compromise. He further contends that America used the atomic bomb against Japan primarily to frighten the Soviet Union rather than to win the war against Japan. Diane Shaver Clemens in *Yalta* (1970) maintains that the United States rather than the Soviet Union violated the Yalta accords. Russel D. Buhite's *Decisions at Yalta: An Appraisal of Summit Diplomacy* (1986), contends that the conference was unnecessary since the decisions could have been resolved by the foreign ministers.

Gabriel Kolko in *The Politics of War: The World and United States Foreign Policy 1943–1945* (1968) takes the position that President Roosevelt sought a liberal – capitalist world dominated by the United States. Kolko sees no difference in the policies of Roosevelt and Truman. Joyce and Gabriel Kolko in *The Limits of Power: The World and United States Foreign Policy, 1945–1954* (1972) contend that the United States used its enormous wealth and military power to dominate its allies, suppress social change throughout the world, and ensure the triumph of the capitalist order.

Lloyd C. Gardner's *Architects of Illusion* (1970) is a scholarly statement of the revisionist position that avoids the polemics of some revisionist studies. Gardner believes that both Roosevelt and Truman sought to maintain the open door throughout the world to ensure the triumph of American capitalism. Walter LaFeber in *America, Russia and the Cold War, 1945–1966* (1968) maintains that because of the military and economic superiority it enjoyed in the post-war period, the United States should have been more willing to seek an understanding with the Soviet Union since its security was not threatened while that of the Soviet Union was.

Martin Sherwin in *A World Destroyed: The Atomic Bomb and the Grand Alliance* (1976) believes that the American reluctance to confide in the Soviet Union during the war, including maintaining nuclear power as an Anglo-American monopoly, increased Soviet intransigence and reduced the possibility of American–Soviet co-operation in the post-war period. William A. Williams in *The Tragedy of American Diplomacy* (rev. ed., 1962) finds that US expansionism was necessitated by the demands of an acquisitive capitalist society.

Early critiques of the revisionist studies are Robert L. Maddox, *The New Left and the Origins of the Cold War* (1973), in which Maddox charges that the revisionists have misused and misinterpreted source materials; and Robert W. Tucker, *The Radical Left and American Foreign Policy* (1971), a scholarly, balanced criticism of the left-revisionist interpretation.

Since the late seventies, Cold War studies have moved away from positions that stress a single cause and have tended to shift responsibility for the Cold War more to Soviet and British actions and personalities. The previously cited works of Mastny, and McCagg reflect this new emphasis. Gaddis's recent work, *The Long Peace: Inquiries into the History of the Cold War* (1986) argues that the United States did not view the Soviet Union as an adversary initially and only came to do so when the Soviet Union's unilateral actions between 1945–1950 undermined the American attempt to resolve issues collectively. Gaddis claims that the United States was reluctant to establish a sphere of influence in Western Europe and did so only in the face of Soviet actions and pressure from Britain and France. Recent studies of British policy support Gaddis's position. Five recent books shift the 'blame' for the Cold War towards Britain. These works are Martin Kitchen, *British Policy Towards the Soviet Union during the Second World War* (1986); Hugh Thomas, *Armed Truce: the Beginnings of the Cold War 1945–46* (1986); Robin Edmonds, *Setting the Mould: The United States and Britain 1945–1950* (1986); Richard A Best, Jr., *Co-operation with like-Minded Peoples: British Influences on American Security Policy, 1945–1949* (1986); and Anne Deighton, *The Impossible Peace: Britain, the Division of Germany, and the Origins of the Cold War* (1990). Two works on Soviet foreign policy that reveal early Soviet intentions to control Eastern Europe are Adam B. Ulam, *Dangerous Relations: The Soviet Union in World Politics, 1970–1982* (1987) and Charles Gati, *Hungary and the Soviet Bloc* (1986).

The ending of the Cold War has allowed archival information to supplement standard analytical treatments. This being the case, John Gaddis's recent *We Now Know: Rethinking Cold war History* (1997) does not fundamentally change his analysis, but broadens the empirical historical context. Similarly, Mel Leffler, *A Preponderance of Power: National Security, the Truman Administration, and the Cold War* (1992), and Charles Maier, ed., *The Cold war in Europe: Era of a Divided Continent* (3rd ed., 1996), add to but do not radically undermine standard accounts.

Many memoirs shed light on the debate over the Cold War. Especially important are the memoirs of George Kennan (cited above); and of W. Averell Harriman, *Special Envoy to Churchill and Stalin 1941–1946* (1976), by W. Averell Harriman and Elie Abel. Insights into Soviet policy can be found in Nikita Khrushchev's reminiscences, *Khrushchev Remembers* (1970); and Milovan Djihas, *Conversations with Stalin* (1962).

Important information and interpretations on Germany can be found in E. Davidson, *The Death and Life of Germany: An Account of the American Occupation* (1959); W. Phillips Davison, *The Berlin Blockade: A Study in Cold War Politics* (1958); J. L. Snell, *Wartime Origins of the East-West Dilemma over Germany* (1959); J. F. Golay, *The Founding the Federal Republic of Germany* (1958); J. P. Nettl, *The Eastern Zone and Soviet Policy in Germany, 1945–1950*

(1951); John H. Backer, *The Decision to Divide Germany: American Foreign Policy in Transition* (1978); and Peter Merkl, *The Origins of the West German Republic* (1965). In *America's Germany: John J. McCloy and the Federal Republic of Germany* (1991), Thomas Alan Schwartz expertly explains McCloy's crucial mediation between the Germans and the British and French and Adenauer's adept securing of Western trust. More recent works include William Smyser, *From Yalta to Berlin: The Cold War Struggle over Germany* (1999); and Peter Alter, *The German Question and Europe: A History* (2000).

Valuable early studies of post-war British foreign policy are M. A. Fitzsimons, *The Foreign Policy of the British Labour Government: 1945–1951* (1953); C.M. Woodhouse, *British Foreign Policy Since the Second World War* (1962) and Victor Rothwell, *Britain and the Cold War, 1941–1947* (1982). A recent edited work of W. Roger Louis and Hedley Bull, *The Special Relationship: Anglo-American relations since 1945* (1986) contains important recent articles with new documentation that provide many insights into Anglo-American relations.

For French foreign policy after the war see John W. Young, *France, The Cold War, and the Western Alliance, 1944–49* (1990). Young argues that the removal of the Communists from the French government in May 1947 resulted from French internal developments, not United States' pressure.

The Soviet takeover in Eastern Europe has generated comparative as well as single country studies. Two outstanding works of events in Eastern Europe after the war are Joseph Rothschild, *Return to Diversity: A Political History of East Central Europe since WWII* (2nd ed., 1993); and J. F. Brown, *Eastern Europe and Communist Rule* (1988). Both authors argue that events in Eastern Europe did not result from any preconceived blueprint but from a combination of Stalinist goals and local conditions. Joseph Rothschild's earlier work, *Communist Eastern Europe* (1964), found that the enforcement of Soviet primacy in Eastern Europe was a result, first and foremost, of Stalin's desire to maintain a monolithic Communist bloc subservient to the Soviet Union. Hugh Seton-Watson, in *The East European Revolution* (1957), takes the position that Stalin and the East European Communist parties had a preconceived plan to communize Eastern Europe. For Stalinist show trials, see G. H. Hodes, *Show Trials: Stalinist Purges in Eastern Europe, 1948–54* (1987).

Robert V. Daniels' *Russia: The Roots of Confrontation* (1985) shows a thorough understanding of Stalin's motives. Daniels contends that national security dominated Soviet decision-making. A comprehensive study of Stalin is Adam B. Ulam's *Stalin: The Man and His Era* (1973). Ulam sees the Sovietization of Eastern Europe as a result of Stalin's paranoia and believes that the Cold War had only a limited impact on Soviet policy. Milivan Djilas's *Conversations with Stalin* (1962); and Nikita Khrushchev's *Khrushchev Remembers* (1970) are two of the few sources containing statements by Stalin as to his motives and policies. Roy Medvedev's anti-Stalinist, pro-Leninist *Let History Judge* (1971) and *On Stalin and Stalinism* (1979) provide further insights into Stalin's policies by revealing information previously unavailable to Western scholars at the time. Recently added to this literature is a history of the period written by two Russian historians, Vladislav Zubok and Constantine Pleshakov, making use of Soviet archival material. In *Inside the Kremlin's Cold war: From Stalin to Khrushchev* (1996), they contend that Stalin was motivated by the twin desires of Communist revolution and global empire.

The Soviet–Yugoslav split is described in Robert Bass and Elizabeth Marbury, eds., *The Soviet-Yugoslav Controversy, 1948–1958: A Documentary Record* (1959). Vladimir Dedijer, in *Tito* (1953) and *The Battle Stalin Lost* (1971), provides a personal account of the Soviet–Yugoslav confrontation. A balanced view of the controversy is presented by Adam B. Ulam's *Titoism and the Cominform* (1952). Coverage of the Communist coup in Czechoslovakia can be found in Josef Korbel, *The Communist Subversion of Czechoslovakia, 1938–1948: The Failure of Coexistence* (1959); Morton Kaplan, *The Communist Coup in Czechoslovakia* (1960); Paul Zinner, *Communist Strategy and Tactics in Czechoslovakia* (1963); and Walter Ullmann, *The United States in Prague, 1945–1948* (1978). Polish affairs can be studies in Hans Roos, *A History of Modern Poland* (1966); and Richard Hiscocks, *Poland: Bridge for the Abyss* (1963). Richard C. Lukas' *The Strange Allies: The United States and Poland, 1941–1945* (1978) concludes that the United States sympathized with Poland's plight but gave little support to the Poles. For details on those involved in the Communist takeover in Poland, see Krystyna Kersten, *The Establishment of Communist Rule in Poland, 1943–1948* (1991). For information on Romania, see Ghita Ionescu, *Communism in Rumania, 1944–1962* (1969). For Hungary, see Bennet Kovrig, *The Hungarian People's republic* (1970) and Stephen Kertesz's *Between Russia and the West: Hungary and the Illusions of Peacemaking, 1945–1947* (1984). For American and British involvement in Hungarian affairs, see S. M. Max, *The United States, Great Britain, and the Sovietization of Hungary, 1945–58* (1985). Also valuable is Thomas Hammond, *The Anatomy of Communist Takeovers* (1975).

Three studies of the role of United States Foreign Service officers in policy making provide additional information on the American role in the origins of the Cold War – Lynn Etheridge Davis, *The Cold War Begins: Soviet American Conflict over Eastern Europe* (1974), Daniel Yergin, *Shattered Peace* (1977); and Hugh DeSantis, *The Diplomacy of Silence: The American Foreign Service, The Soviet Union*, and *The Cold War, 1933–1947* (1980). Against the Davis contention that the Foreign Service advocated co-operation with the Soviet Union and the Yergin claim that they counseled confrontation, DeSantis believes that they tardily advocated 'realistic confrontation.' In effect, DeSantis maintains that they had a limited effect upon US policy due to their inability to reach a consensus.

The many reasons advanced for Marshall Plan aid can be found in John Gimbel, *The Origins of the Marshall Plan* (1976); Alan S. Milward, *The Reconstruction of Western Europe, 1945–51* (1984); and Michael Hogan, *The Marshall Plan: America, Britain, and the reconstruction of Western Europe, 1947–1952* (1987). Hogan believes that America wished to institute a 'neo-liberal' political economy into Europe in order to produce abundance and end ideological strife within and between European countries. But European obstructionism shaped these American ideals to fit their own national objectives. Milward contends that the Marshall Plan resulted from American self-interest not economic chaos, the threat of Communism or idealism. Gimbel believes that the Marshall Plan was a 'crash program' for German economic recovery to occur within a general European recovery programme so that it would be politically acceptable in Europe.

2

From Left to Right: European Politics, 1945–48

> There were a few who simply wanted to return to the institutions of the [French] Third Republic. But, to the great majority, this *ancien régime* was doomed.
>
> Charles de Gaulle, in *De Gaulle* by Alexander Werth

When the Second World War drew to a close in Europe in May 1945, even the victors had little to celebrate. With approximately 14 million deaths in Western and Central Europe, one-half of them civilians, and the transplanting of another 16 million during and immediately after the war, few families escaped the war's suffering. The spectre of economic ruin and famine threatened much of the continent. In Great Britain, wartime debts and post-war shortages cut short the victory celebrations. In France, the destruction of large areas of the northeast as well as chaos in internal social and political affairs boded ill for the nation's future. The restoration of the Third Republic was itself in doubt, as the quote above attests. For the defeated, Germany and Italy, the future seemed even bleaker. In Germany the survivors would have to live with widespread destruction, famine and an economy that had ground to a halt. Germany also had to absorb around 8 million ethnic Germans who fled or were driven out of Eastern Europe. Countries that had been caught between the major belligerents, such as Belgium and Holland, had also suffered severely from the war.

Before Europe could begin to put the pieces together again, political life had to be restored. In Germany and Italy this meant monumental changes. New constitutions had to be written and new leaders had to be found.

The immediate problem was to find individuals capable of establishing democratic governments who had not been associated with previous regimes. Not uncommonly, this search led the occupying powers and European leaders to those who had been on the left of the political spectrum in the pre-war years. The popularity of parties on the left, Communists and Socialists, resulted from their wartime opposition to fascism. After the German attack on the Soviet Union in 1941, Communists had played a major role in the various resistance movements.

Parties on the right had little support in the immediate post-war period. The extreme right had been compromised by its pre-war association with fascism and the conservative parties by their association with depression and economic want during the years between the two world wars. Few people still favoured the conservatives' economic liberalism with its laissez-faire economic philosophy.

Widespread support for economic planning and the nationalization of industry had developed during the war. Only by such measures, many thought, could the economic experiences of the interwar period be avoided. Communist and Socialist parties cooperated in coalition governments in most European countries in the period immediately after the war. But by 1948 on the Continent and 1951 in England, parties of the centre and right – usually Christian Democratic parties – had regained power in most countries, and the left was in retreat. The major reasons for this change were the rapid economic recovery of Europe, the adoption of the welfare-state concept even by conservative parties and the Cold War. The right now seemed more progressive than it had been in the interwar period, and many now associated the left with Soviet expansionism.

Great Britain: The Welfare-State Begins

With the only Labour party in power among major European countries, Great Britain seemed to be the country in which the most fundamental economic and social reforms would be instituted. Indeed, post-war shortages and wartime promises did compel the government to increase social services and to nationalize certain industries and utilities. During the war the Beveridge Report, introduced in the House of Commons in 1942 to boost morale, had promised all citizens a minimum income and a comprehensive system of social welfare. The report was given wide coverage by the press and accepted by the public, but was then shelved for the duration of the war.

Once the war was over, questions of social welfare became the focus of public attention. An opinion poll taken during the first post-war election campaign showed that the respondents were most concerned about housing, full employment and social security.

The election campaign reflected the primacy of social issues over foreign policy considerations. When Winston Churchill, the standard-bearer for the Conservative party, warned that a vote for the Labour party was a vote for totalitarianism, Labour countered with a comprehensive program of social welfare. Despite widespread admiration for Churchill, the voters associated the Conservative party with the pre-war depression, with its soup lines and widespread unemployment. Labour, on the other hand, by filling the home ministries in the wartime National Government coalition, had gained wide spread admiration and support for its mobilization of the home front.

On 5 July 1945, Churchill and the Conservatives were dealt a resounding defeat by the British public. The Labour party, with a majority of 145 votes in the House of Commons, was free to enact its programme. The decisive defeat of the Conservatives indicated that during the war large sections of the middle class had become convinced that the government would have to assume responsibility for the less privileged members of society.

Contrary to Churchill's warnings, the Labour party leadership, with its diverse social composition, proved to be reformist rather than revolutionary. Most of the leaders were interested in pragmatic short-term reforms rather than a complete revamping of the society and the economy. Clement Attlee, the new prime minister, had gained valuable experience as deputy prime minister during the war. He was hardly the flamboyant leader one might have expected from a Labour government, but his low-keyed, pragmatic style of leadership was what Britain needed to overcome its serious post-war economic and social problems.

The right wing of the Labour party was represented by the new foreign secretary, Ernest Bevin, who was part of the trade-union faction of the party. The left wing was led by Sir Stafford Cripps, head of the Board of Trade and later Chancellor of the Exchequer, and by Aneurin ('Nye') Bevan, Minister of Health. Cripps was an upper-middle-class lawyer, while Bevan had been a miner in his youth.

The economic and social program enacted by the Labour party clearly shows the divisions within the party. Revolutionary-minded critics described the Labour measures as the cautious revolution or half-revolution. Certainly the legislation enacted by the Labour government stopped short of being revolutionary in the eyes of the left wing of the party and among most European Socialists, as it did not bring about the expected redistribution of wealth. Moreover, while the government reduced the private sector's share in the direction of the economy, it did not go as far as France or Italy in adopting a plan for long-term development (see Chapter 3). Government investment and planning tended to be short term rather than long term.

But Labour's establishment of the welfare state and its nationalization of major industries and utilities were no small step. The Bank of England and civil aviation were nationalized immediately; the coal and steel industries, public transportation, electricity and gas followed. Nationalization of only one industry, iron and steel, was strongly contested by the House of Lords and the Conservative party. (The Conservatives denationalized it in 1951, only to have it renationalized in 1967 by Labour.) The Lords' opposition was overcome by the passage of an amendment to the Parliament Act of 1911, reducing the power of the Lords to delay legislation to one session. (The 1911 act had abolished the Lords' right to veto money bills passed by the Commons and permitted the Commons to pass *any* bill if it obtained Commons approval in three successive sessions over a period of at least two years.) Some of the nationalizations, particularly of the Bank of England and of public utilities, were less than revolutionary since the government had already exercised considerable control over their activities. In addition, Labour refused to assume full responsibility for the direction of nationalized industries and instead placed them under the direction of autonomous corporations rather than government agencies, as was done in France and Italy.

The initial legislation providing for the creation of the welfare-state consisted of the National Insurance Act and the National Health Service Act, both passed in 1946. The National Insurance Act set up a comprehensive social security program and nationalized medical insurance companies so that the state now subsidized the unemployed, the sick and the aged. The National Health Service Act instituting socialized medicine faced greater opposition but was also in effect by 1948. Doctors and dentists were forced to work with the state hospitals, where the bulk of the patients were going, but they were permitted to retain a private practice. Although the system was very costly – it was the second highest governmental expenditure – it was so widely accepted by the time the Conservatives came to power in 1951 that more than 90 per cent of the medical profession was cooperating with it, and there was no significant effort to repeal it.

No sooner had Labour instituted its programme than it began to lose popularity. Although the welfare programmes helped deplete the British treasury, many of the economic problems were beyond Labour's control. Inherited from the interwar years and the war were a huge debt and an outdated industrial plant that made the balance of trade increasingly unfavourable.

Britain's need to import a large percentage of its foodstuffs and raw materials compelled it to export large quantities of processed goods to pay for them. Unfortunately, the loss of markets during the war and the inability to compete with more modernized foreign industries in the post-war period further reduced its exports and inflated its deficits. Britain had had to sell off many foreign investments during the war and no longer had large returns on such investments to offset the huge trade imbalance. Only with the help of loans from the United States could the government be bailed out.

Economic recovery was hampered in the post-war period by the outlay of large sums in support of foreign policy. Until US President Harry Truman's 1947 proclamation of the Truman Doctrine, which provided economic and military aid to Greece and Turkey, Britain bore the brunt of the effort against the leftist forces in the Greek Civil War. At the same time, British troops were caught up in the hostilities between the Jews and the Arabs in Palestine and between the Hindus and the Moslems in India (see Chapter 5). To add to these woes, Britain spent $60 million in 1946 and another $60 million in the first quarter of 1947 to feed the Germans in its occupation zone.

To carry out these far-flung commitments, Britain still had 1.5 million soldiers in 1947. The decisions to leave India and Palestine in that year and to cut off aid to Greece and Turkey stemmed from economic necessity more than from a genuine desire to retreat from empire. Labour Foreign Secretary Ernest Bevin had in fact long held out against the pressure to withdraw from these areas.

Even the elements seemed to be against Britain during its financial plight. The coldest winter in sixty-six years, with snow piling twenty feet high in some areas, brought the nation to a standstill in 1946–47. The resulting fuel shortages necessitated increased imports of fuel and at the same time cut factory output, which in turn cut exports. The government had no choice; it devalued the pound from $4.03 to $2.80. Although devaluation increased exports and stabilized the value of the pound, the move was unpopular because it increased the price of imported goods and made foreign travel more expensive.

Labour's decreasing popularity became apparent when the 1950 elections reduced its lead over the Tories to a mere seventeen seats.

The issue that finally drove the Labour party from power was rearmament. It caused a battle in the party between a right wing that wanted to rearm and cooperate with the United States and a left wing that wanted to follow a neutral course and not rearm. Ernest Bevin, disillusioned by his dealings with Moscow and convinced that Britain had no choice but to cooperate with the United States, led the rearmament forces to victory. In 1951, in response to the financial demands of the Korean War, the majority of the Labour party decided to cut health care, notably dental and optical payments, and to spend more for rearmament. This shuffling of priorities was apparently done to convince the United States of the Labour government's loyalty. In response, Aneurin Bevan, the Minister of Health, resigned from the cabinet and was followed by a number of others from the left wing of the party. The election of October 1951, called by Attlee to increase the Labour majority, instead produced a slim Conservative victory. Labour would not return to power until 1964.

France: The Fourth Republic

The difficulties facing post-war France were even more complicated than those facing Great Britain. Not only did France have serious financial problems, for which it was dependent on US aid, but it also was faced with more wartime destruction, social dislocation and political turmoil. For example, the destruction of four-fifths of its railway rolling stock hampered transportation. The political division between supporters of the wartime Vichy government and members of the Resistance had no parallel in Britain. The purge of Vichy collaborators, which took thousands of lives, and the inability of the new provisional government to establish its authority outside Paris until October 1944 brought the country close to anarchy. Some Frenchmen used the occasion to carry out vendettas against personal enemies. Over 5000 collaborators were killed by partisans before the new provisional government re-established the legal system.

The leader of the provisional government, General Charles de Gaulle, had not been in France since June 1940, when German troops moved in. A little known secretary of state for the army at the time of the defeat, de Gaulle was soon to become one of the most influential and controversial leaders in the world. As organizer of the Free French movement in exile, his leadership was eventually accepted by the underground Resistance movement in occupied France. Embarrassed by the quick defeat of France in 1940, he sought throughout his life to restore French grandeur. The Anglo-American refusal to acknowledge him as leader of the French government in exile, partially due to Roosevelt's and Churchill's personal dislike of his vain and domineering character, was a humiliating experience for him.

But Churchill and Roosevelt had to recognize his leadership after the Free French movement was established in liberated Algiers in 1943 and de Gaulle had the acceptance of the French underground, including the Communists.

Charles de Gaulle's triumphal return to France in June 1944.
(© Bettmann/Corbis)

Three days before the Allied invasion of Normandy on 6 June 1944, a provisional government was set up in Algiers with de Gaulle at the helm. When he returned to Paris on 25 August 1944, General Dwight D. Eisenhower permitted de Gaulle to take Paris with the Second French Armored Division. Parisians gave him an enthusiastic welcome. In two weeks he set up the French provisional government, then sent large French forces into the battle against Hitler. But stable political life could not be restored until the provisional government could establish its authority throughout the country.

Political turmoil was avoided during the provisional government period because of the co-operation of the Communists and de Gaulle. The political right was completely discredited because of its collaboration with Germany and its association with the puppet Vichy government.

The post-war co-operation of the left and de Gaulle was an outgrowth of the wartime co-ordination of military efforts between the Soviet Union and the Western Allies. The leaders of the Communist party, Maurice Thorez and Jacques Duclos, who were responsible for the co-operation, were both Moscow Communists and followed orders from the Kremlin. Whatever their ultimate goals, they chose initially to support a parliamentary government with de Gaulle as its leader. The Communist party cooperated with de Gaulle in disarming the

Resistance forces that might have been used by the left to gain power in France. At this point, the Communists apparently hoped to come to power in France as part of a left coalition. Some have suggested that without the Cold War and the subsequent polarization of international politics, the Communists would soon have become a genuine national party with no ties to Moscow. While the party's reformist stand and anti-Soviet pronouncements in the 1960s and 1970s tend to support this view, its renewed orthodoxy in the late seventies reject it.

Equally important in promoting national harmony in the post-war period was a consensus emanating from the war and especially from the Resistance movement. A Resistance Charter, accepted by Resistance leaders in March, 1944, advocated major economic and social changes when peace was restored. In order to rid the country of 'economic and financial feudalism,' the charter called for nationalization of key industries and services, economic planning and the establishment of economic and social democracy. Sharing with the left many Resistance ideas, de Gaulle carried out some nationalization (e.g., the coal mines, the four largest banks, civil aviation and a few industries) and initiated economic planning.

By October 1945, sufficient order had been established to hold the first post-war election. The three parties representing the major Resistance forces – the Communists, Socialists, and *Mouvement Republicain Populaire* (MRP) – gained 461 of the 586 assembly seats. At this point the Communists with 26 per cent of the vote and the socialists with 24 per cent were still cooperating. Both wanted a new constitution that would provide a strong assembly with the power to choose and reject a premier.

De Gaulle, seeing in a strengthened assembly a return to the weak Third Republic form of government, hoped for a constitution with strong powers for the executive. The other major Resistance faction, the Christian Democratic MRP, also wanted a strong executive. Although asked to stay on as premier and president, de Gaulle soon realized that the Communists and Socialists who dominated the new constituent assembly were writing a leftist constitution that would strip him of much of his power. He was also aware of the opposition of most parties to his desire for increased military expenditures. Therefore, on 20 January 1946, de Gaulle retired from active political life for the first of three times.

The search for a new premier revealed the growing divisions in the tripartite coalition of Communists, Socialists and MRP. The Communist party proposed a Communist–Socialist government with the Communist Thorez as premier. The Socialists, fearful of being dominated by the Communists, refused to support any premier who did not have MRP approval. The MRP, distrustful of the Communists, refused to support *any* Communist for premier. To break this deadlock, Felix Gouin, the Socialist President of the Constituent Assembly, was named to head the government. Gouin, who was an ineffective leader, was described by a centrist magazine as a 'man of goodwill rather than will'.

The Constituent Assembly's attempts to formulate a new constitution brought about a clash between those who wanted a strong legislature and those who wanted a powerful executive. Essentially the right (MRP, de Gaulle) wanted a strong executive in the American fashion and the left desired an all-powerful legislature. Primarily on the basis of MRP opposition, the first constitution was defeated by a national referendum in May 1946 because it did not provide for a strong executive. Another election the following month, necessitated by the defeat of the constitution, made the MRP the largest party in the tripartite coalition, and its leader, Georges Bidault, was chosen premier, replacing Gouin. When the second constitution, providing for a stronger executive and an upper house in the legislature, was accepted by a national referendum in November 1946, the Fourth French Republic came into existence. The new representative bodies, the National Assembly and the Council of the Republic, resembled the legislative bodies of the interwar period. Dissatisfied with this new constitution, one-third of the electorate abstained from the referendum. The major flaw in the new constitution centered on the selection of a premier: after being nominated by the president, a premier had to present and defend a programme before the National Assembly. It proved difficult to find a premier who could gain and then maintain approval from the Assembly. Searches for new premiers produced extensive party bickering and repeated government inactivity. New governments came to power only after elaborate party negotiating to put together a coalition acceptable to the National Assembly.

In the November elections the popularity of the Communists once again made the French Communist party (PCF) the largest party in the tripartite coalition (see Table 2–1).

The selection of a new premier after the November elections, the exclusion of the Communist party from the tripartite coalition in May 1947, and the massive strike wave in November–December 1947 revealed how inextricably French domestic affairs were entangled with international affairs. As the largest party, the PCF hoped that its leader, Thorez, would become the new premier. But the absorption of the left wing of the Polish Socialists by the Communist party of Poland and the return to France of the anti-Communist Socialist leader Leon Blum from Moscow increased the distrust between the two left parties.

Blum's dislike of the Communists grew out of his association with them in the interwar Popular Front government. He felt that any Communist-dominated government would produce a leftist dictatorship and asserted, 'Without socialism, democracy is imperfect; without democracy, socialism is helpless.'

Table 2–1 Seats won in French elections, 1945–46

Party	October 1945	June 1945	November 1946
Communist (PCF)	161	153	183
Socialist (SFIO)	150	126	105
Christian Democratic (MRP)	150	169	167
Radical	28	32	43
Conservative	64	67	71
Other	33	36	49

Source: Philip M. Williams, *Crisis and Compromise: Politics in the Fourth Republic*, 3rd ed. (Essex, England: Longman, 1964), p. 532. Copyright Philip M. Williams, 1958, 1964. Reprinted by permission of Penguin Books Ltd.

Without Socialist support the Communists had little chance of gaining the premiership, so in January of 1947 they agreed to accept the Socialist Paul Ramadier as the new premier. PCF efforts to keep the tripartite coalition alive were thwarted by three major crises of the Ramadier government: the Indochina War, the Cold War and a domestic labour dispute.

The Indochina War. It was inevitable that France's colonial policy would eventually become an issue in the developing Cold War. Until 1947 the Communist party supported the government's attempt to reimpose its control over Indochina. But only six days after the enunciation of the Truman Doctrine on 12 March 1947, the PCF withdrew its support of France's Indochina policy. Up to this point, Stalin, in keeping with the spirit of Allied wartime co-operation and distrustful of any strong Communist parties outside the Soviet Union, had directed the PCF to cooperate with the other political forces. Now, clearly, the position was reversed. It appears that Stalin told the French Communists to stop supporting a colonial war.

The Cold War. At the heart of the conflict among the coalition parties was the Cold War. Before 1947 the French government had tried to adhere to a neutral position between Moscow and Washington, but the steady deterioration of relations between the two superpowers and the French need of economic aid made this policy impossible.

As late as April 1947 Bidault, now minister of foreign affairs, tried to get Soviet support for the separation of the Ruhr from Germany, French occupation of the Rhineland, integration of the Saar with France and a confederal, decentralized German state. However, after being snubbed by Stalin and Molotov at the Moscow conference in March–April 1947, he turned to the United States.

Accepting US help meant giving up plans to strengthen France by incorporating German territory and accepting American and British plans for the economic revival of Germany. Even before this, some French politicians had recognized the advantages of cooperating with the United States. Pierre Mendes-France, the later Radical Party premier of France, said, 'We must keep up this indispensable Communist scare' since the United States was making a great effort to aid those threatened by Communism.

The End of Tripartism. Ramadier's economic policies precipitated a crisis that resulted in the expulsion of the PCF from the government coalition. The Communist party had denounced strikes as anarchist even through the largest labour union was under its control. But Ramadier's policy of low wages and high prices to promote business recovery precipitated a massive strike at the government-owned Renault automobile factory in April 1947, forcing the PCF to support the workers against the government. After winning a vote of confidence on his economic policy in the assembly, Ramadier demanded that the Communist deputies resign, and tripartism came to an end.

Although the developing Cold War helped undermine the PCF in France, domestic affairs were even more important in excluding the PCF from power. Despite a moderate, conciliatory communist policy after being excluded from office, the Socialists abandoned its coalition with the PCF in October 1947 in the municipalities. As a result, Communist mayors lost 842 mayorial seats when they had lost only three per cent of their vote in the municipal elections. The PCF now turned towards more resolute support of worker's economic demands. PCF support for the massive strikes throughout France in November and December 1947 led to a further defeat for the party. Workers had to return to work when the Socialist minister of the interior called in the army and threatened workers with the loss of their social security benefits. After another attempt to gain a share of power in 1948, the PCF turned to a closer working relationship with Moscow and the Cominform. It approved the communist coup in Czechoslovakia and Stalin directed expulsion of Yugoslavia from the Cominform in 1948.

While the Socialists were engaged in their offensive against the Communists in 1947–48, a new political party of the right appeared. This party, the Rally of the French People (RPF), led by de Gaulle, sought but failed to gain support from the United States as France's bulwark against communism. De Gaulle's arrogant attempt to make the government call a national referendum on his return to power was decisively beaten back, and for the second time de Gaulle had to retire from the political arena. By the spring of 1948 the MRP led government of Robert Schuman, supported by Marshall Plan funds and stabilized by domestic economic recovery, was firmly in control.

Italy: A Policy of Muddling Through

Like France and Great Britain, Italy experienced a wartime and post-war resurgence of the left. Again it was the left-antifascist activities that were responsible for its popularity. The Fascist Grand Council and King Victor Emmanuel III replaced Benito Mussolini with Marshal Pietro Badoglio in July 1943, following the Allied invasion of Sicily. However, Badoglio had to flee to liberated southern Italy when German troops took control of northern Italy (including Rome). In the liberated south, a coalition of anti-fascist parties called the Committee for National Liberation (CLN) challenged Badoglio's claim to the post of head of the Italian government.

The CLN, most of which wanted a republic, clashed with Badoglio over the fate of the monarchy. Under pressure from the Allies, King Victor Emmanuel III promised to step aside in favour of his son, Umberto, who would act as lieutenant governor until a post-war national referendum could decide the fate of the monarchy. Only the Communist leader Palmiro Togliatti's approval of the king's action, apparently a continuation of Soviet-Allied wartime co-operation, convinced the remaining CLN parties to accept Umberto. With the liberation of Rome in June of 1944, the CLN forced acceptance of Ivanoe Bonomi as head of a new government.

Meanwhile, military and political activities in the north had taken a politically more radical turn because of the German occupation. Resistance fighters formed the Committee of National Liberation for Northern Italy (CLNAI) centered in Milan. The CLNAI, dominated by the left of centre – the Communist, Socialist and Action parties – desired a far more radical republic than the Bonomi government in the south was willing to institute. The CLNAI opposition to Bonomi was sufficiently strong to have the leader of the Action party, Ferruccio Parri, appointed premier by Lieutenant General of the Realm Umberto.

In May and June of 1945, immediately before Parri came to power, the weakening of the political left set the pattern for the post-war development of Italy. Throughout the north the leftist-dominated CLNAI permitted the participation of workers in the management of industrial enterprises through so-called management councils. The CLNAI also launched attacks on big business to penalize it for cooperating with fascism and to begin the process of destroying what were considered to be the reactionary forces in Italy.

That the Left was unable to take full control can be attributed in part to Allied intervention. The Left realized that any outright attempt to seize power would be opposed by American and British forces that were then in the country. As the Left attempted to gain Allied acceptance by adopting a moderate reformist position, its basis of strength was systematically destroyed by the Allies. Leftist Resistance groups were compelled to surrender their arms. Workers' councils were disbanded, factory managers were urged to reassert their authority, and local committees of liberation, invariably leftist, were replaced by military government for a few months.

Parri, convinced of the need for radical reforms in post-war Italy, was thus handicapped from the start. His attempts to institute policies favouring small- and medium-size business rather than big business and to redistribute wealth through a more effective tax were defeated by the Liberals and Christian Democrats in his cabinet, considering his policies too radical. After only six months in office Parri resigned, blaming the Liberals and Christian Democrats for sabotaging his programme. His fall signified the end of radical social and political change in post-war Italy and condemned Italy to a policy of muddling through.

With Parri's fall began the post-war domination of Italian politics by the Christian Democratic party that has lasted almost to this day. Although the Christian Democrats, led by Alcide de Gasperi, were forced to share power with the Socialists and Communists, they clearly dominated the coalition. It was fairly easy for the coalition to accept a public referendum in June 1946 ending monarchy in Italy but much more difficult for it to reach decisions on complex economic and social problems. The establishment of regional governments, provided for in the 1948 Constitution of the Italian government, were not fully implemented until 1970 due to Christian Democratic fears that they would create Communist governments across North-Central Italy.

While the Communists and Socialists wanted to nationalize some industry, De Gasperi preferred an essentially private enterprise policy with some state financial subsidization. Although government owned corporations such as IRI (See Chapter 3) extended public ownership to large sectors of industry, De Gasperi and his fellow party members, especially the Catholic clergymen, saw the Communist and Socialist parties as threats to the Church. De Gasperi's attempts to oust the Communists and Socialists from the coalition were helped along by a split in the Socialist party between those like Pietro Nenni who

Election campaign posters in Rome, 1948.
(© Istituto Luce/Gestione Archivi Alinari, Firenze)

favoured co-operation with the Communists and those who did not. The latter, led by Giuseppe Saragat, broke away from the Socialist party in January 1947 and formed the Social Democratic Party (PSDI).

With the left opposition divided, De Gasperi used the growing anti-Communist sentiment stemming from the Cold War to exclude the communists from the coalition government in June 1947. Coming one month after the Communist coup in Czechoslovakia, the April 1948 parliamentary elections became a battleground between the People's Bloc of Communists supported by Nenni Socialists and De Gasperi's Christian Democrats. During the election campaign the Vatican and the United States energetically supported De Gasperi. The United States warned that a Communist–Socialist government would not receive any economic aid and the Central Intelligence Agency actively supported the Christian Democrats. With the Italian electorate anxious about a possible Communist government and the economic consequences this would entail, the Christian Democratic party obtained sufficient votes in the 1948 election, 48.5 per cent of the vote, to govern alone. De Gasperi astutely included representatives of the Social Democratic, Republican and Liberal parties in his ministry, leaving the Communist and Socialist parties isolated on the left. The PCI staged general strike of July 1948, following the attempted assassination of Togliatti, failed when the Communist trade-union leaders folded when confronted with the government threat to use military force.

Until the late 1990s, the Communist party and its working-class supporters were excluded from governing coalitions in Italy. However, the Communists managed in the 1960s and 1970s to gain power in many provinces and municipalities. Their popularity in recent elections won them important positions in the legislature. (This resurgence will be explored in Chapter 12.) Because the basis of support for the Christian Democrats came from the conservative upper and middle classes and the southern peasantry, there was little support for meaningful economic and social reforms.

Spain: An End to Ostracism

A swing to the left was impossible in Spain and Portugal, where strong dictatorships prevented any free political activity. General Francisco Franco had clapped tight police control over his leftist opposition after his victory over the Popular Front government in the Spanish Civil War in 1939. Strong support by Spanish nationalists – and bitter opposition between his opponents, Communists and anti-Communist Republicans – made Franco's task much easier. With a government composed of military men and members of nationalist groups, Franco retained the pragmatic authoritarianism that he had established during the civil war. He feared that the establishment of any clear-cut ideological basis for his regime would alienate some of his nationalist support. Therefore, he opposed the Falange's (Spanish fascist party) attempt to transform his government into a purely Fascist movement.

Concerned that the European democracies might turn on Spain for its adherence to the fascist Anti-Comintern Pact of 1939, Franco declared Spanish neutrality at the outset of the Second World War. But the swift German victory over France produced a marked pro-German attitude among Spanish leaders. Only economic hardships and the possibility that a close identification with the fascist powers would bring crippling economic sanctions kept Spain from openly supporting Germany and Italy at the beginning of the war.

The Nazi attack on the Soviet Union in 1941 caused Franco's vehemently anti-Communist regime to send a force of 20,000 Spanish volunteers to help Germany on the Russian front. Paul Preston's recent biography *Franco* argues that Franco was prepared to enter the war on the Axis side but Hitler was unwilling to agree to a Spanish empire in Morocco at the expense of the then Vichy government of France.

Although Franco continued to be sympathetic to the Axis powers and believed that they would win the war, he was not willing to join them with no expectation of territorial gain and the risk of an Allied naval blockade if he joined them. Spain's involuntary neutralism began to bear fruit when the Allies launched their invasion of French North Africa in 1942. At that time President Roosevelt offered assurances that the invasion was not directed at Spanish holdings in Africa and that the Allies would not intervene in Spanish internal affairs.

Franco overcame the immediate post-war Allied ostracism by again cautiously adapting his policies to satisfy both internal and foreign opponents. At home, he shored-up support among his military, church and monarchist supporters by reducing the influence of his Falangist party followers. The Spanish left, still divided and still closely watched, offered little opposition. On the right, no strong conservative alternative existed to challenge Franco, and the military continued to support him. Heated foreign opposition to his regime had little impact since government propagandists portrayed it as an anti-Spanish rather than an anti-Franco campaign. Franco further strengthened his regime in 1947 by declaring Spain a kingdom with himself as regent and by having it confirmed by a national plebiscite. Although he did not permit the return of the king, he promised the country would be ruled by a king upon his death or retirement. In 1955, he permitted the pretender's son, Prince Juan Carlos, to return to study.

Another factor that helped Franco to hold his domestic critics at bay, and overcome international ostracism, was Spain's growing usefulness to the United States and its allies in the Cold War. In the event of war with the Soviet Union, the United States began to see that the value of military bases in Spain would be immeasurable. By 1948, most of the anti-Communist West had reopened diplomatic contacts with Spain and the United States had begun to provide Spain with financial aid to overcome the serious economic problems. No longer ostracized so completely (Spain was still excluded from NATO), and beginning to recover economically, Franco did not have to alter his internal policies to please republican opponents.

Portugal: Uninterrupted Peace

Before the outbreak of the Second World War Portugal had a dictatorship that was long established and ideologically more consistent than that of Spain. A professor of political economy at the University of Coimbra, Antonio de Oliveira Salazar, had been brought into the military government in 1928 to resolve the acute financial difficulties, and by 1933 Salazar had become dictator of the military regime. The Portuguese accepted his strong, authoritative leadership primarily because of a yearning for peace and security after suffering through twenty-three anti-government revolts between 1910 and 1928.

Salazar overcame the Portuguese fascists, called National Syndicalists, by offering his brand of Catholic corporatism and by concentrating political power in a single government Party of National Union. To provide order and stability he set up a consultative corporate chamber in place of a senate and brought labour under the jurisdiction of government syndicates.

By providing transportation and communication facilities to Franco, Salazar's regime proved to be a valuable aid to the nationalist forces in the Spanish Civil War. But he refused to aid Franco directly and adhered to the international non-intervention agreement. During the Second World War, Salazar initially adopted a policy of strict neutrality. Fearing that the war might bring about a polarization of forces within Portugal, he carried out a comprehensive programme of civic nationalism. A youth organization, an auxiliary militia system, political purges of suspected opponents and a government loyalty oath were among the tools used to stamp out all opposition to the regime.

Owing to Portugal's long-time friendship and treaty of alliance with Britain, Salazar was never so pressured as Spain was to enter the war on the side of

Germany and Italy. This friendship led Salazar to change his policy of neutrality and to grant the United States and Britain use of military bases in the Azores in 1943 and to stop the shipment of strategic material to Germany in 1944.

After the war, Portugal escaped much of the international anti-fascist campaign because of its wartime co-operation with Western allies and because it retained a parliamentary form of government. Moreover, Salazar instituted a liberalization programme to satisfy both foreign and domestic opponents. The programme included the restoration of freedom of the press, amnesty for political opponents of the regime, and new parliamentary elections. However, a reduction in the number of persons eligible to vote and a boycott by the opposition made a sham of the elections.

Although some political unrest was evident in the late 1940s, Salazar was able to maintain his authoritarian rule. Serious economic problems were avoided when his regime received economic aid from the Marshall Plan. Membership in NATO gained Portugal international support. By 1950 Salazar's opposition was limited to a few students and intellectuals, a small group of military men, and some members of the middle class.

The Small Countries: Restoring Order

With the exception of Greece, the smaller European countries concentrated on domestic affairs in the post-war period. Many had suffered extensively from the war and were faced with considerable reconstruction problems. Large sections of Holland, especially Rotterdam, were destroyed by German bombs. Although Belgium had suffered less war damage, it was in the throes of internecine political–cultural conflict between the politically radical, anticlerical, French-speaking Walloons and the politically conservative, Catholic Flemish.

Among the Nordic countries, only Norway and Finland experienced serious wartime losses. Norway lost one-half of its merchant fleet. Finland suffered through a Soviet invasion in 1939, the loss of some territory to the Soviet Union, and the burden of heavy reparations in the post-war period. Nevertheless, the Finns managed to retain their political democracy and won admiration throughout the world for their stout resistance to Soviet domination. The Socialist and the Agrarian parties successfully resisted Communist attempts to gain control of the country. In Norway and Denmark, thousands of German collaborators were arrested at war's end. As in Finland, the Socialist and Agrarian parties dominated the governments as Communist strength waned following the war.

Forced to cooperate with Germany under threat of invasion, Sweden remained neutral during the war and did not, therefore have to face the problems of economic reconstruction and political restoration confronting most European countries. The Swedish Socialist party continued to dominate domestic politics as it had done before the war.

Austria, as an ally of Germany, had suffered extensively from Allied bombing. Not only did Austria have to recover from serious economic destruction and dislocation but it also had to endure a four-power occupation until 1955, when it became an independent, neutral state.

Greece: From Occupation to Civil War

Greece suffered through four years of German occupation (1941–44) and a destructive civil war before political peace was obtained. A Communist-led National Liberation Front (EAM), with its People's Army (ELAS), challenged the exiled Government of National Unity for leadership when Greece was liberated. The ELAS force could have seized power when the Germans withdrew in October 1944, but it refrained because the Churchill–Stalin agreements assigned Greece to Western jurisdiction and because Stalin issued direct orders not to overthrow the British-backed Government of National Unity.

But in December 1944, encouraged by Tito against Stalin's wishes, ELAS seized power when the government threatened a reorganization that would equalize the Communist and non-Communist military forces in a new national army. British troops compelled the EAM–ELAS to capitulate in February 1945. In the anti-Communist reaction that followed, government security agents and vigilante groups hunted down Communists. Again in March 1946 the Communists tried to seize power. Despite guerrilla activity, parliamentary elections were held in March as scheduled. As the Communists had feared, the pro-royalist parties won 206 of the 354 seats in the legislature. This trend continued in the September referendum, when 70 per cent of the voters cast their ballots in favour of a restoration of the monarchy.

The Communist guerrillas, with support from Yugoslavia, Albania and Bulgaria, could not be dislodged from their mountain retreats until funds provided under the Truman Doctrine, totalling $250 million, permitted the build-up of the Greek army in 1948. When the Communist forces shifted from guerrilla warfare to conventional warfare in 1949, they were wiped out by the Greek army.

After nine years of warfare, large sections of Greece were devastated. With support from the Marshall Plan, Greece was able to begin a modest recovery from economic misery. But internal political troubles and the lack of economic resources kept it a poor and troubled country.

Stalin had ordered Tito to stop his support of the Greek guerrillas, and Tito's failure to comply was one of the major reasons for the Stalin–Tito rift in 1948. Yugoslav support for the guerrillas ended in July 1949, when Tito had to concentrate his efforts on resisting Soviet pressures. In any case, Tito could ill-afford to support a guerrilla war that might well spill over into Yugoslavia. He was also desperately in need of economic aid himself, as a consequence of the economic embargo of Comecon.

Popularity of the Left

With the exception of Spain and Portugal, the political left was popular everywhere among the smaller European states. As in France and Italy, leftist parties had led the resistance in the occupied territory or had been popular in the interwar period. The post-war governments of both Belgium and Denmark contained Communists. Without Allied intervention, a left coalition would have undoubtedly come to power in 1944 in Greece. In Belgium, a Communist attempt to gain power in 1944 was beaten back by Allied troops. However, the popularity of the far-Left waned quickly because of its identification with the Soviet Union.

The more successful moderate Left embodied in the Socialist and Social Democratic parties that came to power jointly or separately in Austria, Switzerland, Denmark, Norway, Sweden and in Belgium, the Netherlands and Luxembourg (the Benelux countries) never suffered the political decline experienced by Social Democratic parties in Germany, Italy and France after 1946. The resilience of the Social Democrats in Northern Europe resulted both from their interwar popularity and from the absence of strong Communist scares in the post-war period; in the 1950s Social Democrats were in power, as in Scandinavia, or shared power, as in the Netherlands, Belgium and Austria.

In retrospect, the year 1948 seems to mark a breaking point in the post-war history of Europe. By this time, left-of-centre parties were out of power in the major continental European countries. Only the more reform-minded Labour party in Britain managed to cling to power until 1951. It was also 1948 when foreign funds, primarily through Marshall Plan aid, speeded up the economic recovery of Europe.

Moreover, 1948 and 1949 were the years of the division of Europe into two hostile camps. Beginning with the formation of NATO in 1949, for a decade European countries had to follow the dictates of either the United States or the Soviet Union in foreign affairs.

But 1948 was also a hopeful beginning for Western Europe. It was in that year that rapid economic recovery began. And that year also marked the inception of long-term plans for economic cooperation that eventually developed into the European Common Market.

FURTHER READING

Josef Becker and Franz Knipping's *Power in Europe* (1986) contains many insightful essays with recently available sources on the immediate post-war period. The rest of the readings below cover only the immediate post-war year. Fuller treatments of the first ten or more years are found in the Further Reading section of Chapter 4.

For sympathetic treatments of the British Labour government see Kenneth O. Morgan, Labour People (1987); Keith Hutchinson, *The Decline and Fall of British Capitalism* (1951); C. R. Attlee, *As It Happened* (1954); Maurice Bruce, *The Coming of the Welfare State* (1961); and Emanuel Shinwell, *The Labour Story* (1963). A thorough recent study is Henry Pelling, *The Labour Governments, 1945–51* (1984). Details on British industry under the Labour government can be found in Arnold A. Rogow, *The Labour Government and British Industry* (1955); W. A. Robson, *Nationalised Industry and Public Ownership* (1960); and Andrew Shonfield, *British Economic Policy Since the War* (1958). For more critical accounts see Ernest Watkins, *The Cautious Revolution* (1950); R. H. S. Crossman, *New Fabian Essays* (1952); and Richard Titmuss, *Income Distribution and Social Change* (1962).

For standard thorough accounts of the first years of the French Fourth Republic see Alexander Werth, *France, 1940–1955* (1956); Francois Goguel, *France Under the*

Fourth Republic (1952); Dorothy Pickles, *French Politics: the First Years of the Fourth Republic* (1953); A highly critical account of the first post-war leaders can be found in Ronald Matthews, *Death of the Fourth Republic* (1954). A study by Catherine Gavin, *Liberated France* (1955), heaps most of the blame for the failures of the Fourth Republic on de Gaulle. Irwin Wall, *French Communism in the Era of Stalin* (1983) offers an important reassessment of the post-war Communist party. Wall argues that the PCF did not desire revolution but integration into a broadly based democratic coalition. His *L'Influence americaine sur la politique francaise* (1989) argues that American influence on post-war French politics was much less than previously believed. A particularly insightful analysis of the crisis of French socialism during this period is provided by Bruce Graham, *Choice and Democratic Order: The French Socialist Party, 1937–1950* (1994).

Thorough accounts of post-war Italian politics include M. Grindrod, *The Rebuilding of Italy: Politics and Economics, 1945–55* (1955); Norman Kogan, *A Political History of Italy: The Postwar Years* (1983); H. Stuart Hughes, *The United States and Italy* (Rev. 3rd ed., 1979); and Joe LaPalombara, *Democracy, Italian Style* (1987). For Italian neo-fascist movements see Leonard B. Weinberg, *After Mussolini: Italian Neo-Fascism and The Nature of Fascism* (1979). Joan Barth Urban's *Moscow and the Italian Communist Party, from Togliatti to Berlinguer* (1986) argues that the Italian Communist Party began its independent course from Moscow already in the immediate post-war years. For the United States' role in Italian affairs see John L. Harper, *America and the Reconstruction of Italy, 1945–1948* (1986); James G. Miller, *The United States and Revolutionary Italy, 1940–1950* (1986); and Ronald L. Filippelli, *American Labor and Postwar Italy, 1943–1953: A Study of Cold War Politics* (1989).

For the smaller European countries see W. B. Bader, *Austria Between East and West, 1945–55* (1966); and William T. Bluhm, *Building An Austrian Nation* (1973). The Scandinavian countries are treated in Ander O. Fritof, *The Building of Modern Sweden: The Reign of Gustav V, 1907–1950* (1958); D. A. Rustow, *The Politics of Compromise: A Study of Parties and Cabinet Government in Sweden* (1955); Alice Bourneuf, *Norway: The Planned Revival* (1958); and Harry Eckstein, *Division and Cohesion in Democracy: A Study of Norway* (1966). Post-war Spain is given a balanced treatment in Stanley G. Payne, *The Franco Regime, 1936–1975* (1987). Sheelagh M. Ellwood's *Spanish Fascism in the Franco Era* (1987) provides a useful summary of Falangism. Paul Preston's *Franco* (1994) contains much new information and a reinterpretation of the Franco regime. Portugal is treated in Hugh Kay, *Salazar and Modern Portugal* (1970); and Charles E. Nowell, *Portugal* (1973). The Greek Civil War is competently covered in E. O'Ballance, *The Greek Civil War, 1944–49* (1966); and W. H. McNeill, *The Greek Dilemma: War and Aftermath* (1947). John O. Iatrides treats the first stages of the civil war in *Revolt in Athens: The Greek Communist 'Second Round,' 1944–1945* (1972). Jon V. Kofas' *Intervention and Underdevelopment: Greece During the Cold War* (1989) provides coverage of the post-war period.

3 Economic Recovery in Western Europe

> To present the postwar growth as one of history's unpremeditated happenings would be most unhistorical. For what distinguishes the postwar era from most other periods of economic history is not only its growth but the extent to which this growth was 'contrived': generated and sustained by governments and the public.
>
> M. M. Postan, *An Economic History of Western Europe*, 1945–60

In the two decades following 1948, revolutionary economic changes laid the groundwork for what many observers termed the New Europe. By 1960 Europe had regained its place as the leading trading area in the world, with nearly one-quarter of the world's industrial output and 40 per cent of the world's trade.

Few expected the economic recovery to proceed as rapidly as it did. When the United States was providing some of the initial financing for European recovery through Marshall Plan aid, no one envisioned that a couple of decades later we would be studying the rapid European growth rates in order to find some means to stimulate the US economy. As the quote by Postan suggests, government economic management was a critical factor in this growth.

Equally unexpected was the integration of much of Europe, including some former enemies, in one large economic entity known as the European Economic Community or, more familiarly, the Common Market, which went into effect on 1 January 1958. Although the Common Market failed to achieve all that was expected of it at first and European economic growth rates slowed appreciably in the late 1960s, by the 1980s some of the highly developed European countries surpassed the wealth and affluence of the United States on a per capita basis.

Characteristics of European Economic Recovery

The war, in numerous ways, stimulated economic growth. Amid the rubble that covered large areas of Europe at the end of the Second World War were numerous factories that needed only minor repairs before they could resume operations. Only about 20 per cent of Europe's factories were demolished or seriously damaged.

In some cases the destruction wrought by bombing provided the impetus for long-term economic growth. The systematic bombing of residential areas necessitated the reconstruction of entire cities, which served as a stimulus to the building trades. Moreover, the productive resources of the Second World War belligerents had increased immensely during the war. A team of German researchers estimated that after damages and dismantling, fixed assets in German industry increased by 7 billion German marks from 1936 to 1945. With this increased productive capacity and the shortage of consumer goods throughout Europe, an absence of financial resources remained the only serious obstacle to rapid economic growth.

Wartime destruction of plants, equipment and capital goods proved to be an added benefit; it permitted a modernization that made European industry highly competitive. The destruction of a portion of Europe's transportation network prompted the complete modernization of a number of national railway systems. France closed down unnecessary lines, eliminated pre-war bottlenecks, and electrified one-fifth of its rail network. Now French trains are considerably longer and faster than British trains and can thus ship goods at lower cost.

Marshall Plan Stimulus to Recovery

Some of the capital necessary to finance the initial reconstruction and modernization of European industry was provided by the United States. Western Europe's desperate need for funds in 1947 to keep recovery underway was provided by Marshall Plan aid. Without this aid, ambitious economic expansion programmes begun in 1945 would have been disrupted. The United States offered the aid with the objective of achieving European economic as well as political integration in order to fend off a perceived Communist threat.

There was a considerable amount of self-interest in the decision since a financially sound Europe would provide a large market for US products. But there was also compassion for those suffering from wartime losses as well as the realization that the European countries would have to be helped more than they had been after the First World War. By 1947 the United States had already provided $15.5 billion in aid to Europe, $6.8 billion of that being outright gifts. But the bulk of American aid, $13.7 billion, was provided by the Marshall Plan from 1947 to 1952.

By 1949, when the United States entered a recession, Europe was able to finance its own industrialization. Contributing to this economic recovery was the rapid growth of exports, especially in West Germany. In 1949 German exports doubled over the previous year, and the following year they increased another 75 per cent.

Few expected the rapid economic growth to be more than a short-term phenomenon. But as Table 3–1 indicates, growth rates through the early 1960s were not significantly lower than those of 1948–54. The cyclical fluctuations of boom and bust typical of pre-war economic growth were not characteristic of post-war Europe. It was this long-term, sustained growth that was later studied in the United States with the objective of raising its own growth rates

Table 3–1 Compound rate of growth of gross domestic
product in selected countries, 1949–63 (percentages)

	1949–54	1954–59	1960–63
West Germany	8.4	6.6	7.6
Austria	5.7	5.7	5.8
Italy	4.8	5.6	6.0
Spain	6.4	5.7	–
Switzerland	5.7	4.6	5.1
Netherlands	4.9	4.1	4.7
France	4.8	4.1	4.6
Portugal	4.2	4.0	–
Norway	4.2	2.7	3.5
Sweden	3.5	3.2	3.4
Denmark	3.7	3.4	3.6
Belgium	3.7	2.5	3.2
United Kingdom	2.7	2.3	2.5
United States	3.6	3.3	–
Canada	4.2	4.4	–

Source: David S. Landes, *The Unbound Prometheus: Technological Change and Industrial Development in Western Europe from 1750 to the Present* (Cambridge: Cambridge University Press, 1970), p. 497. Reprinted by permission of Cambridge University Press.

above the 3–4 per cent annual rate of the 1960s. Although some economists have sought to single out one or two primary causes of the high growth rates, there appear to have been a multitude of reasons.

Trade Stimulus to Recovery

Although Marshall Plan aid was an important early stimulus, the ever-increasing foreign trade provided the most important stimulus to economic growth after 1949 by raising foreign sales, personal income and domestic demand. In the 1950s the exports of Germany, Italy and the Netherlands rose more than 10 per cent annually compared to a 6.4 per cent growth rate for world exports. Much of the increase resulted from the worldwide relaxation of trade restrictions.

Most important for Europeans was the easing of trade restrictions under the auspices of the European Payments Union (1950), The Coal and Steel Community (1951), the Common Agricultural Policy's (1950) and the Common Market after 1958 (see Chapter 7). However, Common Market membership was not indispensable for rapid economic growth. One country outside the Common Market, Austria, experienced a growth of industrial output second only to that of West Germany. Even if there had not been a Common Market, the worldwide increase in trade would probably have been sufficient to stimulate European industrial recovery. But the Common Market did provide a number of advantages. It gave European agriculture a much larger internal market and protected it with uniformly high tariffs against foreign, especially US imports. French agricultural exports to Common Market countries increased during the 1950s from about 15 to 41 per cent of the country's total agricultural exports.

Demographic Stimulus to Recovery

Demographic changes provided another important impetus for the rapid economic growth following the war. A rising birth rate coupled with the influx of refugees and foreign workers swelled the population of Western Europe from 264 million in 1940 to about 320 million in 1970. In the immediate post-war years, refugees from Eastern Europe provided much of the labour for West German industry. More jobs were available than there were people to fill them after 1948, and each additional labourer added to European output and demand. The refugees constituted a large supply of cheap labour, encouraging investment in industry since it assured industrialists that manufacturing costs would remain low and Europe's exports would remain highly competitive in the market. When the flow of refugees stopped, foreign workers came from Southern Europe and then from Southeastern Europe, North Africa, the Iberian peninsula and Turkey to man the Western European factories.

Refugees had increased the West German population by 4 million, and foreign workers had added another 3.6 million by 1962. But it was in France that the demographic change was most marked. After more than a century of remaining steady, the French population increased from 42 million in 1950 to about 50 million in 1966, and de Gaulle hoped for a France, including colonies, of 100 million people by the year 2000. Although some of this increase was the result of immigration, most of it was brought about by a rise in the birth rate.

Beginning in the interwar period, French leaders tried to encourage population growth by raising family allowances. In the post-war period France increased family allowances and added rent subsidies because the French leaders saw population growth as a way to revitalize the country. Foreign workers came to France primarily from Algeria, Spain, Portugal and Italy. In Switzerland and Luxembourg, one-third of the labour force came from the less industrialized areas of Europe.

A growing population with the wherewithal to buy new housing and a severe shortage of housing units provided a long-term impetus to industrial expansion. Especially in Germany and Holland, entire cities had to be re-built. From 1953 to 1964 Germany had the highest per capita housing construction in the West: half a million units a year. Some economists see housing construction as the major reason that Europe did not experience a business recession for so long after the war. These economists predicted an end to the building boom and considerably lower growth rates. But massive government support for the

Automobile plant in Birmingham, England.
(© Getty Images)

building trades has prevented a slump in construction on several occasions since the Second World War and was used again during the 1970s to lessen the impact of Europe's worst post-war recession.

At the centre of European economic resurgence is the automobile. As one of the leading economic sectors, it has promoted growth in the steel industry, road building, service stations and countless associated industries. From a production of about 500,000 vehicles in the late 1940s, European vehicle output reached 9 million units a year in the 1970s before encountering Japanese competition in the late seventies. The age when the theft of a bicycle was a tragedy for the European family has passed. Europeans love for their cars and for driving speeds rival those of American adolescents. The automobile was as much a status symbol in Europe in the 1960s as it was in the United States a decade earlier, and Europeans now buy new cars before they improve their housing. Such status seeking has also led to a decline in the European's love affair with the Volkswagen 'beetle' and a growing desire for larger, faster cars. Only the rise in gasoline prices brought about by the increased price of Middle East oil dampened the enthusiasm for larger, more prestigious cars.

The New Capitalism

The fact that European economic growth was not seriously affected by economic slumps in the 1950s, as it was in the pre-war period, resulted from the retreat of laissez-faire economics and the growth of government intervention in the economy. Post-war economic problems were of such magnitude that governments had to intervene to provide basic foodstuffs and raw materials and to prevent unemployment, and reconstruction tasks could often be carried out only by the government. In some cases, governments decided to nationalize industries that were considered indispensable: railroads, airlines, public utilities and some heavy industry. Called modern capitalism or neo- capitalism, it has been characterized by a mixture of private and government initiative in what is essentially a free enterprise system. Government control of banks and budgetary policies had permitted governments to determine the rate of growth of their economies. When European economies seemed headed for recession or inflation, governments stepped in to regulate the economy by manipulating the monetary system as well as supply and demand.

Despite some variations, the new capitalism entailed government acceptance of Keynesian economics and economic planning. Keynes's *The General Theory of Employment, Interest and Money*, written in 1936, provided the theoretical groundwork for neo-capitalism. In recasting the traditional free enterprise system, Keynes contended that full employment led to high consumption and increased productivity. Full employment could be attained, he said, through governmental manipulation of taxation and expenditure that would sustain the demand for goods and services at a high level. He rejected the generally accepted theory that governmental stimulation of the economy would lead to inflation and rising prices, which would in turn lead to economic chaos. Keynesian economists take the position that if workers are provided with high wages, they will consume more and industry will prosper. If labour and management accept such policies, class conflict should diminish as the two sides decide on appropriate wages to maintain economic expansion.

In practice, some countries have implemented full employment policies and have established wage guidelines and incomes policies that have met most labour demands. The implementation of Keynesian economics helped governments avoid fluctuations in the business cycle that brought unemployment and recession. By stimulating demand during periods of recession, governments were able to prevent serious depressions. On the other hand, inflation has been kept in check by restricting credit and raising taxes.

The policy of full employment was soon supplemented by a policy of economic growth. In order to meet the steadily growing expenditures for social services and armaments, as well as the public demand for improvements in the standard of living, governments adopted a policy of rapid economic growth. And, now that economic progress was being equated with high annual growth rates, various forms of economic planning had to be adopted in order to direct investment to those economic sectors that would maximize growth.

To achieve maximum economic growth, most countries drew up long-term plans and centralized planning in government agencies. By 1960 France, Belgium, Austria, Italy, Sweden, Norway and the Netherlands had instituted some form of long-range economic planning. Western planning did not specify production quotas or allocate all raw materials and investment funds, as was done in Eastern Europe and the Soviet Union, but set general guidelines for future economic development and provided financial aid to sectors that would stimulate growth.

The amount of interference in the economies varied considerably in Western Europe. In France the precedents for planning were set under the Popular Front government in the decade before the Second World War. After the war the new planning agency, set up under Jean Monnet, became another arm of the government. The Monnet Plan aimed to use German coal and coke to make the French Steel industry internationally competitive. Once France realized that the Ruhr coal and iron ore resources were not going to be internationalized but returned to German control, the Monnet Plan logic necessitated a close working relationship with Germany in order to obtain coal and coke. This plan led naturally into Robert Schuman's European Coal and Steel Community proposal to integrate the heavy industrial resources of the later Common Market countries.

Great Britain, because of its historic dedication to laissez-faire principles, was slow to institute economic planning. Only after serious economic difficulties compelled repeated government intervention did British leaders become convinced in 1961 that long-term planning was necessary. Soon after the war, Sweden set up a Labor Market Board in which employers and labour planned construction and investment in order to sustain full employment. The one partial exception in this era of planning is Germany. As a reaction to Nazi intervention in the economy, and at the urging of the Allies, post-war West German leaders sought initially to divest the government of control over industry. Yet the government did intervene in the economy every time it granted subsidies, low-cost loans, or tax breaks to favoured enterprises.

One economist has described West German industry as 'organized private enterprise.' Huge industrial corporations commanding enormous sources of capital remain highly competitive in the international market. Instead of government planning, the Federation of German Industry engages in investment planning and long-term forecasting of supply and demand. The federation is dominated by three large banks that obtain agreements among industrial enterprises to avoid competition. Bankers hold important seats on the supervisory boards of the major West German corporations, the big three banks holding more than half the seats.

Industrial Concentration and Nationalization

Planning was made easier throughout Western Europe by the concentration of industry and by government nationalization of important industries. Once a government nationalized the large enterprises in an industry, smaller competitors were forced to cooperate. Compliance with government planning usually brought with it tax relief, state contracts and loans. These advantages and nationalization have promoted the development of huge industrial corporations.

One such corporation, the *Societe Generale* of Belgium, dominates the Belgian economy. As one of its directors put it, 'The *Societe* is not too large;

it's just that Belgium is too small'. By 1960 it had under its control 40 per cent of the iron and steel industry, 30 per cent of coal, 25 per cent of electrical energy and 70 per cent of the insurance companies.

Four huge corporations – Royal Dutch Shell, Unilever, Philips and AKU–dominate the Dutch economy. The annual income of only one, Royal Dutch Shell, is larger than that of Switzerland.

In Italy monopolization and state control permitted the government to participate extensively in long-range industrial planning. Some of the firms that were nationalized during the Fascist period became enormous industrial conglomerates. By 1963, the government-owned IRI (*Istituto per la Ricostruzione Industriale*) consisted of 120 companies with 280,000 employees. Financial resources are firmly under the control of the government; the major commercial bank is nationalized, and the IRI controls over four-fifths of the capital of the next three largest banks. The IRI and the other great public corporation, ENI (*Ente Nazionale Idrocarburi*), were responsible for more than one-third of all capital investment in manufacturing, transportation and communications by 1964. Both ENI and IRI established the necessary infrastructures (inexpensive energy sources, producer goods and roads) that permitted the growth of huge private companies: Fiat, Perelli, Olivetti, etc.

In Austria the nationalized industries accounted for 24 per cent of industrial production and 27 per cent of exports in the sixties. Government control extends also to finance.

In France, jurisdiction over the most important French banks, the *Caisse des Depots* and the *Credit National*, gave the French government control over credit.

A non-economic factor that has contributed mightily to post-war recovery is the belief among industrialists and civil servants alike that economic expansion is not only desirable but attainable. Despite the tendency of some French and English to avoid rapid economic growth lest they be forced to take unnecessary risks to sustain the growth rates, most European industrialists and civil servants have become supporters of what M. M. Postan calls growthmanship. For example, the director of ENI in Italy, Enrico Mattei, while successfully developing Italy's natural gas deposits, pushed production to the point of exhausting Italian resources. As important as the attitude of managers was the attitude of the general public that economic growth is necessary and achievable. Europeans became willing in the sixties to make long-term investments in their economies instead of hoarding their money or sending it abroad in search of profits.

Agricultural Developments

Changes in agriculture have rivalled the revolutionary transformation of industry. Many European countries have made the transition from small-scale subsistence agriculture before 1945 to agricultural production aimed primarily at the much larger urban market. Despite the rapidly growing demand in Europe, a technological revolution in agriculture began to produce massive surpluses by the 1970s.

In 1974, 40 per cent of the bumper 1973 wine crop had to be distilled into alcohol. And the EEC was also compelled to either buy up or dispose of especially large surpluses of dairy products and meat.

Increased mechanization, greater use of fertilizers and insecticides, improved seed and modern equipment have produced the surpluses; the number of tractors in the countries of the EEC rose sixfold from 370,000 in 1950 to 2,330,000 in 1962. The number of farm animals has been increased through artificial insemination, while their size and quality have improved by better feed and selective breeding.

The development of larger, more efficient agricultural units has not kept pace with technological changes primarily because of government policies. Lest they antagonize agricultural voters, governments have subsidized agriculture and have thus preserved many small high-cost farms. In France, Germany, and the Benelux countries, strong organizations of farmers mobilize their members to prevent any change in this policy. Armed with pitchforks, farmers have opposed all EEC attempts to alter their privileged status.

The Common Market perpetuated the system of government protection and high agricultural prices. High tariffs were set against foreign products as tariffs between the EEC members were slowly reduced. To offset lower international prices, an EEC agricultural fund subsidized members' exports. Such protection places a disproportionate burden on the mass of consumers, who have to pay considerably more for their food than consumers in the rest of the world. Third-world countries have accused the EEC of being a rich man's club because of its exclusion of foreign agricultural products. As a result, many agreements have been reached with third-world countries in order not to exclude their products.

One of the major obstacles to British entry into the EEC was Britain's agricultural sector, which is on a larger scale and more productive than those on the Continent. British farms average 200 acres each, compared to a continental average of about 40 acres. But the small total acreage in Britain, necessitating large imports of food, was a sufficient enticement to EEC members once Britain promised it would slowly stop purchasing lower-priced products from its Commonwealth partners.

Membership in the EEC has brought about a major transformation in Italian agriculture. Many peasants who farmed marginal land in the south and central part of Italy were drawn to the industries in Northern Italy, Switzerland, Germany and France. This migration put an end to the tillage of marginal land and thus reduced Italian agricultural output. Italy must now import more food from its EEC partners – at the much higher supported prices – than is produced by the remaining peasant population. While this rationalization of industrial and agricultural production is one of the EEC goals, it has placed a special burden on Italy's balance of payments. In 1974 France felt it necessary to subsidize its exports to Italy when Italy had to reduce food imports to overcome a severe financial crisis. However, Italian firms have profited enormously from the larger European market and began to overcome the imbalance of payments in the eighties.

France: Economic Development

Beneath the surface similarity of post-war economic development there are many national differences. Even within each state there are considerable regional differences and conflicts over the rapid growth of industry. Nowhere is this more apparent than in France. The French economy was encumbered with small businesses and their centuries-old attitude, 'What I have may be small but it is mine.' Small-business opposition to the concentration of French industry was centered in the PME (Unions of Small and Medium-size Business) and the Poujadist movement. Before the PME accepted the so-called new France in 1958 it constantly opposed the concentration of business and industry and upheld the small family enterprise as typically French.

More violent in its support of a static France and in its opposition to the modernization of French industry was the Poujadist movement. Led by a small grocer, Pierre Poujade, the movement opposed the Common Market, fought higher wages for labour, resisted higher taxes and sought government support for small businesses. Although Poujadism itself faded, the movement lived on. In the early 1970s Jean Royer, who is both the mayor of Tours and France's minister of commerce and small business, became the new champion of the small businessman. A bill he proposed gave small businessmen who sit on municipal councils the power to veto the building of huge chain stores or supermarkets in their areas. In 1974, serious clashes occurred in France between the local municipal councils and employees of supermarkets that were prevented from expanding.

But there is the other France, dominated by the new citizenry bent on economic modernization. This is the France of the Caravelle, Concorde, Renault and the Plan. It is also the France of Robert Schuman and Jean Monnet, the architects of Western European economic integration. It is the France of those teams of industrialists, the *missions de productivite*, who studied in the United States after the war to prepare themselves to put France on a modern economic footing. Although Schuman proposed the European Coal and Steel Community primarily to rid Europe of its internecine wars, particularly those between Germany and France, he was also aware of its great economic potential. Jean Monnet's first economic plan concentrated on the long-term reconstruction of basic industries rather than on the alleviation of the housing shortages.

This is also the France that has been renowned for its technical creativity since the nineteenth century. A prime example of this creativity was the conception and production of an excellent jet passenger plane, the Caravelle, long before a similar plane flew in the United States. This creativity also characterized the building of the first supersonic passenger plane, Concorde, in the 1970s. This is, of course, the France that is responsible for the dramatic social and cultural changes that threaten the individualism and uniqueness of the old France. Laurence Wylie's study of change in the small French village of Roussillon, *Village in the Vaucluse*, indicates that this new France has won out over the France of the PME and Poujade. In the 1950s peasants refused to plant orchards lest they be destroyed in the Third World War. In the 1960s the peasants were going into debt to plant olive trees that would not mature for twenty years.

Before Charles de Gaulle returned to power in 1958, the French economic miracle was well under way. As Table 3-1 shows, the French gross domestic product had been increasing at over 4 per cent a year for a decade. Nevertheless, the stability provided by the de Gaulle regime and the propitious timing of the devaluation of the franc in 1958, immediately before a rapid expansion of world trade, increased the nation's exports dramatically. Gold and foreign exchange reserves jumped from a mere 10 million francs in 1959 to 28.6 billion by late 1966.

West Germany: Economic Development

A superficial view of the West German economy might leave one with the incorrect impression that post-war German economic growth was solely the result of laissez-faire economics. While it is true that the German government does not engage in long-term planning as the French government does, other institutions in Germany do engage in short-term planning.

As we have seen, the Federation of German Industry, in concert with the banks, manipulates investment in order to regulate industrial output and control prices, and the German government constantly intervenes in the economy by means of taxation and subsidies. One example of this tactic is the 1951 Investment Aid Act, which taxed German business a billion marks in order to finance reconstruction in heavy industry and to develop energy sources. Another measure, the Housing Act of 1950, provided public subsidized housing projects for low-income families and housing projects with tax preferences for the builders. As a result, before 1961 the government financed more than half the housing construction by direct capital investments and tax reductions granted to builders.

The role of German banks in German industry has grown immensely since 1945. Immediately after the war the Allies divided Germany into eleven states, each with its own budget and taxing power. To prevent the concentration of banking typical of the Nazi period, ties between the banking services of the various states were prohibited. However, the Allied decision to fortify West Germany so as to counter the presumed threat from the Soviet Union led directly to the removal of economic barriers between the German states and the reconcentration of German banking. By 1950 the Deutsche and Dresdner banks were again in control of all their branch banks, and the remaining member of the big three, the Commerz Bank, regained control of its branch banks in 1958. Two years later these three banks controlled about 56 per cent of German industrial shares. The Deutsche Bank, according to a London banker, is equivalent in size to the English Midland, Barclay's, Hambro's, Baring's, Rothschild's and Cazenove's all rolled into one.

The banks and industry cooperate extensively to regulate output and avoid destructive competition. By occupying almost one-fourth of all seats on corporate boards of directors, eleven German banks discourage investments that they consider unproductive or that they think will increase competition among firms associated with them. They have been able to convince companies to produce products cooperatively and have prevented the overproduction of goods. While such regulation by banks, firms and trade associations is never as comprehensive as the national planning in France, it does permit a division of production that is not typical of a true laissez-faire state.

The post-war concentration of industry has permitted closer control. By 1960, the 100 largest firms accounted for 40 per cent of industrial production. Seven West German firms were among the twenty largest European enterprises in the 1960s: Volkswagen, Siemens, Thyssen-Hutte, Daimler-Benz, Farbwerke-Hoechst, Farbenfabriken Bayer and Krupp.

Nationalized until 1961, Volkswagen epitomized the resurgence of German industry. The car that the British considered too ugly and noisy to achieve mass acceptance has been one of the major factors in West Germany's favourable balance of trade since the early 1950s. In 1967 Volkswagen sold more cars in the United States than in Germany. Cleverly merchandised – 'Your second car, even if you haven't got a first' – Volkswagen faced little serious competition from European car manufacturers until the 1960s. Then, it was challenged by producers of larger family cars, primarily Fiat, and its European sales slipped below those of Fiat.

Volkswagen was also falling victim to the status consciousness of Europeans, who no longer thought the Beetle an appropriate status symbol. In the United States, it was challenged by smaller American cars, which offered similar economy. Although Volkswagen's sales remained high into the seventies because of the production of new models and continued high foreign sales, it lost much of its foreign market to Japanese cars in the 1970s. In 1974 VW was offering 7000 marks to any worker who would quit. Of course, the sales of German luxury cars, Mercedes and BMWs in particular, have kept the German automobile sales high. Such luxury cars have become a necessary status symbol among many Americans.

Britain: Economic Decline?

Compared to the high economic growth rates on the Continent, the British economy has experienced a relative decline since 1945. As Table 3-1 indicates, the growth of gross national product from 1949 to 1963 was three times as high in West Germany as it was in Great Britain. French, Italian and Austrian growth rates have been about twice as high. This situation has led one British critic to castigate his country as 'the stagnant society.'

Another indication of the relative economic decline was a very low average annual percentage increase in exports of 1.8 per cent compared to increases above ten per cent in Germany, Italy, the Netherlands and Norway and above six per cent in most other Western European countries. However, when British growth rates are compared to the lower increases of the United States, her economic performance does not appear so bleak. Unquestionably, there has been a relative decline, but it should be pointed out that Great Britain has sometimes been unfairly compared to countries that were much more in need of massive post-war reconstruction – Germany, Italy and Japan.

A large share of the responsibility for Great Britain's discouraging economic performance rests with the government. Both the post-war Labour and Conservative governments were reluctant to interfere in industry. Nationalization was viewed not as a means to enhance efficiency but as a last-ditch effort to save stagnant industries. The vast majority of British firms received little support or direction from the government. Lurking in the back of every Labour and Conservative minister's mind was the conviction that the free enterprise system, which had served Britain so well in the past, would be sufficient for the future. Therefore, contrary to the continental experience, long-term planning was rejected in favour of haphazard short-term intervention in the economy.

One example is a Labour decision to reduce industrial investment in the belief that it would ease the pressure on the external balance of payments. The expectation was that industrial imports would be reduced and more capital equipment would be exported. But instead, output went down and more consumer goods had to be imported.

In some cases, large British firms prevented government intervention in the economy. Development councils, proposed by the Labour government to aid research and promote exports, were rejected by large enterprises on the assumption that small firms would dominate the councils and that the councils were a step towards nationalization.

Industrial management hindered economic growth in other ways. Managers failed to modernize their factories and make their products internationally competitive. One study has shown that American-controlled firms in Great Britain yielded 50 per cent higher returns than the British-managed firms because of lower administrative costs, better salesmanship, higher productivity, and greater concentration of capital investment.

The British automobile industry represents a clear example of Britain's inability to capitalize on its post-war potential. With the continental car companies unable to meet European demand, the British had an excellent opportunity to break into the European market. But English car manufacturers resisted mergers and continued to produce a huge variety of automobiles, none of which could capture a large share of the continental market. Even after two companies merged in 1951 to form the British Motors Corporation, the new firm continued to produce the same old cars. Eventually it did turn out the Mini, thereby breaking the tradition of heavy, rugged cars typical of British automakers. But by this time, other European car manufacturers were meeting the European demand.

A 1968 merger of BMC and Leyland Motors into one huge enterprise called British Leyland Motors, coupled with Britain's entry into the Common Market, did not raise the sales of British automobiles as many expected. Foreign sales of British cars were restricted to a few Europeans and Americans who consider ownership of a Rolls Royce or a Jaguar a status symbol.

Italy: Economic Development

Despite a slow beginning, since 1954 the Italian economic growth rate has exceeded those of all other EEC states except West Germany. However, this growth was restricted to the north, where Italians enjoy a standard of living similar to northern Europeans. Except for small pockets of industrialization, Southern Italy has remained an underdeveloped area.

In the early 1970s a large portion of EEC development money was still going to Southern Italy. Italian politicians and industrialists were at first more intent on developing their markets within the EEC than on developing the south. Fiat, the largest automobile manufacturer in Europe, refused to open plants in the south on the ground that industry had to be concentrated in order to meet modern competition.

To be sure, the concentration of industry and banking has been a major reason for Italy's rapid industrial expansion. The fact that IRI controls a number of banks and 120 companies makes possible a concentration of capital for investment purposes, a reduction of domestic competition, and a focus on the European market. The concentration of oil and gas resources permits ENI to compete with the large American petroleum companies for foreign markets and petroleum resources. Plentiful supplies of labour have kept wages low and Italian products highly competitive in Europe and the international market. In 1966 Italian wages were only about half those in West Germany and Great Britain. Serious labour unrest was avoided through the employment of thousands of Southern Italian labourers in Germany, Switzerland and France.

A rapidly growing domestic and foreign demand and an internal concentration of industry have created a number of mammoth firms. In the 1960s Italy was producing most of the refrigerators used in the Common Market, and Fiat had become the largest automobile manufacturer in Europe. Within Italy the demand for cars continually outstripped the supply. In 1960, one out of every twenty-one Italians owned a car, in 1968, one out of seven. And Olivetti became one of the world's largest producers of office machines.

Post-war Development Patterns

By the end of the 1960s Europe was divided among a variety of economic organizations and exhibited a multitude of economic faces. Wide differences existed between the advanced industrialized west and north and the predominantly agrarian underdeveloped south. Economic change was beginning to transform Spain, but Portugal and Greece had undergone little economic modernization.

Emigration to the labour-hungry factories of the north provided a measure of relief for a small segment of the population, and worker remittances to their families provided some stimulus to the south, but this could not be a long-term substitute for economic modernization at home. In some cases emigration tended to thwart modernization by siphoning off skilled professionals and labourers. In agriculture emigration often brought improvement by removing surplus population from the land, but sometimes large areas were virtually depopulated, agricultural output dropped and costs rose as food had to be imported. The short-term benefits of emigration became apparent in the 1970s when a Western European economic recession forced many migrant workers to return to their native countries.

Western Europe itself was shocked by the high inflation rates and reduced growth rates of the early 1970s, as detailed in Chapter 12. The Keynesian manipulation of the economy no longer produced immediate results, as it had done in the 1950s and early 1960s. European optimism flagged as growth rates dipped and unemployment figures climbed. Countless economic conferences were held to ascertain the problems and provide the remedies for economic stagnation.

But the slump was probably unavoidable. The growth rates had been extremely high for nearly two decades but could not be sustained indefinitely. With consumption levels approaching those of the United States, Western Europe began to experience similar economic difficulties. There were limits to the demand that could be stimulated in order to perpetuate high rates of growth. Europe was more dependent on exports than the United States, but was now facing competition from areas of high output and low labour cost such as Japan. Rising unemployment held down domestic demand. The advanced states of Europe will undoubtedly be hard put to attain the economic growth rates of the past and will have little choice but to endure a certain amount of unemployment. As John Kenneth Galbraith pointed out, demand can be artificially stimulated by convincing people that they must buy unnecessary commodities, but there is a point beyond which the market becomes satiated.

FURTHER READING

Two of the best studies of post-war reconstruction are Alan S. Milward's *The Reconstruction of Western Europe, 1945–51* (1984) and *The European Rescue of the Nation State* (1992). Milward challenges all those who claim that the successful economic and political reconstruction of Western Europe resulted from the idealism of statesmen, by arguing that it grew out of the pursuit of narrow self-interest by all the countries involved. The Marshall Plan resulted from American self-interest and European economic integration was primarily the outcome of French self-interest. The role played by international institutions in Western Europe's recovery – the IMF, the World Bank, the European Coal and Steel Community, the European Payments Union, GATT – are analysed and the relative importance of domestic and international factors in Europe's post-war recovery is weighed in Barry Eichengreen's (ed.) *Europe's Post-war Recovery* (1995).

An excellent older survey of European industrialization with coverage of the post-war period can be found in David Landes, *The Unbound Prometheus* (1970). Another survey, Sidney Pollard's *Peaceful Conquest: The Industrialization of Europe, 1760–1970* (1981) stresses the British industrial experience. Indispensable examinations of the post-war period are Andrew Shonfield, *Modern Capitalism: The Changing Balance of Public and Private Power* (1969); M. M. Postan, *An Economic History of Western Europe, 1945–1964* (1967). A stimulating analysis of the role of labour in promoting post-war growth can be found in Charles P. Kindleberger, *Europe's Postwar Growth: The Role of Labor Supply* (1967). *Power in Europe? Great Britain, France, Italy and Germany in a Postwar World, 1945–1950* (1986), edited by Josef Becker and Franz Knipping, provides many insightful essays on politics, economics and foreign affairs in the immediate post-war period.

For details of French planning see Elie Cohen *L'Etat Brancardier* (1989); Peter Hall's *Governing the Economy* (1986); and Jack Hayward's *The State and the Market Economy, Industrial patriotism and economic Interventionism in France* (1986). An outstanding study of France's economy in the twentieth century is Richard F. Kuisel's *Capitalism and the State in Modern France: Renovation and Economic Management in the Twentieth Century* (1981). Kuisel stresses the role of long-term planning in French economic growth. The British economy is treated in M. W. Kirby, *The Decline of British Economic Power since 1870* (1981); and the immediate First World War years are analysed in Anthony Carew's *Labour under the Marshall Plan* (1987). Kirby provides a summary of reasons previously advanced for Britain's slow growth after 1945. Carew focuses on the implications for British labour unions and their relationship with management. For Germany see Charles Maier (ed), *The Marshall Plan and Germany* (1991); and Anthony Nicholls, *Freedom with Responsibility: The Social Market Economy in Germany 1918–1963* (1994). For Italy see George A. Hildebrand, *Growth and Structure in the Economy of Modern Italy* (1965); and Kevin Allen and Andrew Stevenson, *An Introduction to the Italian economy* (1975). For Sweden, see Steven Koblick, ed. *Sweden's Development from Poverty to Affluence, 1750–1970* (1975).

In *The Marshall Plan: America, Britain, and the reconstruction of Western Europe, 1947–1952*, Michael J. Hogan argues that the United States wanted to 'refashion Western Europe in the image of the United States.' In their edited book *The Americanisation of European Business* (1998), Matthias Kipping and Ove Bjarnar argue that even American management practices were transferred between countries. In *The Marshall Plan: Fifty Years After* (2001), a collection of essays edited by Martin Schain, the key question that is addressed was the relevance of the Marshall Plan for post-war European recovery, and its impact on the shape of post-war Europe. A recurring theme in many of the chapters is the use made of Marshall Plan support by key political leaders in Western Europe to pursue their own political agendas.

Among the many publications of economic statistics are the Organization for Economic Co-operation and Development annual surveys of all member states, OECD *Observer*, United Nations Statistical Yearbooks, and the United Nations annual economic surveys of Europe.

4 Western European Politics, 1948–60s

> France intends to once again exercise sovereignty over her own territory, at present infringed upon by the permanent presence of Allied military forces and by the use which is being made of her airspace, to end her participation in the integrated command, and to no longer place her forces at the disposition of NATO.
>
> Guy de Carmoy, *Les Politiques Etrangeres de la France,* 1944–66

The rapid economic growth in Western Europe and improved East–West relations determined the course of political development from 1948 into the 1960s. Spared serious economic crisis after 1948, the politically moderate and right-of-centre forces in the major Western European countries were not challenged seriously by the left. Growing economic affluence, combined with government extension of social welfare services and full employment policies, stilled demands for a truly revolutionary political change. Parties on the left, kept from office by the improving economic conditions and their own revolutionary rhetoric, began to adopt reformist rather than revolutionary policies. Moderate reformers, such as Willy Brandt in West Germany, emerged as the new leaders of Socialist parties.

Only the Communist parties of France and Italy, which attracted primarily working-class support, continued to pay lip service to revolutionary objectives. But even their revolutionary zeal was dampened by the Soviet Union's suppression of the Hungarian Revolution in 1956. Social Democratic parties gained or shared government office in the 1960s in Italy and Germany only by compromising their former ideals or by breaking away from their revolutionary associates and becoming reformist parties similar to the British Labour party and the Scandinavian Social Democratic parties. In foreign affairs, Europe's economic resurgence and a reduction of Cold War tensions led to a gradual restoration of European self-confidence and the reduction of United States influence in Europe, especially in de Gaulle's France as the opening quote illustrates.

Italian Political Affairs

The impact of economic improvement and the Cold War is clearly discernible in Italy during this period. As described in Chapter 2, the Cold

War and United States influence had led the Christian Democratic party (DC) to drive the Communist party (PCI) from the government in 1947. That same year the reformist issue split the Socialist party into a reformist Social Democratic wing under Giuseppe Saragat and the still revolutionary Socialists (PSI) under Pietro Nenni and Lelio Basso. In a quadripartite government coalition held together only by the parties' shared hostility towards communism, Saragat found that there was considerable opposition to his reformist ideas, especially since the dominant Christian Democratic party based its strength on the Catholic Church, big business, big land-owners, the lower-middle class and the peasantry.

Eventually, with the aid of the left wing of the DC led by Alcide de Gasperi, some of the Saragat-backed reforms were started. In 1949 and 1950 a few large estates totalling 20 million acres were expropriated in the south and sold to the peasants. But after the initial redistribution, the DC failed to push further agrarian reform. Only mass emigration to the industrial areas in the north temporarily relieved the situation. As a result, in the 1953 elections the Communist party gained a million votes in the south. Meanwhile, Nenni had led the Socialist party into close cooperation with the Communist party. But Nenni, never comfortable with this alliance, offered to break with the Communists in 1953 and enter a coalition government with the DC if his PSI were given important cabinet positions. Rejecting this offer, de Gasperi and then a succession of premiers put together bare majorities that reduced the government to immobility for the next five years. Heavily factionalized, the Christian Democrats had to rule as a minority party or find partners among the small centre parties since they would not seek a coalition with a Left or Right party. Governments changed rapidly as one or another faction gained predominance in the DC. Only domestic prosperity and decreasing international tension made such government inaction tolerable.

A leftward trend in successive elections in 1953, 1958 and 1963 resulted from decreasing Cold War tensions, rapid economic growth, and the moderating position taken by Palmiro Togliatti, leader of the Communist party. The Communists were responding to a growing sense of economic well-being which was reflected in labour's selection of more moderate factory and labour union officials. Shocked by the Soviet Union's crushing of the Hungarian Revolution in 1956, Togliatti became convinced that his rightward shift was the proper course.

When Nenni's PSI decided in 1957 to break with the Communist party and seek a coalition with the DC, Togliatti led the PCI even further to the right in order to restore the Left coalition. Despite this, Nenni continued to seek a role for the PSI in a coalition with the DC. The attempt to gain PSI approval for the coalition failed in 1957 when the left wing of the party gained a majority against Nenni. When he finally gained a majority for his position, his left-wing opponents within the PSI broke away and formed the Socialist Party of Proletarian Unity, or PSIUP.

Nenni's efforts finally succeeded in 1962 when DC leaders agreed to a centre–left coalition with the PSI. The left wing of the DC, led by Aldo Moro and Amintore Fanfani, had been trying to arrange an 'opening to the left' since 1958. Although there was a considerable opposition within the DC to a coalition with the PSI, public support for it was growing. A strong trend to the left in the 1958 parliamentary elections indicated that Italians were finding the parties on the left more acceptable and that they were becoming discontented with the government's immobility.

Adding immensely to the public's acceptance of the Socialists and their desire for social reform was the papacy's acceptance of the welfare state in the 1960s. This momentous change in papal policy was a direct result of the election of Angelo Roncalli as Pope John XXIII in 1958. A product of humble beginnings himself, Cardinal Roncalli had gained further knowledge of the world's ills on diplomatic missions to the Balkans and as papal nuncio to France. When he became pope he was determined to bring the Church into line with modern political and social change. This meant a reversal of the papacy's century-old opposition to all forms of socialism and, in the 1960s, adjusting to the institution of the welfare-state throughout Europe. In the 1961 Papal Bull *Mater et Magistra* (Mother and Teacher) Pope John expressed the papacy's approval of the mixed economy, economic planning and social justice. A second major papal encyclical, *Pacem in Terris* (Peace on Earth), confirmed this new papal attitude only a few weeks before the 1963 elections.

Within the DC Moro manoeuvred his party closer to the PSI by encouraging DC–PSI coalitions at the local level. With the support gained from forty such coalitions, Moro and Fanfani convinced the majority of the party to accept the PSI in 1962. The PSI had to accept a pro-Western position, including continued membership in NATO and the EEC, and the DC accepted the PSI plan for the nationalization of electric power and the establishment of more regional governments. The DC had originally opposed the regional governments, fearing the left would control most of them. When the left made further gains in the 1963 elections, indicating an increased desire for reforms, Moro was able to convince the recalcitrant DC deputies that his course was necessary in order to keep the DC in power. After some initial difficulties, Moro put together a left–centre cabinet with Nenni as vice-premier. This leftward trend continued into the 1970s as Cold War tensions declined and the Communist party became even more reformist.

West German Political Affairs

More than any other European country, West Germany reflects the impact of economic prosperity on government and politics. In what is often described as the German economic miracle, the Federal Republic had once again become a major economic power by the sixties. German exports rose from 8.4 billion to 52.3 billion marks between 1950 and 1963 and comprised 11 per cent of world exports. During the same period, industrial production nearly tripled. (See Chapter 3 for comparative growth rates and reasons for the economic recovery.) This rapid recovery permitted Christian Democratic (CDU) Chancellor Konrad Adenauer to rule in an authoritarian manner.

Convinced that the failure of the Weimar Republic in the 1920s resulted from a weak executive and internecine warfare among the many political parties, Adenauer believed with de Gaulle that too much democracy would lead to political failure and economic chaos. Supported by widespread voter approval for his policies of stability and anticommunism, Adenauer instituted a policy of 'chancellor democracy' that circumvented the authority of parliament whenever possible. Few voices were raised in opposition to his extensive use of executive authority lest economic growth be slowed or the delicate position of Germany in international affairs be destroyed.

The government placed increased industrial production above social equalization. But because of the booming economy, industrial workers could boast of higher salaries than those paid in other major continental countries. Sharing in the prosperity, the trade unions dropped all references to Marxism and initiated a form of unionism similar to that of North America (see Chapter 8). Members of the Confederation of German Trade Unions (DGB) take a major part in developing social legislation within the federal parliament, and workers are included on the governing boards of industrial enterprises.

In some respects the Adenauer government provided West Germans with the stability and self-confidence to recover from wartime defeat and destruction and to be accepted by other European states. His staunch anti-Nazism, which led to his imprisonment during the Second World War, and his efficient and honest government restored German pride and European trust in a reconstituted German state. His friendship for France permitted the restoration of the French-occupied Saar region to Germany in 1957 and led to extensive cooperation between France and Germany. Adenauer had favoured merging German military forces with the armies of France, Italy and the Benelux countries in the European Defence Community proposed in 1950 (see Chapter 7).

His foreign policy had a strong pro-Western orientation, and the West needed allies in the Cold War and the Korean War. Together, these led first to German rearmament within NATO, including French acceptance of rearmament when Britain promised to keep troops in West Germany, and ultimately to German independence in 1955. Adenauer also guided West Germany into membership in the Council of Europe, the European Coal and Steel Community, and eventually the EC.

Adenauer's aggressively pro-Western policy led him to reject a Soviet offer in 1954 of German unification in exchange for neutrality. Adenauer also feared that his party would lose office in a reunited Germany since most East Germans, being Protestant, would not vote for the Catholic-based CDU.

Actually, the Soviet Union attached so many conditions to the unification proposal, especially the withdrawal of all Allied troops before elections could be held, that the Allies would never have accepted them. Moreover, both the Soviet Union and the West wanted a Germany created in their own image. Khrushchev wanted a reunited Germany only if it retained the 'political and social achievements' of East Germany. Of course, the Allies and Adenauer were unwilling to accept the extensive social changes already instituted in East

Germany. Finally, neither France nor the Soviet Union was happy at the prospect of a new German state of nearly 70 million people.

Perhaps the greatest change brought about by the sustained prosperity in Germany was the transformation of the German Social Democratic party (SPD). Until the mid-1950s the SPD was led by pre-war Socialists who had suffered severely under the Nazi regime. Their first post-war leader, Kurt Schumacher, had spent ten years in Nazi concentration camps. Under his leadership the SPD favoured reunification, opposed close association with the capitalist West and strenuously opposed NATO, German rearmament and European integration. However, when the party failed to gain major national office or influence political and economic affairs, some of the younger members began to challenge the SPD's orthodox Marxist programme and agitate for a reformist course within a laissez-faire state. At the local level, reformers slowly replaced those desiring more revolutionary change.

The most dramatic change was the election of the reformer Willy Brandt to head the SPD in Berlin in 1958. Large election gains for the CDU in the 1957 parliamentary elections provided the reformers with a major argument for adapting the SPD programme to what they saw as the economic and political realities of the day. At the Bad Godesberg party conference in 1959, Communism was condemned by a reformist majority that declared 'The dictatorship of the proletariat is no longer a reality in our time.'

By a vote of 324 to 16, the conference reversed party policy on almost every important issue. It dropped Marxist terminology, rejected nationalization of industry, approved private property, and accepted the Western alliance and rearmament. The economic success of Ludwig Erhard's social-market economy had overwhelmed those who still favoured a Marxist approach.

The selection of Willy Brandt, the popular Social Democratic mayor of West Berlin to head the party sealed the victory of the reformers. In their eyes, their choice of course was proved right in the 1961 parliamentary elections when SPD seats in the Bundestag increased from 169 to 190 and CDU seats dropped from 270 to 242.

The 1961 elections indicated further that the CDU was beginning to lose its hold on the German electorate. A measure of the disenchantment could be attributed to the slowing of economic growth and the onset of a mild recession. But other factors were political infighting in the CDU and Adenauer's increasingly authoritarian behaviour. In 1959 Adenauer had agreed to take the post of president and give up the chancellorship to Ludwig Erhard. When he realized that Erhard, whom he personally disliked, would be the real ruler in Germany and the presidency would be only a titular post, Adenauer went back on his word. This type of behaviour was tolerated when economic growth was rapid and Germany's future was in doubt; now it became intolerable.

After the election losses in 1961 Adenauer managed to gain support for his plan to form a new cabinet only by promising to retire before the 1965 elections. But before he retired he became involved in another incident that was to blemish his own reputation and that of the CDU. Adenauer's defence minister,

Franz Josef Strauss, irritated when the magazine *Der Spiegel* published what he considered to be secret military information, arrested five members of the editorial staff. When both Strauss and Adenauer refused to take responsibility for the affair, the Free Democratic party members of the cabinet threatened to resign and thus bring down the government. Strauss was eventually forced to resign, and Adenauer promised to resign in the fall of 1963.

This incident brought into question Adenauer's, and indirectly the CDU's, commitment to democratic government. It tarnished Adenauer's reputation and made the ministry of his successor, Erhard, much more difficult. Throughout West Germany it unleashed a spate of criticism of many CDU programmes. Critics contended that Germans had not received the proper education in the principles of democracy because of Adenauer's authoritarian government. The criticism further indicated that the German public did not want a return to arbitrary government.

When Erhard failed to stem the economic recession and the Free Democrats quit the coalition government in 1966, the way was paved for the SPD to share power with the CDU in 1966 and gain power in a coalition with the Free Democrats in 1969.

French Political Affairs

The changes in French socialism and politics have been as dramatic as those in West Germany. As early as 1945 the Socialist party (SFIO) accepted the Western orientation of French foreign policy and coalition with the Christian Democrats (MRP). Socialist leader Ramadier refused to support the candidacy of Communist leader Thorez for French premier. The exclusion of both Communists and Gaullists from the government after 1947 produced an extremely fragile centre–left coalition of the SFIO, MRP, the moderate-liberal Radicals and Moderates. This quadripartite coalition, held together primarily by a shared dislike for the PCF and De Gaulle, could not agree on a unified economic or colonial policy.

The 19 different governments between 1948 and 1958 prevented France from dealing resolutely with its domestic or foreign policy. Only the eight-month government of Pierre Mendes-France can claim much success. This government paralysis, called *immobilisme* in France, resulted from the internal divisions between right and left that prevented a legislative-based executive from acting resolutely over an extended period of time. On the right, traditional conservatives, Gaullists, colonialists and radical-rightist Poujadists battled for the vote, and the left was divided by the Communist and Socialist parties. The centre parties failed to maintain any long-term voter support. For example, the centrist MRP gradually lost support as its left-wing supporters shifted to the Socialists and its right wing joined with moderates or Gaullists. De Gaulle's political support was also not dependable. The national movement he established in 1947, the Rally of the French People (RPF), gained 40 per cent of the vote in the October 1947 municipal elections but then faded as its conservative supporters switched to traditional right-wing groups. The RPF managed to become the largest party in the 1951 parliamentary elections, by altering the proportional election system to permit a party or coalition that won a majority in any constituency to take all the seats in that area. This change in the electoral system led to the displacement of the MRP and the Socialists as the dominant parties by the right-wing Radicals and even more conservative Independents. The MRP lost about half of its following to the RPF in the 1951 elections.

Governments fell rapidly in the 1950s as colonial problems multiplied, but even successes in colonial policy were not always sufficient to insure government stability. Premier Pierre Mendes-France had ended French involvement in the Indochina War (see Chapter 5) and granted autonomy to Tunisia in 1954, but he fell from office the following year when he was unable to change his Radical party's economic policies from laissez-faire to economic planning. A reform-minded Radical–Socialist coalition government of 1956, led by Mendes-France's reformist Radicals and Guy Mollet's Socialists, was overthrown by rightist opposition. It fell in early 1957 when its attempts to reform the tax system were defeated by conservative opposition.

By the mid-1950s, foreign policy – the EDC, Indochina, Suez and particularly Algeria, inflamed political exchange and pushed domestic issues off centre stage. The Algerian rebellion brought down the Fourth Republic, returned de Gaulle to power, and enabled him to change dramatically the French tradition of a dominant legislature. It also thrust de Gaulle and France into a position of European dominance that prompted some observers to dub European history from 1958 to 1968 'the de Gaulle era.' For Europe as a whole, de Gaulle's resolution of the Algerian problem instilled a new confidence and respect that enabled Europe to chart a more independent course.

The Fourth Republic was split over Algeria. The right, including the Gaullists, strenuously opposed any concessions to the Algerian rebels. Support for the right came from more than a million French settlers (*colons*), four-fifths of them born in Algeria, and from a large segment of the French army. The loss of Indochina in 1954, the failure of the Anglo-French force against Egypt's Nasser in 1956 and the granting of independence to Tunisia and Morocco in 1956 made French rightists and the army determined to keep Algeria. The army, numbering nearly half a million in Algeria by 1957, had concluded that the French government could not be trusted to 'save' Algeria for France. Attacks from the right diminished the stability of the Fourth Republic and led to a steady decline in its control over the army.

Ironically, a decisive attempt to resolve the Algerian issue by the normally indecisive Fourth Republic brought about its downfall. On the last day of January in 1956 an Algerian reform bill, providing for regional autonomy and equality of voting for Muslims and Europeans in Algeria, was rendered unworkable by French military action against the Algerian rebels, who now refused to accept the bill. When the Fourth Republic selected a ministry headed by Pierre Pflimlin (MRP) in May 1958, a man the army and the *colons* expected would offer concessions to the Algerian rebels, French army units with *colon* support occupied the palace of the governor-general in Algiers in

May 1958 and set up a Committee of Public Safety with General Jacques Massu at its head. The rightists and certain army officers then began to prepare a paratroop attack on Paris.

This anarchic situation enabled the Gaullists to demand the return of de Gaulle to prevent a civil war in France. After a round of negotiations with President Rene Coty, the national assembly approved de Gaulle as the new premier on 1 June 1958. When de Gaulle told the French Assembly that he had formed a government to preserve the republic, one sceptical deputy warned, 'Today, chamber music. Tomorrow, a brass band'.

The crisis atmosphere gave de Gaulle the opportunity to institute the kind of government that would provide the strong executive authority he desired. Never wavering from his conviction that the French government should not be dominated by the legislature, de Gaulle pushed through a constitution that increased the power of the executive and reduced the authority of the assembly. The constitution that set up the Fifth Republic, approved by 80 per cent of the voters on 28 September 1958, permitted the president to appoint the premier and to dissolve parliament. Although the premier and the cabinet theoretically shared executive authority with the president, de Gaulle now wielded power comparable to that of the American president.

Elections in November further solidified de Gaulle's position by giving the Gaullist UNR (Union for the New Republic) 189 of the 576 seats in the National Assembly. A return to the Third Republic electoral system that required a run-off election in districts where no candidate received a majority succeeded in reducing the representation of the Communists and their allies from 150 deputies to only 10. De Gaulle was selected as president by an overwhelming 78.5 per cent of the votes from an electoral college of over 80,000 voters.

In 1958 de Gaulle's objectives were not yet clear even in his own mind. He was influenced by foreign criticism and the possibility that a United Nations vote of condemnation might thwart his objective of restoring French prestige in the world. Now, armed with the new powers given to him by the new constitution, he could tackle the Algerian problem with increased confidence and bring the army back under the control of the government.

To gain military support, de Gaulle at first kept his aims vague, thus leading the army to believe that he would keep Algeria French. Although he wanted to retain Algeria, he realized by 1959 that the Algerian rebels, led by the FLN (National Liberation Front), would not accept continued French suzerainty. His offer of Algerian self-determination in September 1959 was refused by an ever more confident FLN leadership and violently opposed by the French army leaders in Algeria, who now felt betrayed. In January 1960 a mass uprising against de Gaulle's policies, the Barricades Revolt, failed when metropolitan France rallied to his side.

When de Gaulle began to speak about a possible Algerian Republic after November 1960, the French army and *colons* in Algeria adopted yet more violent tactics. A Secret Army Organization (OAS) was set up in Algeria to intimidate those who would support a free Algeria and to bring down de Gaulle's government by means of terrorism and assassination. In April 1961 the army generals in Algeria rebelled, took over the government of Algeria, and threatened military action against metropolitan France. Only de Gaulle's immense prestige made defeat of the generals possible. Supported over-whelmingly in France, he appealed directly to military units not to support the generals. When the air force and the navy chose to follow him, the army generals had to surrender.

De Gaulle was now determined to resolve the Algerian problem and end military disobedience by granting independence and bringing the army home. On 18 March 1962, negotiators for the FLN and the French government met at Evian-les-Bains and decided to grant Algeria its full independence on 3 July 1962. These Evian Accords granted the *colons* equal rights and provided compensation for the property of those who wished to leave Algeria. Despite widespread OAS terrorism to keep the French settlers in Algeria, within a year only 100,000 remained. With the Algerian problem resolved and the French army firmly under his control, de Gaulle could now turn to his goal of making France the leader of Europe.

To increase French prestige and strength, de Gaulle believed the authority of the president had to be increased further and the power of the political parties had to be reduced. He viewed political parties as divisive forces and therefore tried to circumvent them by appealing to the populace through national refer-endums. To strengthen the office of the president he held a referendum in 1962 on the direct election of the president. Despite the opposition of the National Assembly, which had not approved the referendum, it won the support of 67.7 per cent of the voters.

Now de Gaulle no longer had to please the electors, who were associated with political parties, in order to stay in power. When the assembly censured his ministry, with Georges Pompidou as premier, de Gaulle dissolved the assembly and called new elections. Often he threatened to resign, and often he warned of the weaknesses of parliamentary government. These ploys helped the Gaullists to gain 250 of the 480 seats and an absolute majority in the assembly.

Despite the election success, de Gaulle's popularity soon began to decline. Many resented his blocking of British entry into the EEC in 1963. Others shifted their support away from de Gaulle when it became apparent that he wished to reduce French democracy to a facade. A growing number felt that France should not try to develop an independent French military deterrent – as we shall see – but should concentrate on domestic problems. The vote in the 1965 presidential elections reflected a shift towards the left. In the first popular election of a president since 1848, de Gaulle captured only 44 per cent of the votes; François Mitterrand, candidate of the newly formed Left – Federation (Socialists, Communists and Radicals) carried 32 per cent; and the other major candidate, Jean Lecanuet, representing a Centrist coalition, received 16 per cent. France was not yet ready for a Socialist president, how-ever. In the run-off election against Mitterrand, de Gaulle gained 54.5 per cent of the vote. Despite this victory, popular resentment against de Gaulle would

Algerian independence rally.
(© Getty Images)

soon reduce Gaullist support and steadily increase the strength of the left in French politics.

Even before de Gaulle had resolved the Algerian problem he began to implement another of his major goals, the reduction of United States influence in Europe. Since de Gaulle was little influenced by ideologies, except for his dislike of the French left, he did not believe in a struggle between Communism and capitalism for world dominance. He viewed Soviet actions in terms of old-fashioned balance of power considerations rather than from the American perspective. In other words, he felt that Soviet expansionism was limited to Eastern Europe and therefore posed no threat to Western Europe. What is more, he believed a reduction of American influence in Western Europe would not lead to a sovietization of Western Europe but would enhance French power in Europe.

In March 1959 de Gaulle began to withdraw French naval units from the NATO Mediterranean Command as the first step in the French withdrawal from NATO. The United States humbling of the Soviet Union in the Cuban missile crisis in 1962 and subsequent United States/Soviet steps towards detente convinced de Gaulle that his perception of the Soviet 'threat' was accurate.

In order to establish France as an independent third force between the two superpowers, de Gaulle undertook the development of an independent French nuclear force. In 1964 he refused to sign the nuclear test ban treaty sponsored by the United States and the Soviet Union since it would prevent France from developing its own nuclear force. In 1965, France pulled out of the Southeast Asia Treaty Organization (SEATO) and refused to participate in NATO military manoeuvres. In 1966 French forces were withdrawn officially from NATO, and its headquarters was transferred from Paris to Brussels. Contributing to this show of independence was an economic upsurge that brought France a $6 billion gold reserve by 1965.

Despite these actions, de Gaulle was unable to resolve European–Soviet differences unilaterally. By this time, Soviet leaders were more interested in dealing directly with the United States to resolve world and European problems. Still, de Gaulle had begun the gradual loosening of United States/ European ties, and other countries followed suit in the late 1960s and 1970s as the United States became mired in the Vietnam War.

British Political Affairs

After defeating a divided, ideologically confused Labour party in 1951, Great Britain's Conservative party retained office until 1964 through the acceptance of the welfare-state, the impact of several periods of rapid economic growth, and the continued division in the Labour party. Returning to power at the age of 77, Winston Churchill changed little of the previous Labour government's programmes. Improving economic conditions permitted Churchill to end food rationing, an issue that had contributed to Labour's defeat, and to carry out the Conservative campaign promise to build more than 300,000 houses a year to relieve Britain's housing shortage and stimulate the economy.

Now convinced that the British wanted the welfare-state, Churchill did no more than increase medical fees slightly and reverse Labour's nationalization programme only in the iron and steel industry and in road transport. The Conservatives did, however, change Labour's policy of raising income taxes to achieve a more equitable distribution of wealth. The Conservatives hoped that the reduction of income taxes would also stimulate the economy.

When a heart attack forced Churchill to retire in 1955, Anthony Eden became prime minister. A business boom in 1954 and 1955 and another reduction in income taxes put an even larger Conservative majority into the House of Commons in the 1955 elections.

Within a year after Eden assumed power he was called upon to deal with Egyptian leader Gamal Abdel Nasser's nationalization of the Suez Canal (see Chapter 5). Backed by the majority of the Conservative party and by France, Eden tried to force a reversal of Nasser's policy. In the face of stiff United States and United Nations opposition, Britain was forced to back down. Before the crisis had passed, Eden suffered a nervous breakdown and was replaced by Harold Macmillan.

'Supermac' proved to be a more capable leader than Eden. Supported by improving economic conditions, Macmillan spent little time on domestic affairs. He travelled more than 80,000 miles in eighteen months in an attempt

to ease Cold War tensions and restore British respectability after the humiliation of Suez. At home, his government slowed investment in the economy and
restricted credit in order to avert another devaluation of the pound. Although
these measures eventually put the brakes on economic growth and added to the
unemployment rolls, a renewed business boom in 1958 and 1959 gave the
Conservatives an even larger majority in the House of Commons in the 1959
elections. Labour's support for an expansion of welfare programmes apparently
contributed to its resounding defeat.

The Labour party was plagued by divisions over social welfare and rearmament throughout the decade. Led by Aneurin Bevan, the left continued to
demand more attention to social welfare. The right, under the leadership of
Hugh Gaitskell, a former Oxford University economics don, and Clement
Attlee, opposed an extension of welfare and the growth of the bureaucracy it
would bring about. After the 1959 elections, the right wing convinced the party
to jettison nationalization in favour of expanding economic growth through
full employment and periodic stimulation of the economy.

Leftist intellectuals writing for the *New Left Review*, shocked by the Soviet
suppression of the Hungarian Revolution, began to emphasize democratic
socialism in place of class conflict and economic controls. The Labour support
for British development of the hydrogen bomb in 1957 produced a new left
movement, the Campaign for Nuclear Disarmament (CND). The CND and the
left wing of the party finally got Labour to reverse its stand on nuclear
weapons but not its drift towards a more moderate political and social
programme.

An economic downturn after 1959, reflected in a growing inflation rate and
an unfavourable balance of trade, undermined Conservative support. Although
Macmillan resorted to a wage freeze, increased indirect taxes, and initiated
some very unconservative economic devices to overcome the economic downturn – even including a modified form of economic planning – he was unable
to turn the economy around.

The economic malaise stemmed from a variety of shortcomings in the
British economy described earlier (see Chapter 3), as well as from growing
competition from the continental European countries and Japan. Adding to
Conservative woes in 1963 was de Gaulle's veto of British entry into the
Common Market. Although Britain's entry would certainly not have brought
immediate relief to the British economy because of the dislocations accompa-
nying entry, it was a severe blow to Macmillan's much-publicized plans for
British entry.

Then Macmillan's Secretary of State for War, John Profumo, became the
subject of a scandal. As banner headlines reported day after day, he was
involved with a call girl, and she had been asked by a naval attaché of the
Soviet Embassy to get all the information she could from Profumo on Britain's
nuclear arsenal. Although Macmillan demanded and got Profumo's resignation,
he was himself compelled to take some of the responsibility. This scandal and
his increasing bad health led him to tender his resignation.

Macmillan was replaced by Sir Alec Douglas-Home. Even though Douglas-Home lacked the charisma of Macmillan and of the Labour candidate, Harold Wilson, he won the election by a slim four-seat margin. Despite all of the Conservatives' problems, there was still considerable anxiety about a Labour government.

Nordic Political Affairs

There was little anxiety about left-of-centre governments in Scandinavia. With the exception of Finland, where the Agrarian and Socialist parties shared power, the Scandinavian countries had Socialist-dominated govern-ments from the end of the war until the mid-1960s. Only Denmark had a brief interruption, from 1950 to 1953, of Social Democratic or Labour party lead-ership. The Social Democrats might have gained power in Finland were it not for the Soviet Union's preponderant influence and its distrust of the Social Democrats. As the conservative parties in Western Europe had profited from the post-war economic resurgence, so did the Socialist parties in Scandinavia.

Economically, Western Europe had been divided into two blocs, the European Economic Community (France, Italy, West Germany and the Benelux countries) and the European Free Trade Association, or EFTA (Austria, Denmark, Great Britain, Norway, Portugal, Sweden and Switzerland). This caused some eco-nomic dislocations, but in general the Scandinavian countries profited from the expansion of both. In 1960 about one-third of Swedish exports were going to partners in EFTA and another one-third to the EEC. Denmark, always a major exporter of farm products, managed to bring its industrial exports abreast of its agricultural exports by means of a concerted industrialization programme coupled with tariff reductions among EFTA countries.

The Norwegian Labour party and the Swedish and Danish Social Democrats, which had been in power since the interwar years, increased their popularity during the rapid economic expansion by extending social welfare services. Sweden adopted compulsory health insurance and pension plans, family allowances and other social measures that cost the country $3 billion a year (see Chapter 8). By 1965, Denmark and Norway had similarly become social welfare states.

The economic resurgence had contributed to Socialist success in the 1950s, and the economic downturns in the 1960s undermined their leadership. An economic slowdown in Denmark in the mid-1960s, caused by the high tariff walls erected by the EEC, resulted in a devaluation of the kroner. Adding to the Socialist woes were exceedingly high direct and indirect taxes, needed to support the welfare-state, that were increasingly resented by the population. When both the Social Democrats and their coalition partner, the Socialist People's party, lost votes in the 1968 elections, a group of centre parties formed a governing coalition.

Labour's thirty-year rule in Norway, weakened also by the EFTA-EEC split, ended when the Conservative, Liberal and Centre parties formed a coalition cabinet. However, these changes had little effect on domestic policies since all Scandinavian parties accepted the welfare state.

Benelux Political Affairs

Politics in the Benelux countries are incredibly complex because of the plethora of parties – ten parties won parliamentary seats in the 1963 elections in the Netherlands – and because ethnic and religious differences intrude into the political arena.

In Belgium the division between Flemish (Dutch)-speaking Belgians and French-speaking Belgians (Walloons) often cuts across party lines. In general the Flemish support the Catholic party – the Social Christians – whereas the Walloons favour the Socialists and the Liberals. State support for Catholic schools became a major issue in the 1950s and was resolved only through a compromise that permitted the state to supplement the salaries of teachers in church-sponsored schools. Controversy over Louvain University (the Flemish wanted it to be exclusively Flemish), was resolved only by a division of the university into separate Flemish and Walloon institutions, called Leuven and Louvain-le-Neuve, respectively.

Relatively slow economic growth – the gross national product, or GNP, grew at a rate of only 2.7 per cent in the 1950s – exacerbated the ethnic–linguistic division. The Walloons, who had dominated the country in the interwar period, suffered most from the economic stagnation. Most new industry was built in the Flemish region because of its superior transportation facilities, and the southern Walloon area bore the brunt of the economic decline because the coal resources in that area had been exhausted. When the government tried to revitalize industry in 1960 by applying austerity measures, including reductions in welfare benefits and public works as well as various aids to industry, a twenty-seven-day general strike brought down the government.

In the 1960s the Flemish–Walloon division continued to inhibit government attempts to resolve the nation's economic problems. Ministries fell in 1965 and 1968 primarily over the language issue. There was some relaxation of tension late in the decade as EEC aid ended the economic stagnation and encouraged a greater sense of community. Moreover, the economic impact of losing the Belgian Congo and Rwanda-Burundi was offset by the improving economic conditions. The creation of dual ministers for education, culture, economy and community problems further reduced the Flemish–Walloon acrimony.

Despite the multiplicity of parties in the Netherlands and the division of most institutions along religious lines, rapid economic growth has tended to keep the turmoil down to manageable proportions. Although the Netherlands had suffered severely from German bombardment during the war, its geographic location at the mouth of the Rhine and its traditional focus on commerce contributed to its rapid recovery as world trade picked up and German industry expanded. Rotterdam has become the leading seaport in Europe and the Dutch, the major EEC shipping nation. The loss of Indonesia in 1949 had little effect on the Dutch economy, as evidenced by the doubling of industrial output from 1954 to 1964 and by the growth of commercial activities.

The Catholic People's party and the Labour party dominated the political scene throughout the 1950s and 1960s. A Labour and Catholic People's party coalition ruled the country until 1958, when Labour lost support by its unorthodox policy of wage-fixing. After 1958, the Catholic People's party in coalition with two Protestant (Calvinist) parties took over the premiership. Both major parties lost votes and suffered internal splits in the mid-1960s, but they continued to dominate the coalition governments or renew their association, as they did in a ministry in 1965 and 1966.

Austrian Political Affairs

The easing of Cold War tensions, coupled with rapid economic growth, had a singular impact on Austrian political affairs. Occupied by the wartime Allies since the Second World War, Austria had had no chance to regain its national sovereignty during the Stalin era because Stalin considered Austria to be of strategic importance in Central Europe. But in 1955, Khrushchev, in a move to reduce Cold War tensions, agreed to end the occupation of Austria in return for an Austrian pledge of permanent neutrality.

At first, Austrian politics was changed little by the sudden end of occupation. The Social Democrats and Christian Socialists, which had shared political office and civil service jobs in direct proportion to their votes since the occupation began, continued their coalition for eleven years after the occupation ended. Both parties were cautious about resuming normal political activities lest there be a dangerous polarization of the kind that had erupted in civil war during the 1930s. However, rapid economic growth and the Social Democrats' adoption of a reformist rather than revolutionary course soon stilled fears of political chaos. With the restoration of political confidence, the coalition was ended in 1966 when the Christian Socialists gained sufficient votes to rule independently.

Iberian Political Affairs

In Southern Europe, where economic transformation was minimal, political affairs remained authoritarian. Spain and Portugal, under the dictatorships of Francisco Franco and Antonio Salazar, stoutly resisted political and social change into the 1960s. Opposition political parties continued to be banned in Spain but Franco was unable to prevent them from forming or put a stop to their clandestine activities. Despite opposition to his regime among the citizenry, Franco continued to receive support from the Catholic Church, the army and the Falange (the official party of the regime).

When opposition developed within the church and the army, Franco was obliged to permit limited reforms. Liberals among the Catholic clergy grew more outspoken in their opposition to Franco's authoritarianism; and young army officers, eager for faster promotions and economic modernization, agitated for change. A group of militant Catholics in the Opus Dei movement, including some government ministers, urged both economic modernization and closer association with the EEC. Bolstered by a strong position it won in the universities after the war, the anti-socialist, pro-monarchist movement sought to modernize Spain through a rejection of corporatist autarchy favoured by the Falange and the adoption of capitalism. After gaining Franco's support in 1957, Opus Dei technocrats directed Spain towards economic incorporation within the Western economic system. Spain's application for membership in the EEC in 1962 owed much to the Opus Dei insistence that Spanish modernization demanded Western capital, trade and expertise.

Franco's strongest opposition came from separatists in the Northern Catalan and Basque regions, who increasingly resorted to violence to achieve more autonomy. But the opposition groups, including the political parties, were unwilling to undertake a cooperative challenge of the regime. In the 1960s Franco weakened some of his opposition when he granted limited reforms. He relaxed press censorship, abolished military courts, gave the minorities greater rights, divided the executive powers between himself and parliament, and permitted the free election of 100 members of the 600-member parliament.

The regime was further strengthened when the long period of economic stagnation was brought to an end. Increased investments by the United States, Germany and France provided the necessary industrial capital. In return for permitting American bases in Spain, Franco received both economic and military aid. And as an added fillip, the Spanish economy got a boost from the flood of tourists who came to savour the sunny Mediterranean beaches and low prices.

The Economy in Political Affairs

As the Cold War's significance in domestic politics dwindled, economic factors predominated as determinants of political success or failure. While rapid economic growth in the 1950s had kept the right in the ascendant in the major European countries and had sustained social democracy in Scandinavia, economic downturns in the mid-1960s generated strong and sometimes successful challenges from political adversaries. Labour replaced the conservatives in Great Britain and the German Social Democrats gained a share of the Christian Democrats' political power.

Although the Italian Christian Democrats remained the dominant political party, they faced a growing challenge from parties to their left. Since the French economy did not begin a serious downturn until the late 1960s, and since de Gaulle's diplomatic successes were still fresh in the minds of the French up to that time, the Gaullist-led UNR remained strong until then. But centre and left coalitions formed, and de Gaulle's margin in 1965 was much narrower than expected, heralding the beginning of the challenge to Gaullist political dominance. In Scandinavia, only the Swedish Social Democrats managed to stay in power in the 1960s. The ruling Norwegian Labour party and the Social Democrats in Denmark fell from power primarily as a result of economic issues.

A particularly significant factor in the changing political fortunes of Europe's ruling parties was social welfare. In many of the major states the electorate was demanding extended welfare programmes and reforms, whereas in Scandinavia the electorate was demanding a halt to the extension of even more elaborate welfare programmes. In countries where social welfare and an economic downturn were combined issues, the parties in power were seriously weakened or were supplanted as the dominant parties.

FURTHER READING

Important studies of British politics are Samuel H. Beer, *British Politics in the Collectivist Age* (1965) and *Britain Against Itself: The Political Contradictions of Collectivism* (1982); R. Rose, *Politics in England* (1964); and R. M. Punnett, *British Government and Politics* (1968). Valuable analyses of the relationship between politics and the social structure of Britain are provided in Kingsley Martin, *The Crown and the Establishment* (1963); D. V. Glass, *The British Political Elite* (1963); and Anthony Sampson, *Anatomy of Britain Today* (1965). For the period during the first Labour government, see Peter Hennessy, *Never Again: Britain 1945–1951* (1992). British elections are treated in general by Pippa Norris, *Electoral Change in Britain Since 1945* (1997). Individual national elections are treated in the following: David E. Butler, *The British General Election of 1951* (1952) and the *British General Election of 1955* (1956); David E. Butler and Richard Rose, *The British General Election of 1959* (1960); David E. Butler and Anthony King, *The British General Election of 1964* (1965). Conflicting studies of the British Labour Party are Barry Hindess *The Decline of Working Class Politics* (1977); and Tom Forester, *The British Labour Party and the Working Class* (1976). Forester rejects Hinders' thesis that the British Labour Party experienced a de-radicalization and increasing control by the middle class. A more recent analysis of the Labour Party, situating its experiences in the 1950s and 1960s from the perspective of the 1990s is Eric Shaw, *The Labour Party Since 1945* (1996). On the Conservative party see John Ramsden, *An Appetite for Power: a History of the Conservative party Since 1830* (1998).

Valuable background studies of the development of French political ideologies and alignments and the relationship between society and politics can be found in Gordon Wright, *France in Modern Times* (1981); David Thomson, *Democracy in France* (1958); and Sudhir Hazareesingh, *Political Traditions in Modern France* (1994). Post-war French Fourth Republic politics are analysed in Philip Williams, *Crisis and Compromise: Politics in the Fourth Republic* (1964); and J.-P. Rioux, *The Fourth Republic, 1944–1958* (1987); subsequent and more general politics is covered by Philip Williams and Martin Harrison, *Politics and Society in de Gaulle's Republic* (1971); Lowell G. Noonan, *France: The Politics of Continuity in Change* (1970); Stanley Hoffmann (ed.), *France: Change and Tradition* (1963) and *In Search of France* (1965); Raymond Aron, *France: Steadfast and Changing*

(1960); Jacques Chapsal, *La Vie Politique en France depuis 1940* (1966); and Francois Goguel and Alfred Grosser, *La Politique en France* (1964).

Valuable studies of de Gaulle are Alexander Werth, *De Gaulle: A Political Biography* (1966); Jean Charlot *The Gaullist Phenomenon* (1970); and Brian Crozier *De Gaulle* (1973). Crozier's study is a lengthy and valuable synthesis that is critical of De Gaulle. French communism is treated in Charles A. Micaud, *Communism and the French Left* (1963); George Lichtheim, *Marxism in Modern France* (1966); Ronald Tiersky, *French Communism, 1920–72* (1974); and Irwin M. Wall, *French Communism in the Era of Stalin: The Quest for Unity and Integration, 1945–1962* (1983). For an important study on the dilemma of the French Socialists during this period, see Harvey Simmons, *French Socialists in Search of a Role, 1956–1967* (1970). Frank L. Wilson's study of the re-grouping of the non-Communist left is excellent, *The French Democratic Left, 1963–1969: Toward a Modern Party System* (1971). For further information on Christian Democracy see Mario Einaudi and Francois Goguel, *Christian Democracy in Italy and France* (1952); M. P. Fogarty, *Christian Democracy in Western Europe* (1957); and R. E. M. Irving, *Christian Democracy in France* (1973). R. Gildea also has a good discussion of the Christian democratic party in France, the MRP, in *France Since 1945* (1996).

The best studies of Italian politics after the war are S. J. Woolf, *The Rebirth of Italy, 1943–1950* (1972); Giuseppe Mammarella, *Italy After Fascism: A Political History, 1943–63* (1964); Norman Kogan, *A Political History of Post-war Italy* (2 vols., 1966 and 1981); Joseph LaPalombara, *Interest Groups in Italian Politics* (1963); and Donald Sassoon, *Contemporary Italy: Politics, Economy & Society since 1945* (1986). The Italian Communist party is competently treated in Donald Blackmer, *Unity in Diversity: Italian Communism and the Communist World* (1968); and Sidney Tarrow, *Peasant Communism in Southern Italy* (1967). The Christian Democratic party is covered in Mario Einaudi and Francois Goguel, *Christian Democracy in Italy and France* (1952); and M. P. Fogarty, *Christian Democracy in Western Europe* (1957).

For further information on the nature of West German politics during this period see Lewis J. Edinger, *Politics in Germany* (1968); Edward Pinney, *Federalism, Bureaucracy and Party Politics in Western Germany* (1963); and Uwe W. Kitzinger, *German Electoral Politics* (1960). The most informative but concise history of the Federal Republic is Michael Balfour, *West Germany: A Contemporary History* (1982). For a comparison of East and West German politics see Arnold J. Heidenheimer, *The Governments of Germany* (3rd ed., 1971).

The workings of the West German parliament are treated in Gerhard Loewenberg, *Parliament in the German Political System* (1967). The transformation of the Social Democratic party is analysed in Douglas A. Chalmers, *The Social Democratic Party of Germany: From Working Class Movement to Modern Political Party* (1964); and, more recently, Gerard Braunthal *The German Social Democrats Since 1969* (1994). For the Christian Democratic Union, see Geoffrey Pridham, *Christian Democracy in Western Germany: The CDU/CSU in Government and Opposition, 1945–1976* (1977). Two important studies of Adenauer are Arnold J. Heidenheimer, *Adenauer and the CDU: The Rise of the Leader and the Integration of the Party* (1960); and Richard Hiscocks, *The Adenauer Era* (1966). A more critical and controversial treatment of Adenauer and German politics is presented in Ralf Dahrendorf, *Society and*

Democracy in Germany (1969). An important study of German foreign policy is David Calleo, *The German Problem Reconsidered* (1978).

Valuable surveys of Franco's Spain are Stanley G. Payne, *Franco's Spain* (1967); Max Gallo, *Spain Under Franco* (translated from the French by Jean Stewart, 1974); and Raymond Carr and Juan Pablo Fusi Aizpurua, *Spain: Dictatorship to Democracy* (1979). Political dissent under Franco can be studied in Jose Maravall, *Dictatorship and Political Dissent: Workers and Students in Franco's Spain* (1978). Maravall shows how attempts to grow and develop through more liberal and open policies while maintaining authoritarian institutions led to worker and student dissent. Also valuable is Paul Preston, ed., *Spain in Crisis: The Evolution and Decline of the Franco Regime* (1976).

For the small states of Western Europe see D. A. Rustow, *The Politics of Compromise: A Study of Parties and Cabinet Government in Sweden* (1955). Norway is treated in Harry Eckstein, *Division and Cohesion in Democracy: A Study of Norway* (1966). For the Netherlands see Arend Lijphart, *The Politics of Accommodation: Pluralism and Democracy in the Netherlands* (1968); and Ken Gladdish, *Governing from the Centre: Politic and Policy Making in the Netherlands* (1991). Hugh Kay, *Salazar and Modern Portugal* (1970); and Charles E. Newell, *Portugal* (1973) cover Portugal during this period. For Austria see W. T. Bluhm, *Building an Austrian Nation* (1973); Gunter Bischof, *Leverage of the Weak: Austria in the First Cold War, 1945–1955* (1999); and Kurt Steiner, *Politics in Austria* (1972). For Belgium, see John Fitzmaurice, *The Politics of Belgium* (1994).

5   The End of European Empire

We prefer self-government with danger to servitude in tranquility.

Kwame Nkrumah, *Autobiography*

During the two decades following the Second World War, Europe lost its Asian and its African empires. The Asian empire was the first to go because of national liberation movements that began before the First World War. By 1965, most of Africa had followed the Asian countries to independence. Over forty countries with one-quarter of the world's population had overthrown colonialism in this brief span of time.

Although the Second World War had provided a powerful stimulus to the independence movements, many of the liberation struggles, especially those in Asia and the Middle East, were well under way before the war. Japan's successful challenge of Russian imperialism in the 1905 Russo-Japanese War provided an early impetus to nationalist groups throughout Asia by convincing them that the European powers were not invincible.

During the Second World War the European powers weakened themselves by promoting nationalist movements against each other: Germany encouraged Arab nationalism against the French in the Maghreb; and the British and French promoted nationalism in the Middle East against Germany's ally, Turkey. Wartime promises of concessions in return for aid against their enemies further loosened the grasp of Europe's nations on some colonies. As the First World War drew to a close, the anti-imperialist propaganda campaign launched by Lenin after the Bolshevik Revolution in November of 1917 instigated a countermovement in the West. US President Woodrow Wilson's support for self-determination in his Fourteen Points was followed by British Prime Minister David Lloyd George's pledge in 1918 that self-determination was applicable to the colonies as much as it was elsewhere.

But the First World War also provided a stimulus to the victors who enlarged their colonial empires. During the interwar years, Europe's dominance was challenged by colonial elites in some areas but not broken. The economic strain of the Second World War and the post-war years would force the colonial powers to relinquish their dominance due primarily to a lack of resources and the growing strength of the anti-colonial forces. The colonial powers' responses to the decolonization movements varied. The British put up less resistance than other powers because of the post-war economic exhaustion. Nkrumah, for example, achieved his 'self-government' peacefully. Still, the Labour government tried to hold on to areas such as the Middle East through a policy 'partnership' with the elites. The French refused to grant the colonial elites any share of power and clung tenaciously to their colonial empire. Only military defeat (Indochina), savage guerrilla warfare (Algeria) and worldwide pressure (Suez) forced France to quit her colonial possessions. The responses of Britain, France and other colonial powers to the anti-colonial movement were, indeed, so different that no single pattern exists.

Stages on the Road to Independence

National independence movements commonly passed through three stages before independence was achieved. During the first stage, traditional elites tried to stave off westernization and preserve the native culture and institutions. Tribal chieftains in Africa, for example, engaged in ineffective protests against the vastly superior military might of the colonial powers. Only in Ethiopia and Morocco did leaders of this first, so-called proto-nationalist stage, manage to retain power after independence.

The second, or bourgeois, stage was a direct result of Western modernization of native economies and societies. Except where it was deliberately held back, as in Vietnam, a Western-educated middle class emerged to challenge and in time replace the traditional native elites. In order to destroy the old social order, the colonial powers usually encouraged these middle-class groups, in the expectation that they would remain loyal because of their acceptance of Western ideas, techniques and institutions. The First World War led to a rapid expansion of this Westernized elite.

When the colonial powers concentrated all their efforts on the First World War in Europe, a native industrial class grew rapidly. This new elite occupied an ambivalent position in the colonial countries. Despite superior training, the members of the group were allowed to fill only the subordinate positions in the colonial administrations. Denied equal status with the European administrators on the one hand and separated from the traditional society on the other, they were often frustrated in their attempts to bring about the changes they desired or find positions that fit their training. India's Jawaharlal Nehru, who later adopted a more revolutionary posture, aptly described their ambivalent feelings: 'Indeed, 1 often wonder if I represent anyone at all, and I am inclined to think that 1 do not, though many have kindly and friendly feelings toward me. I have become a queer mixture of the East and West, out of place everywhere, at home nowhere'.

Although the members of this group eventually demanded independence for their countries, their social base remained narrowly middle class. They refused to appeal to the masses of workers and peasants for support, thus generally

*Mahatma Gandhi (*right*) chats with Jawaharlal Nehru in July 1946.*
(© Empics)

permitting leadership of the independence movements to pass to more revolutionary countrymen. Independence came during this second phase of the liberation struggle only when the colonial powers withdrew because of financial and international pressures, as in Nigeria and Tanganyika.

For the most part, national liberation movements succeeded during the third, or mass revolutionary, stage. Nationalist leaders such as Mahatma Gandhi and Jawaharlal Nehru in India, Mao Zedong in China, Ho Chi Minh in Vietnam, Kwame Nkrumah in Ghana and Achmed Sukarno in Indonesia mobilized the masses of peasants and workers to overthrow their colonial overlords. Gandhi's policy of massive civil disobedience, adopted in the 1920s, presented the colonial powers with an insurmountable obstacle to their continued rule and provided subsequent nationalists with techniques that were invaluable in their own liberation struggles. Both Gandhi and Mao established elaborate ties between the masses and revolutionary leaders that were adopted by nationalists elsewhere. While this three-stage struggle went on for more than a half-century in India, it was telescoped into less than fifteen years in Africa due primarily to the debilitating impact of the Second Word War on the colonial powers.

India's Independence Movement

The parent of all independence movements was clearly that of India. Beginning in 1885 with the Congress party movement, India provides one of the best examples of the three-stage division of nationalist movements. The first leader of the Congress party, G. K. Gokhale, accepted British rule and asked only for greater integration of educated Indians in the colonial administration. After 1905 a Western-educated elite led by B. G. Tilak rose to leadership in the party. This is the group that ultimately rejected piecemeal reforms and British suzerainty and demanded independence. However, the group's failure to appeal to the Indian masses left the independence movement in the hands of students and a few middle-class leaders. Britain had, in fact, promoted the build-up of a Western-educated elite to support it against the traditional nationalists.

The First World War and its aftermath irretrievably weakened the British hold on India. From this point on the British could only engage in delaying tactics as they watched the nationalist movement gather momentum and pass into the third stage. To maintain their influence, in 1917 the British promised the gradual development of self-governing institutions and in 1919 they committed themselves to internal self-government by instalments. But the British massacre of Indians at Amritsar in 1919 showed that internal self-government would not come soon. By this time the Congress party was demanding independence on its own terms.

When Gandhi organized the party on a mass basis with the Nagpur Constitution of 1920, it had a chain of command stretching to the district and village level. His policy of massive civil disobedience stymied the British despite their superior resources. Congress's other leader, Nehru, overcame rightist opposition within the party and pushed through a social reform programme that tied the masses to the new leadership. Winston Churchill seriously misread the Congress party's new revolutionary programme and its impact on the masses when he said in 1931: 'They merely represent those Indians who have acquired a veneer of Western civilization, and have read all those books about democracy which Europe is now beginning increasingly to disregard.'

Other British leaders had by 1935 become sufficiently convinced of the strength of the Congress party to pass the Government of India Act, which provided for the election of provincial legislatures and the establishment of provincial cabinets. By granting local rights and maintaining control over foreign affairs and other national issues, Britain hoped to stop the independence movement. But the Congress party would now be content with nothing less than complete independence.

Efforts to secure Indian cooperation against Germany during the Second World War finally convinced British leaders that they had no choice but to grant India its independence. When Britain requested Indian aid in 1939, the Congress party not only refused but also withdrew its representatives from the provincial parliaments. Britain responded by jailing many of the Congress leaders. However, the Japanese march through Indochina and Burma forced the British to seek an accord in 1942.

For its cooperation the British representative, Sir Stafford Cripps, offered India full dominion status within the British Commonwealth after the war. Gandhi, mindful of earlier promises that went unfulfilled as well as of Britain's predicament in the war against Germany, would not compromise. Instead, the party passed a Quit India Resolution that promised cooperation if independence was granted, or massive resistance if it was refused. Again Congress leaders were put in jail, where they remained until the end of the war.

The absence of the major leaders of the Congress party permitted the Moslem League, led by Mohammed Ali Jinnah, to build up its strength. Street clashes between Moslems and Hindus increased in number and intensity as the Moslem League pushed for its own separate state once independence was achieved.

With the Labour party victory in the 1945 British elections, independence for India awaited only the resolution of the Moslem–Hindu dispute. In the elections for a central legislative assembly set up by a sympathetic Labour party, the Moslem League and the Congress party captured most of the seats. But the Moslem League refused to take part in a cabinet headed by Nehru.

While the British engaged in fruitless attempts to bring the two sides together, continued street clashes divided the two sides even further. Convinced by February 1947 that a unitary Indian state could be achieved only if the two factions were compelled to resolve their differences, Britain announced that it was pulling out of India by June 1948. Realizing that no compromise was possible, in July 1947 Britain passed the India Independence Bill that set up two independent states: India and Pakistan.

After a massive migration of Moslems and Hindus and considerable blood-shed, India and Pakistan became independent states in August 1947. Both were given the option to turn their backs on the British Commonwealth; both decided to remain within it. Despite the partition, India became a powerful symbol for countries still under colonial domination. After studying Gandhi's policies, Nkrumah said it 'could be the solution to the colonial problem'. In fact, many nationalist leaders adopted the same policy of passive resistance and appeal to the masses. Shortly after India gained its independence, nationalist pressures in Ceylon and Burma, in combination with financial problems at home, led Britain to relinquish its jurisdiction over these two countries.

China's Independence Movement

Although China remained independent during the imperialist period, it was unable to prevent the European powers and Japan from establishing hegemony over most of its coastal areas major cities. The three-stage national-ist pattern is associated in China with three people: Kang Yu-wei, Sun Yat-sen and Mao Zedong.

During Kang's period of activity, the late 1800s, the Manchus ruled China. The Manchus were a Mongol people who invaded in 1643 and stayed on to found the Manchu dynasty. Then, in the Sino-Japanese War of 1894–95, China had suffered defeat at the hands of Japanese forces. Furthermore, before the turn of the century Western powers were clamouring for economic concessions.

Kang stirred up popular sentiment against aliens, and promoted enthusiastic but ill-planned and ill-directed attacks on foreigners. Most notable of these was the Boxer Rebellion in 1900, which the Western powers crushed with singular brutality.

Realizing the futility of such tactics, a new reform group sought to rid China of the Manchus. This is the group, led by Dr. Sun Yat-sen, which later came to be called the Kuomintang. In 1911 Sun succeeded in overthrowing the Manchus and establishing the Republic of China. Before the First World War, Sun had been convinced that a Western-style democracy could modernize China and eliminate foreign influence. He won the support of the growing Chinese business class, which wanted a stronger government to protect it against foreign competition.

By 1919 Sun no longer believed that a narrowly based liberal government could counter Western influence. Adopting passive resistance and the boycott of foreign goods, Sun began the transition to the third stage of nationalism. This transition was completed when he reorganized the Kuomintang as a mass party with an army aimed at revolution and aligned the Kuomintang with the Communist party led by Mao Zedong.

When Sun died in 1925 the nationalist movement split between the followers of Mao and the more conservative followers of Sun's successor, Chiang Kai-shek. Chiang rejected social reform, whereas Mao proclaimed an agrarian revolution in 1927. Now Chiang, leading the Kuomintang forces and supported by businessmen, financiers and landlords, attacked Mao's Communist forces, pushing them back into the far north of China. While Mao built up Communist strength in Shensi province in the 1930s the corruption-riddled Kuomintang split into factions as the Japanese took over control of most of the heavily populated areas of China.

During the Second World War a three-cornered war broke out between Mao, the Kuomintang and the Japanese. When the Japanese empire collapsed in

Nikita Khrushchev, Mao Zedong and Ho Chi Minh at a banquet in Peking (Beijing).
(© Underwood & Underwood/Corbis)

1945, the United States tried to arrange a coalition between the Communists and the Kuomintang. Neither side was willing to cooperate and civil war broke out again in 1946. Although Chiang's forces controlled most of the cities, they could not subdue the countryside. Despite more than $2 billion in American aid, Mao's forces gradually pushed southward, gaining the support of China's peasants with their policy of land reform.

Mao said, 'Whoever wins the support of the peasants will win China; whoever solves the land question will win the peasants.' Now his prophecy was borne out. Winning the support of the peasantry as they advanced, the Communists took control of Beijing in January 1949 and proclaimed the Chinese People's Republic in October. By 1950 the Kuomintang was driven off the Chinese mainland onto the island of Formosa, now called Taiwan. Mao's organization of the peasantry and guerrilla warfare tactics were to provide the theories and techniques for the conquest of power in other under-developed countries. Despite Mao's consolidation of power, the final Western colonies or enclaves in China, Hong Kong (British) and Macao (Portuguese) were not returned to Beijing until the end of the twentieth century.

Indochina's Independence Movement

The lesson of China was not lost *on* Ho Chi Minh, the Indochinese nationalist. As early as 1925 he formed the Revolutionary League of the Youth of Vietnam to exploit popular discontent over French colonialism and to organize the peasantry and workers. Groups representing the first two nationalist stages existed in Indochina but were never strong enough to challenge the revolutionaries. A proto-nationalist Constitutional party, formed early in the century, opposed both social revolution and demands for independence, and it refused to support nationalistic uprisings in Tonkin and Annam in 1930 and 1931. No democratic–liberal group could gain major support. French colonial policy restricted business activity to French and Chinese entrepreneurs, thus thwarting the development of an indigenous middle class that might have favoured a moderate nationalist course.

The Vietnamese National Party (VNQDD), a liberal nationalist group formed in 1927, gained the support of only a small group of intellectuals. Denied legal existence by the French and ideologically incapable of appealing to the peasantry or workers, it joined Ho Chi Minh's Communists in the abortive revolts in Tonkin and Annam. Remnants of the VNQDD fled to the Kuomintang in China and did not return to Indochina until the Second World War.

The Communist party, which Ho had formed in 1930, also suffered severely when the French crushed the Communist-led Annam revolt in 1930 and 1931. French Governor General Pasquier declared, 'As a force capable of acting against public order, Communism has disappeared.' Ho Chi Minh fled to Moscow, where he remained until 1941. The Indochinese Communists were permitted a legal existence between 1933 and 1939, but a three-way division into Trotskyites, Stalinists and followers of Ho, together with close French scrutiny, prevented a serious challenge to French rule.

The Communists were forced into hiding again in 1939 after the signing of the Stalin–Hitler pact led to the outlawing of the Communist party in France. But, as in China, the outbreak of the Second World War was to have a major impact on the Liberation struggle. After an initial abortive Nationalist–Communist attempt to overthrow the French, the Communists and many VNQDD supporters united under the banner of the League for the Independence of Vietnam, or Vietminh, to resist the Japanese invaders. Hitler's invasion of the Soviet Union and Japan's attack on Pearl Harbour propelled the Vietminh into a new role as opponents of fascism.

During the war the Japanese permitted France's Vichy government to continue the administration of Indochina. Ho and the Vietminh, supported by Chiang Kai-shek after 1942, refused to make an all-out effort against the Japanese because they feared that Japan might destroy them; they chose instead to wait for the expected defeat of the Japanese, which would give them the opportunity to assume power. The Japanese paved the way for the Vietminh by disarming and imprisoning the French, who were supplied by the Free French Forces of Charles de Gaulle and were planning an attack on the Japanese. When Japan capitulated on 15 August 1945, the Vietminh assumed power under the banner of the hastily organized National Liberation Committee of Vietnam. Ho Chi Minh proclaimed the independence of the Democratic Republic of Vietnam in September 1945. Bao Dai, the former emperor of Annam under the French, acknowledged Ho's leadership.

Distrusting Ho Chi Minh, the Western Allies had other plans. They assigned administration of the area north of the sixteenth parallel to the Chinese Nationalists and the area south of the sixteenth parallel to the British. The British immediately released the French soldiers and administrators from prison and helped them reestablish their control over the Saigon area. Fearing Chiang Kai-shek, the Vietminh wanted a close association with the French. The left-dominated government in Paris reached an agreement with Ho Chi Minh in March 1946 that recognized his government as a free state within a French federation in Indochina.

But the French administrators and military in Saigon sabotaged the agreement by setting up the free state of Cochin–China in the south. In response the Vietminh established a dictatorship in the north. In December 1946 war broke out, and the French drove the Vietminh back to their guerrilla bases in the mountains. The military justified the attack by reporting that the Vietminh had tried to kill all the Europeans in Hanoi. What Paris was not told was that the Vietminh action followed on the heels of a French naval attack on the Vietminh quarter of Hanoi that killed 6000 Vietnamese. The French now set up Bao Dai as the puppet ruler of all Vietnam and granted Cambodia and Laos independence in internal affairs. France hoped it would later be able to set up a federation of states under French hegemony in Indochina.

French attempts to wipe out the Vietminh were frustrated by Vo Nguyen Giap, who had mastered guerrilla warfare tactics while fighting with Mao's Communist forces in China. Guerrilla warfare continued until 1949, when Mao's victory in China permitted him to start supplying the Vietminh. As fighting shifted to more conventional warfare after 1950, the United States began to supply the French. Viewed as a part of the worldwide Communist expansion, the Truman administration considered Ho Chi Minh a puppet of the Chinese and the Soviet Union.

American financial aid increased from $150 million in 1950 to $1.3 billion by 1953. In spite of this aid, the French attempt to challenge the Vietminh in their mountain strongholds failed in 1954. At the battle of Dien Bien Phu a French force of 16,000 had to capitulate to the Vietminh after an eight-week siege. The United States provided no military aid at this time because it had just negotiated an end to the war in Korea and President Eisenhower was opposed to another land war in Asia.

The Geneva Conference, called before the battle of Dien Bien Phu, was meeting to bring the war in Indochina to an end when news of the defeat came. The announcement put France in a very weak negotiating position. The French agreed to withdraw from north of the seventeenth parallel, and the Vietminh agreed to pull their troops out of the south. Elections were to be held in 1956 to decide on a government for all of Vietnam. The United States representative at Geneva, John Foster Dulles, refused to take part in the agreement. Following Geneva, the United States pushed aside the French and assumed a preponderant influence in South Vietnam. In 1956, when South Vietnam refused to hold elections, the move had the United States support.

The second stage of the struggle to liberate all of Vietnam began after 1956, with the United States protecting South Vietnam against the Vietcong nationalists in the south and against North Vietnam. Another long war ensued. The Vietcong and North Vietnamese resorted to guerrilla warfare against vastly superior American military power. And, despite US efforts to set up a stable government in South Vietnam, a succession of incompetent, corrupt administrations could not win the support of the South Vietnamese. Eventually, international and domestic criticism of the American role in Vietnam forced the United States to withdraw in 1973.

Indonesia's Independence Movement

The impact of the Second World War was even more decisive in Indonesia, where the nationalist movement never completely reached the third stage. Neither the Sarekat Islam movement led by Tjokro Aminoto nor the Partai Nasional Indonesia (PNI) formed by Achmed Sukarno in 1927 made a successful appeal to the peasantry. Led by students and members of the professions, the PNI could not withstand the Dutch military attacks.

But the power of the Dutch was broken by the German conquest of the Netherlands during the Second World War and the Japanese occupation of the East Indies. When Japan was defeated and the Second World War came to a close, before the Japanese pulled out of Indonesia they encouraged Sukarno, who had cooperated with them, to set up an independent state. The Dutch, weakened by war, had no choice but to acquiesce when Sukarno proclaimed Indonesia a republic in August 1945. When the Dutch regained their strength, they tried to divide the nationalists and destroy the independence movement by occupying the cities and imposing an economic blockade. Although they managed to capture Sukarno and other nationalist leaders in 1948, the United States exerted overwhelming diplomatic and economic pressures on the Dutch to relinquish their East Indies' empire. Since Sukarno and other nationalists had crushed a Communist regime set up in Maduim in September 1948, the United States evidently hoped it would obtain a strong anti-communist ally by supporting an independent Indonesia under Sukarno.

In August 1949 the Dutch, realizing that they lacked the military strength to defeat the rebels, agreed to the establishment of the United States of Indonesia within a larger Netherlands-Indonesian Union. However, Sukarno was unhappy with this federalized solution and the continuing ties to the Netherlands, and in 1950 he set up the unitary Republic of Indonesia. Since the nationalists were divided when independence came and the masses had not been included in the nationalist movements, a long struggle then ensued to destroy regional loyalties and weld Indonesia's masses into a modern nation-state.

Middle East Independence Movements

Most of the Arab states in the Middle East and North Africa had gained a measure of independence long before nationalism had developed into a third stage. As a result of the collapse of the Ottoman Empire during the First World War and the increased influence of Great Britain and France throughout the Arab world, these new states emerged under native dynasties or aristocratic oligarchies but with special ties to the British or French. Iraq, Palestine and Transjordan were under a British mandate, and Syria and Lebanon under a French mandate from the League of Nations. Morocco and Tunisia were French protectorates. The other areas were directly controlled (French Algeria and Italian Libya), dominated (British Egypt) or independent (Saudi Arabia and Yemen).

During the interwar years Britain and France employed several methods to head off middle-class nationalism: propping up existing dynasties, granting quasi-independence or creating territorial divisions. Britain preferred to support existing dynasties or grant quasi-independence. Immediately after the First World War it supported Reza Khan in Iran and King Farouk in Egypt, and it installed Feisal as king in Iraq. France used the territorial division method in Syria when it destroyed the unity the Syrians had achieved under the Ottoman Empire by dividing the country into six administrative zones. One of these later became the present state of Lebanon. These divisions created a heated Syrian nationalism that was suppressed only through large-scale imprisonment and exile of Syrian leaders. To this day Syria remains a principal centre of Arab nationalism and opponent of Western imperialism.

Three Syrian political groups – the Muslim Brotherhood, the League of National Action and the Baath party – led the struggle for a united Arab Islamic Empire and emancipation from colonial rule. However, by remaining narrowly intellectual and pan-Arab, these parties were unable to tap the energies of the masses. As a result, France had little difficulty in overcoming the nationalistic movement in the interwar years.

Despite British and French opposition, middle-class nationalism grew. In Tunisia, Habib Bourguiba's middle-class, nationalist Neo-Destour party replaced the Islamic-inspired Destour party that desired reforms within a French-dominated Tunisia. By 1943 the nationalist Moroccan Istiqlal party, based on the middle class, rose to prominence. In Iraq and Egypt, middle-class opposition came primarily from the military; many educated Arabs joined the military because they found little opportunity to use their talents elsewhere in their underdeveloped traditional societies. Military leaders in Iraq, Egypt and Syria began reforms after successful revolts against traditional rulers.

Arab-Israeli Conflict   Immediately after the Second World War, British and French influence began to crumble in the Arab world. With de Gaulle cynically remarking that their actions 'stank of oil,' Britain and the United States forced the French out of Syria in 1946. But the event that led to a general attack on Western colonialism by shocking much of the Arab world into the third stage of nationalism was the Arab–Israeli War in 1948–49.

The war was partially a result of British policies that stretched back to the First World War. In order to obtain Jewish and Arab support against the Central Powers, Britain had made promises to both. The Balfour Declaration of 1917 promised the Jews a national homeland in Palestine, yet the Arabs believed all of Palestine had been promised to them by Sir Henry McMahon, British high commissioner for Egypt during the First World War. The British mandate over Palestine, granted by the League of Nations in 1923, instructed the British to establish a Jewish national home in Palestine and facilitate immigration. The mandate promised a home, not a state. The Arabs began to protest the influx of thousands of Jews into their midst.

As anti-Semitic policies in Europe increased the flow of Jewish immigrants in the interwar period, Britain reacted to the Arab opposition by trying periodically to curtail Jewish settlement. Despite British actions, the Jewish population of Palestine increased by about 350,000 during the interwar period. When Britain put limits on the number of immigrants permitted during the Second World War, Jewish terrorist groups resorted to violence in order to force the British to accept more of the Jewish refugees fleeing persecution in Europe. Caught between Arab demands to limit Jewish immigration to Palestine and Jewish violence to prevent any such limitation, in 1947 Britain asked the United Nations to resolve the dilemma.

The United Nations decided to partition Palestine into a Jewish state and an Arab state and to internationalize Jerusalem. In May 1948, when Britain pulled out its troops, war broke out between the new state of Israel and the neighbouring Arab states. Although vastly outnumbered, Israel relied on superior organization to achieve victory in February 1949. Now Israel encompassed not only the area assigned to it by the United Nations but the city of Jerusalem, a corridor to the coast, and the remainder of Galilee as well. Nearly a million Arabs, primarily Palestinians, fled Israel in the wake of rumours of impending massacres and orders by their leaders to leave. In subsequent clashes with the Arabs the Israelis captured more Arab lands, including the West Bank, the Gaza Strip and East Jerusalem. Permanently alienated from what they considered to be their lands, the Palestinians remained refugees, symbols of Arab humiliation and a permanent irredentist force that has never accepted the new Israeli state.

Some hope for a resolution of the Palestinian problem came in 1993 when the Israeli head of state, Yitzhak Rabin, and the main Palestinian leader, Yasser Arafat, agreed to begin Palestinian self-rule in the Gaza Strip and West Bank area. This gained Israel official recognition from the neighbouring state of Jordan. However, this initiative encountered heated opposition from radical Palestinians who want no compromise with Israel and right-wing Israeli parties determined not to compromise with Arafat's PLO and other radical Palestinian groups. At this writing, a resolution of the dilemma is complicated by the continued presence of Israeli settlers in the West Bank and division among the Palestinians, although Arafat's death in 2004 signalled a renewed effort at peace under a new Palestinian president, Mahmoud Abbas.

The Arab defeat, blamed on the traditionalist regimes in the Arab world, generated military revolts in Syria, Jordan and Egypt. The Syrian and Jordanian revolts failed initially to replace the existing regimes with a modernizing leadership. But in Egypt the corrupt, British-supported regime of King Farouk was overthrown by General Mohammed Naguib and Colonel Gamal Abdel Nasser, an act that was to have a far-reaching impact in the Arab world. Naguib abolished the monarchy and began the modernization of Egypt by replacing the old elite with fellow officers. He was supplanted by the more energetic Nasser, whose interests focused on more revolutionary changes in society and the ouster of the British from the Suez Canal.

Nasser eliminated all opponents, put an end to parliamentary government, and adopted a single mass organization to arouse and channel political consciousness. With these measures he set a pattern for many of the one-party governments that followed political liberation throughout Africa. Nasser's ultra-nationalist dictatorship and those that followed were grounded on the premise that political democracy without social democracy is meaningless.

The Suez Crisis   One of Nasser's ways of providing more social democracy was to improve the lot of the peasantry by building the Aswan High Dam, which regulated the flow of the Nile River. This led him into conflict with Britain and France over the Suez Canal.

Nasser expected aid from Britain and the United States for building the Aswan Dam. When aid was refused, Nasser responded by nationalizing the Suez Canal on 26 July 1956. Nasser had purchased arms from Czechoslovakia because the West would not provide him with the type or quantity of weapons he wanted. Also, he had recognized Communist China in 1955. Now the United States denied him aid because of what it considered to be his anti-Western attitude. In the Cold War milieu of the 1950s, the United States equated neutralism with opposition and viewed Nasser's actions as setting a dangerous precedent of playing off West against East. Britain, angry at Nasser's seizure of the canal, sought to punish him and give a warning to other Arab nationalists.

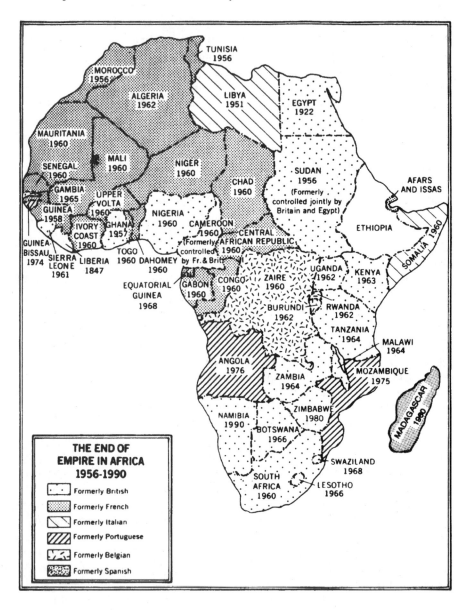

THE END OF
EMPIRE IN AFRICA
1956-1990

Formerly British
Formerly French
Formerly Italian
Formerly Portuguese
Formerly Belgian
Formerly Spanish

The French were happy to join with Britain because they hoped to cut off the material support being provided by Nassar to the Algerian rebels.

England and France decided on joint action to capture the Canal Zone, coordinated with an Israeli attack ostensibly to destroy guerrilla bases in the Sinai Peninsula. The effort was a dismal failure. Israel captured a large part of the Sinai and Anglo-French forces captured Port said, but United States and international pressure forced a halt to the attempted seizure of the Canal Zone. (The United States feared that the Anglo-French invasion would have a deleterious effect on Western popularity and influence in the Middle East. Further, because the United States was leading the attack in the UN against the Soviet Union's invasion of Hungary, it could not at the same time approve the invasion of Egypt.)

The subsequent withdrawal of Anglo-French forces rid Egypt of all foreign influence, left it in control of the canal, and greatly enhanced Nasser's reputation, especially among third-world countries. It now seemed possible to oppose the militarily superior colonial powers by appealing to the United Nations and world opinion. The Suez fiasco provided a major impetus to national liberation movements in sub-Saharan Africa. In the Middle East, Nasser's military junta served as a model for similar governments in Syria and Iraq.

Africa's Independence Movements

The weakened international position of Britain and France after 1956 accelerated the process of national liberation in Africa. Indochinese and Algerian pressures on France and a national resistance movement centering around the traditional sultan brought independence to Morocco before the three stages of nationalism had fully developed. The middle-class Istiqlal party had led a national resistance movement against the French since 1943. But it was the exile of the sultan in 1953, inspired by French *colons*, that promoted mass resistance of the kind usually associated only with ultranationalists, in support of the sultan's traditional regime. The sultan, Mohammed V, had the support of his people not only because of his reform programme but also because the sultan was by tradition the country's Islamic leader. The French *colons* set up a puppet government, but the populace demanded the return of the legitimate ruler. When the traditionally anti-sultan Berber tribes transferred their support from the puppet government to the exiled sultan and began to attack European settlers, France reinstated the sultan in November 1955 to end the growing anarchy. In March 1956 France granted Morocco full independence. Faced with a *fait accompli*, the other protecting power, Spain, was forced to acquiesce.

During the next five years Mohammed V tried to change Morocco to a modern constitutional monarchy. But the challenge of the ultra-nationalist Neo-Istiqlal party headed by Ben Barka led Mohammed and his son, Hassan II, to depose the left-leaning government of Premier Abdallah Ibrahim and slow Morocco's progress towards genuine constitutional government. A struggle ensued in the 1960s between the more conservative middle-class Istiqlal party and the social revolutionary Neo-Istiqlal party under the watchful eye of the kings.

Again, in Tunisia, independence came before the nationalist movement reached the ultra-nationalist stage. The bourgeois Destour party had led a movement for greater independence from France since 1919. Although led by the middle class, it differed from the bourgeois second stage in that it was willing to accept administrative reforms and greater middle-class participation under French auspices and Islamic influences. The secular Neo-Destour party, formed in 1934 under Habib Bourguiba's leadership, adopted a mixture of bourgeois and ultra revolutionary aims. Bourguiba's party appealed to the masses through a revolutionary reform programme but stopped short of the ultra-nationalist, anti-Western aspects of the typical third-stage nationalists. This pattern also characterized the independence movements in the Gold Coast, Nigeria and Tanganyika.

Bourguiba was often hard-pressed by more radical Arab and African nationalists, especially in neighbouring Algeria, to justify his pro-Western stance. Nevertheless, his programme led to national independence in 1956 because the masses identified with his leadership and because France's position weakened after 1956. The French settlers feared they would lose their privileged economic status if Tunisia gained independence. The punitive actions they instituted, which included the exile and imprisonment of Bourguiba, instigated a mass reaction among the Tunisian populace in 1954. Alarmed by the outbreak of partisan warfare, Premier Mendès-France promised Tunisia internal autonomy only one week after he negotiated an end to French involvement in Indochina. Bourguiba was returned to Tunisia and independence was proclaimed on 20 March 1956. Because Tunisia achieved its independence under what was essentially second-stage leadership, it has retained a parliamentary, democratic form of government and a pro-Western political orientation.

The rush to independence of sub-Saharan African states after 1956 was the result of many factors that instilled a new confidence in African nationalists. Independence for Morocco and Tunisia in 1956, the successes of the Algerian rebels and the Suez debacle were obvious immediate factors. While these events speeded up the liberation process, the independence movements had already reached the ultra-nationalist stage in Ghana and the bourgeois stage in several colonial areas.

The Second World War had already seriously weakened the control of Europeans over their colonies. Africans came into contact with nationalists in India and with African nationalists serving in the British and French military during the war. The defeat and occupation of France convinced many Africans that their European overlords were not invincible.

At home, increased economic activity in support of the Western war effort increased the size of the native lower-middle class – nurses, teachers, mechanics, artisans and so on. After the war, these people were frustrated by their inability to find jobs and by the Europeans' monopoly of the top administrative positions. In addition, the Cold War led the United States and the Soviet Union to seek support among Third-World countries by encouraging independence movements.

The events of 1956 were instrumental in ending France's dream of assimilating French colonial areas within a greater France and in convincing the British that granting independence was the only alternative. Before the war, assimilation into a greater French Union had been accepted by many

African nationalists. In 1936 an Algerian nationalist, Ferhat Abbas, asserted,

> Six million Moslems live on this soil which has been French for a hundred years; they live in hovels, go barefoot, without clothing and often without bread. Out of this hungry mass we shall make a modern society ... elevate them to human dignity so that they may be worthy of the name of Frenchmen.

By the time Ferhat Abbas became premier of the provisional government of the Algerian Republic in 1958 he had become a staunch advocate of Algerian independence.

Britain's system of local administration permitted its colonies to make a smoother transition to independence. Having been brought into colonial administrations in the nineteenth century, many Africans had become capable administrators. When Britain's Asian empire was lost in the late 1940s, most British leaders recognized that African independence was inevitable. As British administrators gradually relinquished their control, well-trained Africans easily picked up the reins of government.

In late 1956, most French colonies demanded and received the *loi-cadre* (semi-autonomy) from a weakened France. Because of the weakness of the European powers, independence often came to sub-Saharan Africa when the ultra-nationalist groups were just forming. In cases where the nationalist movement had reached the third ultra-nationalist stage, the transition from the second to third stage may have taken only a few years. The Belgian Congo provides a perfect example of this telescoping of the nationalist movements. In 1956 Patrice Lumumba's demands were for more liberal measures for the educated Congolese; two years later he formed the *Mouvement National Congolais*, a mass ultra-nationalist party.

Unfortunately, the independence movements often were splintered by regional and tribal differences that were overcome only through civil war. These divisions encouraged and in some cases forced the new states to set up one-party governments or military regimes in order to overcome the opposition.

In Ghana (Gold Coast) ultra-nationalists had gained control of the independence movement before independence came in 1957. Ghana provides the best example of the three-stage nationalist transition, with the Aborigines' Rights Protection Society, the Gold Coast Convention (GCC), and the Convention People's Party (CPP) representing the three stages. Typically, the CPP, headed by Kwame Nkrumah, became dissatisfied with the moderate leadership of the GCC and formed its own mass-based political party. Nkrumah claimed that 'a middle-class elite, without the battering-ram of the illiterate masses' would never be able to 'smash the forces of colonialism'. His 'positive action' campaign of strikes and boycotts was deeply influenced by his training in Marxian economics in the West and by Gandhi's tactics in India.

Finding Nkrumah's policies too revolutionary, Britain imprisoned him in 1950. A British Commission Report in 1948 said, 'We have no reason to suppose that power in the hands of a small literate minority would not tend to be used to exploit the illiterate majority.' It recommended that Britain retain control over Ghana until literacy and political experience had reached a stage whereby the masses could not be exploited. However, when the CPP won an overwhelming victory in the 1951 elections, Britain decided that it was politically expedient to release Nkrumah from prison and include him in the government.

Granted self-government in 1951, Ghana's leaders had considerable experience when full independence came in 1957. Despite this advantage, Ghana has suffered from regional and tribal opposition to the central government since independence. Nkrumah's attempt to build up support among his countrymen, including assuming adulatory titles such as saviour, increased middleclass opposition to his government. In order to curb the opposition, he became president in 1960 under a new CPP constitution that permitted him to rule without parliament. Several years after he forbade the existence of other political parties, Nkrumah was overthrown by a military coup that was supported by his middle-class opponents and the powerful Ashanti tribe. The Ashantis had gained important positions in the military and among Nkrumah's political opponents.

The Nigerian nationalist movement, split among strong tribal lines, was a more complicated but perhaps a more typical example than Ghana of the African independence struggles. Not one but two proto-nationalist groups emerged, the Nigerian National Democratic party led by Herbert Macauly and the traditionalist Muslim Northern People's Congress (NPC) based on the Fulani-Hausa tribe in the predominantly Muslim north. At first the NPC opposed independence since the powerful Muslim leaders did not desire integration with the more Westernized non-Muslim south and west.

Among the Ibo tribe in the east a Westernized group, the National Council of Nigeria and the Cameroons (NCNC), was set up by a newspaper publisher, Dr Nnamdi Azikiwe, in 1944. Azikiwe had gained popularity before the war when he spoke out against British control and for independence.

In the more urban west, dominated by the Yoruba tribe, Chief Obafemi Awolowo put together the Action party. Basically a middle-class-led group, the Action party at first followed a pro-Western moderate course towards independence. After gaining independence, Awolowo switched to a neutralist and more radical programme of Nigerianization. But he stopped short of any Nkrumah-style ultra-Africanism with its strong appeal to the urban and peasant masses.

Independence necessitated bringing these disparate groups together by satisfying regional and tribal differences. Britain, fearful that it might alienate the Muslim north by granting autonomy prematurely, encountered increasing resistance from Azikiwe and Awolowo. NPC resistance was overcome when younger NPC members persuaded their colleagues to form and NCNC–NCP coalition, which chose NPC leader Abubaker Tafawa Balewa to be the first prime minister of Nigeria. The organization of Nigeria on a federal basis permits considerable local autonomy; for example, the Muslim leader in the Northern Province, Sir Ahmadu Bello, was able to retain much of his local authority. Azikiwe, who at first favoured a coalition with the Action party, accepted the NPC coalition because of pressure from within his own group. This compromise permitted Azikiwe to become governor-general of independent Nigeria in 1960. Awolowo, as a member of the opposition in the new government, resorted to more radical policies and was imprisoned in

1963. After independence a genuine ultra-nationalist Nigerian Socialist party formed.

In British East Africa, Tanganyika obtained independence in 1961 under the leadership of the Tanganyika African National Union (TANU) headed by Julius Nyerere. When independence came, TANU stood somewhere between the bourgeois and ultra-nationalist stages of nationalism. It was organized on a mass basis but it lacked the social revolutionary and anti-Western aspects of a genuine ultra-nationalist programme.

Not until 1966, after Tanganyika had merged with Zanzibar to form the new state of Tanzania, did Nyerere adopt a revolutionary programme that included nationalization of banks and industry and a cooperative agricultural programme. Tanganyika was spared the divisive tribal rivalries characteristic of most African states because none of its 120 tribes were large enough to challenge the government.

Nyerere's government was similar to many others in Africa in that no organized opposition was permitted. However, considerable differences were to be found within TANU. Before 1966 a strong left wing, composed of the trade union and cooperative movements, was critical of Nyerere's moderate social policies. This group was instrumental in swinging Nyerere's policies to the left in 1966. Differences such as this, which exist in many one-party governments in Africa, have led political observers to conclude that the decision-making process is often as democratic in these states as it is in some multi-party systems. In foreign affairs, Nyerere chose to keep his country in the British Commonwealth along with the other seven former British colonies and protectorates in East and West Africa.

With the exception of Guinea, the French territories in Africa followed a similar path to independence. All had experienced the French policy of assimilation to 1956 that reduced tribal authority and administered the eight colonies of French West Africa and the four in Equatorial Africa and Madagascar from the administrative centres at Dakar and Brazzaville.

The events of the mid-1950s crushed French hopes that these territories could ultimately be incorporated into a greater France as Guadeloupe, Martinique, French Guiana and Reunion already were. With the granting of the *loi-cadre* in 1956, the colonies were given the right to exercise full executive power through their local assemblies and cabinets. In 1958, de Gaulle gave the colonies a choice: autonomy within a community of French nations, complete independence, a continuation of their present status, or incorporation within France as a department. Twelve of the colonies chose autonomy within the French community and Guinea opted for complete independence. Beginning in 1960, the twelve colonies that had chosen autonomy were granted their independence as de Gaulle recognized the futility of trying to keep them in a larger French community. Nevertheless, most of them retained close economic and cultural ties with France after independence.

Only Guinea, under the ultra-African leadership of Sekou Toure, deviated from an essentially moderate Westernized leadership common to all the French territories. Most leaders in French Africa had acquired their political education in the

Rassemblement Démocratique Africain (RDA), the strongest of the African political parties represented in the Chamber of Deputies in Paris. Except for a period
of Communist influence from 1948 to 1954, the RDA remained in the hands of
moderate Francophile leaders such as Felix Houphouet-Boigny from the Ivory
Coast. Houphouet-Boigny, a member of the Mollet cabinet and leader of the
RDA, was the main author of the *loi-cadre*. Once the colonies received autonomy, the RDA often became the leading party in the individual states.

Only in Guinea and Senegal did the RDA lose out to more Socialist,
Africanist parties. After independence, power fell to a Westernized elite that
normally set up the one-party state dominated by a strong personality, such as
Houphouet-Boigny in the Ivory Coast or Leopold Sedar-Senghor in Senegal.

With Portugal's loss of its colonial empire in the 1970s, the fall of the white
minority government in Rhodesia in 1980 (now called Zimbabwe), South
Africa remained the only African country with a white minority government in
the eighties. Although this white minority government was not formally a
colonial power since it was not tied to any foreign government, its oppressive
rule resembled that of the colonial powers in other areas. Moreover, the resistance of the oppressed majority, although divided by tribal rivalries, had
reached the third mass stage of national liberation by the 1980s. Despite international economic sanctions and political isolation, the Boer (Dutch settlers)
government maintained a strict separation of whites and blacks (Apartheid)
until 1989. But a change in the leadership of the ruling National Party in 1989
brought Frederick W. De Klerk to power and a dramatic change in policy. De
Klerk ended most apartheid restrictions, released the leader of the opposition
African National Congress, Nelson Mandela, from prison, and reached an
agreement with Mandela over a transition of power to the black majority.
Although violence between the ANC and the Inkatha Freedom Party threatened to disrupt the transition, elections brought Mandela's ANC to power in
1994. Although South Africa faces serious economic and social problems, in
particular the great income disparity between whites and blacks, the resumption of trade with the outside world and the lessening of internal strife hold out
the promise for a better future.

Decolonization and Immigration in Britain and France

The process leading from self-rule to independence for Europe's colonies,
however conflict-ridden, did not mean the end of strong ties between former
colonial ruler and newly independent countries. Britain's relations with new
Commonwealth countries and France's ties with West African countries
remained dense, in terms of economic, security and social links. One aspect
of this linkage was the turn to these former colonies in the 1950s and 1960s
for labour in economies experiencing fast economic growth coupled with
labour shortages. In the case of France, in the first decade after the Second
World War, other European labour filled the job vacancies. But by the 1960s,
this European migration, mostly Southern European, began to drop off, and

attention turned to South Asia and the Caribbean for Britain, and Africa, including Algeria, for France.

The impact of immigrant labour is explored in Chapter 8, but it should be noted that this immigration flow during this period contributed in a major fashion to the creation of the multi-cultural nature of Britain and France today. The numbers speak for themselves. In the case of Britain, after a government mind-set that opposed the permanent settlement of non-white foreigners was changed with the Commonwealth Immigrants Act of 1962, the numbers of immigrants from Pakistan, India and the West Indies shot up. From 1955 to 1959, the annual net estimates of inward movement of persons from the West Indies fluctuated between 27,000 and 15,000. From 1960 to 1963, however, it ranged from 49,670 in 1960 to 66,290 in 1961, and was already 31,800 just for the first half of 1962. For France, the migration of Algerians, which slowed during the Algerian war, resumed an upward trend with the signing of the Evian agreement, which ended the war. Between 1962 and 1965 111,000 migrants entered France, compared to the average of 11,000 per year during the war. Other North and West African countries followed. 67,000 Moroccans entered France between 1962 and 1966, after bilateral agreements were signed in 1963. The end of empire, then, had effects upon the colonizing country as well as the colonies, different in nature of course, but its legacy still evident today.

FURTHER READING

For an outstanding concise interpretation of the politics of national liberation see the chapter on decolonization in Geoffrey Barraclough, *An Introduction to Contemporary History* (1967). For a more detailed description see F. Mansur, *Process of Independence* (1962); and M. E. Chamberlain, *Decolonization: The Fall of European Empires* (1985). R.F. Holland's *European Decolonization, 1918–1981: An Introductory Survey* (1985) challenges the interpretation of Barraclough and Mansur. Holland argues that the colonized areas were not liberated by disinterested modernizing elites but by small urban elites hungry for power and wealth. The timing of decolonization resulted from the actions of these urban elites and the colonizing powers' more beneficial returns from cooperating among themselves in such organizations as the Common Market. A recent full account is F. Ansprenger, *The Dissolution of Colonial Empires* (1989). A general but comprehensive overview of decolonization is found in Muriel Chamberlain, *The Longman Companion to European Decolonisation in the Twentieth Century* (1998).

The decline of the British Empire is described in Rupert Emerson, *From Empire to Nation* (1960); Eric Estoric, *Changing Empire: Churchill to Nehru* (1950); and John Strachey, *The End of Empire* (1960). John Gallagher's *The Decline, Revival, and Fall of the British Empire* (1982) argues that the First World War permitted the victorious powers to absorb vast new overseas territories and that any retreat from empire in the interwar years resulted from lack of resources rather than lack of will. J. Darwin's *End of Empire* (1990); and *Britain and Decolonisation: The*

Retreat from Empire in the Post-War World (1989) provides a recent, full account
of British decolonization. French colonialism and its decline is described in Guy
De Carmoy, *The Foreign Policies of France 1944–1968* (1970). The role of the
French army in the colonial territories is covered in John Ambler, *The French Army
in Politics, 1945–1962* (1966). France's Algerian Policy is excellently treated in
Alistair Horne, *A Savage War of Peace: Algeria, 1954–62*; and Tony Smith *The
French Stake in Algeria, 1945–1962* (1978). Smith contends that the collapse of
the French Fourth Republic was more the result of its efforts to keep Algeria
French than its internal institutional defects. Horne's work provides a comprehensive history of the conflict itself, but needs to be supplemented with a fuller
historical background.

For the collapse of colonialism in Asia see K. M. Pannikar, *Asia and Western
Dominance* (1953); J. Romein, *The Asian Century: A History of Modern
Nationalism in Asia* (1962); Truong Buu Lam, *Patterns of Vietnamese Response to
Foreign Intervention; 1858–1900* (1967); P. Spear, *India, Pakistan and the West*
(1961); Gowher Rizui, *Linlithgow and India: A Study of British Policy and the
Political Impasse in India, 1936–43* (1978); B.R. Tomlinson, *The Political
Economy of the Raj, 1914–1947: The Economics of Decolonization in India*
(1979); Ellen Hammer, *The Struggle for Indochina, 1940–54* (1955); and
G. M. Ziadeh, *Nationalism and Revolution in Indonesia* (1952).

The course of national liberation in the Middle East is described in M. Rowlatt,
Founders of Modern Egypt (1962); Philip K. Hitti, *Islam and the West* (1962); and
John Campbell, *Defense of the Middle East* (1960). More recent studies of Islamic
liberation movements include D. Pipes, *In the Path of God: Islam and Political
Power* (1983); and F. Ajami, *The Arab Predicament: Arab Political Thought and
Political Practice since 1967* (1992).

Nationalism and the stages of the independence movements in Africa are analysed
in Immanuel Wallerstein, *Africa: The Politics of Independence* (1961); George W.
Shepherd, *The Politics of African Independence* (1962); and Thomas Hodgkin,
Nationalism in Colonial Africa (sixth impression, 1968). For a comparative study
of European rule in Africa see A. J. Hanna, *European Rule in Africa* (1961). Two
studies that describe the three-stage pattern of nationalism in Africa are D. E.
Apter, *The Gold Coast in Transition* (1955); and J. S. Coleman, *Nigeria:
Background to Nationalism* (1958). Political decolonization in West Africa has
been treated recently by John D. Hargreaves, *The End of Colonial Rule in West
Africa: Essays in Contemporary History* (1979). Hargreaves shows how the British
retained much of their former political initiative by collaborating with the new
urban national movements. British policy in East Africa has recently been examined in Cranford Pratt's, *The Critical Phase in Tanzania 1945–1968: Nyerere and
the Emergence of a Socialist Strategy* (1976). Two edited volumes with much
information on the African independence movements are P. Gifford and
W. R. Louis (Eds.) *The Transfer of Power in Africa: Decolonization, 1940–1960*,
(1982) and *Decolon-ization and African Independence: The Transfers of Power,
1960–1980*, (1988).

Decolonization's impact on internal affairs in Britain and France is expertly
described in Miles Kahler's *Decolonization in Britain and France: The Domestic
Consequences of International Relations* (1984). Kahler explains both how external
relations affect domestic politics and internal politics influence foreign policy. He

argues that the British liquidated their colonial empire with less internal disruption than the French because the French right had still not accepted defeat at the hands of Nazi Germany and hoped to redeem French honour by retaining her colonies. Kahler also points out that the more heated settler resistance in the French colonies resulted in greater French domestic turmoil. In terms of how Britain and France handled immigrants from their former colonies, and the social consequences, see Gary Freeman, *Immigrant labor and Racial Conflict in Industrial Societies: The French and British Experiences, 1945–1975* (1979). For Britain in particular, see Ian Spencer, *British Immigration Policy Since 1939: The Making of Multi-Racial Britain* (1997) Randall Hansen, *Citizenship and Immigration in Poatwar Britain: The Institutional Origins of a Multicultural Nation* (2000). For France, see Maxim Silverman, *Deconstructing the Nation: Immigration, Racism and Citizenship in Modern France* (1992) and Gary Cross, *Immigrant Workers in Industrial France* (1983).

6 The Soviet Union and Eastern Europe in the 1950s and 1960s: The New Course and Polycentrism

> The heart of Lenin's comrade-in-arms and the inspired continuer of Lenin's cause, the wise teacher and leader of the party and the people, has stopped beating. Stalin's name is boundlessly dear to our party, to the Soviet people, to the working people of the world.
>
> *Pravda*, 5 March 1953

The above announcement signalled the end of an era, but several years were to elapse before the nature of the new era became clear. Between Stalin's death and the denunciation of his so-called cult of personality that Nikita Khrushchev made at the Twentieth Party Congress in 1956, a struggle for power raged between the Stalinists and the proponents of a 'new course.'

The Stalinists continued to support heavy industry, the collectivization of agriculture, the extreme centralization of economic planning, and, in foreign policy, continued hostility towards the West. The followers of the so-called new course stressed increased production of consumer goods, light industry, decentralization of economic decision-making, relaxation of internal political controls and the achievement of an understanding with the West.

This internal Soviet division, combined with national communist movements (domesticism) and what the Soviet Union classified as 'revisionism,' was to lead to a weakening of Soviet hegemony in Eastern Europe. Although the Soviet Union still had military control over most of Eastern Europe in the 1960s, the Soviet satellites had gained a large measure of independence. Furthermore, where only one leader of world communism had been acknowledged before 1948, at least three centres existed by the 1960s: the Soviet Union, Communist China and Yugoslavia.

Post-war Society under Stalin

During the Second World War Stalin relaxed his dictatorship in order to rally popular support for the war. After the massive purges of the 1930s when almost all the old Bolshevik leaders had been wiped out, the war years brought a partial reprieve from fear and insecurity. Loyalty to the state rather than loyalty to Stalin became the major criterion for social acceptance. Emphasis was placed on the fatherland and past Russian heroes. The Russian Orthodox Church escaped persecution for the duration of the war. When the Communist party relaxed its admittance requirements in 1943, party membership swelled from 3.4 to 6 million. The army experienced a similar relaxation when the Communist party commissars who had formerly shared command with the army officers were limited to an advisory role.

Such relative freedom led many Soviet citizens to expect that the quality of life would improve in the post-war period. They were in for a rude shock. Soviet society grew more repressive after the war. Instead of relaxation, citizens were faced with a conservative restoration, a return to total orthodoxy. The immediate post-war period has become known as the Zhdanov era, after anti-intellectual party bureaucrat Andrei Zhdanov, who reimposed the ideological uniformity that had existed before the war. The secret police (NKVD), headed by Lavrenti Beria, rounded up all people classified as enemies of the state and exiled them to Siberian labour camps run by the NKVD. War heroes such as Kliment Voroshilov and Georgi Zhukov were demoted to minor posts, and party control over the military was reestablished.

These acts reflected Stalin's apparent fear that a complex society with many centres of authority would threaten his authoritarian control. He considered himself responsible for the Soviet victory over Germany and particularly resented the praise heaped upon the Soviet generals. By humbling these generals – he made Voroshilov ask permission to come to each Politburo meeting – he could enhance his own feeling of importance.

In the arts, the post-war period was marked by a return to socialist realism. Creativity was sacrificed to a pervasive uniformity. Writing had to sing the praises of Soviet society and the Communist party. Writers, social scientists, even natural scientists had to follow the party line. One of the greatest sins was cosmopolitanism; composers Dimitri Shostakovich and Sergei Prokofiev and film director Sergie Eisenstein were adjudged guilty of this sin. In all fields, particular emphasis was placed on Stalin's role as the saviour of the Soviet Union. It was this Caesarian worship that Khrushchev denounced as the cult of personality.

When Stalin died in 1953 he apparently had been planning another major purge. The arrest of some prominent doctors, most of them Jewish, for plotting to kill government officials seems to have been the opening move in a much broader purge. Stalin is reported to have told Minister of State Security E. Ignatiev, 'If you do not obtain confessions from the victims, we will shorten you by a head.' Khrushchev charged that among the intended victims were some of the top members of the party: Anastas Mikoyan, Voroshilov and Vyacheslav Molotov.

The Post-war Economy under Stalin

The Soviet Union experienced a post-war economic restoration of Stalinism similar to the social one. As in the 1930s, supply, demand and investment were directed by an extensive bureaucracy, with headquarters in Moscow. Stalin again stressed heavy industry at the expense of agriculture and consumer goods. Agriculture was to provide the necessary capital for industry; it contributed one-third of the gross national product but received only 15 per cent of total investments.

Soviet production figures, which were always inflated until the late 1950s, reported that industrial output had reached the 1940 level by 1953. Despite this growth, the standard of living remained among the lowest in Europe. Real wages rose 83 per cent in the Soviet Union (according to inflated Soviet statistics), but doubled in Western Europe between 1950 and 1966. Moreover, the concentration on producer goods caused serious shortages of consumer goods. Bread rationing, for example, continued through the 1950s.

Most industrial products were either of poor quality or outdated. In part this was because there was no competition and no need to please the customer. And in part it was because some of the quotas set by the central planners left factory managers no choice but to turn out inferior products. According to Khrushchev, most Soviet leaders were aware of these problems but were afraid to go counter to Stalin's view that only centralized control could make things work. As a result, local factory managers were deprived of all decision-making power.

The Choice of Stalin's Successor

At the time of Stalin's death, no one had sufficient support to fill his dictatorial shoes. When Soviet leaders asked the citizenry not to panic they revealed their own fears. As Nikita Khrushchev remarked later, 'If you put fifteen of us [in the Presidium] end to end, it would not make a Stalin.' It was not clear at this point whether the next leader or leaders would come from the Communist Party organization or the state organization, since Stalin's dictatorial regime had severely curtailed the authority of the party.

It soon became apparent that the supporters of the new course were in the majority. The closest followers of Stalin soon lost out in the power struggle. Beria, who was head of the secret police and best qualified to assume Stalin's position, was liquidated on both real and trumped-up charges. But another close follower, Molotov, was to remain as one of the top policy makers until 1955, when his hard-line foreign policy objectives were defeated.

Soviet leaders soon began to stress the collective nature of leadership. Georgi Malenkov succeeded Stalin as both party secretary and chairman of the council of ministers, but he was removed as party secretary after only a few weeks by the Central Committee. This move heralded the greater diffusion of power and the revival of the Communist party's role as the major decision-making body. Stalin, with the aid of the secret police, had limited the party's power to merely rubber-stamping all of his decisions. Now, after Beria was liquidated, it was the power of the secret police that was severely circumscribed.

Until Khrushchev became dominant, the party Presidium made all policy decisions. Throughout the 1950s, party organs made major decisions on leadership and policy changes. Khrushchev realized the importance of the party; in 1957 he defeated his opponents by appealing a Presidium decision against him to a meeting of the party's Central Committee. The decision to remove Khrushchev from power seven years later was made by a majority of the Presidium and the Central Committee. True, some decisions had already been reached before the meetings of the government organs, but they were not always final, as the reversal of the 1957 Presidium decision attests.

Nikita Khrushchev's rise to power corresponded to Georgy Malenkov's fall. The battle was waged over Malenkov's advocacy of the new course and Khrushchev's support of heavy industry and agriculture. In stressing improvement in the standard of living through concentration on light industry, housing and consumer goods, Malenkov promised 'an abundance of food for the people and of raw materials for consumer goods industries in the next two or three years.' A struggle then ensued between Khrushchev and Malenkov over the economy and ultimately over party leadership.

Malenkov's programme would have required a massive shift in economic priorities, thus reducing investment in heavy industry and armaments. Khrushchev was able to convince most of the party members that such a course would imperil Soviet security since there was not enough money for heavy industry and armaments as well as for agriculture and consumer goods. And, Khrushchev argued, huge investments in machinery were needed so that enormous new territories in Kazakhstan and Western Siberia (virgin lands) could be opened up to agriculture. Although this virgin lands project was ultimately to fail, it provided Khrushchev with a means to defeat Malenkov.

With the majority of the party behind him, Khrushchev became first secretary of the party in September 1953 and finally forced Malenkov to resign as chairman of the council of ministers in February 1955. With the appointment of Nikolai Bulganin as Malenkov's successor, Khrushchev had established his ascendancy.

Struggles for leadership followed Stalin's death in many East European countries as well. The initial division of party and government leadership that had ensued in the Soviet Union, occurred in Czechoslovakia and Hungary in 1953 and in Bulgaria and Poland in 1954 at Soviet insistence. The Hungarian division left Matyas Rakosi as party secretary and brought the 'new course' reformer Imre Nagy to the premiership. Such seeming indecision in the Soviet Union and elsewhere left a public impression of weakness among the leadership. This division among party officials contributed to labour unrest in Czechoslovakia, East Germany and Bulgaria in 1953. Instructed by Soviet leaders to institute a new course in East Germany, the East German leadership divided over the extent of the reforms. They failed to rescind increased work demands on East German workers decreed in May. When the government, led by Stalinists such as Walter Ulbricht, the secretary general of the party, resisted worker demands, the strikers increased their demands from a rescinding of the increased work norms to include free elections, parliamentary democracy and reunion with West Germany. When the police failed to quell the rioting, the Soviet military stepped in to crush the uprising.

Khrushchev's Leadership

Once Khrushchev gained the upper hand in the Soviet Union he tried to find a new way to establish Soviet hegemony in Eastern Europe. It had become clear to Khrushchev that some relaxation of Stalinist orthodoxy was necessary to prevent massive upheaval in Eastern Europe. Therefore, in 1955 and 1956, he launched a campaign to put the Soviet Union in the forefront of this relaxation. As a first step he had to counteract Tito's influence in Eastern Europe, for Yugoslavia had taken the lead by abandoning collectivization in 1953, initiating worker self-management in industry, and turning the Communist party into a broader, more popular organization called the League of Communists.

The Khrushchev offensive began with a 20,000-word denunciation of Stalin at the Twentieth Party Congress of the Soviet Union in February 1956. The official reports from the congress contained little surprising information. His acceptance of Yugoslavia's different 'forms of transition' to socialism was expected. But in a secret speech to a closed session of the congress Khrushchev charged Stalin with the murder of loyal party leaders and with alienating Tito. By making Stalin the scapegoat for all the evils in Eastern Europe, Khrushchev hoped to take the onus off the present Soviet leadership and discredit his internal opponents. This policy was, of course, dangerous since any criticism of former leaders could reflect on him and on the party as well. Even some West European Communists, such as Togliatti, expressed alarm at the harshness of the criticism. Fearing that the criticism had gotten out of hand, the Soviet Central Committee on 30 June partially exonerated Stalin by claiming that strict discipline and centralization was needed during his time in office.

Khrushchev's dissolution of the Cominform in April 1956 confirmed his earlier promise to Tito that ideological uniformity would not be imposed on the East European countries. Finally, his announcement of the doctrine of diversity at a meeting with Tito on 20 June seemed to put the Soviet stamp of approval on different roads to socialism. It was not long before Khrushchev's new policy was to be put to the test.

The Polish October

Only eight days after Khrushchev's meeting with Tito, riots erupted in Poznan, Poland. These riots were not solely the result of Khrushchev's policies; primarily, the workers were protesting their low standard of living, which had its roots in earlier Soviet pressure to concentrate on heavy industry. Malenkov's new course, which was urged on Polish leaders to improve relations with the masses, actually divided the leadership into Stalinists and followers of the new course; and at the same time it accelerated worker demands for economic improvement. Revelations by Khrushchev and the Polish secret police further undermined the credibility of Polish Stalinists: Khrushchev reported at the Twentieth Party Congress that Soviet agents had destroyed the Polish Communist party leadership in 1938 and remade the party to conform to Soviet desires. These revelations followed those of a Polish secret service agent who had escaped to the West in 1954 and revealed extensive corruption, terror and favouritism among the Polish leadership. The 1954 revelations led to a purge of the secret police and the release of the previously discredited Wladyslaw Gomulka from detention.

Even before Khrushchev's 1956 offensive, Polish intellectuals had become increasingly critical of the hard-line Polish leadership. Following the onset of the new course, they had discussed the inappropriateness of agricultural collectivization in Poland and the lack of worker participation in industrial management. Undoubtedly, Yugoslav 'deviationism' in agrarian and industrial policies had a further impact upon the Polish debate.

Among the noteworthy consequences of the Polish revolt were the ending of collectivization in Polish agriculture and the establishment of workers' councils in Polish industry. The workers' revolt for bread and freedom and the refusal of the police and army to fire on them left the Polish leadership with two options: to comply with popular demands or depend on Soviet troops to put down the rioters.

The reform movement had had its effect. Polish leaders, in an unprecedented move, apologized to the workers for their poor conditions and promised reforms. At a meeting of the Central Committee between 18 and 28 July attended by Soviet leaders Nikolai Bulganin and Georgi Zhukov, Polish leaders tried to pick their way between two equally undesirable extremes: an anti-Communist revolution or Soviet intervention. Bulganin told the Poles, 'Every country can go a different way to socialism' – as long as it did not break-up the Soviet bloc. This was rejected at the meeting, but it became the basis for the final settlement.

During the next three months, the Polish leadership came to the conclusion that only the return of the recently discredited national communist leader, Gomulka, could resolve the crisis. While the Stalinists wished to use Gomulka merely to quiet revolutionary ferment, Gomulka said he would return to the Polish leadership only if he were empowered to implement his programme. During these three months Poland had obtained the support of Communist China for its national communist course by convincing the Chinese that the Polish national road was not to be similar to the Yugoslav one. The Soviets also had to consider the masses' growing identification with Catholicism after the massive pilgrimage to the Jasna Gora monastery to commemorate Poland's delivery from another foreign army's siege 300 years before. Early in October worker intervention helped the Polish leaders survive an attempted coup by Stalinists. With the Polish Stalinists defeated, Soviet leaders decided it was time to come to an understanding with the reformist forces.

On 19 October Khrushchev, Lazar Kaganovich, Anastas Mikoyan and Vyacheslav Molotov flew unannounced to Warsaw. Before the Soviet delegation arrived, the Polish leadership chose Gomulka as first secretary in order to satisfy the masses and save Polish communism. Khrushchev accused the Polish leaders of misleading him about the internal situation, but the recently rehabilitated Gomulka convinced the Soviet leaders that Poland was going to remain within the Soviet bloc and that Poland's anti-Stalinist views were no more radical than those of the Soviet Union. Moreover, he convinced Khrushchev that only a somewhat revisionist course would be acceptable to the Polish masses. Khrushchev accepted Polish assurances since he did not want to intervene in Poland at the same time that he was dealing with Hungarian revolutionaries, he did not wish to sacrifice his recent understanding with Tito and he could find no other Polish leader who could preserve Polish communism without a civil war or Soviet intervention. The Polish masses were convinced not to push their demands beyond what Gomulka had obtained by the Soviet crushing of the Hungarian Revolution in November, 1956. Gomulka released the Catholic Primate Stefan Cardinal Wyszynski from monastic internment to help convince the Polish masses to accept the compromise.

The Soviet visit was not altogether in vain. Since Khrushchev had previously enunciated a policy of diversity and had accepted the Yugoslav revisionists, the Polish promises of support for Soviet foreign policy and continued control of the Communist party in Poland were sufficient to allay Soviet fears.

Despite Soviet acquiescence on the Polish demand for decollectivization of agriculture and de-emphasis of heavy industry, there was little else about the Polish policy that was revisionist from a Soviet perspective. Until Gomulka fell from power in 1970 he followed a pro-Soviet course, in part because he realized that Poland's geographic position demanded a close working relationship with the Soviet Union, and in part because he disliked radical revisionism.

Gomulka continued to oppose Titoism and a liberalization of the press in Poland. Eventually, he stilled most of the voices that had demanded greater liberalization, or the so-called 'Polish spring' in October. His orthodoxy extended even outside his own country. He joined in the denunciation of the 1956 Hungarian Revolution that followed on the heels of the Polish revolt and ironically was inspired at least to some extent by Poland's defiance of the Soviet Union and he also helped crush the 1968 Czech Revolution.

The Hungarian Revolution

The Hungarian Revolution presented a much more serious challenge to the Soviet Union than the Polish uprising had done. While Poland threatened to establish its own brand of national communism, the Hungarian Revolution ultimately threatened the very existence of the Communist party. Poland continued to acknowledge the supremacy of the Soviet Union in Eastern

Europe, but Hungary aimed to chart a neutral course by severing its ties with the Soviet Union. If this uprising had been allowed to succeed it might have engendered similar revolutions throughout Eastern Europe.

Hungarian political and economic developments prior to the 1956 revolt mirrored those of the Soviet Union. Malenkov's new course was followed in Hungary by Imre Nagy's new course. Appointed premier in July 1953 at Soviet insistence to correct the worst aspects of Stalinism, Nagy saw as his task the restoration of economic stability and confidence in the Communist regime. His predecessor as premier, Matyas Rakosi, who retained his position as leader of the Communist party, had brought Hungary to the brink of economic catastrophe by his Stalinist emphasis on the build-up of Hungarian heavy industry at the expense of the rest of the economy. Nagy began to divert the country's resources to light industry and stopped the forced collectivization of agriculture.

The economic relaxation led to a corresponding intellectual relaxation. Intellectuals began to discuss not only the nature of the changes in Hungarian communism but also the value of a communist system. A group of intellectuals gathered in the Petöfi Circle – named after a nineteenth-century nationalist poet and established by the Communist party in March 1956 as what the party hoped would be a harmless escape valve – and debated the possibility of achieving democracy in a Communist state. Nagy and the intellectuals appear to have been influenced by the independent course in Yugoslavia, believing it possible for Hungary to achieve the same independent position.

Nagy's plans were cut short by the fall of his Soviet protector, Malenkov, in February 1955. Rakosi now seized the opportunity to regain leadership over both the state and the party, reinstituting a Stalinist hard line. Nagy gave in without a fight, perhaps because he expected Rakosi would fail in his attempt to reimpose ideological conformity.

Yet Nagy could hardly have expected the shake-up in the Soviet bloc that was to result from Khrushchev's denunciation of Stalin at the Twentieth Party Congress in February 1956. While Rakosi tried to reestablish his authority, Khrushchev was exonerating Bela Kun, a discredited former Rakosi rival and a national communist. Buoyed up by Khrushchev's action, Hungarian intellectuals demanded an investigation of Rakosi's past, especially the part he had played in the liquidation of the national communist, Laslo Rajk. Rajk had been accused of Titoist deviationism and had been executed during the Stalinst purges in 1949. In March 1956 Rakosi conceded Rajk's innocence.

Three months later the Hungarian Writers Union and the Petofi Circle, inspired by Gomulka's successful stand in Poland, openly opposed Rakosi in the columns of the party newspaper *Szabad Nep*. The Soviet Union opposed Rakosi's plan to silence his opposition by arresting Nagy and 400 intellectuals, both because the plan might fail and because it certainly would not endear the Communist party to the Hungarian population. Rakosi was handcuffed by the Soviet directive to reintroduce Stalinist economic priorities without the Stalinist terrorist methods that would have made such changes a possibility.

Wanting a more popular leader for the Hungarian Communist party (CPH), the Soviet leaders chose Erno Gero as Rakosi's successor, but he was not acceptable to the majority of the anti-Stalinst intellectuals. According to Tito, distrust of Nagy led the Soviet leaders to make it 'a condition that Rakosi would go only if Gero remained. And this was a mistake, because Gero differed in no way from Rakosi'. Had the Soviet leaders supported Nagy at this point when he still had a chance to put himself at the head of the reforming forces, they might have prevented the more radical revolution that was to follow.

The first stage of the revolution was touched off when a group demonstrating in support of the Polish insurrection was fired upon by the Hungarian police on 23 October 1956. Several mass demonstrations had already been held by the Petofi Circle to demand a new party congress and the reinstatement of Nagy. For example, three days earlier, 200,000 people marched in Budapest, chanting the Petofi verse, 'We will never again be slaves.' Hungarian revolutionaries had mistakenly viewed the reinstatement of Gomulka in Poland as a Soviet surrender to the forces of change in Eastern Europe.

Gero made his most serious mistake on that fateful day when he called on the Soviet army to put down the demonstration. In the minds of most Hungarians this act completely discredited the party and increased their desire for a non-Communist Hungary. Although Soviet troops halted their intervention once they realized that workers had joined the student demonstrators, their presence stimulated a violent reaction. Workers set up anti-Soviet, anti-Communist workers' councils throughout Hungary. In the countryside student parliaments and socialist revolutionary councils arose spontaneously, demanding free elections, the withdrawal of Soviet troops and the dissolution of the security police.

When segments of the Hungarian army joined the revolt, Soviet leaders decided that only a Communist government headed by Nagy as premier and Janos Kadar as first secretary could survive without Soviet support. The Soviets expected that Kadar would satisfy the more orthodox Communists as well as moderate Nagy's more radical objectives. On 28 October Soviet troops began to withdraw from Budapest, and Nagy set up a new government.

By now, hatred of the Soviet Union and the Hungarian Communist party had reached such intensity that even Nagy would have found it difficult to install a solely Communist government, had he wanted to do so. Nagy not only permitted the re-establishment of opposition parties but also set up a coalition government with Social Democratic, Smallholder and National Peasant party participation. By 31 October he had withdrawn Hungary from the Warsaw Treaty Organization, proclaimed Hungarian neutrality, and requested United Nations protection.

These acts confirmed Khrushchev's fears about Nagy. Hungary had presented the Soviet Union with a challenge to its authority that it could not ignore. If the Hungarians were permitted to continue, the Soviets faced the prospect of more anti-Communist revolts in Eastern Europe and an end to Soviet hegemony in Eastern Europe. Even Tito approved the crushing of the 'fascist counter-revolution' in November since Nagy's programme threatened the very existence of the Communist Party. Despite the valiant opposition of most of Hungary's population, the Soviet army soon smashed all resistance. Before being hanged for his part in the revolution, Nagy prophetically remarked,

> If my life is needed to prove that not all Communists are enemies of the people, I gladly make the sacrifice. I know that one day there will be another Nagy trial that will rehabilitate me. I also know I will have a reburial. I only fear that the future oration will be delivered by those who betrayed me.

His reburial came on 16 June 1989 but those responsible were not his betrayers but a Committee for Historical Justice that was seeking his exoneration.

Because the next Hungarian Communist party and government leader, Janos Kadar, called on the Soviet Union to put down the revolution, he was termed 'a standing affront to national memory and pride'. But after the revolution he led Hungary to its own form of national communism. Having been imprisoned by Rakosi for his nationalism, Kadar was not unaware of the desires of his countrymen. If we compare conditions since the early 1960s in Hungary and Poland, where Gomulka instituted a more orthodox regime, we might wonder whether it was the Hungarians or the Poles who won in 1956. Kadar removed the Stalinists from the party and concentrated on promoting economic development and raising the standard of living. The Hungarian people eventually came to accept Kadar as the result of improved economic conditions in the 1960s and seventies but an economic downturn in the eighties forced him from power (see Chapter 11).

The Hungarian Revolution seriously eroded Khrushchev's support in the Soviet Union. The cost of putting down the revolt and financing the recovery of Hungary put the brake on Soviet economic growth. Certain of Khrushchev's enemies, Bulganin among them, used the financial crisis and the Hungarian debacle as grounds for challenging Khrushchev's position. In defence, Khrushchev tried to blame the highly centralized government agencies for the economic failures. His proposal for lodging economic decision-making in regional economic commissions, called *Sovnarkhozy*, gained the support of a majority of the Central Committee in May 1957.

Since local party officials then were given more say in local economic affairs, support for Khrushchev increased among party members. But in June 1957, while he was on a trip to Finland, his opponents managed to gain a majority in the Presidium. When he returned, he was vigorously attacked by Malenkov, Molotov and Bulganin, for creating economic problems and violating the principle of collective leadership. Undaunted, Khrushchev had the entire Central Committee called together in June 1957 and gained a majority over his opponents. As a result, a so-called anti-party group, including Malenkov, Kaganovich and Molotov were expelled from the Presidium of the party. Such an exercise of party democracy, not used since Lenin, indicated the changed nature of party leadership.

Polycentrism

Khrushchev faced an equally serious challenge to Soviet leadership of international communism. The revolts in Hungary and Poland as well as Yugoslav 'deviationism' threatened Soviet domination in Eastern Europe. In fact, international communism underwent a three-way division in the 1950s among 'revisionists,' dogmatists (Stalinists), and national communists. The split left the Communist world with several centres of power, a state of affairs known as *polycentrism*.

The revisionists, mainly Yugoslavia, rejected the Soviet model in its entirety, contending that it was the Soviet Union – not Yugoslavia – that had strayed from the path of Marxism-Leninism. They began to decentralize economic and political decision making to prove that they were closer to the communist society envisioned by Marx than the highly centralized dictatorial government in the Soviet Union.

The Yugoslav revisionists were labelled deviationists and were vehemently opposed by the dogmatists, especially Communist China and Albania. In international affairs the dogmatists supported a continuation of the struggle with capitalism and violently rejected peaceful coexistence. At home they opposed a relaxation of Stalinist principles. Therefore, they viewed Khrushchev's de-Stalinization efforts as revisionist.

The *national communists*, led by Gomulka, stressed Communist solidarity in foreign affairs but insisted that each state be permitted to achieve communism in its own way. They held that local conditions were sufficiently different to preclude adoption of the Soviet economic and social model without adjusting it as needed. In practice, most of the states led by national communists retained much of the Soviet model.

Revisionism in Yugoslavia   It was the 'revisionist' Yugoslavs who offered the most serious challenge to the Soviet model. There the establishment of the League of Communists reduced the strong centralized control of the party. Economically, many capitalist practices were adopted to stimulate the economy (see Chapter 9). Some Communist critics, in fact, viewed Titoism as nothing more than Western European social democracy. Much of Yugoslavia's unorthodox mixture of Communist and capitalist practice has grown out of an ideological need to defend itself against charges of deviationism and a fundamentally pragmatic approach to Communist economic practices.

Khrushchev's denunciation of Stalinism and confirmation of separate paths to socialism in 1956 seemed to clear the way for a rapprochement between the Soviet Union and Yugoslavia. However, the Soviet's crushing of the Hungarian Revolution, which each blamed the other for causing, and subsequent efforts to achieve greater unity among Communist Bloc countries encouraged Tito to maintain more stoutly the principle of national independence. Khrushchev ignored Tito's demand that the Soviet Union act against Stalinist leaders throughout Eastern Europe. In fact, Stalinism became more rigid in Eastern Europe after the Hungarian uprising. Led by Walter Ulbricht in East Germany and Antonin Novotny in Czechoslovakia, Eastern Europe became more dogmatic than the Soviet Union. Attacks on Yugoslavia in the Soviet and East European press and accelerated economic pressures led Tito to take a much more militant ideological position.

The 1958 draft programme of the Yugoslav Party Congress asserted that Yugoslavia was closer to Marxism–Leninism than the Soviet Union was. With worker self-management and the diffusion of political power to local communes, the 1958 programme stated, the League of Communists 'will gradually, in the long run, disappear with the developing and strengthening of ever more inclusive forms of immediate socialist democracy'.

Furthermore, the programme asserted Communist parties were not the only creators of socialism. This was an apparent attempt to solidify Yugoslavia's position as a bridge between East and West by implying that Western European welfare states were also finding their way towards socialism. Although the programme suggested no major change in Yugoslav policy, it was anathema in China, Albania and Romania.

Dogmatism in China What China considered to be Khrushchev's coddling of deviationsim became the immediate cause for the division of the Communist world into three major centres – the Soviet Union, China and Yugoslavia – and many minor centres.

However, the development of the Sino-Soviet-Yugoslav split had long been evident. The Chinese had been disenchanted with Khrushchev's leadership since his denunciation of Stalin in 1956 and had long been opposed to the Soviet Union's territorial acquisitions in Asia, its monopoly of economic power within the Communist bloc, and its policy of peaceful coexistence. Mao Zedong was, in fact, always independent of the Soviet Union but had adopted Stalinist totalitarian methods to maintain his authoritarian government. Therefore, any denunciation of Stalin was a condemnation of Mao's rule as well.

China especially resented the favoured economic position of the Soviet Union among the other Communist countries. Stalin had treated China the way he had treated the East European countries: as economic dependencies of the Soviet Union. In his view, China's function was to provide cheap raw materials to the Soviet Union and to serve as a buyer of Soviet manufactured goods. Stalin had also refused to help the Chinese develop nuclear weapons. Rejecting a subordinate role, China propagandized that the Soviet Union should have raised all other Communist states to the Soviet Union's economic level.

Since Stalin and Khrushchev were more interested in developing the Soviet Union than in fomenting world revolution, they were not interested in building up China. In fact, Stalin and Khrushchev were more afraid of China than of the West. Soviet propaganda against the Chinese smacked of the late nineteenth century, when westerners were warning of the 'yellow peril'.

Chinese and Soviet claims to the same territory – Sinkiang, Amur, Sakhalin, Transbaikalia – were much more immediate than Western threats. The failure of the Soviet Union to back China against India in 1962 was seen by Chinese leaders as further evidence of Soviet revisionism. However, to say, as some have done, that the Sino-Soviet rift is national and not ideological is to overlook a major element in the conflict.

The Chinese tolerated Khrushchev's denunciation of Stalin only because they thought the world Communist movement should be unified around the Soviet Union. From 1956 to 1958, they tolerated Soviet revisionism because they were much more afraid of polycentrism. In 1957 and 1958, as Khrushchev implemented his own pragmatic brand of communism in the Soviet Union, China attempted the Great Leap Forward to collectivize and communize China completely. When this experiment failed, even greater emphasis was placed on Stalinist orthodoxy (except for the Stalinist emphasis on industry at the expense of agriculture) in order to assure unity at home and save face abroad. Khrushchev's unsuccessful attempt to unseat Mao in 1959 by instigating a party revolt exacerbated relations.

At a series of conferences and party congresses from 1960 until Khrushchev's fall from power four years later, the Soviet Union tried to discredit China. At the Twenty-second Party Congress in Bucharest during June of 1960, Khrushchev succeeded in obtaining majority support for his condemnation of Chinese factionalism. Unsubdued, the Chinese continued to charge that the world Communist movement was threatened by compromise with the enemy. Khrushchev's attempt to obtain 'peaceful coexistence' with the United States at the summit conferences at Camp David (1959) and Paris (1960) were vehemently denounced in Beijing.

The Soviet decisions to remove Stalin's body from the Kremlin, where it had rested in state next to Lenin's body, and to expel the pro-Chinese Albanians from the world Communist movement at the Twenty-second Congress of the CPSU in 1961 were an indirect slap at the Chinese. The gap became virtually unbridgeable with the withdrawal of Soviet forces from Cuba in 1962 and the signing of the Nuclear Test Ban Treaty a year later. The Chinese saw these actions as final proof that the Soviet Union would use nuclear weapons only to further its own interests and not to achieve world revolutionary aims.

National Communism in Romania The establishment of a form of national communism in Romania in 1963 and 1964, influenced by the growing divisions in world communism, was even more clearly the outcome of Soviet economic policies and Khrushchev's anti-Stalinist offensive. In response to Soviet de-Stalinization in 1953 Gheorghe Gheorghiu-Dej set Romania on a new course by instituting collective leadership, and, with Soviet permission, abolishing the hated Soviet-Romanian joint companies (sovroms). Inspired by Malenkov's new course in the Soviet Union, Romania also sought to obtain a more diversified economy by increasing expenditures on the production of consumer goods and on agriculture.

Responsibility for Romania's decision to follow an independent course can be laid at the feet of Khrushchev, whose drive to obtain economic and diplomatic unity in Eastern Europe after the Hungarian Revolution, provided a major impetus to Romanian national communism. Throughout the 1950s Romania drew closer to China as both nations resisted Khrushchev's policy of de-Stalinization within the Communist world. Gheorghiu-Dej and Mao resented Khrushchev's continuing denunciations of Stalin and his pressure on them to follow suit. The Stalinist line in Romania hardened, and the likelihood of integration within the Soviet bloc dwindled.

When a pro-Khrushchev force in Romania allegedly challenged Gheorghiu Dej's leadership in 1957, a campaign ensued to remove all revisionists – that is,

Khrushchevites – from power. In order to strengthen the regime at home and continue Romania's drive towards economic independence from Moscow, Gheorghiu-Dej stepped-up his efforts to obtain aid from the West. Trade with the West reached 25 per cent of Romania's total foreign trade in 1960. By 1960, Gheorghiu-Dej had strong support from the Romanian masses for his independent course. His death in March 1965 brought little change to Romania policies since his successor, Nicolae Ceausescu, had been groomed to fill is shoes.

Council for Mutual Economic Assistance (Comecon) and Economic Nationalism The final shaping of Romanian national communism stemmed from Khrushchev's attempt to make Comecon a supranational economic agency with jurisdiction over the economies of each member state. Khrushchev saw Comecon as an answer to the growing economic division of labour in the European Economic Community. Only by achieving a similar division of labour in Comecon could the Communist countries keep pace with economic growth in the West. Romanian fears that the Comecon envisioned by Khrushchev would frustrate its own industrialization were well founded. Khrushchev planned to have Romania continue as a supplier of raw materials to the more developed Comecon countries – Czechoslovakia, East Germany and the Soviet Union.

Khrushchev's determined drive in 1962 and 1963 to integrate all the East European economies was to founder on the rocks of economic nationalism. In advance of a meeting in July 1963 to determine whether Comecon was to be a supranational body, Romania got the support of both China and Yugoslavia to keep it international – and also received promises of financial support from the West. As an international agency, Comecon can suggest integrative measures but cannot enforce them as a supranational body could do. At the meeting, not only was supranationalism defeated but the right of member states to develop independently was upheld.

Now embroiled in his dispute with China and Albania, Khrushchev could not force the majority of East European states to accept a reinvigorated Comecon. Because of a continued friendship with China as well as with the Soviet Union, Romania attempted in 1963 to mediate the differences between the two. Romania's independent stand reached its apogee in 1968 when Ceausescu, not only refused to join other Warsaw Pact states in the invasion of Czechoslovakia but also publicly denounced the invasion.

Strong support of Soviet foreign policy in recent years has taken the sting out of Romania's earlier rejection of economic co-operation: it subscribed to Khrushchev's policy of peaceful coexistence and backed the Nuclear Test Ban Treaty. Coexistence suited Romania's goal of developing trade with the West in order to promote economic independence. Yet the Romanians may in fact have been saved by a more fundamental change – the unexpected fall of Khrushchev in October 1964.

Khrushchev's Fall from Power

Failures in both domestic and foreign policy led to Khrushchev's fall. The weakening of Soviet hegemony in Eastern Europe, the growing disagreement with China and the Cuban fiasco had undermined Khrushchev's position. His opponents were especially upset by his hasty decision to set up missile sites in Cuba and the humiliation of having to dismantle them.

Added to his foreign policy debacles were a number of economic failures. Especially harmful was the failure of Khrushchev's agricultural Virgin Lands project, which did not provide the promised amount of food. Despite a 17 per cent increase in the acreage sown to crops from 1960 to 1963, massive imports of Canadian wheat and rationing of bread were necessary in 1963. Rather than increasing the acreage, Khrushchev should have concentrated machinery and fertilizer on the existing arable land.

The failure of the sixth five-year plan added to Khrushchev's woes. The attempt to keep the Soviet Union's space programme ahead of the United States while investing heavily in new plants and equipment overtaxed Soviet resources. As defence spending rose by one-third between 1959 and 1963, the rate of industrial growth declined. The GNP growth rate declined from 10 per cent in 1958 to about 3 per cent in 1962 and 1963. Khrushchev also lost the support of the military and the heavy industry advocates in 1964, when he began to emphasize the production of consumer goods.

But it may have been Khrushchev's political reforms that were decisive in his fall, since they stripped even Central Committee members of their security. Khrushchev's proposed reforms would have forced a turnover in governing party bodies of one-third at every election. As a result, party functionaries (*apparatchiki*) would suddenly be deprived of life-time bureaucratic posts. Another unpopular innovation, the 1962 division of regional party administration into industrial and agricultural sectors, cut local party functionaries' authority in half. Such tampering with party functionaries' livelihood cost Khrushchev much of the support he had previously had in the Central Committee. Party faithful were no longer assured of continuing local political office and, if they became a local party secretary, of national political office and economic security. A local party secretary now had to compete with his industrial or agricultural counterpart for a seat in the Central Committee and with his counterpart and local government (Soviet) officials for a seat in the Supreme Soviet of the USSR. The result of this local division of authority was not greater efficiency through new leadership but confusion and economic decline.

Despite these setbacks, Khrushchev's opponents had to manoeuvre his fall while he was vacationing in the Crimea. Called back by the Presidium, he was unable to turn the table on his opponents by appealing to the Central Committee as he had done in 1957 because his supporters were now in the minority there. Two days after his removal from office, *Pravda,* the Soviet newspaper, denounced his 'hare-brained scheming, immature conclusions, hasty decisions, and actions divorced from reality'.

Although the post-Khrushchev period is often called the Brezhnev era, the policies pursued until Brezhnev's death in November 1982 were normally the result of collective decisions of the 14-member Politburo of the Communist Party. In order to prevent any one person from monopolizing power as Stalin and Khrushchev had done, the Politburo reduced the Central Committee of the Party and the Party Congress to a mere rubber-stamping of decisions already reached in the Politburo. Brezhnev's position as Party Secretary did not permit him to pack the Politburo with his supporters; after 18 years as Party Secretary, only 5 members of the Politburo were indisputably his political protégés and they were not the more powerful members. As a result, Brezhnev had to put together a majority in the Politburo for any decision or policy.

During Brezhnev's early years as Party Secretary, the Soviet Union achieved internal stability, military parity with the United States and international recognition as a true superpower. Domestic stability was obtained by scrapping Khrushchev's administrative reforms: his decentralization of authority, his division of regional Party administration into agricultural and industrial sectors and his rejection of seniority as the primary means for advancement. With local Communist Party officials regaining full authority, local administrative conflicts were reduced. Also, de-Stalinization ended with Khrushchev since the Politburo apparently determined that a continuing public criticism of former leaders was undermining the present leadership. This newly found order was obviously comforting to the leadership but it reduced local initiative and added to the enormous bureaucratic machine at the centre. As will be discussed in Chapter 9, the economy suffered from this excessive centralization of authority.

Although Khrushchev fell from power in 1964, the consequences of his rule were to play an immediate role in the Czech uprising in 1968 and a long-term role in the undermining of totalitarianism within the Soviet Union. His attempts to reform the ossified party cadres in the Soviet Union set in motion a similar questioning of bureaucratic party structures and centralized decision making in Czechoslovakia (Chapter 10). His efforts also stimulated national Stalinist movements in Romania and Albania that were further aided by the great schism between China and the Soviet Union. The 1968 revolt in Czechoslovakia also gained momentum as a result of Soviet concentration on its own domestic problems after 1964 and its indecisiveness once the Czech unrest began in 1968.

FURTHER READING

Soviet internal affairs are analysed in Merle Fainsod, *How Russia is Ruled* (2d ed. 1963); Leonard Schapiro, *The Communist Party of the Soviet Union* (1964); Robert Conquest, *Power and Policy in the U.S.S.R.* (1961); Adam B. Ulam, *The New Face of Soviet Totalitarianism* (1963); and John Reshetar, *The Soviet Polity* (1971). Robert Daniel's *Is Russia Reformable? Change and Resistance from Stalin to Gorbachev* (1988) provides valuable information and analysis of Soviet domestic affairs between Stalin and Gorbachev. For more recent events and policies see Donald D. Barry and Carol Barner-Barry, *Contemporary Soviet Politics* (2nd Edition) (1982); and Jerry Hough's enlarged and revised edition of Fainsod, *How the Soviet Union is Governed* (1979).

For the Soviet role in world affairs see Alvin Z. Rubinstein (ed.), *The Foreign Policy of the Soviet Union* (1960); Louis Fischer, *The Soviets in World Affairs* (1960); David Dallin, *Soviet Foreign Policy After Stalin* (1961); Philip Mosely, *The Kremlin and World Politics* (1960); and Adam Ulam's *Dangerous Relations: The Soviet Union in World Politics, 1970–82* (1983).

The best studies of the changing nature of the Soviet bloc in the fifties and sixties are Zbigniew Brzezinski, *The Soviet Bloc, Unity and Conflict* (rev. ed., 1967); and Ghita Ionescu, *The Break-up of the Soviet Empire in Eastern Europe* (1965). Some perceptive short studies of polycentrism are in Kurt London (ed.), *Eastern Europe in Transition* (1966); Alexander Dallin (ed.), *Diversity in International Communism* (1963); Paul Zinner (ed.), *National Communism and Popular Revolt in Eastern Europe* (1956); and Stephen Fischer-Galati (ed.) *Eastern Europe in the 1980's* (1981). Also useful are P. Lewis, *Central Europe Since 1945* (1994), Sabrina Ramet, *Eastern Europe: Politics, Culture, and Society Since 1939* (1998), and G. Stokes, *From Stalinism to Pluralism: A Documentary History of Eastern Europe Since 1945* (1991).

Scholarly treatments of Khrushchev are found in Edward Crankshaw, *Khrushchev: A Career* (1966); Carl A. Linden, *Khrushchev and the Soviet Leadership* (1966); Abraham Blumberg (ed.), *Russia Under Khrushchev* (1962); and Roy A. Medvedev and Zhores A. Medvedev, *Khrushchev: The Years in Power* (1976) and William Tompson, *Khrushchev: A Political Life* (1995). For an insider's view see Fedor Mikhailovich Burlatskic, *Khrushchev and the First Russian Spring: The Era of Khrushchev through the Eyes of His Advisor* (1991).

For the period after Khrushchev see Seweryn Bialer, *Stalin's Successors: Leadership, Stability and Change in the Soviet Union* (1980) and *The Soviet Paradox: External Expansion, Internal Decline* (1987). Bialer emphasized the differences between the generation of leaders from the 1930s and those of the post-Stalinist period who initiated reforms in the period before Gorbachev. Also useful is Michel Tatu, *Power in the Kremlin: From Khrushchev's Decline to Collective Leadership* (1969) and George Breslauer, *Khrushchev and Brezhnev as Leaders: Building Authority in Soviet Politics* (1982).

Competent studies of the Romanian separate road and Romanian communism are Ghita Ionescu, *Communism in Rumania, 1944–1962* (1964); Stephen Fischer-Galati, *The Socialist Republic of Rumania* (1969); and David Floyd, *Rumania: Russia's Dissident Ally* (1965), R. R. King, *History of the Romanian Communist Party* (1980) and T. Gilberg, *Nationalism and Communism in Romania: The Rise and Fall of Ceausesçu's Personal Dictatorship* (1990).

For Poland see Hansjakob Stehle, *The Independent Satellite: Society and Politics in Poland Since 1945* (1965); James F. Morrison, *The Polish People's Republic* (1969); Richard Hiscocks, *Poland, Bridge for the Abyss* (1963); and Nicholas Bethell, *Gomulka: His Poland, His Communism* (1969). For a thorough historical background see Norman Davies, *God's Playground: A History of Poland, Vol. II: 1795 to the Present* (1982). For information on the early post-war years, see Krystyna Kersten, *The Establishment of Communist Rule in Poland, 1943–1948* (1991). On the antecedents for the rise of Solidarity, see M. D. Simon and R. E. Kanet, *Background to Crisis: Policy and Politics in Gierek's Poland* (1981).

The Hungarian Revolution is detailed further in Paul Kecskemeti, *The Unexpected Revolution* (1961); Ference A. Vali, *Rift and Revolt in Hungary*

(1961); Paul E. Zinner, *Revolution in Hungary* (1962); Bennet Kovrig, *The Hungarian People's Republic* (1970); Tamas Ceczel, *Ten Years After: The Hungarian Revolution in the Perspective of History* (1967); and F. Feher, *Hungary 1956 Revisited: The Message of a Revolution* (1983). A good analysis of the relationship of Hungary to the Soviet Union is provided in Charles Gati, *Hungary and the Soviet Bloc* (1986). For personal accounts of the Hungarian Revolution see Sandor Kopacsi, *In the Name of the Working Class: The Inside Story of the Hungarian Revolution* (1987).

7 European Unity

> The creation of a large internal market is indispensable to make it possible for Europeans to take their place in the world again.
>
> Jean Monnet, *Les États-Unis d'Europe Ont Commencé: Discours et Allocutions, 1952–1954*

> What we need now is an intelligent synthesis between the market and the state which can help Europe win and not lose in the face of globalisation.
>
> Jose Manuel Barroso, President of the European Commission, 4 June 2005, *The Financial Times*

The omnipresent fear and impotence of small nations in a world dominated by superpowers, the desire to incorporate Germany into a federated Europe so as to prevent a recurrence of war and its attendant devastation, the longing for the economic advantages thought to be inherent in a larger economic unit – together, these provided the initial impetus for European integration. The unification movement had slowed by the 1950s, but then the Soviet Union crushed the Hungarian Revolution, the British and French failed at Suez, and Europe lost its colonial empire. All these now convinced a growing number of Europeans who had originally opposed union that closer cooperation might be their only salvation. Externally, the United States pressured Europe to cooperate so that it could pay for more of its own reconstruction, restore its markets for American goods, and prevent calamitous political developments similar to those that followed the First World War.

As French author and critic André Malraux noted, Europe was united only under Rome and under Christianity in the medieval period. By the end of the First World War the triumph of the national state was complete. Few questioned the right of the national state to command the obedience of the people living within its borders. Nineteenth-century philosophers such as Hegel justified the carving up of Europe into smaller national states that began in earnest with the French Revolution. The French Revolution had shown how brittle empires were and how powerful a political entity could be when supported by its citizenry.

Hegel and the romantics found in the national state the proper vehicle for the full development of a people's genius. In their view, the empires and Christian Europe had impeded the full development of this genius. To them, true creativity in literature, music and the other arts was no more than the ability to express this folk genius embodied in the national state. Nationalism became one of the major forces in the disruption of the Ottoman and Hapsburg empires before and during the First World War. Nevertheless, as the opening quotes suggest, politics and markets in the late twentieth-century became driving forces of the 'new' European integration process.

The Beginnings of Unity

Until after the First World War, few questioned the legitimacy of the national state. Count Richard Coudenhove–Kalergi, an aristocrat brought up in the Habsburg monarchy, was the strongest advocate of European unification in the interwar years. Others, such as French Foreign Minister Aristide Briand, had prepared a memorandum for a united Europe in 1930, but Europe was already on its way to an unlooked-for union under the jackboots of Adolf Hitler's Third Reich.

From the sufferings of the Second World War emerged a much more broadly based desire for some form of European Union. Countless wartime resistance fighters decided that the Europe of nation states should be replaced by a unified and therefore less warlike Europe. A Dutch resistance publication of 1944, *De Ploeg*, visualizing a divided post-war Europe under the influence of either the United States or the Soviet Union, had this to say: 'We Dutch are Europeans and we believe in a future for Europe. We do not belong to the Americans, who see Europe as senile and who from the outset are dividing it up into an Asiatic and an American sphere of interest.'

European leaders of the stature of Winston Churchill, Pope Pius XII, Paul-Henri Spaak, Alcide de Gasperi, Robert Schuman and Konrad Adenauer added their voices to the outpouring of support for a united Europe. Numerous organizations, Britain's United Europe Movement and Coudenhove–Kalergi's European Parliamentary Union among them, sprang up in support of European union.

In addition to the desire of Europeanists to avoid wars, the economic arguments for European union were compelling. Integration of the European economy would promote large-scale, low-cost production that would lead to greater economic output and an improved competitive position in the world market. Moreover, a customs union would enlarge the European market for member countries by bringing down the high tariff walls that separated them. Europeanists were convinced that a primary factor in American productivity and competitiveness was the huge American common market of 160 million people. Despite these advantages, many Europeans were unwilling to relinquish a measure of national sovereignty in order to attain economic integration. Two outside influences were dominant in breaking down resistance to European economic integration: the Cold War and American pressure in support of European integration to block possible Soviet expansion into Western Europe.

The first major step towards integration was taken in 1947 when the United States asked for the establishment of a common European organization to plan the distribution of American aid under the European Recovery Programme, known more familiarly as the Marshall Plan. Presented with the possibility of forestalling a severe post-war economic crisis, 17 European nations, acting in concert, set up the Organization for European Economic Co-operation (OEEC) to distribute the funds and promote trade among the member nations. Only the East European countries, pressurized by Stalin, refused to take part. Since the OEEC was to remain an international rather than a supranational organization – the United States eventually became a full member – there was never any possibility that a participant would have to sacrifice its national sovereignty.

The rapid expansion of trade across European borders – it doubled between 1948 and 1955 – convinced many Europeans of the OEEC's value. But attempts to expand it into a European customs union, with common external tariffs against non-members, encountered the resistance of Britain, which did not want to jeopardize its own economic ties with its Commonwealth partners. To those who wanted further European unification it became clear that the OEEC was incapable of achieving this. Still, it had brought Europeans together to discuss their economic needs and had in this way helped break down some opposition to integration.

The Council of Europe

The second major step towards integration was taken with the establishment of the Council of Europe. In May 1948, European federalists convoked a Congress of Europe that was attended by 750 delegates, including some of Europe's leading statesmen: Churchill, Spaak, de Gasperi, Schuman and Léon Blum. This body's proposal for the political and economic unification of the Continent led a year later to the establishment of the Council of Europe, a permanent European assembly that was to plan some form of European integration.

The Council's attempts to put together some form of union encountered serious resistance. Once again, none of the Eastern European states joined in the deliberations. Britain signed the agreement reluctantly because of the governing Labour party's concern for Britain's Commonwealth partners and its disapproval of what it considered to be the anti-Soviet orientation of the Council. Beneath the surface was Britain's feeling that it really did not belong to Europe and that its interests would be best served by acting as a middleman between Europe and the United States.

As a result of British opposition, the Consultative Assembly of the Council of Europe was limited to the right of recommendation and had no true deliberative power. A Committee of Ministers, comprising the foreign ministers of the member states, was the sole decision-making body. Obviously, the foreign ministers would act as representatives of their individual states rather than as spokesmen for a new sovereign body. Thus, the Council was reduced to making recommendations and offering advice rather than moving towards any real supranational integration of the European states.

The first president of the Council of Europe, the Belgian Prime Minister and Foreign Minister from 1948 to 51 Paul-Henri Spaak, angrily denounced those who thwarted the establishment of a meaningful supranational body when he resigned his office in 1951. In his words, 'If a quarter of the energy spent here in saying no were used to say yes to something positive, we should not be in the state we are in today.'

Had the movement for European integration stopped with only the OEEC and Council of Europe to its credit, there would be little need today to speak of a possible united Europe. However, there were strong pressures for decisive action. Especially instrumental in promoting tighter bonds was the unstable international situation and the reemergence of a German state. The 1948 Communist coup in Czechoslovakia convinced many opponents of integration that a larger European community was necessary to forestall Communist thrusts into central and western Europe. The United States, searching for support in the Cold War with the Soviet Union, encouraged a stronger economic and military organization.

When the Soviet Union exploded its first atomic bomb in 1949, the general sense of insecurity increased. The outbreak of the Korean War lent new urgency to pan-European deliberations because it seemed to some a clear indication of the Communist world's intentions, and to many more it imparted fears for German security. While the United States was tied down in Asia, the reasoning went, American troops would be in short supply in Germany, and that would make Germany a tempting target for Soviet aggression. Europeans were, of course, aware that the United States wanted to rearm Germany in order to steel her defenses against the Soviet Union. This step the other European countries did not favour unless there was some larger European organization to control a rearmed Germany.

The European Coal and Steel Community

France took the lead in the negotiations for a genuine supranational body. Led by two of its greatest statesmen, Commissioner of Planning Jean Monnet and Foreign Minister Robert Schuman, Monnet proposed in 1950 the Schuman Plan a pooling of Europe's coal and steel resources that would, in his words, make war between France and Germany 'not only unthinkable but materially impossible'. France's desire to gain security against Germany provided the major impetus for European integration. Once France realized that Germany would not remain a weak, fragmented entity as she had hoped and Britain would not remain on the continent as a counterweight to a revived Germany, she had no alternative but to seek some form of French–German association. British failure to cooperate in the European Payments Union (EPU), set up in 1950 to handle financial transactions between states, pointed towards the 'little European' (France, Germany, Italy and the Benelux countries) solution to economic reconstruction. Britain feared the impact any common financial arrangements would have on her sterling trade area.

In the summer of 1952, Monnet's proposal for a pooling of coal and steel resources came to fruition when France, Germany, Italy and the Benelux countries put into force the agreement setting up the European Coal and Steel

Community (ECSC). Britain refused to join because of what it considered to be the excessive power given to the six-member High Authority of the ECSC, whose decisions were binding on all members. Britain, with fewer economic problems at the time and with important ties to the United States and to its Commonwealth associates, was not prepared to sacrifice its national sovereignty. Had Britain joined the ECSC, the integration of its coal, steel and iron industry with the six would have made avoidance of the next step, the European Economic Community, almost impossible. Many British Labour leaders continued to see such supranational organizations as a conspiracy of big business to circumvent the demands of national labour movements.

The European Defense Community

Strangely enough, attempts to form a common European military force encountered opposition not only from the British but ultimately from the very country that had initially proposed it: France. In October 1950, French Prime Minister René Pleven proposed, as a military counterpart to the ECSC, a unified European army made up of small national contingents from each member nation. France was under pressure from the United States to agree to the rearmament of Germany because of US fears that the Soviet Union might put pressure on or even attack in Europe to help North Korea by diverting US troops from Asia. France therefore offered the Pleven Plan to avoid the establishment of an independent German military force. Even in Germany there was support for the proposal, because German leaders hoped a common European military might bring an end to Allied occupation.

Perhaps a new supranational army with recruits from all states could have been realized if the former national contingents had been left intact. Yet it is difficult to see how even that proposal could have succeeded without a supranational political organization, and that was never a possibility.

In any case, the Pleven Plan for a European Defence Community (EDC) became the victim of events. The need for a European army diminished with Stalin's death and the thaw in Soviet–Western foreign relations. Although the United States Secretary of State John Foster Dulles continued to threaten to cut military aid to Europe if the EDC was not accepted, the United States demands for a European force became less insistent with the end of the Korean War. As for the French change of heart, there were several motivations for it. After France's defeat by the Vietminh at Dien Bien Phu in May 1954, and the subsequent withdrawal of all French forces from Southeast Asia, many French leaders saw surrender of jurisdiction over its army as yet another disgrace. The French premier at this time, Pierre Mendès–France, was not a strong supporter of the EDC. He found it too anti-Soviet and too drastic a move towards supranationalism.

The English refusal to cooperate in the EDC was the final blow, because France feared an EDC that did not have the participation of British forces to offset those of Germany. On 30 August 1954, the French National Assembly rejected the EDC by 319 to 264 votes. With the EDC defeated, the only way to deal with a German military force was to integrate it into the North Atlantic

Treaty Organization (NATO) forces. This integration was brought about through the Western European Union (WEU) a body that provided for the stationing of British troops on the continent. Since all the signatories were members of NATO, it was agreed to incorporate the WEU into NATO. As a condition of its membership within the WEU, West Germany agreed to limit its military forces and armaments to levels determined by WEU members. Once French fears of a rearmed Germany were allayed by Britain's promise to keep its forces on German soil indefinitely, German military contingents joined NATO in 1955.

The European Economic Community

Fortunately for the Europeanists, economic integration was not stymied by the failure to reach a military agreement; the apparent success of the Coal and Steel Community in promoting production and trade was a persuasive argument for those advocating further economic integration, even though the ECSC had encouraged overproduction of steel and had thereby lost the support of some industrialists. With production increasing twice as fast among the six as in Great Britain from 1950 to 1955, many former opponents of European economic co-operation became ardent supporters of further economic unification.

Foreign affairs were again significant in marshalling support for closer economic cooperation. The extent of the decline in France's importance was made abundantly clear by Nasser's nationalization of the Suez Canal in 1956. This action triggered speculation as to whether Europe would be cut off from its supplies of fuel. Monnet's new Action Committee for the United States of Europe said that Europe's life might 'in the near future, ... be paralyzed by the cutting-off of its oil imports from the Middle East.' British and French attempts to make Nasser return ownership of the canal to the original stock- holders met resistance not only from Egypt but also from the United States, which sought to prevent war in Egypt. Even French and British bombardment of Egypt, coordinated with an Israeli attack into the Sinai desert, failed to produce the desired results.

The cutting off of oil imports to France led to a winter of unheated homes and immobilized automobiles and made French leaders starkly aware that France could not act alone and that its alliance with the United States did not guarantee unconditional support for any French action. Britain attempted to obtain the United States financial support so as to stabilize its finances after its military action had caused a worldwide run on the pound, but it was turned down. That the Soviet Union was unhampered in crushing the Hungarian Revolution was further proof that, individually, Europe's nations were helpless in the world of superpowers.

Recognizing the weakness of the individual nations of Europe, the French now threw their support to plans for expanding the ECSC into a common market that would include all industrial and agricultural production.

The Council of Ministers of the ECSC had already begun negotiations for a further integration of Europe's economy. Led by Paul-Henri Spaak, the

Benelux countries took the initiative in these discussions. Belgium, the Netherlands, and Luxembourg had already been brought together in a customs union in 1948; now the objective was to establish an area free of internal tariffs similar to that in the Benelux countries and the United States. At a meeting in Messina in 1955 the council decided to discuss the possibility of a common tariff among the ECSC member states. This was the initial step towards economic unity. The organization it led to was the EEC, or Common Market. The Rome Treaties of 1957, the founding treaties of the EEC, envisioned the elimination of customs barriers by 1967 and the development of an economic unit that could compete with the United States.

Authority in the EEC was lodged in four bodies – a Council of Ministers representing the interests of each member state, an appointed Commission representing the supranational interest, a Court of Justice and a Common Assembly (renamed European Parliament in 1962). The founders realized that the members would not be willing initially to sacrifice all national jurisdiction over their separate economies.

The Council of Ministers, made up of the foreign ministers (or their representatives) from each member state, considered and voted on proposals from the Commission. The size of each member's vote was determined by the size of the state. France, Germany and Italy had four votes each, Belgium and the Netherlands two and Luxembourg one.

The Court of Justice was comprised of seven judges appointed by the separate governments for a maximum term of six years. The court settled disputes among the member nations.

The European Parliament (EP), to which delegates from national parliaments are sent, and which Europeanists hoped would soon blossom into a genuine supranational assembly, could only question the Commission members and force the resignation of the Commission by a two-thirds vote. Normally, decisions were reached through a rather exhausting process of having the Commission submit and resubmit proposals before they were accepted by the Council. In the 1950s this system provided a good balance between national and supranational interests, but in the 1960s de Gaulle's narrow view of EEC duties and authority severely reduced the power of the Commission and thus the hopes for a united Europe.

In 1960 Europe was far from the unity envisioned by many EEC founders. In fact, it was divided into three economic areas: the EEC, the Eastern European Comecon countries and a new British-led European Free Trade Association (EFTA) consisting of Britain, Sweden, Denmark, Norway, Portugal, Switzerland and Austria. EFTA's primary aim was to remove trade barriers between member countries. Before the formation of EFTA in 1959, Britain had tried to set up a larger free trade area that included the EEC. But EEC members were fearful that it would keep them from their goal of making the EEC a fully integrated economic area. EFTA did not, for example, include a common external tariff.

In practice, EFTA had a very limited impact on the redirection of trade in Europe. Austria, Sweden and even Great Britain traded more with EEC members than with members of EFTA. Richard Mayne, an EEC official, correctly perceived it as 'partly a salvage operation, to secure whatever benefits were possible on a smaller and more scattered basis' than the EEC envisioned. Given Britain's close ties to the United States and the Commonwealth and rather ambivalent feelings about its European-ness, in 1959 an organization such as EFTA seemed the only possibility.

Only two years later, convinced by the EEC's economic success and discouraged by its own economic problems and declining role in the world, Great Britain decided to seek admittance to the EEC. The British were especially concerned with reports that the EEC had decided to institute political as well as economic co-operation, which would exclude Great Britain from any possibility of future integration with the six. A communiqué from a meeting of the six in July 1961, setting up a committee to draft a political treaty, announced that the EEC sought 'to give shape to the will for political union already implicit in the Treaties establishing the European Communities.' The British need not have worried. This statement was issued by the Fouchet Committee, which later failed to reach an agreement on political co-operation.

Britain's conception of itself as an intermediary between the United States and Europe was undermined by President John F. Kennedy's grand design to bring Europe and the United States closer together and prevent the imposition of high tariffs between the United States and the EEC. The so-called Kennedy Round of tariff negotiations, which resulted in the United States Trade Expansion Act of 1961, did reduce tariffs 30 to 50 per cent (depending on the commodity) on trade between Europe and the United States. Included in the trade expansion act was a clause that would have permitted President Kennedy to cut tariffs even further if Great Britain had been an EEC member.

President Kennedy, as well as his predecessors, hoped to see Great Britain join the EEC. In March 1961 George Ball, US under-secretary of state for economic affairs, told Edward Heath, later to be prime minister, 'So long as Britain remains outside the European Community, she is a force for division rather than cohesion, since she is like a giant lodestone drawing with unequal degrees of force on each member state.' He went on to say that British membership in the EEC would lead to 'a unity that can transform the Western world.' So with a mixture of anxiety over its economic and political position, fear that Europe would go it alone, and assurance that the United States approved, on 10 August 1961, Great Britain asked to negotiate with the EEC.

Fourteen months later, with the basis for British entry not yet completely settled, de Gaulle intervened. On 14 January 1963, he informed the world:

England in fact is insular, maritime, bound by her trade, her markets, her supplies to countries that are very diverse and often far away ... The nature, the structure, the situation that are peculiar to England are very different from those of the continental countries. How can England, as she lives, as she produces, as she trades, be incorporated into the Common Market as it was conceived and as it works?

Fifteen days later the negotiations were brought to a close by a French veto of the British application.

De Gaulle disapproved of British entry into the EEC for a variety of reasons. Perhaps most important was the likelihood that it would destroy France's domination of the organization. The EEC had made it possible for France to play a much larger role in the world than its own resources warranted. After the loss of its colonial empire, de Gaulle hoped to regain in Europe what France had lost in the world. Furthermore, de Gaulle resented Britain's close relationship with the United States. He resented Britain's refusal to cooperate with France in developing nuclear weapons and her acceptance of American weapons. De Gaulle could not say in so many words that France did not want to share its leadership of the EEC, but he could say the British were acting as a 'Trojan horse' for the Americans.

A final roadblock to British entry was a number of conditions that Britain wanted taken into consideration, including protection for its agriculture and special consideration for the interests of its Commonwealth and EFTA partners. De Gaulle was not alone in opposing the special conditions, for if every member had been given such consideration, there would have been no EEC. Still, it was the brusque manner of de Gaulle's rejection, without warning, that so embittered the British and impaired EEC operations in the mid-1960s.

The difference between de Gaulle's conception of Europe – as a springboard for French designs – and that of the European federalists became the subject of a 1965 struggle to decide which of the EEC governing bodies should have precedence. The trigger for the power struggle was a reform of the funding of the Common Agricultural Policy (CAP) and a strengthening of the EP, and pitted de Gaulle against the German head of the EEC Commission, Walter Hallstein. De Gaulle needed EEC support for his policy of grandeur (see Chapter 2) but he did not want to have any economic decision making taken out of French hands. Hallstein had proposed, as part of a sweeping reform of the EEC, majority voting in certain cases. De Gaulle refused to give the Commission and chairman Hallstein the authority they desired.

Hallstein persisted, and although the other EEC members stood firm against de Gaulle, they could not compel the French to accept an increase in the authority of the Commission. On 1 July 1965, de Gaulle went so far as to recall the French permanent representative in Brussels and announced no participation in the Council or other committees thus, the aptly named 'empty chair' crisis. The crisis was resolved in 1966 when the six governments signed the Luxembourg Agreement stipulating that the EEC Commission must consult the individual states before making major proposals. Further, the agreement provided that no member nation could be overruled in the Council of Ministers on an issue that that nation saw as affecting its vital interests. The conflict between de Gaulle and the federalists proved a serious setback to the supra-national concept of Europe, and it would be over 20 years before a renewed attempt at enhancing supranationality.

The period from 1967 to 1971 was dominated by new British attempts to enter the Common Market. Prime Minister Harold Wilson tried to reopen negotiations in 1967 and was again turned back by de Gaulle, but a series of later events combined to make British entry possible. Foremost among these events was the change of government in France when de Gaulle retired in 1969. His successor was Georges Pompidou, a supporter of a confederated Europe who was not as firmly opposed to British membership since his goals for France were not as exaggerated as those of de Gaulle.

Equally persuasive in shaping the new French attitude was the growing power and independence of West Germany. When de Gaulle and the Francophile Konrad Adenauer were in power, France had little difficulty in dominating the EEC. But after forced wage increases in 1968 and a growing trade deficit, French financial reserves, once a threat to the United States, began to dwindle. De Gaulle tried to get Germany to revalue its currency higher so as to keep France from having to devalue. That he failed, was a severe blow to his prestiege and the first indication that West Germany's politics would no longer be tied to French coat-tails.

When the Social Democrat Willy Brandt came to power, the change became even more apparent. Brandt's *Ostpolitik*, or Eastern policy, pointed to an independence in foreign affairs that could unify Germany and make it an even stronger economic and political entity. In addition, Brandt's attempts to resolve difficulties with the Soviet Union and Eastern Europe stole the thunder from de Gaulle's attempts at detente.

The French reaction to Brandt's designs reflected growing fears with regard to Germany. A final blow to French pride was a German unilateral decision to let the strong German mark float against other currencies in May 1971. One Gaullist deputy was quoted as saying, 'The importance of the power of Germany now makes the French people think that Great Britain will be very, very useful in the Common Market.'

Britain's economic woes made entry into the Common Market seem daily more desirable. The hope was widespread that EEC membership could step up Britain's economic pace and cut its persistent trade deficits. Politically, Prime Minister Edward Heath realized that the EEC concept of confederation would mean no significant sacrifice of Britain's sovereignty. Now Britain's view was that the EEC, stripped of its supranational tendencies, could strengthen Britain's economy and restore a measure of its dwindling stature.

The negotiations for British membership, which began in July 1970, were concluded within one year. The British were now willing to forgo some special privileges; for example, instead of a six-year transition period before its agriculture had to meet all the requirements of membership, Britain now agreed to a three-year transition. It also accepted a diminished world role for sterling in order to insure the equality of all EEC currencies. In 1972 the remaining obstacles to entry were cleared up, and Britain joined two other nations, Ireland and Denmark, in assuming membership in the EEC.

After the acceptance of Britain, Ireland and Denmark in 1972 the economic crisis brought on by the cutbacks in Arab oil production temporarily brought any further integration to a standstill. The 1980 deadline for European union that was agreed to at the Paris Summit Conference of the nine heads of state

John McCormick, *Understanding the European Union, 3rd Edition,* 2005, Palgrave Macmillan, reproduced with permission of Palgrave Macmillan.

in 1972 had become a laughing matter only a year later as each country tried to find its own way out of the economic recession that began in that year. The common energy policy that was proposed at the Copenhagen Summit by the nine heads of state in 1972 had also failed to materialize.

Perhaps most disheartening for those Europeanists who had fought so hard for unification was members' refusal to act like genuine economic partners. During the fuel crisis that was an aftermath of the Arab–Israeli War in 1973, the nine went their separate ways, trying to make unilateral deals for oil and refusing to stand behind the Netherlands, which was denied Arab oil because of its support of Israel. Nor did the EEC countries seek a common solution to the economic recession that began in the late seventies. One European diplomat's remark, 'These countries are so different that it's very hard to put the same saddle on all ten horses', pointed out the great differences between member countries.

Nor did British entry promote European unity; instead, it actually retarded integration. Britain dragged its feet on full economic integration because the newly elected Labour government of 1974 was dissatisfied with the terms of entry into the community and because British leaders feared that the EEC wanted a share of the oil discovered in the North Sea. Although a British referendum favouring participation in the EEC passed by a two-to-one majority in 1975, later opinion polls swung decisively against participation. The British blamed increasing food prices on the high EEC farm subsidies that artificially created high prices. They were also the largest net contributor to the EEC's budget. Perhaps most important, the EEC had not been the economic panacea for Britain's economic woes that many British expected. If Labour had won the British elections in 1979, they would have had popular support for their threat to pull Britain out of the EEC. Greece also proved disruptive when it sought to renegotiate the terms of its entry in 1981.

A special 15 member EEC committee set up to investigate the outlook for economic and monetary union reported in April 1975: 'Europe is no nearer to economic and monetary union today than when it was proposed six years ago, largely because of lack of political will.' The report attributed this to the international monetary crisis that began in the late 1960s, the financial problems caused by the sharp rise in oil prices in 1973, and the tendency of each government to search for its own way out of the crisis. A high-ranking EEC official expressed similar pessimism in 1981 when he remarked, 'People in general just don't believe anymore that the Community can deal with their real problems.'

One factor that preserved economic co-operation among EEC members during this time of troubles was the network of economic ties that had developed over the past two decades and the fact that extensive trade co-operation did indeed exist. Between 1958 and 1968, trade quadrupled among the six original members of the EEC. Even with the European Community's increasing trade with the Third World and developed Asian countries, the Community's trade with other members increased from 51 per cent in 1979 to 60 per cent in 1992. The Italians would be as reluctant to give up the huge tariff-free zone for their refrigerators and wine as the other members would be to lose this advantage for their own national specialties.

Not only had the two oil crises of 1973 and 1979 hindered further co-operation in the seventies, but vague plans for greater political union went far beyond the vision of most EEC members. The EEC had gotten away from the earlier directives of Robert Schuman and Jean Monnet that Europe had to be built on concrete agreements and timetables that were more limited in their goals. The Fouchet Plan of 1961 that envisioned a joint European foreign policy struck too deeply at the sovereignty of members. A plan for Economic and Monetary Unity (EMU) of 1970 also frightened those countries wishing to maintain financial independence. The British could not accept surrendering the pound, nor the French the franc. What the EEC needed was more clearly designed plans for further economic co-operation that would move the countries closer together without compromising their political independence.

The Re-launch of the European Union: From the Single Market to Maastricht and Beyond

This impetus came with the appointment of Jacques Delors as president of the Commission in 1985. Delors had already brought about major economic improvement in the French economy as finance minister by reducing inflation and cutting foreign debt. By presenting the member states with a more limited programme for developing internal trade further, Delors began to move the EEC forward. Delors was aided by a general European feeling that they were falling behind Japan and the United States of America in the important areas of computer technology and the United States of America in space related technology and that greater European co-operation was needed to meet the challenge. Delors had a white paper prepared that listed 300 measures that were necessary to achieve a true customs union such as that in the Untied States of America. He and his vice-president Lord Cockfield set the end of 1992 as a reasonable deadline for implementing these measures. Although the total number of measures declined during discussions, the more precise goal of eliminating barriers to the free movement of goods, services, capital and labour seemed achievable and did not violate member countries sense of sovereignty as much as the political goals had done. Delors' initiative resulted in the passing of the Single European Act (SEA) of 1987 that bound member countries to the goal of a single EEC market by 1 January 1993. Critical to the goal of progress towards further economic union was the permitting of majority voting rather than unanimous voting in the Council of Ministers on issues related to the implementation of the Single Market.

One aspect of the SEA that caused a great deal of footdragging was financial unity and a common European currency under the auspices of EMU. While the creation of a European super economy would undoubtedly require financial unity, member countries such as Britain would not easily discard their own currency. Consequently, the SEA focused on market enhancement measures, putting off until later more grandiose schemes such as a Euro-currency. The move towards a barrier-free internal market was aided by European Court of Justice decisions that struck down national decisions that restricted trade between EEC members. Essentially the court decided that the movement of goods and services could not be blocked except for reasons of health, fiscal supervision, fair trade or consumer protection. Even a German demand to maintain high purity demands for its sausages (wurst) was struck down by the court.

While the SEA provided a further stimulus to economic integration, new initiatives emerged to promote political co-operation, mostly as a result of

German unification. German Chancellor Helmut Kohl's belief that further European political integration was needed in order for Europeans to accept the unification of a larger Germany and French desires for greater political unification to offset this greater Germany, provided the impetus for movement towards monetary union, a common foreign and defence policy and co-operation on home affairs. Deliberations began in late 1990s and reached their fruition in Maastricht, Netherlands in December 1991, when two treaties, on Economic and Monetary Union and on Political Union, popularly known as the Maastricht Treaty, were agreed to. Agreement was concluded only when the United Kingdom was permitted to opt-out on implementing common social policies. A major aspect of Maastricht was to work towards a EU utilizing the existing office of the EC and adding new inter-governmental offices on home affairs and justice and foreign and security policy. A common European citizenship was also established, allowing citizens of one EU country, for example, Spain, who live and work in another EU country, for instance Italy, to vote in Italian local and European Parliament elections. A Common Foreign and Security Policy (CFSP) was set up alongside the EC. In order to get approval for the CFSP, it was set up on a inter-governmental rather than a supranational basis. In effect, national governments would have to agree on common policies. The WEU will serve as the defence arm of the new European Union. How the WEU will relate to existing organizations such as NATO remains to be seen. If the federalists have their way, it will obviously replace NATO in the future as a purely European defence organization.

The real continuity with the Single Market initiative, though, was the Treaty on Economic and Monetary Union (EMU). The now renamed European Union (EU) member states agreed to adopt a single currency and central banking system for Europe and become part of a EMU by the end of the decade. Strict requirements for membership in EMU were set (budget deficits within three per cent of GDP, annual inflation to within one and a half percentage points of the average of the lowest three nations and EMS qualifications). A European Monetary Institute began to monitor European financial affairs in 1994 and the creation of a fully functioning European Central Bank and common currency came into force in 1999.

Maastricht's framers hoped that EC members would ratify the proposals by 1 January 1993. The European Parliament approved in April 1992 but then Denmark rejected the Treaty in June in a popular referendum (50.7 to 49.3). The rejection shocked those in favour of Maastricht to launch a campaign to convince citizens that Maastricht was beneficial. The Irish gave overwhelming support in a popular referendum later in June 1992 despite the fears of many Irish that Maastricht would impose some unpopular social policies on such issues as abortion. A French referendum in September, called by President Mitterrand to divide his internal opposition and provide support for Maastricht, drew strong opposition from nationalists, farmers and political opponents of President Mitterrand and won by only a slim 51 to 49 per cent margin. But with the exception of Denmark and the United Kingdom, the other EC countries ratified Maastricht by the Edinburgh Summit in December 1992

(From John McCormick, Understanding the European Union, 3rd Edition 2005,
Palgrave Macmillan. Reproduced with permission of Palgrave Macmillan)

(although the German legislature approved the treaty, a court challenge held up final ratification until October 1993). In addition to the principle of subsidiarity, Edinburgh also set limits to EC power by permitting countries to opt-out of certain policies – both Denmark and the United Kingdom have not joined the EMU and Denmark not the Western European Union. Edinburgh also raised the number of seats in the European Parliament from 518 to 567 to accommodate the former East Germany. Finally, Denmark, in a second referendum, and the United Kingdom by a vote of Parliament, ratified the Maastricht Treaty, and it formally entered into force on 1 November 1993.

Deepening, Widening or Both?

If the unification of Germany was an added incentive in launching the single currency, then the enlargement of the Union in 1995 to include Austria, Sweden and Finland (bringing the EU up to 15 members), brought institutional reform that much closer. The EU's basic rules governing the inter-institutional relations between Commission, Council and Parliament, were designed for the original six founding members. The increasingly cumbersome decision-making process was bad enough with 12, but now with

15 members, plus the realization that it was probably within ten years or so that eastern European countries would be joining, reform was now a pressing issue. An inter-governmental conference (IGC), begun in 1996, produced a slight reform, signed by the political leaders in June 1997 in Amsterdam. This so-called Amsterdam Treaty expanded the policy areas in which the EP shared co-equal decision-making with the Council, and also expanded the number of policy areas in which Qualified Majority Voting (QMV) could pertain in the Council, that is, a further diminishing of the national veto. Certain Justice and Home Affairs (JHA) policies were moved from Third Pillar decision-making, that is, purely national government's decisions, to the First Pillar, the Community method. These areas included visas, asylum and immigration. Police cooperation and judicial cooperation on criminal matters remained with national governments.

This IGC took place against the backdrop of the wars in the former Yugoslavia, and so it should not be a surprise that the CFSP was looked at again, especially in light of what seemed European powerlessness to many in terms of intervention. Even so, this area of national sovereignty remained a difficult issue for member states to make substantial change. Nevertheless, some modest reform was made, such as a 'constructive abstention' by member states and an 'emergency brake', both regarding decisions by others on joint action taken by QMV. Overall, the verdict by many was that Amsterdam did not substantially reform the EU, but simply made changes at the margins. In the years soon after the ratification of the Amsterdam Treaty, the Balkans were again in turmoil, this time in Bosnia and Kosovo, and again CFSP, as consti- tuted, did not result in critical EU action. Thus, for those waiting to see the EU pursue increased integration, or deepening, much was still to be done to make the EU a foreign policy actor in security affairs.

As the 1990s came to an end, and pre-accession negotiations had begun with many of the states of central and eastern Europe, including Cyprus and Malta, the pressures to resolve decision-making rules in the Council became urgent, as the next enlargement could possibly add up to another ten members. Consequently, an IGC was called for in 2000, and in December of that year, in Nice, France, one of the most acrimonious summits took place. At stake was the weighting of member states votes in the Council of Ministers and the number of Commissioners each member state could have.

The backdrop to Nice is important to bear in mind. First, the usual recalci- trance of the United Kingdom towards further EU institutional power was softened due to the election of the Labour Party in 1997, led by Tony Blair. Seeking to be more constructive in EU matters, although certainly not 'feder- alist' in any sense, the United Kingdom was prepared to compromise on certain matters. Second, the long leadership of Helmut Kohl in Germany had come to an end in 1998, when the SPD leader Gerhard Schroeder became chancellor, supported by a government coalition partner, the Greens (Die Grünen), whose leader Joshka Fischer became foreign minister. Although Germany continued to be supportive of European integration, Schroeder decided the time had come for Germany to be more assertive of its interests in the political realm. In France, Jacques Chirac became president in 1995, so the

Franco–German relationship now had two different individuals at its head. However, the 'chemistry' that contributed to the personal dimension of the relationship, first between Schmidt and Giscard d'Estaing from 1974 to 1981, and with Mitterrand and Kohl from 1983 to 1995, was not repeated between Schröder and Chirac. Finally, a new Commission had taken office following the resignation of the Santer Commission in 1999 and the EP elections later that year. The former Italian prime minister Romano Prodi was named president of the Commission, and he saw as his mission to prepare the EU for the next enlargement, which looked like 2004 or 2005 at the latest. Reforming the weighting of votes in the Council was difficult, as it meant that some of the current member states would see their influence decline as part of the re-weighting, in anticipation of the number of new states. Two specific problems emerged. First, Spain, which had the second highest number of votes in the Council, after the United Kingdom, France, Italy and Germany, would see its influence proportionally diminish. This it opposed. Second, the blocking minority of votes, after a next enlargement in which most of the member states would be relatively small (the exception being Poland), could mean that a minority of countries representing less than a majority of the EU's population could frustrate the others. Thus, national prestige, tactical voting in the future, etc., was at stake at the Nice summit which attempted to break the logjam of the IGC on these issues. The Commission preference was resolved by allowing only one Commissioner per member state, so that France, Germany, Italy and the United Kingdom lost one each. The summit was extended by one day and in the end the Council voting weights were minimally adjusted (with Poland and Spain both just below that of the biggest states) but with the added proviso that the majority also had to represent at least 62 per cent of the EU population, thus slightly favouring the more populous states. Some drama was imparted later when the Irish, in a referendum in June 2001, voted against the new Treaty by 54 per cent. In a second attempt – this time with the full and explicit support of the Irish political and business establishment, the Irish then adopted the Treaty.

The Nice Treaty, as with the Amsterdam Treaty, did not finally settle the outstanding issue regarding a wholesale change in the way the Union operated, in other words the 'deepening' of the EU before 'widening' (enlargement). The Nice summit did, however, commit the Union to another IGC in 2004, and following a summit hosted by the more federalist-minded Belgian government in December 2001 in Laeken, it was decided that 'a deeper and wider debate about the future of the European Union' should precede the 2004 IGC. This debate was organized as the Convention on the Future of Europe. The Convention was launched in Brussels in February 2002 and lasted until July 2003. Its mission was soon understood to be to draft a constitution for the EU. It was chaired by former French President Valery Giscard d'Estaing, and was composed of: one representative of each head of state or Government; two representatives from each national parliament; 16 members of the EP (representing the different parliamentary groups in it); and two Commission representatives. The accession candidate countries were part of the representation also. So, roughly hundred members set about trying to simplify the accumulated Treaties (the so-called *acquis communitaire*) into a manageable document, incorporate a Charter on Fundamental Rights, produce a more precise delimitation of powers between the EU and its member states, and link national parliaments into the EU decision-making process.

The Convention produced a draft Constitution that was delivered to the leaders of the member states, representing the basis on which the IGC debated. This IGC produced a revised text, and was adopted in June 2004. The political leaders did amend certain aspects of the Convention draft, namely weakening some of the supranational aspects in favour of member state prerogatives. Other issues that arose concerned the mention of religion, in particular reference to 'God', in the preamble. Reference to the heritage of European civilization caused a debate between secularists and those who wished to have an explicit reference to Christianity. This debate was waged at the same time as political debate on immigration, and in some countries this meant Muslim immigrants.

In the end, the Constitution was sent out for ratification among the 25 member states beginning in late 2004. Some countries opted for ratification by referendum in addition to a parliamentary vote, about ten of the twenty-five. Matters appeared to be going smoothly, with some of the new member states, such as Estonia, approving the Constitutional Treaty by an overwhelming parliamentary vote. In February 2005, the first country to use a referendum for ratification, Spain, also approved it. Then matters turned for the worse. Britain and France had both voluntarily opted for a referendum in addition to a parliamentary vote and the reason for this had much to do with domestic political factors. Once Blair decided to submit the treaty to a referendum, Chirac soon chose the same route. On 29 May 2005, the French voted *against* the treaty by 55 to 45 per cent, though many commentators were quick to point out that a good portion of the 'no' vote was not anti-European in nature, but rather against what many on the left interpreted as a 'right-wing' treaty. The following week, the Netherlands, in a referendum, also rejected the treaty by an even wider margin, 60 to 40 per cent. It appeared that the Constitutional Treaty was 'dead in the water'. Over a summit – in some cases an emergency summit due to the No votes of France and the Netherlands – in Brussels 16–18 June 2005, the process of ratification was for all intents and purposes put on hold, though individual EU member states could decide to continue with their ratifications, as Luxembourg decided to do. The summit was noteworthy for also not being able to approve the next multi-annual budget for the EU, and the meeting seemed to pit Blair on one side, demanding a complete re-think of the budget, and Chirac on the other, demanding solidarity with the rest of Europe. On 1 July 2005, Britain took over the rotating presidency of the EU, and in the eleventh hour of 18 December 2005, Blair succeeded in producing an EU budget acceptable to all 25 member states, though at the price of reducing the rebate that Thatcher had negotiated in the 1980s.

FURTHER READING

For thorough and insightful and reasonably up-to-date accounts of the launch and subsequent history of the European integration process, see Desmond Dinan, *Europe Recast* (2004); and John Gillingham, *European Integration, 1950–2003: Superstate or New Market Economy?* (2003). Alan Milward's *The European Rescue of the Nation–State* argues that integration itself was the result of a series of specifically situated historical choices made by national political elites to enhance national sovereignty, not to weaken it. See also his *The Reconstruction of Europe, 1945–51* (1984).

Since the renewal of European integration in the mid-to-late 1980s, there has been a corresponding profusion of works analyzing various dimensions of this phenomenon. In particular, students should consult the appropriate texts published by Palgrave in their European Union series. In terms of the operation of the EU, a good and brief introduction is John McCormick, *Understanding the European Union* (3rd ed., 2005). Michelle Cini's edited collection *European Union Politics* covers institutions and policies of the EU. *Development in the European Union 2* (2004), edited by Maria Green Cowles and Desmond Dinan, addresses recent EU policies as well as EU foreign economic and security policies. Regarding the EU's non-security foreign policies, see C. Bretherton and J. Vogler, *The European Union as a Global Actor* (2006). They consider the EU's actions in policy areas such as environment and development cooperation.

The enlargement of the EU to the east in 2004, that is, to the post-communist countries, and the impact of the EU on its member states domestic politics are two important themes to emerge in recent years. On the former, see M. Baun, *A Wider Europe: The Process and Politics of European Union Enlargement* (2000), Fraser Cameron, *The Future of Europe: Integration and Enlargement* (2004); A. Mayhew, *Recreating Europe: The European Union's Policy Towrads Central and Eastern Europe* (1998); and D. Papadimitriou, *Negotiating the New Europe: The European Union and Eastern Europe* (2002).

As for the impact of the EU on its member states, a good introduction to the concept of 'europeanization' and a survey of the 15 member states before the 2004 enlargement is Simon Bulmer and Christian Lequesne, eds., *The Member States of the European Union* (2005). Other works include Wolfgang Wessels, Andreas Maurer and Jurgen Mittag, eds., *Fifteen Into One? The European Union and Its Member States* (2003); Maria Green Cowles, James Caporaso and Thomas Risse, eds., *Transforming Europe: Europeanization and Domestic Change* (2001); and, at a more advanced level, Kevin Featherstone and Claudio Radaelli, eds., *The Politics of Europeanization* (2003).

8 Post-war European Society: A Consumer Society and Welfare State

> What people really pay attention to here is the same as in all the rest of France – TV, auto, and *tierce* [the Sunday triple bet].
>
> Laurence Wylie, quoted in 'The French Are In,' Flora Lewis,
> *The New York Times Magazine*, 28 October, 1973

Jacques Delors, president of the European Commission from 1985 until 1995, often spoke of a 'European model of society'. By this, he meant a model of society in which the state provided a welfare system that was more than simply a safety net, an economy in which the social partners cooperated rather than conflicted, and a principle of economic activity summed up by the term 'social market economy'. The Western Europe reconstructed after WWII and developed since, is not a perfect representation of this model. But in some key areas, Delors' vision is closer to reality than, say, America's, often the model of society that Delors and other Europeans, especially on the left, have warned against (in France this model is often simply referred to as the 'anglo-saxon model'). Western European countries have indeed entered a new socio-economic and political era. The poverty of the immediate post-war period has been replaced in much of Europe by a material well-being that rivals and in some cases surpasses that of the United States. Wylie's observation is relevant for much of Europe, not simply France. Added to this material well-being are welfare systems that provide extensive protection to all citizens. Although there is now movement to cut back extensive welfare systems that have threatened economic efficiency, all political parties support the welfare state. Affluence forced socialist and even the communist parties to drop their revolutionary rhetoric and programmes and support the welfare state. The contemporary struggle defining left and right in this matter is between the two models of society, that is, preserving and modernizing the European model, or allowing globalization to promote the American model. In this chapter, we pay special attention to the characteristics of the society that emerged in the first several decades after the war. Globalization, the enlargement of the EU to eastern and central Europe and other social trends are stimulating a new evolutionary phase in contemporary Europe, and will be explored in Chapter 14.

Europe's Class Structure

Although the old pre-war class divisions have vanished except in some sections of southern Europe, even though many workers are sharing in the new affluence, sizeable income differentials still exist and some workers in countries such as France and England continue to think in terms of 'us' and 'them.' The emergence of the affluent society brought important socio-economic changes but did not bring about the equality that some forecast would provide equal opportunity for all. Now, as before, political power and industrial management rest solidly in the hands of the upper-middle and middle-middle classes that is difficult to enter for those born outside these classes.

An immediately apparent difference between pre-war and post-war Europe is the occupational composition of the population. As Table 8–1 shows, the service class has outpaced the industrial class and left the agrarian sector considerably diminished. By 1972, the proportion of the working population engaged in service had surpassed the proportion employed in industry in France, Great Britain, Belgium, the Netherlands, Switzerland and Scandinavia and in Germany and Italy by 1980. The rapid growth of government bureaucracy and increasing number of service industries in highly industrialized societies led to the proliferation of white-collar employment. Europe has undoubtedly moved in the direction of the United States, where the service class now comprises about 70 per cent of the working population. Such a change in the class structure makes it difficult to accept the revolutionary polarization of society between bourgeoisie and proletariat predicted by Karl Marx unless a large segment of the service class is categorized among the proletariat. A closer examination of the class structure, then, is fundamental to any understanding of the concept of a new European society.

Despite social change and unprecedented affluence, Western Europe can still be analyzed in terms of differences in income, education, housing, and socio-political attitudes. To be sure, these factors have become less clear indicators of social status for several reasons.

For one thing, income, educational possibilities and the distribution of consumer goods have risen at all levels of the population. For another thing, the traditional isolation of social classes in their own neighbourhoods, once a clear indication of class, has now given way in most northern European countries to a widespread mixing of classes in the new suburbs and new towns. While this mixing has led to a reduction in class consciousness, important national differences remain. The final factor is demographic. As the proportion of young people in the population grew rapidly immediately after the war, a youth cult emerged that did not accept traditional class differences. This has tended to break down class attitudes somewhat.

Table 8–1 Percentage of the working population in three economic sectors

	First Sector (Agriculture, Forestry and Fishing)	Second Sector (Industrial)	Third Sector (Services)
France			
1954	28.2	37.1	34.7
1962	20.7	40.1	39.2
1973	12.2	39.3	48.5
1980	8.8	35.9	55.3
1992	5.2	28.9	65.9
2003	3.7	24.0	72.2
West Germany			
1950	24.6	42.9	37.5
1962	13.5	49.0	37.5
1973	7.5	49.5	43.0
1980	6.0	44.8	49.2
1992	3.1	38.3	58.6
Germany			
2003	2.6	33.1	64.3
Italy			
1954	39.9	32.8	27.3
1966	28.0	41.0	31.0
1973	17.4	44.0	38.6
1980	14.2	37.8	48.0
1992	8.2	32.2	59.6
2003	5.3	32.1	62.6

Sources: Figures for 1973, 1980 and 1992 are from the OECD *Observer* 74 (March–April 1975): 21, 115 (March 1982); and 188 (June–July 1994). Figures for 2003 are from the OECD Quarterly Labour Force Statistics, Vol. 2004/4, 73, 79 and 95. All other figures are from M.M. Postan, *An Economic History of Western Europe, 1945–1964* (1967), 191.

Because of the wide socio-economic gulf separating northern and southern Europe, generalizations about one, are true only in part, or not true at all, for the other. Western Europe can be categorized into two separate socio-economic regions: highly developed Scandinavia, the Benelux countries, Great Britain, France, West Germany (before unification), Switzerland, Austria and Italy; and developing Spain, Portugal, Greece and Ireland. There are, of course, great economic-social differences within these countries. Southern Italy in 1978, for example, had a per capita GDP only about half the north (a ratio of 66 to 128 with Italy as a whole at 100 in 1978) and double the unemployment.

One means of estimating Europe's economic resurgence is to compare per capita domestic product with that of the United States. As Table 8–2 shows, per capita domestic product at market exchange rates place six countries

Table 8–2   2005 (estimated) GDP per person in dollars

	At Market Exchange Rates	Purchasing Power Parities
Austria	39,292	32,292
Belgium	37,730	31,549
Denmark	49,182	34,718
France	35,727	29,203
Germany	35,075	30,150
Greece	21,017	21,529
Ireland	50,303	40,003
Italy	31,874	29,414
Luxembourg	77,595	66,821
Netherlands	38,320	30,363
Norway	61,852	41,941
Portugal	18,105	19,949
Spain	27,074	24,803
Sweden	42,392	29,537
Switzerland	52,879	33,168
United Kingdom	38,098	30,309
United States	41,917	41,557

Source: International Monetary Fund, World Economic Outlook Database, April 2005.

above the United States with Luxembourg nearly double that of the United States as a result of its very strong currency and the exclusion of cost of living factors. If, however, cost of living factors are taken into consideration, more realistic Purchasing Power Parities (PPPs) eliminate price differences between countries and produce quite different positions. PPPs, by including the higher GDP of the United States in volume terms and the higher cost of living in many European countries, leave only oil-rich Norway and Luxembourg above the United States. But no matter which measure is used, Table 8–2 shows that three countries – Spain, Greece and Portugal – ranked much below the highly developed Western European countries. Spain is advancing rapidly, however, and should close this gap rapidly as EU development aid continues to spur economic development. Ireland was for a long time included in the lesser-developed Western European countries, and a similar table just a dozen years earlier would certainly have it categorized as such. But its impressive economic growth, coupled with EU development assistance, a phenomenon dubbing it a 'Celtic tiger' in the 1990s, means that it is now in league with other developed countries.

Wages and Fringe Benefits

While the gap between rich and poor has remained wide, as in all industrialized economies, few would dispute that wages have increased more than costs since the Second World War. In most European countries, government and industrial leaders have adopted a new attitude towards labour because of their acceptance of the welfare state. They now promote higher wages for labourers, in line with the conviction that this will increase the demand for consumer goods and avoid industrial conflict. This new attitude is often reflected in the guidelines set by the government to guarantee wage increments. In Sweden, labour leaders, employers and government officials negotiate annual contracts for the work force. This so-called incomes policy assures labour of annual increases to meet rising costs even during periods of limited economic growth.

European wages increased most during periods of rapid economic growth and low inflation. Between 1953 and 1965, real wages rose 36 per cent in the United Kingdom, 58 per cent in France, 80 per cent in Italy, and 100 per cent in Germany. Despite these increases, wages remained comparatively low in France, and took longer in the United Kingdom and Italy to reach and surpass those of the United States. Although Table 8–3 gives the average wage in manufacturing for each country, it does not include expenditures for social services or benefits received by workers, both of which are higher in European countries than in the United States. By the 1980s, in most western European countries, where workers receive high fringe benefits along with high wages, workers' living standards reached or surpassed those of labourers in the United States.

The gap between the upper income groups and manual and service-class workers is narrowed somewhat by state benefits – tax rebates, pensions, family allowances, rent assistance, and so on – that go primarily to low income groups. Although still a major portion of a worker's income, they have diminished since the early seventies. Using data for 1972, the Organization for Economic Co-operation and Development calculated that state benefits increased the disposable income of a worker with two children and a

Table 8–3   Average hourly wages in manufacturing (in current US dollars)

	1960	1971	1974	1980	1988	1992	1997	2002
United States	2.28	3.57	4.40	7.27	10.30	11.50	13.17	15.30
Sweden	1.14	2.88	4.02	7.72	10.00	12.92	14.14	16.51
Belgium	1.00	2.34	N. A.	7.45	8.50	9.90	18.00[a]	
Norway	0.90	2.29	3.50	7.84	13.00	15.60	19.92	—
West Germany	0.82	2.49	3.44	7.25	10.60	12.76	17.21	19.41
Great Britain	0.82	2.14	2.66	5.62	6.89	9.17	14.11	18.50
France	0.51	1.24	1.86	4.37	6.75	7.79	10.86	—
Italy	—	1.10	1.87	5.57	6.60	8.44	14.95[b]	—

Notes: [a] denotes 1999 value.
[b] denotes 1995 value.
Sources: Bulletin of Labor Statistics (Geneva: International Labor Office, 3rd quarter, 1975), 57–62. *Worldwide Economic Indicators: Comparative Summary for 131 Countries* (Business International Corporation, 1982 Annual). *Bulletin of Labor Statistics* (1989–1992), 100–105. 1992 figures calculated from average annual increases reported in basic Statistics: International Comparison in OECD Economic Surveys: Greece 1995.

nonworking wife to 106 per cent of gross pay in France, 102 per cent in Spain, and 96 per cent in Italy. In 1983 Workers in Austria, France and Luxembourg received more than 90 per cent of their gross earnings compared to between 70 and 80 per cent in Finland, Germany, Italy, the Netherlands, Sweden and the United States.

Health care has been one of the prime differences between the European and American Welfare State. Whereas many Americans purchase private health care, millions are at risk because they cannot afford these policies. They are dependent upon state coverage in Medicare (directed at retired people) and Medicaid (directed at the poorest, and varies state by state). The west European welfare state, as a matter of principle, is based on universal coverage, either through state sponsored insurance schemes or an outright government–run medical establishment, for example, the National Health Service in Britain. Public funding is the main source of health funding in all OECD countries, apart from the United States and Mexico. Focusing on trends since 1990, the role of public funding has increased considerably in several lower-income countries in Europe, such as Portugal and declined in some higher-income countries, such as Finland, Italy and Sweden.

By the early 1990s, however, the trend towards more generous benefits overall had stopped. The retrenchment of welfare programmes and spending experienced in the United States during the 1980s under the Reagan and Bush administrations began to characterize even the affluent countries of northern Europe. Still, we are speaking in relative terms, and compared to the United States even pared-back programmes seem luxurious. The long recession in the early 1990s in Western Europe did change some perspectives on the relationship between government support and economic growth. Consequently, budget cutting was accompanied by rhetoric about getting individuals off welfare and back to work. According to a Social Affairs Ministry official in the Netherlands speaking in 1993 – 'Before, the top priority was protection for people. Now the priority is avoiding fraud, getting people back to work as fast as possible, and encouraging citizens to supplement national insurance with private insurance policies' (NYT, 9 Aug 1993).

Status of Women

While women's status has improved since 1945, they are still treated as second-class citizens in many European countries. But compared to the nineteenth century, when women were employed primarily in domestic service, they now make up a large segment of those employed in white-collar occupations and an increasing number of those in blue-collar occupations.

Table 8–4 shows that both the present participation rate of women in the labour force and the female share of the labour force has increased since 1950 except in the less developed countries where it remains low. Women comprised from about 44–48 per cent of the labour force in the developed European states in 2003. This transformation has come despite a traditional

Table 8–4 Labour force participation rates and female share of labour force

	1950		1990		2003	
	Participation Rate	Share of Labour Force	Participation Rate	Share of Labour Force	Participation Rate	Share of Labour Force
Austria	51.0	38.5	55.4	41.0	61.5	44.6
Belgium	32.8	27.9	52.4	41.6	51.4	—
Denmark	49.6	33.6	78.4	46.1	70.5	46.6
France	49.5	35.9	56.6	42.9	56.7	46.3
Germany	44.3	35.1	56.6	40.7	58.7	44.8
Greece	41.4	32.1	43.0	37.1	44.0	—
Ireland	36.9	25.5	38.9	31.6	55.4	41.8
Italy	32.0	25.4	44.5	36.8	42.7	39.1
Netherlands	28.5	23.4	53.0	39.2	64.9	—
Portugal	26.3	22.4	61.3	42.9	60.6	45.9
Spain	17.6	15.4	40.9	34.8	46.8	40.5
Sweden	35.1	26.3	81.1	48.0	72.8	48.0
United Kingdom	40.7	30.7	65.1	42.8	66.4	44.6

Sources: Figures for 1950 are from the OECD *Observer* 104 (May 1980). Figures for 1990 are from the OECD *Observer* 176, supplement (June–July 1992), and the OECD *Economic Outlook Historical Statistics, 1960–1990.* Figures for 2003 are from the OECD Factbook, 2005.

attitude that a woman's proper place was in the home. John Ardagh's findings in 1987 that 'to have a wife who does not work is often a status symbol' among the poorer classes seems to be an attitude that has nearly vanished in the highly developed European countries. Esping-Andersen found, in *Changing Classes: Stratification and Mobility in Post-Industrial Societies*, that for unskilled women by the 1980s there was a 'closed mobility circuit between unskilled services, (low-end) sales and (low-end) clerical work.'

Women's unemployment rates are invariably higher than those of men since they lack job seniority and are more involved in part-time work. When economic difficulties occur, women are the first to lose their jobs.

Women's wages have continued to be lower than men's because of discrimination, the segregation of women into 'women's jobs' and differences in qualifications and work experience. The income gap is most apparent among white-collar employees. The German Institute for Economic Research reported in September 1994 that women's pay had suffered a relative decline from 1980 to 1993: the average gross monthly income for men was $580 higher in 1980 than the pay for women in similar jobs and $1,480 more than women in 1993. This reflects the fact that few women reach the top management positions. In the United Kingdom, there remains something of a 'glass ceiling' for women in access to the very top positions in British society, only one per cent of women account for top company chief executive officers and 17 per cent of company directors.

In many cases family responsibilities have prevented women from obtaining the proper training and have removed them from the job market during maternity leaves. But, as shown in Table 8–5, gender differences in pay within the EU had narrowed substantially since 1970. As late as 1974, the EU rebuked Britain, Ireland and Denmark for their unequal treatment of women. The other EU states had established equal-pay-for-equal-work guidelines, although in practice the gaps have not been closed. By 2002, women's earnings narrowed the gap further: in Belgium, Denmark, France, Norway, Italy, Greece, Luxembourg and Sweden women's wages reached over 80 per cent of those of men, but those in Germany, the United Kingdom, the Netherlands, the United States and Ireland had reached at least 70 per cent

Table 8–5 Women's earnings as a percentage of men's average hourly earnings

	1970	1975	1986	2002
Belgium	66.7	69.7 (1979)	73	84.0
Denmark	72.4	83.2	82.2	80.2
West Germany	69.2	—	73	77.5
France	78.8 (1973)	79.2 (1979)	82.2	82.4
Greece	—	—	67.2	80.1
Ireland	56.2	60.9	67.6 (1981)	—
Italy	74.2	78.7	83.2 (1980)	—
Luxembourg	57	63.3	64.7 (1980)	80.0
Netherlands	73.3	79.5	77.9 (1980)	75.5
Norway	75.1	78	81.9 (1980)	—
Sweden	—	—	91 (1985)	86.9
United Kingdom	—	72.1	74 (1985)	69.9
United States	—	58.9 (1977)	64.3	—

Sources: 'Closing the Wage Gap: An International Perspective,' National Committee on Pay Equity, Washington, DC, October 1988. Figures for 2002 taken from Eurostat publications 'Average gross annual earnings for women in industry and services' and 'Average gross annual earnings for men in industry and services'.

of men's wages. As women's work becomes more like that of men – more full time and skilled work – the gap will tend to narrow as it has through the 1990s.

The status of women in government and elected office is another area that has witnessed change, albeit slow and geographically diverse. As Table 8–6 shows, there is a clear difference in western European parliaments concerning seats held by women. Scandinavian countries all have sizable percentages of seats held by women, ranging from 30 to 45 per cent. By contrast, France, Italy, Greece, Ireland, Portugal and the United Kingdom are all under 20 per cent. The picture is somewhat different when we look at regional or sub-national elected bodies. In the United Kingdom, the Scottish Parliament in 2005 contained 37 per cent women, and the Welsh Assembly could boast 50 per cent. When we look at non-elected government positions, that is, in government administration, the picture is also mixed. In France, a country with a low number of women in the National Assembly, the OECD reports that in 1998, women made up 53.5 per cent of senior managers in central government, up 10 per cent since 1990. In Greece, for the same position, women made up 30.1 per cent, also up since 1990 by 20 per cent. Yet in other countries, Ireland for example, women only made up 12 per cent of central government senior managers in 2000.

Another important reason for women's limited role among the elite has been their under-representation in graduate and professional schools. While the proportion of women attending universities rose by the mid-1980s (about half of the total students in Denmark and France and between 40 and 50 per cent elsewhere), their under-representation in professional schools and in mathematics and the physical sciences throughout their schooling leaves them at a disadvantage. A recent OECD report shows that four successful candidates out of every five for the French humanities baccalaureat in 1983 were women, compared to only one of three for the mathematics and natural sciences

Table 8–6   Percentage of legislative seats held by women, 2005

Scandinavia		Rest of Europe	
Denmark	36.9	Austria	33.9
Finland	37.5	Belgium	34.7
Iceland	30.2	France	12.2
Norway	38.2	Germany	32.8
Sweden	45.3	Greece	14.0
		Ireland	13.3
		Italy	11.5
		Netherlands	36.7
		Portugal	19.5
		Spain	36.0
		United Kingdom	18.1

Source: Inter-Parliamentary Union website, (http://www.ipu.org/ english/ home.htm), 'Women in Parliaments'.

baccalaureat. These patterns then, naturally continue into higher education. While a university degree alone would have provided a graduate with an excellent opportunity for a good position previously, the type of degree and school that issued it now conditions one's job possibilities. For example, the proportion of women studying at the French advanced professional schools has increased but still comprises only 15 per cent of the students at the School of Administration (ENA) and 10 per cent at the *Ecole Polytechnique*. These percentages would, however, be large in comparison to women's participation in advanced professional education in southern Europe.

Status of Immigrant Labourers

Only partially profiting from the new affluence are the thousands of immigrant labourers who flocked to Northern Europe's factories in the 1960s (see Chapter 3 for details). When the employment of foreign workers reached its peak of about ten million in Western Europe, before the recession following the 1973 Arab oil embargo led to mass firings, over one-third of the Swiss labour force consisted of foreign workers. Filling initially the least desirable jobs in municipalities and on assembly lines, they constituted an underpaid, neglected segment of the working class; they swept streets, collected garbage, cleaned rest rooms and did unskilled work in factories. But they gradually came to fill many of the semi-skilled jobs in manufacturing; about 80 per cent of the assembly line tasks at the Renault factory near Paris, were performed by foreign labourers in the seventies.

When their labour was essential during the economic boom years and their numbers were relatively small, they were accepted by Europeans with only the occasional protests. But the economic slow down that began in the seventies combined with the sizeable numbers of immigrant workers, led to the resentment of the foreign workers. The growing unemployment and the willingness of foreign workers to accept lower wages than northern European workers led to popular agitation to limit their numbers. To prevent a further influx of Italian workers in the 1970s, some Swiss resorted to fear tactics and hate slogans: 'Would you like to share a hospital room with a Sicilian?' Governments began to reduce the number of foreign workers in the seventies by offering them departure payments and reducing the inflow of immigrants. But the number of foreigners continued to increase since many families stayed on, some even starting small businesses, and their families increased in size. While West Germany decreased the number of foreign workers from 2.6 to 1.9 million between 1973 and 1983, the total number of foreigners rose from below 4 million to 4.4 million in 1986 or 7.4 per cent of its population (by 2002, unified Germany had 8.9 per cent of its population foreign-born). OECD figures show that immigrants and their families comprised 5.6, 8.2, 38.1 and 19.9 per cent of the French, Belgian, Luxembourg and Swiss populations respectively by 2002. Many nursery and elementary schools are now filled with immigrant's children because of their large families and the exceedingly low northern European birth rates.

Some rightist political groups have sprung up with the reduction of immigrants a major aspect of their appeal. Much of Jean-Marie Le Pen's and his National Front's appeal in France, 'Send them back home', has come at the expense of the foreign workers, who are blamed for taking jobs from 'true' Frenchmen at a time of high unemployment. The unexpected success of Norway's rightist Progress Party in the 1989 elections can be mainly attributed to the resentment of foreign workers.

In order to save money to buy a car, support their families, and set themselves up when they return home, many of the immigrants were willing to live in slums. In France shanty towns, called *Bidonvilles*, sprang up on the outskirts of the major cities in the sixties to house most of the foreign workers. Many moved into more permanent residences after bringing their families to their place of work. But this often created ghettos since the previous residents moved out and left only the immigrants. While many of the Italian and Greek workers have obtained acceptance in northern Europe, the Turks, who remain rather exclusive and the Arabs have not gained acceptance. Recently Arab immigrants have suffered most severely due to the fear of terrorism and the dislike of Muslim fundamentalism. For the most part, northern European workers show little concern for this 'subproletariat'. A semiskilled worker in West Germany rationalized his renting a small house to several families of these foreign workers with the excuse that they were accustomed to such overcrowding in their home countries.

Governments, on the other hand, have instituted many programmes to speed the integration of foreign workers who wish to stay in northern Europe. They have allocated funds for language instruction, for improved housing, and for cultural adaptation. Germany abolished rules that had set quotas on foreign habitation of urban areas and reduced the time needed for a foreigner to gain permanent residence from ten to eight years. Sweden has given foreigners the right to vote and stand for election at the local and regional level in 1978.

But the immigrant issue took a new turn in the post-Cold War period. With German unification, Turkish immigrants now found themselves the scapegoat of former East German citizens, themselves experiencing unemployment for the first time in their lives. Germany also became a destination of choice for Romanians, Poles, Croats and others seeking a better life from the crumbling economies of the former Communist East European regimes. Many of these people declared that they were fleeing political persecution, and therefore asked for asylum. In 1989 the number seeking asylum in Germany was 121,318, in 1991 the figure rose to 256,112 and then to 438,191 in 1992. This led in 1992 to a new German law restricting the granting of asylum, which became effective on 1 July 1993. Under the new conditions, foreigners who enter Germany from a safe third country may no longer invoke this basic right, except for those with German heritage from east European countries, for example, Ukraine.

The immigrant issue also became entangled in the process of European integration (see Chapter 7). The so-called Schengen Agreement of 1990 among nine of the twelve EU countries was to have enabled the free movement of their nationals by discontinuing border controls. The implementation of the Agreement, however, was stalled for many years due to fear on the part of some countries that it would facilitate the entry of illegal immigrants and illegal drugs into their country. A December 1994 summit meeting fixed 26 March 1995 as the date for the belated accord to come into force.

The affluence experienced by the majority of Europe's inhabitants has benefited little a primarily migrant urban underclass in even the most wealthy north European countries. Technological advances, economic downturns since the seventies, and the migrants lack of skills and education have produced large differences in unemployment rates: in Holland 35 per cent of Turks and 42 per cent of Moroccans compared to seven per cent of ethnic Dutch were unemployed in early 1994. (Economist, 30 July–5 Aug 1994) This underclass is similar to America's in that, crime, drug abuse and single parent families increasingly define it. But Europe's underclass is better off than America's because of Europe's more generous social and health benefits and the fact that there is less urban decay. This European underclass has little possibility of finding employment since there are few part-time or low-paying full-time jobs in Europe of the type that have cut the unemployment rate in the United States. Of course, such jobs do not permit the American poor to live at an acceptable level.

The Standard of Living

Throughout most of the post-war period, Europe trailed the United States in the level of consumer goods used. The more industrialized European states now enjoy affluence equal to that of the United States. As smaller per centages of their wages have been used up on clothing, food and rent, workers have had considerably more money to spend on the kind of consumer goods known as durables because they are longer lasting. During the 1990s, ownership of telephones, refrigerators, television sets and cars began to reach levels near that of the United States in the more developed countries as Table 8–7 demonstrates. Not that the different nations had the same priorities for consumer goods. As a case in point, the Scandinavian countries, with a standard of living near that of West Germany, had about one-third more telephones per capita. The ownership of passenger cars is perhaps more reliable, although not conclusive, as an indicator of standard of living (of course, more extensive public transport, especially, trains, mean that many Europeans are less reliant on cars than Americans). Yet by the beginning of the twenty-first century, car ownership in Italy, France, Germany and Switzerland had outstripped the United States (with Sweden not very far behind).

Before the Second World War, workers tended to spend about half their income on food. By the mid-1980s, food and clothing expenditures in the developed European countries reached only between 20 to 24 per cent of total household consumption according to the World Bank. As Table 8–8 shows, the amount of work time needed to purchase food and clothing had declined markedly since 1950 in Germany.

Table 8–7 Ownership of consumer durables (number per 1,000 inhabitants)

	Telephones			Passenger Cars			Television Sets		
	1969	1985	2003ᵃ	1969	1990	2002	1969	1990	2003
United States	567	800	1164	427	573	481	399	815	938
Sweden	515	890	1716	275	426	452	300	474	965
United Kingdom	253	521	1432	205	341	384	284	435	950
Switzerland	457	832	1587	206	449	507	184	407	552
West Germany	212	621	1442	208	386	516	262	570	675
France	161	608	1262	238	405	491	201	406	632
Italy	160	448	1502	170	476	542	170	424	—

Note: ᵃFigure includes mainline and mobile telephones.
Source: OECD *Economic Surveys* (1976, 1981–2); OECD *Observer* 74 (March–April): 75; OECD *Observer* 56 (February 1972); OECD *Observer* 115 (March 1982); Eurostat, Basic Statistics of the European Community (1988); *The Economist*, 'Economic Indicators' (December 25, 1993-January 7, 1994), 39 and the World Development Indicators handbook 2005, published by the World Bank.

Table 8–8 Work time needed to buy commodities in Germany

	1950	1960	1992	2002
Milk (1l)	14 min.	8 min.	3 min.	2 min.
Butter (1 kg)	4 hrs., 24 min.	2 hrs., 40 min.	20 min.	12 min.
Pork (1 kg)	2 hrs., 50 min.	2 hrs., 8 min.	31 min.	21 min.
Man's shoe	19 hrs., 36 min.	12 hrs., 29 min.	6 hrs., 14 min.	4 hrs., 27 min.
Rye bread	17 min.	15 min.	9 min.	7 min.

Source: Facts About Germany (Frankfurt/Main, Germany: Societäts-Verlag, 1993), 241. 2002 figures taken from 'The Purchasing Power of Working Time: An International Comparison', published by the International Metalworkers' Federation (http://www.imfmetal.org/main/files/PP2004-English.pdf).

Nevertheless, it is important to remember that countries differ markedly in enjoying this new affluence. While unskilled workers and low-paid white-collar workers in northern Europe can now afford to spend more of their income on consumer goods, those in Greece and Portugal still spend a large portion of their incomes on food and drink. Food and clothing consumed 38 per cent of total Greek consumption and 44 per cent of Portuguese consumption between 1980 and 1985 according to the World Bank. Many workers in these countries migrated to the richer northern countries. With increasing subsidies by the European Union and its single internal market that began after 1992, these inequities diminished over the decade.

Both the improvement in the standard of living and the wide gap between Northern and Southern Europe are revealed in the rise in per capita private consumption since 1955. Table 8–9 shows the countries' rankings according to private consumption in 1973, 1980, 1990 and 2002; the figures agree

Table 8–9   Per-capita private expenditure (in current US dollars)

	1973	1980	1990	2003
Denmark	3,050	7,270	13,112	18,469
Switzerland	3,640	10,128	18,881	22,328
Sweden	3,240	7,630	13,798	16,415
France	2,913	7,690	12,732	16,093
Belgium	2,810	7,540	11,946	15,957
West Germany	3,000	7,340	12,717	17,076
Netherlands	2,430	7,200	10,987	12,715
United Kingdom	1,960	5,581	10,749	19,729
Norway	2,530	6,600	12,583	22,199
Austria	1,870	5,650	11,303	17,613
Italy	1,620	4,270	11,701	15,272
Ireland	1,370	3,310	6,719	13,656
United States	3,840	7,370	14,465	24,959

Sources: OECD *Economic Survey: Germany* (Paris, 1975), International Comparisons; OECD *Economic Surveys, 1981–1982: Germany Statistical Annex* (June 1982); OECD *Economic Outlook: Historical Statistics, 1960–1990*; and World Development Indicators handbook 2005, published by the World Bank.

fairly closely with previous figures on income and the ownership of consumer goods. However, if the higher prices in the top-ranked countries are taken into consideration (PPP's), the differences between consumers in the countries at the top and the bottom of the ranking are reduced somewhat. Table 8–10 measures disparities in private consumption per capita in PPP's. Some of the disparity between the United States and Europe results from the higher saving rate in Europe compared to the United States.

The Work Week and Vacation

For most workers reduced working hours and paid holidays and vacations have relieved the boredom of the factory. The working week has declined from 48 hours in the pre-war period to less than 40 hours throughout Europe. The Bulletin of Labour Statistics of the International Labour Office (ILO) reports that the hours of actual work per week for wage earners in manufacturing declined to 40 or below by the 1990s. In the following countries, the ILO reports that in 2003, the hours worked were: Norway (36), Belgium (32.9, 1994), Austria (36.9), Spain (36), France (35), Italy (39.2) and Germany (40; this includes former east Germany).

Even more responsible for reduced work time has been the extension of paid vacations to four and often five weeks a year (Table 8–11). Since vacations are seldom based upon seniority, labourers can expect these long vacations during their first years of work. French workers get two days vacation

Table 8–10   Private consumption per capita using current PPPs

	1990	1992	2003		1990	1992	2003
United States	14,465	15,637	24,959	Germany	9,883	11,186	14,002
Switzerland	11,982	13,043	14,513	Sweden	8,733	8,907	12,147
Norway	8,028	9,189	14,651	Denmark	8,628	9,120	12,005
France	10,516	11,144	13,196	Spain	7,360	8,083	12,162
United Kingdom	9,948	10,397	16,770	Ireland	5,904	7,443	9,559
Belgium	10,153	11,420	13,563	Greece	5,317	5,929	11,172
Italy	9,907	10,936	13,439	Portugal	5,294	6,124	7,943
Netherlands	9,276	10,213	10,680				

Sources: OECD *Economic Surveys: Switzerland, 1988/1989* (Paris, 1989), Basic Statistics: International Comparisons, OECD *Economic Outlook: Historical Statistics, 1960–1990*, and World Development Indicators handbook 2005, published by the World Bank.

Table 8–11   Minimum paid vacation mandates for full time workers who have worked for one year (2003)

France	35
Sweden	35
Spain	30
Germany	28
Ireland	28
United Kingdom	28
Netherlands	28
Belgium	20
United States	12
Japan	10

Source: Keller, William L., Timothy J. Darby, and American Bar Association. *International Labor Law Committee. International Labor and Employment Laws.* 2 vols. Washington, D.C.: Bureau of National Affairs, 1997, 2002 Supplements.

for every month on the job or about five weeks vacation a year. In Germany, where two-thirds of the workforce gets about six weeks of paid leave annually, workers prize leisure time as much as advancement. In a recent opinion poll, family, time off, and friends ranked ahead of their job. In the United States, where vacation time depends on the time of service with a company, most workers receive only two weeks paid vacation a year. European governments and businesses also provide extra vacation bonuses and low-cost holiday excursions for workers. Austrian workers receive two extra months pay as bonuses each year. France's state-owned Renault automobile firm provides support for 30 vacation villages. Most companies throughout Europe now provide additional vacation bonuses for their workers.

Because of higher incomes and paid vacations, entire countries come almost to a standstill at certain times of the year. In one of the richest countries in Europe, Sweden, three out of four residents take a vacation outside their place of residence each year. In August the only people left in Paris are the poorer workers, tourists and those few unfortunates who are left behind to serve the tourists. Vienna has now worked out a staggered vacation plan so that the tourist trade will not be adversely affected by the massive departure of the populace, and the windows of closed restaurants display signs directing tourists to nearby restaurants that have remained open.

By the early years of the twenty-first century, with the introduction of low-cost, no-frills airlines, many Europeans were leaving on vacation – many of them so-called package holidays – to a variety of southern European and Mediterranean resorts. Parts of mainland Spain, along the Costa del Sol, have become enclaves of British holidaymakers, some of who now buy property along the coast. Spanish islands such as Ibiza, in particular, attract younger people from all across Europe.

The Voices of Labour

Affluence, full employment, and diminished economic crisis in the most developed European countries have changed the goals of labour unions and labour parties from revolutionary to reformist. Some union activists still pay lip service to Marxism, but unions and labour-oriented parties now concentrate their demands on higher wages, full employment, fringe benefits and price stability. French and Italian unions have changed their goals as reform-oriented German and Scandinavian unions have succeeded in improving the position of the workers in their societies.

Swedish, German and Austrian labour unions work closely with business leaders and government officials in negotiating working conditions, wages and fringe benefits. In the 1980s, Swedish unions, together with the Social Democratic party, did propose a plan by which worker ownership of industries would have radically changed the nature of industrial relations in Sweden. This so-called Meidner plan was never implemented, and although by the late 1990s relations between the union federation, the LO, were not as close as during most of the post-war years, Sweden remains a country with relatively low levels of industrial strife. German and Austrian industrial relations remained committed to consensual bargaining.

German labour leaders sit on the Boards of Directors of the top German industrial enterprises. The Confederation of German Trade Unions (DGB), which speaks for about 32 per cent of German workers in 1994, operates schools, banks, and insurance companies. The head of the DGB maintains, 'You can't stop progress – our job is to see that workers get the benefit of it.' Since the DGB is not affiliated with any political party, it is a strong, independent political force. German labour leaders stoutly defend their gradualism against more militant French and Italian unionists by pointing to the much larger number of workers organized in Germany, the much lower wages of workers in France and Italy, and the near absence of industrial conflict.

German labour leaders believe profits must be high so that they can negotiate for higher wages. They also do not try to keep workers on the job in obsolete industries. Workers who become unemployed because their jobs are mechanized or because their industries are in a decline are immediately retrained at union and/or company expense. More recently, in the present era of globalized competition, it is the fact that jobs are going overseas – what the French call delocalisations – that spurs militant union action.

Labour unions that cling to revolutionary goals have lost their effectiveness. In France, where unionism is divided among the Communist *Confederation Generale du Travail* (CGT), the Socialist-leaning *Confederation Francais Democratique du Travail* (CFDT) and a moderate *Force Ouvriere*, only about ten per cent of the workers are organized. Moreover, the CGT continues to lose members while the more moderate Force Ouvriere has gained members. Despite considerable theoretical militancy, in practice, French labour unions have been much less militant than their rhetoric would indicate. In fact, the CGT actually restrained workers during the 1968 national strikes.

The general picture of industrial action, as measured by indicators such as working days lost through industrial action per 1000 employees, shows that since the late 1990s, a period of relative industrial peace has occurred in many European countries (see Table 8–12). According to the European Industrial Relations Observatory (EIRO), in the first half of the 1980s, countries such as Greece, Ireland, Italy, Spain and the United Kingdom averaged over 400 days lost per 1000 workers annually (data from Eurostat). At the same time, countries such as Denmark, France, Luxembourg and Portugal averaged over 100. By the late 1990s and early 2000s, the average for the EU and Norway was 67.1. Within this figure, we still see variation – and of course a particular event or episode will affect a country's average. There are three groups of countries: those with low levels of industrial action, averaging under 20 working days lost for every 1000 employees – Austria, Germany, the Netherlands, Poland, Portugal, Slovakia, Sweden and the United Kingdom; those countries with moderate levels, averaging 20 to 70 working days lost per year for every 1000 workers – Belgium, Finland, France, Greece, Hungary, Italy and Luxembourg; and those countries with relatively high levels, averaging over 70 days lost per year for every 1000 workers – Denmark, Ireland, Norway and Spain. The three main reasons accounting for industrial action are pay, employment – which includes issues such as dismissals, redundancies and job losses and issues arising out of the bargaining process.

Although the more militant unions have lost support during the last three decades, union membership in general declined further as the various interests in society became fully integrated in the new Europe. According to the OECD, most European OECD countries experienced a decline in the number of union members making up the workforce from 1980 to 2002 (see Table 8–13). In addition, defensiveness on the part of trade unions has developed due to

Table 8–12 Working days lost to strikes and lockouts

	1996	2003
France	1439	2131 (2001)
Denmark	930	681
Italy	904	710
Spain	830	678
Australia	543	643
Canada	330	266
Portugal	265 (1997)	17
United Kingdom	244	133
Japan	193	47
Greece	171	–
Finland	94	112
New Zealand	72	28
Belgium	60	75 (2000)
Turkey	38	22
United States	37	14
Ireland	32	24
Norway	18	5
Netherlands	12	16 (2001)
Sweden	9	11
Switzerland	3	8
Austria	0	4 (2000)

Source: International Labour Organisation statistics.

three general trends. The first has been the impact of technological innovation on production. Higher rates of productivity were achieved in the early 1990s with fewer workers. Upturns in economic performance have not been matched with a lessening of unemployment, in particular that of the young. Second, there have been the effects of the EU Single Market, allowing more freedom for companies to move plants to lower labour-cost countries. This fact was brought home in a much publicized manner in France when in 1993 the American company, Hoover, closed a plant near Dijon in order to relocate the positions to its facility in Scotland, taking advantage of lower wages and flexible work rules. The particularly striking aspect of this move was that neither country's union knew that Hoover was playing each union off against each other in order to receive the best deal. Finally, in those

Table 8–13   Trade union membership as a
percentage of wage earners

	1980	1990	2000
France	18%	10%	9%
Spain	25	11	18.6 (1995)
United States	24	16	13
Netherlands	35	26	25
Germany	36	34	26
Italy	50	39	35
Great Britain	51	39	29
Austria	56	48	37
Ireland	58	50	45
Belgium	56	52	53
Norway	58	57	57
Denmark	78	74	76
Sweden	80	83	82

Source: The Economist, 'Economic Indicators' (23 July, 1994),
102, reporting OECD approximate figures, and the International
Labour Organisation's World Employment Report 1997/8.

countries that have a large nationalized industrial sector, growing government privatizations has ended some of the entrenched organized relations between unions and employers. Private owners are much more ready to cut losses by closing down unprofitable enterprises than governments. Consequently, unions now face a much different type of bargaining environment than they have since the early 1980s. This has become especially true in Britain, France, Spain and Italy.

Finally, if we turn to working conditions, the fact that western Europe is characterized by stronger unions than the United States does not exempt workers from experiencing some of the same trends in affecting the workplace. In 1996, the European Foundation for the Improvement of Living and Working Conditions interviewed a representative sample of 1000 workers in each of the EU's (then) 15 member states (15,800 persons in total). The survey revealed that the pace of work is increasing all the time; between 1991 and 1996 the per cent of workers exposed to high-speed work increased from 48 to 54 per cent. Workers are expected to learn new skills in order to adapt to changing technologies. Seventy-four per cent in the survey said their work involves acquiring new skills. Computers feature strongly as well: 39 per cent of all workers and 41 per cent of all employees now use them. Although it was pointed out above that many workers are consulted about work matters, there are still wide disparities between countries. The survey reported that in Finland and the Netherlands, 68 per cent of employees are consulted on organizational changes, whereas in Greece, Spain and Portugal, the percentage respectively is 38, 34 and 31.

Social Levelling

Much has been written on the blurring of class lines brought about by the improved standard of living of the working class and the growth of the service class. It is said that European society is undergoing an *embourgeoisement* – the word used for the drift of the working class into the middle class – and that classes as we know them now will cease to exist.

Service-class workers are salaried (a traditional status symbol) and usually have more education than blue-collar workers, but they often live in the same neighbourhoods and acquire the same status symbols that have traditionally divided the middle and working classes.

Because of the continuing expansion of the service class and the declining proportion of manual labourers in the working populations, blue-collar workers and their offspring are moving into white-collar work. Approximately one-third of the offspring of industrial workers in Western Europe in the 1970s rose into non-manual categories, predominantly the service and professional classes. At the same time a smaller but not insignificant group of white-collar workers moved down into working-class occupations. The results of surveys taken between 1976 and 1979 in Scandinavia (Table 8–14) showed that the children of manual labourers had the best chance in Sweden to move to a salaried white-collar position: 34 per cent compared to Denmark's 23 per cent and Finland's 18 per cent. But it also indicated that it was difficult in the seventies for the offspring of a manual labourer to move to a senior salaried position even in socially advanced countries such as Sweden (6 per cent), Denmark (5 per cent) and Finland (4 per cent). Table 9–13 also shows that the children of salaried employees occupy a high percentage of the salaried and senior salaried positions. But the continued growth of the service class (shown in table 9–1) and the relative decline of manual labourers in the total work force resulted in a rise in the number of workers who moved into the service class.

A study of Swedish employees work-life mobility between 1979 and 1989 by Michael Tåhlin determined that despite the egalitarianism existing in Swedish society, stratification 'remains heavily class-structured despite the rise of the service industries, the public sector and new "post-industrial occupations." ' He found that social class, sex and age were the main determinants of wage inequality and the quality of work. Educational attainment still tends to inhibit movement from manual to service class occupations and from lower-level service to managerial positions among service class employees.

New housing and intermarriage have also brought the service and working classes closer together. Living in the same areas, and no longer divided by dress as they were in the nineteenth century, youth ignore social class differences. Many new towns and suburbs are not socially segregated, as the major cities still tend to be. This is especially true in the more developed countries. In the new model housing areas in Sweden, middle-and lower-class families are deliberately mixed, by providing the poor with rent

Table 8–14 Social mobility of the population 35–64 years by father's socio-economic group

Own Socio-economic Group	Workers			Salaried Employees			Farmers			Entrepreneurs		
	De	Fi	Sw	De	Fi	Sw	De	Fi	Sw	De	Fi	Sw
Workers	38	41	35	19	20	15	32	26	29	24	24	21
Salaried employees	23	18	34	50	53	58	18	16	27	37	31	29
Senior salaried employees	5	4	6	24	34	21	5	5	5	15	20	11
Farmers	2	5	1	1	2	1	18	23	14	1	3	2
Entrepreneurs	8	4	7	7	2	9	7	6	8	14	10	10
Other	29	32	22	24	23	17	26	29	23	24	36	19
Number (thousands)	617	535	1269	238	195	446	469	718	636	233	140	402

Source: Nordic Council / Nordic Statistical Secretariat, 'Level of Living and Inequality in the Nordic Countries' (Stockholm, 1984), 197.
Note: De = Denmark, Fi = Finland, Sw = Sweden.

supports. The pervasiveness of modern advertising and cheaper mass-produced goods have also reduced the differences between working-class and middle-class homes and furnishings. And the behavioral pattern of manual workers in their new surroundings has changed as well. They tend to spend less time in pubs and more time at home watching television. The fact that working-class children in socially integrated neighbourhoods attend the same schools as middle-class children has a further levelling effect.

Despite this social levelling, class distinctions remain very much a part of European society, especially in Great Britain, France and southern Europe. There has been little mingling of working class and middle class in the South. Even within social classes in Europe, divisions continue to exist. Divisions between skilled and unskilled labourers are often greater than those between the working and the middle class. This is even more true in Europe today since most of the unskilled workers are immigrants.

This is similar to the split found between the upper levels of the service class (administrators) and lower-level clerks. Most of the service-class workers consider themselves members of the middle class and pursue practices common to the middle class. In a recent French random survey, 51 per cent of the respondents rated a lower-paid clerical worker higher than a foundry worker. Based upon income, lower-paid clerical workers do comprise a 'white-collar proletariat' according to Rosemary Crompton and Gareth Jones, but their own perceptions of their status, their extended paid vacations and the wide social net common to all developed European countries

Affordable apartments in new Europe during the postwar economic resurgence.
(© Keystone/Getty Images (UK) Ltd)

separates them from the misery associated with a true proletariat. Also about half of the low-paid women clerical workers are married and with their spouse's income enjoy a middle-class standard of living.

In 1969 Cambridge University sponsored a sociological study of 70 British working-class families. The report, entitled *The Affluent Worker in the Class Structure*, revealed 'no more than one or two of the seventy couples in question here could be realistically represented as being even on the road to a middle-class pattern of social life.' This study, drawn from a relatively affluent working-class area, concluded that the *embourgeoisement* thesis had limited validity in Great Britain in the sixties. The researchers found that only seven couples followed middle-class life-styles and had middle-class friends from other than family or work associations. The same author's study of British social mobility in the eighties contends that 'the class position of individuals in the present-day population and their class origins remains essentially the same in its extent and pattern as that which existed in the inter-war period' (Goldthorpe). Again, in 1999, Heath and Payne of Oxford University reported in *Twentieth Century Trend in Social Mobility in Britain* that only around 10 per cent of boys from working-class backgrounds ended up in the service class, with a similar proportion of sons of service-class fathers ending up in the working class. So, although the relative size of the service class and laboring class has changed, the distance between them changed little. A large comparative study published in 1992 also including the United States and Japan, *The Constant Flux* by Erikson and Goldthorpe, found that such mobility patters are common to most Western industrial societies. Their book shows how, despite substantial changes in the class structure of major European nations, the United States, Australia and Japan, the *relative* chance of social mobility remains remarkably constant.

A Ruling Elite?

No single term can fully describe the ruling elites in Europe and the United States. Some observers still subscribe to the idea of a ruling class. Others have adopted one or another of the more sophisticated concepts: an establishment, a military-industrial complex, a power elite, or a cadre. No matter which concept is used, all believe that European societies are ruled by a relatively small elite, that preserves its position through various combinations of wealth, family eminence and educational advantages. But most believe that this elite has been transformed, that it has replaced the traditional nineteenth century elites that had retained power until the Second World War.

However, European countries are sufficiently different from the United States and from one another to warrant the use of several descriptions of their societies. For instance, one can speak of an establishment in Great Britain because of the continued influence of former elites and the similar training of government leaders. The leaders of British government and society have been trained primarily in the same schools – private secondary schools such as Eton, then Oxford or Cambridge – and retain their social ties (the old-boy network) long after their formal schooling ends.

In France, the dominant bourgeoisie of the pre-war period has been replaced to a large extent by a new professional-technical elite, the French prefer the term cadres, who are trained in cadre-dominated secondary schools (*lycées*) and exclusive professional schools (*grandes écoles*). Individuals who follow the prescribed path to power may fill a diversity of government and economic positions merely because they have been initiated and accepted into the ruling circles.

None of the other developed nations in Europe have as clearly defined ties that bind the ruling circles together. For the remaining developed European countries, it seems best to adopt the theory of a more accessible but still rather exclusive ruling stratum. The more open German ruling elite is, according to Lewis Edinger, composed of 'a few thousand elected and appointed, co-opted and anointed leaders.' Much of Germany's traditional aristocratic and bourgeois elite was eliminated by Hitler's regime and the carnage of the Second World War. But all ruling strata consist primarily of middle-aged, well-educated males from the highest social stratum.

Composition of the Elite

Although the composition of the ruling stratum has changed since 1945, power is still exercised by a small, privileged, slow-changing elite in most European societies. The new French technocratic elite (*cadres supérieuers*) has maintained its monopoly of power in France since DeGaulle. This technocracy maintains its exclusivity through its monopoly of French technical education in the grande ecoles (see below) and its tendency to marrying only within the same group. John Ardagh cites a 1961 study of 2,000 eminent people in France that showed that 68 per cent were recruited from the top 5 per cent of the population and 81 per cent from the top 15 per cent of the population. This technocracy draws mainly from the upper and middle-middle class and seldom gets recruits from the lower middle class or the lower class. About two decades after the 1961 study, a survey of the 2500 most famous or powerful French people showed that only 3 per cent came from manual labourers' homes. Mendras and Cole, in *Social change in modern France* (1991) maintain that 'access to the ruling elite was more socially bound at the end of the 1980s than it had been ten years earlier.' It is important to remember, however, that both the peasantry and manual laborers now comprises a small percentage of the population and that the possibility of someone from either group entering the ruling elite has diminished.

Studies of the British elite over the last three decades indicate that leadership there has experienced little alteration. Guttsman's 1963 study, *The British Political Elite*, showed that about 'two-thirds of the members of the highest occupational groups, comprising less than three percent of the population, are the sons of men who belonged to the same group.' Marwick's 1982 work, *British Society since 1945* estimated that a British upper class comprising 'two percent or so' of the population still dominates leadership positions in the mid-eighties. Finally, the continuation of this upper class is substantiated by a survey by *The Economist* (19 Dec 1992) that compared Britain's 'top' 100 people in 1972 and 1992 and found that most were male (96 per cent), two-thirds went to private schools and more than one-half of them attended Oxford or Cambridge. Moreover, there has been a reversal of an immediate post-war trend to choose parliamentary members from the working class. Now more and more British Labour party leaders are chosen from the professions.

Only in Scandinavia, where the Social Democrats have long been in power and there are fewer educational and class obstacles to advancement, has there been a more marked democratization of the elite. More than half the ministers serving in the Swedish Social Democratic cabinet from 1956 to 1968 had lower-class social origins. In Sweden, for example, most youth attend the same primary school for nine years, and about 80 per cent continue on in an integrated secondary school. Robert Erikson believes this egalitarian education system, along with a high rate of income equality, is responsible for Sweden's democratization of its political leadership.

Anthony Sampson's sixties observation that 'The chances of the son of a working man reaching a position of power are almost – but not quite – as remote as they were in 1789' seem to still be true for Europe in the eighties with the exception of the Scandinavian states. It should be noted again, however, that the structure of these societies is quite different today than it was then. Today, a much broader middle stratum of professionals and technicians supplies many of the leadership positions, and manual labourers have become a small portion of the working population.

Former British Prime Minister Margaret Thatcher (left) and Norwegian Prime Minister Gro Harlem Brundtland at 10 Downing Street, the British government leader's residence.

(© Empire)

Education of the Elite

Immediately after the war, a thorough democratization of Europe's ruling circles seemed imminent as more elite positions – especially those requiring advanced training – were filled by students from presumably more democratic educational systems. Confirming that the route to the top was indeed through higher education, a 1961 study showed that nearly 85 per cent of a large sample of the French ruling stratum had received a university education (including *grandes écoles*), and that 63 per cent of a smaller group from German ruling circles had had at least some university training. Still, postwar Europe still lagged far behind the United States in access to higher education.

Advanced schooling continues to be the preserve of children of the upper-middle and middle classes. However, even in the most class-based educational system, the wall of social privilege started to break down in the late 1960s and early 1970s. Nevertheless, the various European countries differ sufficiently to necessitate the separate study of the major educational systems.

British Ruling-class Education   Success in British government has normally proceeded from the exclusive private secondary schools – Eton, Winchester, and so on – to Oxford or Cambridge universities. A 1973 study by the National Foundation for Educational Research showed graduates of the twenty-six leading private secondary schools had as large a share of the elite positions in Britain as they had had in 1939. The *Economist*'s survey of Britain's 100 top people found that 67 or 100 went to private school in 1972 and 66 or 100 in 1992. In 1964, slightly over one-third of the House of Commons members had attended Oxford or Cambridge – or Oxbridge, as they are referred to collectively. These schools are even more closely connected to the Conservative party. Four-fifths of the university-educated Conservative candidates for parliament between 1950 and 1966 were Oxbridge graduates. By 1987, Oxbridge graduates still made up 44 per cent of Conservative Party Members of Parliament (MPs) and only 15 per cent of Labour party MPs. The 1992 *Economist* survey of their 100 top positions found that in 1972 52 per cent of the 100 had attended Oxbridge compared to 54 per cent in 1992.

Although Oxbridge graduates retain an inordinate share of the important positions of power in Britain, changes in education, even at Oxbridge, indicate that such a monopoly does not have the same social significance as it once did. For one thing, an increasing percentage of the university student body now comes from the less privileged. In 1981, Anthony Sampson found that Oxford admitted slightly more than half new students from state secondary schools than from the private schools, a trend that has continued to the present day. For another thing, university education is becoming a more decisive factor than class in the competition for positions of power and influence. So graduates who have lower-class origins will undoubtedly fill a greater share of the important positions in the future. The elite schools also face increasing competition from the less prestigious universities, most of which were not established until after the war. The transformation of polytechnics into universities by the early 1990s certainly expanded the number of those graduating with a university degree, and thereby expanding their employment prospects. Still, an Oxbridge degree retains an exclusive allure.

At the secondary level, comprehensive, or common secondary, schools are gradually increasing their share of students. But the comprehensive schools have not equalled across the board the academic excellence of the grammar schools. Labour's attempts to put all secondary students in comprehensive schools encountered stiff opposition from the middle-class-dominated grammar and public schools. The opponents maintain that placing all students in comprehensive schools of the American type will mean the end of excellence in British education. Under New Labour, the comprehensive school was further pressured by the creation of so-called city academies, which allows private funding of schools and an opting out of the national curriculum.

French Ruling-class Education   As in Great Britain, both France's top industrial positions and government service, has been dominated by the upper-middle and middle classes. The *haute bourgeoisie* now dominates government service not merely because of social position but also because of their children's better education, which their wealth and social position make possible.

The persistence of social divisions in France has resulted from the ruling stratum's monopoly of an elite educational system. The domination begins in the state secondary schools, the *lycées*. In 1968 John Ardagh wrote, in *The New French Revolution*, 'State *lycées*, though in theory free and open to all, are in practice still largely a preserve of the middle class, and they alone provide a passport to higher education and the best jobs.' In his 1987 revised edition, *France Today*, Ardagh wrote that 'social barriers and prejudices are such that the more prestigious of them (*lycées*) – such as Louis-Le-Grand in Paris – have in practice been almost as much the preserves of a certain class as the English ... public [private] schools; and even in the average *lycée* the children of workers were always much under-represented.' Bourgeois society itself has been divided between those who have obtained a *lycée* diploma (*le baccalaureat*) and those who have failed. With *le bac* the student was prepared to attend the university or – for the fortunate few who proceed beyond *le bac* – one of the *grandes écoles*, where the future leaders of the nation are trained. Normally, two to three years of study beyond the *lycée* is needed in order to pass the rigorous entrance examination for the *grandes écoles*. Only about one of twenty students in higher education attends a grande ecole.

Leaders of business and government have long been recruited from these bastions of privilege, especially the *École Polytechnique*, the *École Normale Supérieure*, and the post-war École National d'Administration (ENA). Graduates of the *École Polytechnique*, affectionately called "X" because of its emblem of two-crossed cannon, go on to more specialized post-graduate grandes écoles and from there to government posts. While the grandes écoles were first set up to provide government servants, many graduates are now buying themselves out of government service in order to take lucrative jobs in business.

Both the students' brilliance – the selection process is one of the most rigorous in the world – and their connections make such a choice possible for them. In fact, an old-boy network similar to the British one has existed for *grandes écoles* graduates. In 1967, seven of the eleven top positions in the Ministry of Finance, and sixteen of the twenty-nine cabinet minister positions, were held by ENA graduates or enarques. In Mitterrand's first cabinet in 1981, eight out of 44 members were ENA graduates. Enarques held about two-thirds of the leading civil service positions in the early 1990s. Set up in the post-war period, ENA was intended to democratize recruitment to the higher administration. However, the competition for entry has restricted access to the elite. Only about one in ten graduates of the Lycée make it into the prestigious grandes Écoles. In the case of ENA, most recruits come from a few Parisian lycees that specialize in preparing persons for the entrance examinations. One must agree with Anthony Sampson that ENA has provided 'an old-boy net or a 'Mafia' which makes others – the Harvard Business School, Balliol (an Oxford college), or even the *Polytechnique* – seem amateurish.' But ENA and other grandes écoles graduates are now facing competition from French graduates of foreign business schools and administrators moving up through industry and business. Michel Crozier and Bruno Tilliette's 1995 study, *La Crise de l'Intélligence*, found that ENA, the *École Polytechnique*, and the *École des Hautes Études Commerciales* provide 60 per cent of French CEOs and that only four per cent are promoted from within these enterprises.

Of those entering the *grandes écoles* in 1967, only two per cent came from the working class and four per cent from the peasantry. In the same year, 57 per cent of the students in higher education had professional parents while 17 per cent came from the industrial and commercial bourgeoisie. In the mid-eighties no *grande école* had more than ten percent workers and peasants in the student body. Henri Mendras and Alistar Cole's 1991 study found that 'the elite which emerges from the school system tends to be composed of children of the existing social elite' and this shows how the reforms have failed to increase the educational opportunities of children from less privileged social backgrounds. Of course, many French prefer this more elitist system and will continue to place obstacles in the way of any more equalitarian reforms that the socialist government has in mind. But the trend has been in the direction of greater equalization of opportunity.

German Ruling-class Education In Germany no schools or families unite the ruling circles. Entry into the ruling stratum has come primarily through study at a university and, more specifically, through the study of law; Ralf Dahrendorf's 1967 study, *Society and Democracy in Germany*, calculated that 85 per cent of the civil servants in all government ministries had law degrees in 1962. Since university study was restricted to the upper and middle classes in Germany even more than in France, a narrow social basis of the ruling stratum was assured.

Traditionally, higher education has long been considered appropriate for only the talented few; four-fifths of the students still left school at age 14 in the early sixties. As in France, few children from working-class homes passed from the primary school (*grundschule*) into the select secondary school (*gymnasium*). But entry into German universities, and therefore German elite positions, has been opened up since the WWII. About 44 per cent of German youth began post-graduate studies in 1990 (27 per cent in the universities) compared to about 16 per cent in the 1970 (see Table 10xx). Whereas only 4 per cent of the university students came from wage-earner families in 1952–53, 18 per cent of those in 1977/78 came from such families. This change has been brought about through government grants to students, the building of twenty additional universities since 1965, and increasing the number of gymnasium students. The number of gymnasium graduates increased from 48,000 in 1965 to 204,000 in 1978 to over 1.5 million in 1989 (before unification) or 23 per cent of the relevant age group.

Recent changes making university study available to more students – university study will be possible for those who chose the secondary technical or vocational track – will increase those coming from lower social strata. Not all Germans are happy with the increased number entering the universities. With fewer choosing the vocational track at age 15 – the number of youths seeking apprenticeships declined from 765,000 to 600,000 between 1984 and 1990 according to the Economist (21 November, 1992) – some Germans fear that Germany's highly skilled labour force will be jeopardized. In addition, many university graduates specialize in the liberal arts and can often not find work once they have finished the university.

Scandinavian Ruling-class Education   The Scandinavian countries have the most socially progressive educational system in Western Europe. Modelled on that of the United States, Swedish education is free and open to all up to the university level. All students receive their primary and secondary education in the same common *comprehensive schools*, but here the similarity with the United States ends.

Despite thirty years of Social Democratic party equalization measures, the percentage of manual laborers' children obtaining a university education has risen very little. Some of this is due to the decline in the percentage of manual labourers in the population, but also the cultural deprivation of lower-class children in the home has prevented them from performing as well as middle-class children in the common secondary schools. Children of a senior white-collar employee are still more than three times as likely to continue academic studies beyond age sixteen as the children of unskilled workers, according to a 1988 study in *The Economist*. Of course, some of the disparity can be further explained by the availability in the Swedish educational system of an outstanding vocational track from age 16 to 18 that much better prepares Swedish youth to enter the labor force.

The Plutocrats

In the prewar period the upper-middle class, numbering 2 to 3 per cent of the population, was distinguished primarily by its dominance of political power, its

Table 8–15   Portion of total income received by the top 10 per cent of families before taxes

	1938	1954	1964	1981	2000
United Kingdom	38	30.4	29.3	23.4 (1979)	28.5 (1999)
France	—	34.1	36.8[c]	26.4 (1975)	25.1 (1995)
West Germany	39[a]	44.0[b]	41.4	24.0 (1978)	22.1
United States	36	30	28	23.3 (1980)	29.9
Sweden	—	—	—	28.1	22.2

Notes: [a] Data for all Germany in 1936.
[b] French data for 1956, German for 1955.
[c] Data for 1962.
Sources: Stanley Rothman, *European Society and Politics* (New York: Bobbs-Merrill, 1970), 137. World Bank, World Development Report 1988, 273. 2000 figures taken from World Development Indicators 2005, published by the World Bank.

wealth, and its life-style. Now it has to share power with a much broader segment of the middle class. This new ruling stratum, comprising at most ten per cent of the population of any Western European country, has at its disposal a major share of the wealth. Table 8–15 indicates that its share of total income declined between 1954 and 1981. In 1978 the upper ten per cent of French families received 26.4 per cent of all take-home income compared to only 5.5 per cent for the lowest 20 per cent. The Mitterrand government initially struck hard at this plutocracy with new income and luxury taxes. But there was much successful evasion of those taxes, as is typical in France and the conservative premier, Jacques Chirac, reversed many of these taxes during his premiership between 1986 and 1988. The Socialists' turn to modernization rather than equalization after 1983 has made them less interested in increasing taxes.

Other indicators of wealth, such as taxable income and possession of private property, confirm the existence of a relatively small plutocracy in most European countries. According to the British Inland Revenue Board's estimate of ownership of wealth (based upon inheritance taxes) from 1960 to 1968, the number of those owning over 50,000 had doubled while the number owning less than 5,000 had declined by only 16 per cent. A recent study by the British institute for Fiscal Studies calculated that in 1977 the income of the richest 20 per cent of Britons was four times larger than that of the poorest 20 per cent while in 1991 it had grown seven times larger. This increasing income disparity was primarily a result of Prime Minister Thatcher's lowering of direct taxes of wealth.

On the other hand, in Germany, Scandinavia and several smaller countries there has been a redistribution of income in favor of employees. Pay differentials in Germany narrowed during the eighties because of the strong trade unions. Sweden, paradoxically, has the most egalitarian allocation of wealth and the smallest group of extremely wealthy families; Micael Jungblut calculated that 15 families and two large banks controlled 90 per cent of the country's private industrial capital in the early 1970s. This situation came about primarily because high income taxes prevented the bulk of the population from investing in industry and because many Socialists wanted to keep the financial elite intact but small so that it would offer little resistance to Socialist programs. Sweden's taxes are so high that a jump in income from 20,000 to 40,000 kroner a year will produce a real income increase of only 3000 kroner.

In Norway, even higher taxes on income and property forced about 2,000 wealthy Norwegians to pay taxes in excess of their 1973 incomes. Now, however, the Socialist majority in parliament has apparently decided to return to an earlier law limiting taxes to a maximum of 80 per cent of one's income.

In West Germany, where class lines are not as distinct as in France or Great Britain, there are reports of the beginnings of a service-class society. According to this view, all who hold service jobs – soon to be the majority of the employed – from the clerk to the top government minister, are involved in the exercise of power and can no longer be divided into distinct social classes. Yet service-class workers do not behave as a class or think as a class; they behave and think as individuals. There are also great disparities in the authority exercised by upper and lower level service class workers. Although the German class structure is certainly less distinct than those in France and Great Britain, the service-class thesis seems somewhat premature.

Class demarcations in wealth and the exercise of political power remain clear in West Germany. In a study of the 'rich and superrich in Germany,' Michael Jungblut singled out a new 'oligarchy of wealth' numbering some 50,000 families. In 1960 each family had more than 10 million marks, and as a group they controlled 16 per cent of the country's capital shares and seven per cent of the individual wealth. A slightly larger group, 1.7 per cent of the population, possessed 35 per cent of the country's wealth. A survey of the top ten billionaires in Western Europe in 1994 counted six Germans, including the number one spot. But wealth is probably less necessary to obtain power than in the United States. Many leaders of the Social Democratic Party and the powerful labour unions came from humble beginnings. Willy Brandt, for example, the illegitimate son of a shop clerk, rose to head the West German government and the Social Democratic Party.

Political Attitudes and Social Class

With some exceptions, it was generally acknowledged that the working class voted for pro-labour parties – whether they were called communist, labour, socialist or social democratic. This was certainly the case in the first few decades after the war. But a combination of factors combined to see a decline in class voting (see Table 8–16). On the one hand, this means that the major parties of the center-left and center-right can no longer take for granted the votes of large sections of the electorate. On the other hand, some of the features that parties then characterize themselves in order to appeal to wide portions of the electorate are less class-based and more media-driven, for

Table 8–16   The decline in class voting[a]

	1945–1960	1961–1970	1971–1980	1981–1990
Austria	—	27.4	28.9	18.3
Belgium	—	25.4	17.9	16.4
Britain	37.3	38.3	24.3	23.4
Denmark	39.8	52.0	28.1	20.9
Finland	48.4	50.2	36.9	35.7
France	24.4	18.3	17.0	11.7
Germany	36.0	24.8	14.9	13.4
Ireland	—	14.1	8.7	7.3
Italy	26.6	14.5	17.8	13.1
Netherlands	14.0	14.7	21.8	15.5
Norway	52.5	32.0	33.8	20.5
Sweden	51.0	40.7	37.3	32.7
Mean (n)	36.7 (9)	29.4 (12)	24.0 (12)	19.1 (12)

Note: [a]Values are those of the Alford index, measuring the difference between the percentage of manual workers voting for left-wing political parties and the percentage of non-manual workers voting for these same parties; the higher the index, the stronger is class voting.

Source: Paul Nieuwbeerta (1995), *The Democratic Class Struggle in Twenty Countries, 1945/1990*, Thesis Publishers, Amsterdam, p. 53.

instance a focus on the qualities of the leader. Expansion of the middle class, a decline in religious voting, decline in identification with groups linked to parties, such as unions, etc, are reasons given by political scientists of the decline in class voting.

In the 1979 British parliamentary elections 36 per cent of labour voted for the Conservative party and another 14 per cent for the Liberals. Even in France, support for the Communist party has declined among workers; the labour vote for the Communists dropped from 49 per cent of the total labour vote in 1951 to 20 per cent in the 1986 parliamentary elections. In those same elections 34 per cent of the workers voted for the moderate socialists and 29 per cent for the middle-of-the-road RPR/UDF coalition. In the 1990s, the French Communists lost a good portion of their working class vote to the far-right National Front. All major parties of the center-left nowadays reach out to their working class supporters as well as white-collar employees. This is the only way that they can hope to win a majority or plurality of votes in order to form governments.

In Sum ... It is difficult to generalize about the thesis of a new European society throughout Western Europe because of the wide variety of conditions and attitudes. However, one can draw certain conclusions. In Scandinavia, West Germany, the Benelux countries and France a new society has emerged. The standard of living bears little resemblance to the prewar period. Most workers are no longer underpaid, overworked and without voice in the determination of their working conditions or wages.

The concept of a new Europe is less applicable to a number of smaller developing states. Certainly, a much larger section of the population now is upwardly mobile and is sharing in the new-found affluence. Although social deprivation continues to exist, especially for more recent immigrants, the role of the welfare state has made this condition less harsh than in the pre or interwar period.

There is considerably less mixing of social classes in these countries than in Scandinavia or the United States. Nevertheless, remarkable progress has been made since the war. The majority of their populations now have vastly improved housing, more consumer goods and the money to buy them, more free time, and income enough to enjoy annual vacations that amount to a month in most countries.

FURTHER READING

The works listed below portray the changing social structures of Europe as well as the evolution of the welfare state. Some of the social issues that have also become politicized over the past ten years such as immigration are handled in Chapter Twelve's Further Reading. Two books that provide an overview of socio-economic facts about Europe since WWII are Antony Sutcliffe, *An Economic and Social History of Western Europe since 1945* (1996), and Göran Therborn, *European Modernity and Beyond: The Trajectory of European Societies, 1945–2000* (1995), which is an invaluable analysis.

On the welfare state, the work of Gøsta Esping-Andersen has been influential, especially *The Three Worlds of welfare Capitalism* (1989), in which he argues that the forces of change are mediated by national models of welfare. Also see his edited volume *Welfare States in Transition* (1996). A more recent comparative work is Allan Cochrane et al., eds., *Comparing Welfare States: Britain in International Context* (2001), which compares the British welfare system with those of the United States, Germany, Sweden and Ireland. Exploring the impact of the European Union's social policy on welfare systems is Mark Kleinman, *A European Welfare State? European Union Social Policy in Context* (2001).

One of the key points in the chapter has been the change in social stratification between pre- and post-war Europe. An excellent and comprehensive work with which to begin exploring this phenomenon is Colin Crouch, *Social Change in Western Europe* (1999). He compares a wide range of social institutions: work and occupations, the structure of the economy, the family, education, religion and nationality and ethnicity. On social mobility in particular, see Robert Erikson and John H. Goldthorpe, *The Constant Flux* (1992), which is a critical study of social mobility arguing that there is a wide variation among countries. It has the added value of including some Eastern European countries. The endurance of class-based voting is analyzed by Geoffrey Evans, ed., *The End of Class Politics? Class Voting in Comparative Perspective* (1999).

There is of course an intimate connection between social policy and economic change, and the chapter has addressed this phenomenon. Two important works in this area are G. Esping-Andersen, *Social Foundations of Post-industrial Economies* (1999), in which he analyzes post-industrial diversity, and Colin Crouch and Wolfgang Streeck, *Political Economy of Modern Capitalism* (1997). On the development of the post-war European economy up to the end of the 1970s, what some have called the 'golden age' of capitalism, see Andrew Shonfield, *Modern Capitalism: The Changing Balance of Private and Public Power* (1980). From the perspective of the late 1980s, the modern capitalism began to appear less healthy, and this is reflected in Stephen A. Marglin and Juliet R. Schor, *The Golden Age of Capitalism: Reinterpreting the Post-war Experience* (1990).

The role of women in th eworkforce and in politics has been another key issue raised in the chapter. Among many useful works are the following: Joni Lovenduski, *State Feminism and Political Rrepresentation* (2005), which evaluates governments' responses to women's demands for inclusion in multiple areas of public life. Ruth Henig and Simon Henig, *Women and Political Power: Europe Since 1945* (2000) is a very useful point of reference. Finally, on the theme of women and politics, Richard E. Matland and Kathleen Montgomery, eds., *Women's Access to Political Power in Post-Communist Europe* (2003) is excellent in its coverage and analysis of women and politics in Eastern Europe. A good source for information about women in the workforce, and changes over the past few decades, see Jill Rubey et al., *Women's Employment in Europe: Trends and Prospects* (1999). The authors explore the impact of economic, social and cultural changes on the pattern of women's employment. The implications of EU policy for women is covered by M. D. Garcia-Ramon and J. Monk, eds., *Women of the European Union: The politics of Work and Daily Life* (1996).

The role of organized labour in Europe has been affected by post-industrial trends. Informative studies on the changing fortunes of trade unions include: Miriam Golden and Jonas Pontusson, eds., *Bargaining for Change: Union Politics in North American and Europe* (1992), and more recently, Andrew Martin and George Ross, eds., *The Brave New World of European Union: European Trade Unions at the Millennium* (1999). For an analysis of how unions have attempted to regain lost territory, see John Kelly and Carola M. Frege, eds., *Varieties of Unionism: Strategies for Union Revitalization in a Globalizing Economy* (2004). For a selection of individual country studies, see Chris Howell's authoritative study on British trade unionism in *Trade Unions and the State: The Construction of Industrial Relations Institutions in Britain, 1890–2000* (2005). For France, see Herrick Chapman, Mark Kesselman and Martin Schain, eds., *A Century of Organized Labor in France: A Union Movement for the Twenty-First Century?* (1998). For West Germany see Andrei Markovits, *The Politics of the West German Trade Unions* (1986), and for post–1989 Germany, see Rebecca Harding and William Paterson, eds., *The Future of the German Economy* (2000).

9

Economics and Society in the Communist World

[In East Germany] the society of inherited status has largely given way to a society of achieved status.

Ralf Dahrendorf, *Society and Democracy in Germany* (1979)

During the immediate post-war decades, the East European countries and the Soviet Union made good on their promise to bring about a greater equalization of income. Their economic policies, however, while initially inducing greater levels of industrialization, lowered dramatically the standard of living for the vast mass of their populations by the 1980s, and contributed to the collapse of these regimes in 1989–90. They achieved greater social equalization after the war through the abandonment of private ownership of property, through the nationalization of industry and through a greater equalization of educational opportunity. But in place of an elite based upon private ownership emerged an elite based upon special privilege. Moreover, economic difficulties forced these countries to reintroduce income differentiation in order to bring about the economic reforms necessary to stimulate economic performance. While the income disparities were not as great as they are in the West, the higher income and greater privileges of the elite has brought about social disparities and popular resentment in the East. This chapter will examine economic and social development within the Soviet Bloc and Yugoslavia between 1945 and 1989.

With the exception of Yugoslavia after 1952 and Albania and Romania after the early sixties, the East European states generally followed, or were forced to follow, Soviet economic and social patterns. But the Soviet model was difficult to follow since it experienced three major transformations, associated with Stalin, Khrushchev and Gorbachev, and many minor changes. Immediately after the war, government imposed social levelling measures brought about a much greater social egalitarianism than in the West as Dahrendort suggests. The expropriation of property from the landed classes (especially in Hungary and Poland) and the nationalization of industry eliminated the nobility and capitalist entrepreneurial class. But a new elite of party bureaucrats and technocratic managers soon replaced this former elite. A technocratic elite also arose as a result of the economic modernization that swept through Eastern Europe. The social disparities that re-emerged in all countries, with the possible (exception) of economically underdeveloped Albania, were based less on income than on benefits received by this new elite. The privileged position of the party elite, known as the Nomenklatura in the Soviet Union and Poland, continued up to the final demise of these regimes despite attempts to alter their power.

The Soviet Economy

Although the Soviet Union had made considerable progress in the interwar years, the Second World War set back its industrialization momentarily. Much of the industry in the South and West and half of the total pre-war railway network had been destroyed. The wartime deaths of millions had also reduced the skilled labour supply. Nevertheless, the war provided some lasting benefits to Soviet industrialization, for entire industries had been set up beyond the Urals to escape German destruction. With these industrial areas intact and the older ones rebuilt, the country's industrial potential was immensely increased. By 1953, the Soviet Union had surpassed its pre-war levels of production in much of the heavy industry sector. Production of steel rose from 18.3 million metric tons in 1940 to 38 million metric tons in 1953. Concentration on heavy industry put the nation in a position to challenge the United States in the production of raw materials and military equipment – though not consumer goods – by the 1970s. But growing economic problems in the late seventies and eighties severely limited any further Soviet economic advances and undermined both the whole course of Soviet economic development and leadership.

Khrushchev's Decentralization

After Stalin's death, the Soviet economy experienced three markedly different periods of development: the first under Khrushchev, the second under his successors, Brezhnev and Kosygin, and the third under Gorbachev. All three periods were reactions to Stalinist centralization and his concentration on heavy industry.

Beginning in 1958, Khrushchev instituted a major reorganization of the Soviet economy along regional lines. The rationale for this decentralization was sound. The extreme Stalinist centralization was adequate for a small developing economy but not for an increasingly complex developed one. The rigid centralized plans, long-term goals and resource allocations led to wasted resources and shoddy manufactured goods.

However, because Khrushchev's decentralization was hastily instituted, it created new difficulties. Overall co-ordination and control of 100 regional areas was extremely difficult. Local factory managers were hampered by greater interference than they had endured under Stalin since they now received endless directives, many of them conflicting, from the newly empowered local and state agencies. Nor was the factory manager freed from the exaggerated production goals typical of the Stalinist period, since Khrushchev was equally determined to catch up with American industrial output. Because production goals were still couched in terms of volume or weight, managers went on meeting their quotas by hoarding materials, falsifying records, and turning out inferior products. The Soviet publication *Krokodil* once lampooned the system of output measurement and factory management by showing a nail factory that had met its quota by producing one giant nail. Since transport goals were expressed in ton-kilometres, transport firms made useless trips in order to fill their quotas.

Khrushchev's determination to raise agricultural production also misfired. The concentration on increasing corn and wheat production forced local officials to adopt monoculture. To raise production, fallowing was banned almost entirely. This led to weed infestation, wind erosion and falling yields. And Khrushchev's emphasis on raising production in certain fertile areas left the land in less fertile areas with little fertilizer and little capital.

When Khrushchev realized that his policy of decentralization was failing, he resorted to further divisions of authority in order to stimulate competition among officials and thereby promote greater efficiency. As detailed in Chapter 6, he divided the party into agricultural and industrial groups, thereby further complicating an already confused situation. Local Communist party officials were extremely resentful when the new division of responsibility deprived them of half their authority. Nor were things better at the national level, where both the Soviet *Sovnaskhov* (Economic Council) and the Supreme Council of National Economy were given the authority to issue directives in the same industrial sectors.

Khrushchev forced most of the East European countries into an economic division of labour with the establishment of Comecon: under this plan East Germany, Czechoslovakia and the Soviet Union were to concentrate on heavy industrial production while the other countries would supply raw materials and light industrial products. The latter would, therefore, be permitted to develop only a portion of their economies. Naturally, this plan met much opposition from countries such as Romania that wished to develop their heavy industry but were not permitted to according to the new division of labour.

Economic Policy from Kosygin and Brezhnev to Gorbachev

The second major shift in economic policy began after Kosygin and Brezhnev instituted reforms in 1965. They abolished regional administration and returned to centralized direction of the economy. But this was not a Stalinist centralism with its complete control over all aspects of production, investment, and resource allocation. To be centrally determined were major investments, volume of sales, basic assortment of output, total wages fund, amount of profit and profit rate on capital, and payments to and allocations from the state budget. Local managers were to have the authority to handle most factory labour questions except gross wages and to authorize all minor investments out of their profit. Most important, volume of sales and profitability replaced gross output as indicators of the success of enterprises. Central controls now tended to be indirect rather than direct: taxes, subsidies, interest rates, rents, price ceilings and profit rates.

The economic lag of the early 1960s came to a temporary end as a measure of order was restored in the economy. But growth rates turned down again after 1973 due to inefficiency, lack of technology, a too rigid central allocation of material and labour and the concentration of investment on military spending. Khrushchev's boast that the Soviet Union would overtake the United States never materialized economically; Soviet Gross National Product per capita reached only about 41 per cent of that of the United States in 1987 according to United States Department of State. In fact, much of the Soviet demand for consumer goods was met by the underground economy. Economists estimate that about 20 per cent of all consumer purchases were made on the underground economy. Authorities permitted this 'second economy' to exist since it supplied scarce goods, reduced discontent and even supplied goods needed by the official economy. Widespread pilfering from government run industries was overlooked. There was a popular Soviet and East European view that those who are not cheating are cheating their own families. Soviet managers hamstrung by the shortage of centrally allocated material, turned to this underground economy for material if they wished to meet their production goals. Certainly, the sharp difference in the living standards of American and Soviet citizens was not a good advertisement for the superiority of communism. Much of the support for Gorbachev's reforms resulted from the failure of centralized economic planning.

Serious economic difficulties in the early 1980s convinced Gorbachev and other reformers that economic reforms were absolutely essential to prevent a weakening of the Soviet Union. They believed that the free flow of information in a society was the basis for the economic strength, and ultimately political and military strength, of a country. Therefore, Gorbachev's efforts at restructuring, openness and Demokratia were aimed at removing obstacles to reform, such as the ossified bureaucracy, and freeing up economic activity at the local level. His desire to increase local initiative and industrial output encountered stubborn opposition from communist party conservatives and the entrenched bureaucracy who feared a loss of local authority. As a result, Gorbachev was driven to even greater demands for economic freedoms in order to achieve reforms. Gorbachev's drive to establish a strong economy through market socialism demanded a destruction of the conservative party forces that profited from the previous system. He needed to reform the party with its gigantic officialdom in order to remove obstacles to his economic reforms. By encouraging popular involvement everywhere he hoped to defeat the conservative forces and tap the energies of the masses. However, he was not able to achieve economic reforms in time (see Chapter 11) to prevent a conservative counterrevolution against the reforms and to save his regime.

East European Economic Modernization

The basis for much of the transformation of Eastern Europe in the post-war years has been economic modernization. Most of the countries have made the transition from peasant societies to diversified economies. Having a good economic balance of agricultural and industrial output, East Germany made particularly rapid strides until the 1980s. With a population of only 17 million, East Germany became the tenth leading industrial country in the world in the seventies. Despite the loss of over a million skilled workers to the West, East Germany maintained its reputation as one of the world's leading producers of optical and photographic equipment and became a leading producer of chemicals, and iron and steel products.

But East Germany existed in the shadow of the much more successful West German economy where consumer goods were abundant. East Germany's concentration on heavy industrial products led to serious consumer goods' shortages. The immigrants who poured into West Germany after 1989 complained about inferior products and severe shortages with delivery of automobiles taking about ten years (see Table 9–1). The loss of many skilled workers to the West further reduced industrial production and cut services. With the entire economy on the brink of collapse in early 1990,

Table 9–1   Comparing purchasing power in East Germany (GDR) and West Germany (FRG), April 1, 1990 (in hours of work by an average industrial worker)

Item	East Germany (GDR)	West Germany (FRG)
Color television	739 hrs.	84 hrs.
Washing machine	347 hrs.	53 hrs., 13 min.
Refrigerator	215 hrs.	30 hrs.
Rent (monthly)	11 hrs., 19 min.	22 hrs., 18 min.
Coffee (1 kg.)	10 hrs., 32 min.	1 hr.
Cheese (1 kg.)	1 hr., 25 min.	48 min.
Butter (1 kg.)	5 hrs., 48 min.	28 min.
Bread (1 kg.)	5 min.	10 min.
Pork cutlet (1 kg.)	1 hr., 12 min.	35 min.
Beer (1 l.)	14 min.	6 min.
Postage (domestic letter)	2 min.	3 min.

Source: Adapted from *German Unification in the European Context* by Peter H. Merkl. University Park: The Pennsylvania State University Press 1993, 258. Copyright 1993 by The Pennsylvania State University. Reproduced by permission of the publisher.

only massive aid from the West or unification with West Germany could have prevented collapse.

Romania, with its important mineral resources, also made impressive economic gains until the seventies: its economic growth rate averaged 10 per cent annually between 1950 and 1973. Romania's rejection of the role of mere raw materials supplier to the Soviet Union and the other members of Comecon led it to develop its own manufacturing industries. But raw material, energy, and agricultural shortages combined with a dogmatic insistence on developing heavy industry, led to a sharp economic downturn in the late seventies and eighties. Communist Party leader Ceaucescu imposed a severe Stalinist centralization plan to overcome the economic problems. His attempt to export most of what Roman produced in order to obtain investment funds and cut the deficit, created extreme hardship, massive food and consumer goods shortages, and mounting internal and foreign opposition. These economic problems helped undermine his leadership and contribute to his overthrow in December 1989. His successors faced a long and difficult task in restoring economic stability.

The economic development of the other Communist Bloc countries has been more checkered. In the 1960s their output fell far behind their goals. Czechoslovakia, with an advanced manufacturing sector, suffered from overzealous planning, political turmoil and a labour shortage. Although political stability between the Prague Spring (see Chapter 10) and the overthrow of the Communist government in 1989 promoted economic improvement, highly planned resource allocation, worker apathy and energy shortages severely inhibited economic growth.

Yugoslavia's self-management system, instituted by Tito to give workers a voice in industrial management and to win the ideological battle against Stalin, became increasingly ineffective in the 1970s and 1980s. Worker's councils in factories proved to be inept managers. Also the necessity to treat each republic and autonomous area equally resulted in a ruinous duplication of production. Efforts to establish a free market economy by the economically advanced republics of Slovenia and Croatia encountered the opposition of most other areas who feared the unemployment and greater inequality it would bring. As a result, all efforts to establish a free market were stymied by central government intervention. Lack of capital and technological backwardness impeded international competitiveness and industrial solvency. Efforts to resolve the conflict between the free-market north and the Serb dominated south resulted in a further political fragmentation. Legislation passed in 1988, intended to move toward a free market and return management to factory managers, fell victim to civil wars that tore Yugoslavia apart in the 1990s.

As a whole, the Eastern Bloc economies maintained a rapid economic advance in the early 1970s; from 1971 to 1973 every country's industrial growth rate topped 6 per cent. But higher energy costs, scarce raw materials, shortages of investment capital and reduced exports curtailed economic growth after 1973. In addition, the East Bloc countries buy much of their technologically advanced equipment needed to promote industrial expansion from the West. The costs for countries attempting to establish competitive industries – East Germany, Romania, Hungary – were enormous. By 1981, East Germany's debt to the West ($12.8 billion) was second only to Poland's $22.6 billion that was brought about to a large extent by its internal political turmoil (see Table 9–2). Romania managed to retire most of its $10 billion

Table 9–2   The estimated hard-currency debt of the Soviet Union and East European states, 1990 (billions of US dollars)

	1975	1980	1984	1985	1986	1987	1988	1989
Bulgaria								
gross	2.6	3.5	2.8	3.2	4.7	6.1	8.2	9.2
net	2.3	2.7	1.4	1.2	3.3	5.1	6.4	8.0
Czechoslovakia								
gross	1.1	6.9	4.7	4.6	5.6	6.7	7.3	7.9
net	0.8	5.6	3.7	3.6	4.4	5.1	5.6	5.7
The GDR								
gross	5.2	13.8	11.7	13.2	15.6	18.6	19.8	20.6
net	3.5	11.8	7.2	6.9	8.2	9.7	10.3	11.1
Hungary								
gross	3.9	9.1	11.0	14.0	16.9	19.6	19.6	20.6
net	2.0	7.7	9.4	11.7	14.8	18.1	18.2	19.4
Poland								
gross	8.4	24.1	26.5	29.3	33.5	39.2	39.2	40.8
net	7.7	23.5	24.9	27.7	31.8	36.2	35.6	36.9
Romania								
gross	2.9	9.6	7.2	6.6	6.4	5.7	2.9	0.6
net	2.4	9.3	6.6	6.2	5.8	4.4	2.1	21.2
Eastern Europe								
gross	24.2	67.0	63.9	71.0	82.7	96.0	97.0	99.7
net	18.8	60.5	53.2	57.4	68.1	78.4	78.2	79.9
The Soviet Union								
gross	10.6	23.5	21.4	25.2	30.5	40.2	46.8	52.4
net	7.5	14.9	10.1	1.1	15.6	26.1	31.4	37.7
Comecon								
gross	34.8	90.5	85.3	96.1	13.1	136.2	143.7	152.1
net	26.3	75.5	63.3	69.5	83.8	104.5	109.7	117.6

Note: Theses figures are Western estimates based on officially reported data. In the case of the GDR, in particular, internal figures that became available after unification indicate that these estimates understated the net debt. The table nevertheless gives a sense of orders of magnitude.

Source: Comecon Data 1990, Macmillian Ltd (Vienna Institute for Comparative Economic Studies), 1991.

debt to the West in 1989 but only by severe rationing measures that brought extreme hardship. Hungary avoided serious economic setbacks in the 1970s by diverting some industrial endeavour from large state-owned enterprises to more efficient local and private companies and by introducing incentives and cost accountability. But the 1980s brought economic decline to Hungary as well. Efforts to reduce costs by allowing technology to replace labour encountered stiff resistance from more orthodox Communist officials who prized full-employment more than profitability. As new governments emerged throughout Eastern Europe in the 1990s, cost accountability and profitability was necessary so that Eastern European companies could be competitive internationally.

Per capita Gross National Product rose steadily since the early 1960s. But as Table 9–3 shows, there was considerable variance from one country to another. Although Bulgaria advanced rapidly in the 1980s, only East Germany, the Soviet Union and Czechoslovakia could be considered mature industrial societies. The World Bank report of 1988 classified Poland and Hungary as intermediate developed economies. A 1987 study of *Equality and Inequality in Eastern Europe* found that two of the more advanced countries in Eastern Europe, Hungary and Czechoslovakia had fallen far behind their next-door neighbour Austria since the interwar period: in 1938 per capita income in Hungary and Czechoslovakia reached 66 per cent and 118 per cent that of Austria compared to 1978 GNP per capita of only 47 per cent and 63 per cent that of Austria. The economic dislocation after 1987 obviously produced an even greater disparity.

The economic reforms needed to make East European economies competitive in the world economy required changes to previous economic practices that the communist authorities were incapable of making. Left communists

Table 9–3   Per-capita GNP (in 1977 US dollars)

	1967	*1977*	*1987*
East Germany	3,093	4,363	11,860
Czechoslovakia	3,293	4,198	9,715
Soviet Union	1,554	3,976	8,363
Hungary	2,235	2,747	8,260
Bulgaria	1,795	2,511	7,222
Poland	1,917	2,888	6,890
Romania	1,787	2,766	6,358

Sources: US Department of Commerce, *Selected Trade and Economic Data of the Centrally Planned Economies* June 1979, 2. Central Intelligence Agency, *World Factbook 1989.* These estimates of per-capita GNP by the CIA are considered to be too high by many economists (Jan Winiecki, *The Distorted World of Soviet-type Economies*) and by the World Bank. The 1987 per-capita GNP is taken from Department of State, Bureau of Intelligence and Research, *Indicators of Comparative East-West Economic Strength 1987*, 196 (December 30, 1988).

opposed market forces as leading to capitalism while many workers opposed them because they did not have to work hard while receiving a government-supported wage. For example, economic reforms in 1987 that would have permitted higher incomes in the Soviet Union were thwarted by government bureaucrats who imposed exceedingly high taxes on private businesses and cooperative owners. Private tourist business on Romania's Black Sea coast vanished when government officials decided such ventures would produce some wealth among these small private owners. Workers became impatient with the pace of change in the eighties. Many believed that they worked more for less under Gorbachev and similar reformers. This attitude led to major coal miners strikes in July 1989, that Gorbachev defused only by granting wage increases. The Soviet Railway system, where many workers received only about $35 a month pay in 1989, was plagued by massive absenteeism (150,000 did not report for work each day). A railway worker commented in 1989 that Soviet leaders were oblivious to their suffering because 'they don't taste the gravy of real life'.

Agricultural Problems

Some of the Soviet Union's industrial progress, particularly in the Stalin period, was made at the expense of agriculture. A noted economist, Arcadius Kahan, called Soviet policy one of calculated subsistence for agriculture. Despite the increased attention given to agriculture by Khrushchev and Gorbachev, it still suffered from inadequate mechanization, low fertilization, skilled labor shortages, and poor transportation. With about 75 per cent more sown land in the early 1960s, the Soviet Union produced only about 63 per cent of the United States' crop of major grains. By 1980, Soviet farm output reached 80 per cent of that of the United States but with a much higher investment of labour and capital: eight times as many farm workers as the United States (23 per cent of work force) and five times the capital investment (one-quarter of all investment capital). Only under extremely favourable climatic conditions could the Soviet Union feed its population.

Khrushchev's attempts to raise agricultural production failed because they were primarily restricted to tilling new marginal virgin land and trying one short-term project after another in order to raise production, instead of undertaking long-term efforts to modernize farming methods and provide adequate machinery and fertilizers. The post-Khrushchev planners invested more in agriculture and raised the wages of agriculture workers, but despite their efforts, Soviet food needs could not be met. From 1971 to 1973, the average growth of Soviet agricultural output was only 3.4 per cent. The failure of the Soviet grain crop in 1972 necessitated huge grain purchases from the United States.

Brezhnev shifted even large investment of funds to agriculture at the expense of the consumer-goods industry; agricultural investment increased from about 19 per cent of total government investment in the early sixties to about 24 per cent between 1976 and 1978. Much of this increased investment went to enlarge livestock herds and for land reclamation and improvement. But, for ideology's sake, Brezhnev did not attempt to reduce the amount of collectivized land, which was much less productive than the privately owned plots due to mismanagement and an excessively over-centralized allocation of resources.

Soviet planners were faced with another major agricultural problem – the migration of agricultural workers, especially the young, to the cities. A 1967 survey showed that 65 per cent of those described as job transients were under 30 years of age. The Communist youth organization, Komsomol, was not able to slow this migration. A 1966 survey of the Smolensk region showed that the number of Komsomol members working on state farms had halved in five years; on collective farms it had dropped even more, from 21,043 to 8,778. In order to harvest vegetables, urban residents were forced to help with the harvest. Students often spent as much as six weeks in the fields during harvest time in the 1960s. Still, much of the produce was not harvested; one third of the potato crop in 1980 remained unharvested. Total potato output declined 12 per cent from 1966 to 1980.

Gorbachev's reform of agriculture was designed to increase local initiative by reducing centralized decision-making. Profitability was to govern agricultural ventures. Farming units were permitted to sell all produce above an existing target at market prices. Gorbachev's policy of increasing lease-holding encountered strong opposition from state-farm bosses who feared their loss of power and collective farmers who did not want to give up their security for the free market. Gorbachev did not want to force farmers into private farming but he intended to reduce collective farming where peasants worked little for their wages. Gorbachev remarked that No fool is going to work on a lease contract as long as he can have a salary without earning it (*NYT*, 14 Oct, 1988).

Eastern European Agriculture

Agriculture underwent a deeper transformation than did industry in Eastern Europe after the war. Most land was first divided into state-owned and cooperatively owned sectors with agricultural workers receiving a wage. These wages rose even more rapidly than industrial wages at first.

In an attempt to satisfy land-hungry peasants, land was distributed in small private plots immediately after the war. Later, as governments came under Communist domination, the land was either taken over by the state or organized into cooperatives. The cooperatives ranged from those where the peasant owned nothing and was paid a wage to those where property was individually owned but cooperatively farmed. Fierce peasant resistance to collectivization in Poland, combined with the leaders' reluctance to collectivize, led to the establishment of over three million small private farms. In Hungary, huge cooperative farms with productivity bonuses replaced almost all the state-collective farms. In order to maintain the rural labour supply, peasants were not issued rural passports that permitted them to travel: Soviet peasants began to receive such passports only after 1974.

Population density on the land retarded the development of agriculture; one study fixed the population density in the private sector at forty to fifty workers for every 250 acres. In Western Europe the agricultural population is well under 10 per cent of the working population, but it remained over 20 per cent in all East European countries as of 1982, except East Germany (4 per cent), Czechoslovakia (14 per cent), and former Yugoslavia (5 per cent). By 1993, Hungary, Slovakia and the Czech Republic had 10 per cent or below.

Collectivized agriculture did not provide the answer to East Europe's agrarian problems. By the mid-1960s, Poland's agricultural output had risen more than that of any other East European country because of its small farms, whereas output in collectivized East Germany, Czechoslovakia and Hungary was actually lower than the 1938 production. In the mid-1970s a Polish farmer proudly remarked, 'It is amusing to us to see high-ranking Russian officers going home carrying sacks of potatoes.' Among the countries with collectivized agriculture, only Romania produced a slight increase in agricultural production since the war. Collectivized agriculture in Yugoslavia provided a higher yield mainly because the most fertile land is in large state farms in the Voivodina area north of Belgrade, whereas individually owned farms (not larger than 25 acres) were located in infertile mountainous terrain. After the mid-1970s, only Hungarian agriculture continued to increase production sufficiently to meet their needs. The Polish practice of keeping food prices low in order to satisfy industrial workers led to low agricultural prices, reduced output, and black marketeering. In 1980 all Eastern European countries except Hungary imported more grain than they exported. Of course, official trade figures do not include the enormous underground economy in Eastern Europe. Much of the agricultural output as well as some industrial products were sold on the black market. In Hungary, private plots, comprising about 12 per cent of the arable land, produced most of the vegetables and fruit and about half of the pork and poultry in 1980. Most of the remaining produce and most of the grain was produced on co-operatives where workers received a salary and bonuses for exceeding production goals. This combination made Hungary the only East European country able to meet its own food needs. Other Eastern European countries began to follow the Hungarian practices in the early 1980s especially after Brezhnev praised the Hungarian performance in 1981. But the real solution to the agricultural problem, free-market prices for produce, resulted in extreme opposition from populations accustomed to low agricultural prices. Higher wages for industrial workers could have offset price increases but it would have also made industrial products less competitive in the world market. This dilemma produced extensive suffering no matter how enlightened the reforms.

Living Standards

Economic changes did not bring about a standard of living in the Soviet Union and Eastern Europe anywhere near that in Western Europe. Throughout the 1970s and 1980s the Soviet Union suffered from falling rates of productivity and excessive defence spending that reduced outlays for consumer goods and health care. As a result, the infant mortality rate rose dramatically in the 1970s; it increased by more than a third between 1970 and 1975. Although better registration could account for some of the apparent decline, the infant mortality rate in 1979 was 39 per 1000 live births compared to 14 in the United States and 13 in the United Kingdom. Some improvement was registered by 1990, when infant mortality rates fell to 24 per 1000 live births.

Male life expectancy rates actually decreased 4.3 years between 1965 and 1980 according to Chesnais. Chesnais also calculates that a Soviet and Japanese male could expect to live about the same number of years in 1960 (66.2 in the Soviet Union compared to 67.7 in Japan) but by 1980 Soviet male life expectancy had declined to 61.9 years compared to 73.6 years in Japan. The Soviet Union's poor economic performance in the 1980s only increased this discrepancy.

In terms of equalizing income, the Soviet Union achieved a greater equalization than most of the West European states with the exception of Scandinavia. Table 9–4 indicates that top managers, physicians and lawyers were not paid the huge sums characteristic in the West in the 1960s but that political leaders received a much higher salary than the average worker. Matthew's study of 1972 income calculated that the Soviet elite received official income of 3.1 to 3.8 times the average pay compared to an American average of eight times the national average. However, additional fringe benefits and incomes added an extra 100 per cent to the Soviet elites official income. Since Stalin renewed income differentiation in the early 1930s to promote production, Soviet leaders have apparently felt that wage differentials are necessary in an industrialized society. It is noteworthy that men constitute only 40 per cent of physicians, probably because of the extensive training required and the comparatively low salaries. The lure of becoming a party bureaucrat with its higher income and special perquisites in the form of better housing, food, and consumer goods (see below) is more appealing.

The concentration of Soviet resources on heavy industry and the armaments and space programs left little for consumer goods. Until recently, Soviet leaders were little interested in providing consumer goods: Khrushchev asserted, 'A person cannot consume, for example, more bread and other products than are necessary for his organism .... Of course, when we speak of satisfying people's needs, we have in mind not whims or claims to luxuries, but the healthy needs of a culturally developed person'. Soviet per capita consumption of consumer goods was only 40 to 60 per cent of that in France, West Germany, and the United Kingdom in 1962. It is unlikely that there has been any improvement in this ratio since the 1960s. Between

1970 and 78 Soviet annual rates of growth of per capita consumption trailed even that of the struggling United States' economy: the Soviet rate was 2.5 per cent compared to the 2.7 per cent for the United States. In comparison to the 50 telephones per 100 inhabitants in Western Europe in 1985, only Czechoslovakia, Bulgaria and East Germany had more than 20.

Despite Brezhnev's efforts to raise meat consumption, Table 9–5 shows that Soviet citizens consume far less meat then do East European and Western inhabitants. Another measure of economic well-being that is more meaningful than monetary comparisons (the Soviet Union set the rate of exchange of the ruble) is the amount of work required to purchase commodities. Radio Liberty estimated that in 1982 it cost a Moscow inhabitant 46.8 hours of work to purchase the same weekly basket of consumer goods that it took a Washington, Munich, Paris and London inhabitant 16.3, 20.4, 19.4 and 22.5 hours respectively to purchase. The Soviet journal USA estimated that in 1988 the average Soviet inhabitant worked 10 times longer

Table 9–4   Basic wage differentials in the Soviet Union, 1963 (in US dollars per year, before taxes)[a]

Cabinet ministers, republic government	9,125
University professor	7,070
Factory director (machine building)	6,240
Doctor of science, head of department in a research institute	5,730
Master foreman (machine building)	5,028
Engineer (oil industry)	4,238
Technician	3,724
State-farm manager	3,530
Average for all workers and employees	1,445[b]
Lawyer	1,376
Physician	1,260
Coal miner	1,092
Steel worker	872
High-school teacher	824
Construction worker	746
Machine-tool operator	746
Textile worker	679
Office typist	588
State-farm worker	586
Collective farmer (1962)	574

Notes: [a] Rubles converted into dollars at 1:1.11 ratio.
[b] Total wages received, including bonuses. Bonuses are not included in the other figures in the table.

Source: J. P. Nettl, *The Soviet Achievement* (New York: Harcourt Brace Jovanovich, 1967), p. 254. Reprinted by permission.

than the average American to buy a pound of meat, 4.5 times longer to buy a quart of milk and three times as long to buy a pound of potatoes. Forty per cent of Soviet households existed on less than 100 Rubles a month (a Ruble was officially being exchanged at six to the dollar in 1989 but its real worth was about ten cents).

It is, of course, important to remember that consumer goods were more equally distributed in the Soviet Union than in France, West Germany, and the United Kingdom. For example, in housing there were few socially and economically differentiated neighborhoods like those in the West; the special housing and dachas of the powerful and influential were an exception. The size of a dwelling usually depended on the size of the family. Since rents were low – only about 12 per cent of an individual's income was spent on rent in 1982 compared to 51, 24, 39, 28 per cent respectively for an inhabitant of Washington, Munich, Paris and London-there were fewer economic barriers to entry into certain neighborhoods than there were in the West. The living space per capita was, however, much lower in the Soviet Union than in the West: it was only about 8.6 square meters per capita in 1979.

As in Western Europe, the standard of living varied considerably among East European countries, being highest in East Germany, Czechoslovakia and Yugoslavia. Tito boasted in 1974 that every fifth Yugoslav had a car. Typical Yugoslavs spent only 37 per cent of their income on food and drink in the mid-1970s compared to over 50 per cent in the early 1960s. There is little doubt that these figures would not be so favorable if many Yugoslavs had not become guest workers in more affluent countries in the north.

Within Yugoslavia there was a radical difference in the standard of living between north and south. The north, with a standard of living near that of Austria, resented having to help the underdeveloped areas of Macedonia and Montenegro in the south. In Czechoslovakia the standard of living varied too, being much lower in the primarily agrarian Slovakian east.

Regional differences have been a long-standing problem in Eastern Europe, especially in Czechoslovakia and Yugoslavia. During the interwar years the Bohemian-Moravian areas in Czechoslovakia, like Croatia and Slovenia in Yugoslavia, had much more developed economic areas and considerably higher standards of living than other sections. The inhabitants of the Czech lands also held most of the government positions during the interwar years and in the post-war Communist government.

As in the Soviet Union, the Eastern European countries offered low-cost housing and services. In East Germany and Hungary, apartments and houses cost an average of $14.50 per month in the sixties; but public transportation costs were a fraction of those in the West; and medical services were free. However, the low costs were often offset by poor quality goods and inadequate housing. Many apartments lacked bathrooms, kitchens and other features common to housing in Western Europe.

Because consumer goods were still expensive and of poor quality, visitors from Western Europe often found that their clothing attracted interest and sometimes prospective buyers. East Europeans normally waited for extended periods to obtain consumer goods. A Bulgarian in 1984 had to wait 20 years to receive an automobile that had to be paid for in advance. Hungarians flooded into Austria in 1989 to buy consumer goods because of the scarcity and poor quality at home. An East German who fled to West Germany in 1989 complained that he had waited ten years to receive a car he had paid for in 1979.

Status

Despite Soviet and East European efforts to upgrade the status of the worker, the gap between theory and practice remained. The prestige of many jobs was little different from that of the same positions in the West. Service-class jobs, especially those of the new technocracy, continued to be more respected among the workers. A Hungarian woman's choice of a lower-paying administrative position over that of a textile worker became a cause for concern among communist officials in 1973. Industrial progress naturally demanded highly trained experts; their jobs were more prestigious and their incomes higher.

An increase in leisure time was one device used by Eastern European countries to meet workers' demands for a life-style similar to that in the West. Every worker received one month's paid vacation per year. Factory-owned resorts in the mountains and on the Baltic Sea and Black Sea gave workers the kind of vacation they could only dream about fifteen years earlier; an East German worker could spend two weeks on the Baltic for as little as $20 in the early seventies. Eastern European travelers, overwhelmingly academics who bolstered their income by teaching in the West, were being seen in increasing numbers in the West. However, even when Eastern Europeans were permitted to travel outside their country the West was still too expensive for most of them.

The Role of Women

Despite the egalitarian ideals of Communism, women possessed no more real power in the Soviet Union then they did in the West. The 15-member Politburo, headed by Brezhnev, had no female members. Only eight women were among the 287 full members of the Central Committee of the Communist party. Men headed all the government ministries and committees. Women were, however, well represented in the professions – about 70 per cent of the Soviet doctors and 79 per cent of all schoolteachers were female. But these were low-paying professions not desired by men. The heads of hospitals and schools were almost always male. Women comprised 51 per cent of the work force but two-thirds of them were involved in manual labor in 1980. Women's hourly pay of about 68–70 percent that of men was lower than most Western European countries.

Women occupied an inferior place in the home. Even among those who held jobs on the outside, most still did all the housework. And because they lacked labour-saving devices and seldom dined out, their household work was much more arduous than in the West. The comment of a divorced woman – one of three marriages end in divorce – captured the frustration felt by many overworked women, 'I doubt that I will ever marry again. Why should I? Having a husband is like having another baby in the apartment.'

Added to the household duties were the long lines in the shops. Soviet women spent as much as two hours each day waiting in lines and a 1985 average of 27 hours a week on shopping and housekeeping compared to six hours for men. A Polish survey found that the amount of time queuing increased from 63 to 98 minutes a day between 1966 and 1976. It is true that child-care centres leave wives free to work, but this often simply means that a woman works both day and night without the satisfaction that comes with raising her own child. Except for the annual vacations, leisure is an unknown concept for Eastern European women.

Women have also suffered at the hands of central planners. With only one factory producing condoms and a very limited supply of birth-control pills, Soviet women chose to undergo from four to six abortions in their lives rather than face increasing poverty. A 1985 estimate of only official abortions placed them at 2.08 for each birth.

Social Structure

Post-war economic modernization and Communist-inspired social changes transformed the East's social structure. In the Soviet Union Stalinist purges destroyed the former ruling classes during the interwar period. In Eastern Europe they lost their privileged positions after 1945.

Poland provides a clear example of the decline of a former ruling aristocracy. Those aristocrats who did not flee Poland as World War II drew to a close lost both their property and their political power. Some are now part of the professional and service classes. Perhaps the best example of this transformation is the experience of the famous Potocki and Radziwill families.

In the interwar period, the Potocki family owned nine million acres of land and eighteen towns and employed countless peasants. When the Communists expropriated their land after the war, one member of the family, Ignacz Potocki, became a common laborer. But he had had a superior education and by the late 1950s the government's fear of the former aristocracy had declined. So Potocki, who was an expert on medicinal springs, became chief geologist of the Ministry of Health and Social Welfare. Many of the prominent Radziwills have also found employment – as engineers, accountants and book publishers.

Hungary and Romania, which had had large and wealthy aristocracies, experienced a similar social revolution. But in Bulgaria, Yugoslavia and Albania, where land was owned primarily by the peasants, no such social transformation occurred.

All the Eastern European countries were primarily agrarian – 60 to 75 per cent of the working population was engaged in agriculture at the end of the second World War The nationalization of industry therefore had far less impact on the social structures than did the destruction of the landed aristocracy. Only in Czechoslovakia and East Germany did the nationalization of industry displace a significant segment of the population.

Changes in Education

Nowhere were the social changes more dramatic than in education. Some Eastern states were ruthless in their determination to eliminate social privilege in education. In the 1950s university quotas were introduced for each social group throughout Eastern Europe. In East Germany, which Ralf Dahrendorf called the first modern society on German soil, at least half the student populations in all secondary schools had to be workers' and peasants' children. This requirement, along with the elimination of private property, succeeded in eliminating the grasp of the former elite on advanced education. By 1963, one-third of all university students and half the students in technical colleges came from working-class families.

This change meant that a much larger percentage of professors, judges, generals and industrial managers came from working-class backgrounds. In comparison with the West, especially France and West Germany, Table 9–6 shows that the number of children from labouring-class backgrounds in universities was much higher in Eastern Europe by the 1960s.

However, Soviet and East European leaders retreated from the view that working-class children should have preference in higher education. Soviet leaders argued that all citizens are now socially equal. Though preferential points are still allocated for social origin, points were also allocated for political attitude and for work experience obtained after secondary school. This system permits influential *Nomenklatura* families to gain preferential treatment for their children. These practices tended to favor the children

Table 9–5 Per-capita meat consumption in 1978 and 1989 (in kilograms)

	1978	1989
USSR	49	67
East Germany	68	—
Hungary	72	—
Poland	86	—
West Germany	87	—
United States	116	—

Sources: John L. Sherer, ed., *USSR: Facts and Figures Annual*, vol. 6 (1982), 298. Wikrasik, ed., *USSR: Facts and Figures Annual*, vol. 17 (1992), 291.

of the elite. In 1971, children of blue-collar workers – numbering about 60 per cent of the population – comprised 36 per cent of those in higher education, compared to almost 60 per cent for children of white-collar workers. East Germany dropped the 50 per cent clause in order to provide sufficient competent managers for its rapidly industrializing economy. By 1981–82, only 10.2 per cent of Soviet youth entering the university were rural residents. In Poland, working-class children comprised 39.1 per cent and peasant children 24.2 per cent of those reaching higher education in 1951–52 but only 24.8 per cent and 12.2 per cent respectively in 1976–77. The proportion of the working class in the population increased from 39.3 to 40 per cent during this time while the peasantry decreased from 36.7 to 30.4 per cent.

Higher education became more selective with only 11 per cent of Polish and 7 per cent of Czechoslovak youth of the appropriate age group entering higher education, or figures much lower than the proportion entering higher education in the United States and most Western European countries. As in the West the children of the elite had higher aspirations than those below them and prepared themselves in special courses for the entrance examinations. In Poland in 1976–77, 60 per cent of teachers and researchers' children had such preparation while only 25 per cent of workers' children received such preparation. In spite of this trend to select future leaders from a more privileged sector of society, the number of children from working-class homes still considerably exceeded that of the West.

The Elite

Critics of the Communist regimes have charged that a new elite class replaced the former elites throughout Eastern Europe. Central to the question of a new class was the distribution both of rewards and of power. Was there, in fact, a small privileged elite that siphoned off a major part of the wealth and privileges of the Soviet Union and Eastern Europe? The Communist ideal was that what each person gets is determined by his or her need. Was this changed so that what each person gets is determined by his or her relationship to the ruling elite? Was power monopolized at the top in a totalitarian fashion, or was it distributed among various groups within the society? In sum, were the promises of Communist society realized?

There is no escaping the fact that a new ruling stratum replaced the old ruling classes. But it was similar to the old ruling groups primarily in its monopoly of political power and privilege, not in its monopoly of wealth. There were no individuals in the East compared with millionaires in the West. Property and inheritance were limited to personal real estate and belongings, and it was difficult to profit from personal savings; therefore, inherited wealth could not be the basis for a new capitalist class. But what of the concept of a new class popularized by Milovan Djilas, a close associate of Tito and formerly vice-president of Communist Yugoslavia? If the new-class label is restricted to those who exercised political power and benefited more than others from their favored position, then the theory has considerable validity. Top political,

Table 9–6   Worker and peasant students at Czech, East German
and Polish universities

	Czech Lands (Student Body)	East Germany (Student Body)	Poland (Freshmen)
1945–46	—	10.1	—
1946–47	18.4	—	—
1947–48	18.0	16.8	41.7
1949–50	—	34.0	45.6
1950–51	36.8	38.6	62.2
1951–52	—	41.0	59.9
1952–53	—	45.4	59.4
1953–54	37.3	—	57.8
1955–56	37.0	54.8	53.9
1956–57	38.4	56.6	48.5
1958–59	41.5	57.7	44.7
1960–61	37.8	56.0	44.5

Sources: Connelly, J. (2000), *Captive University: the Sovietization of East German, Czech, and Polish Higher Education, 1945–1956*, (The University of North Carolina Press: Chapel Hill and London), p. 252.

administrative, military, and economic officials had such special privileges as special stores, paid vacations at select sites, and preference in education and jobs for their children. These special privileges became apparent to eastern Europeans only after the overthrow of these regimes in 1989–90.

Marshal Tito became highly critical of the life-styles of some people in the Yugoslav ruling stratum. In 1973 he said it was time for Yugoslavia to rid itself of the deformations that had 'brought shame to a Socialist society.' To avert the development of a new 'oppressive class', Tito stole a page from Chairman Mao's book. He removed about 100,000 members from the League of Communists and ordered all elected officeholders to retain their previous jobs while carrying out their new duties in their spare time.

Like political parties in the West, Communist parties became more professionalized and less worker-oriented. In a 1980s survey, 70 per cent of the Communist party members in one Soviet province were found to have come from white-collar occupations – managers, technicians, and government and party bureaucrats. Eastern societies could not change this trend radically, since they found it impossible to industrialize without leaders who had the knowledge and training that could be provided only by the professional classes.

The Beginnings of Pluralism?

A final important question concerning Communist bloc countries is whether these new ruling strata were relatively open. Did they monopolize power in totalitarian fashion as former rulers had done, or were decisions influenced by interest groups that had no strong party connections? Contrary to interest groups in the Western pluralist societies, we find that leaders of the various interest groups were often closely affiliated with the Communist parties. However, as these various interest groups became more professionalized, they tended to be less closely associated with the party.

The dominance of the Communist parties over decision-making was tied rather closely to economic development. Where the economies could still be described as underdeveloped, as in Bulgaria, Albania and Romania, the party rigidly dominated political and economic decision-making. But in the more developed societies, such as the Soviet Union, East Germany, Poland and Hungary, decision making spread beyond the narrow confines of the party bureaucracy.

Despite Soviet attempts to block or limit discussion of issues, decision-making moved from the narrow court politics of Stalin. Whereas Stalin issued orders after consulting only his closest associates, Khrushchev opened up debate to a much larger segment of the society. His successor, Brezhnev, again restricted decision-making to a small oligarchy of Politburo members and a few influential military and industrial leaders. But Gorbachev launched a campaign to modernize the Soviet Union through the free flow of information that he believed responsible for economic advance in the West. Ironically, Gorbachev's opening up of debate in the press over his economic reforms, discussed in Chapter 11, ultimately contributed to his loss of power when the discussion went beyond the reforms he intended.

In the developed Eastern European states, the decision-making process was never as closed as it was in the Soviet Union. In countries such as Poland, the Communist party never achieved complete control over the Roman Catholic Church, the peasantry, or labour. Opposition to agrarian collectivization was so stout that the political authorities eventually had to drop their plans to eliminate private farming. Polish intellectuals continued to criticize the regime even during the Stalinist Gomulka regime.

Labour unions and business groups were much more powerful in Poland than in the Soviet Union. Unions nominated business leaders who had a veto power over the decisions of the state economic planning executives. The violent strikes of 1956 and 1970 and the Solidarity Movement of the 1980s and the changes they precipitated are a further indication of the limits of the party's power. Throughout Eastern Europe, the Communist parties' monopoly of power was challenged in the late 1980s before the regimes collapsed.

In Yugoslavia, where economic decision-making was decentralized, the League of Communists lost power rapidly after Tito's death. Tito, in fact, had second thoughts about decentralization since in his opinion it led to a revival of regionalism and 'social democratic' thinking. He removed most of the Croatian party leaders in the early 1970s because of their desire to concentrate on Croatian rather than Yugoslav development. They opposed sending a part of the profits from Croatian industry and tourism to the poorer areas in the south. After Tito's death, a collective leadership with a presidency that alternated among party officials from the various republics was unable to stem a growing regionalism and may have contributed to the disintegration that occurred in the 1990s. Finally, without the intervention of the Soviet Union, most Eastern European countries would long ago have developed pluralistic societies in the pattern of Western Europe.

As this chapter has argued, public debate over national priorities occurred even before the events of the late 1980s. Eastern European societies had already stepped up the production of consumer goods in the face of increasing public demand. But these concessions had not changed the power structure significantly. In fact, the attainment of some economic freedom from the rigid centralization and collectivization common in the East was often permitted as a sort of safety-valve to obscure the lack of independence. Hungary's rather successful private or 'secondary economy' long existed in a society totally controlled by a small party elite at the top. Once pronouncements by Gorbachev indicated that they were free to introduce greater democratization, the democratic forces soon began to dismantle the Soviet-supported regimes as discussed in Chapter 11.

FURTHER READING

Several edited studies have been particularly helpful in the preparation of this chapter: Pierre Kende and Zdenek Strimiska (ed.) *Equality and Inequality in Eastern Europe* (1987); Richard Sakwa *Soviet Politics in Perspective* 2nd ed. (1989) and Seweryn Bialer (ed.), *Politics, Society and Nationality inside Gorbachev's Russia* (1989). The Kende/Strmiska volume provides several excellent studies of education (Janina Markiewicz-Lagneau), political power (Strmiska) and social mobility (Strmiska). Also useful as a reference is Stephen White (ed.) *Political and Economic Encyclopaedia of the Soviet Union and Eastern Europe* (1990), which provides entries over a wide range of actors, institutions, policies and events.

The views expressed by Alex Inkeles and Raymond A. Bauer in *The Soviet Citizen* (1959) are voiced in later works. They maintained that Soviet citizens accept the Soviet way of life even though they may reject certain leaders. They want the security that comes with collectivism, central planning, comprehensive socialization and single-party rule. More recent studies of Soviet society are John G. Eriksen, *The Development of Soviet Society* (1970); David Lane, *Politics and Society in the USSR* (1971) and *Soviet Economy and Society* (1985).

Criticisms of Soviet society from Soviet citizens include the sharp denunciations of Andrei Amalrik, *Will the Soviet Union Survive Until 1984?* (1970); and Aleksandr Solzhenitsyn, *One Day in the Life of Ivan Denisovich* and *The Gulag Archipelago*. For less polemical criticisms see Roy Medvedev, *On Socialist Democracy* (1975) and *Let History Judge* (1971). The most important non-Russian criticism came from Milovan Djilas in *The New Class* (1957) and *The Unperfect Society: Beyond the New Class* (1969). Works about dissent in the Soviet Union include: Ludmilla Alexeyeva, *Soviet Dissent: Contemporary Movements for National, Religious and Human Rights* (1985); Rudolf Tokes (ed.), *Dissent in the USSR: Politics, Ideology, and People* (1975); and Marshall Shatz, *Soviet Dissent in Historical Perspective* (1980). Social conditions are examined in Mervyn

Matthews, *Privilege in the Soviet Union* (1978) and James Miller (ed.), *Politics, Work and Daily Life in the USSR* (1987). Corruption in the Soviet Union analyzed by Konstantin M. Simis, *USSR: The Corrupt Society* (1982). Much of his evidence comes from his 17 years experience as an advocate in Soviet trials.

The standard work on the Soviet economy is Alec Nove, *The Soviet Economic System* (3rd ed. 1981). Outstanding studies of the Soviet economy under Gorbachev are Anders Aslund, *Gorbachev's Struggle for Economic Reform* (1991); Marshall Goldman, *Lost Opportunity: Why Economic Reforms in Russia Have Not Worked* (1995); and Paul Gregory and Robert Stuart, *Soviet and Post-Soviet Economic Structure and Performance* (5th ed., 1993). A dated but still valuable study is David Granick, *The Red Executive: A Study of the Organization Man in Russian Industry* (1960). For Khrushchev's agricultural policies see Martin McCauley, *Khrushchev and the Development of Soviet Agriculture: The Virgin Land Programme, 1953–1964* (1976). McCauley believes Khrushchev's error was not in planting virgin lands but in doing it in excess.

The Soviet worker is presented in A. Brodersen, *The Soviet Worker* (1966); Robert Conquest (ed.), *Industrial Workers in the USSR* (1967); David Lane and F. O'Dell, *The Soviet Industrial Worker: Social Class, Education and Control* (1978); and L. Shapiro and J. Godson (eds.), *The Soviet Worker: From Lenin to Andropov* (1984).

For Soviet women see Feiga Blekher, *The Soviet Woman in the Family and in Society* (1979); Alena Heitlinger, *Women and State Socialism* (1979); Alastair McAuley, *Women's Work and Wages in the Soviet Union* (1981); Gail W. Lapidus, *Women, Work, and Family in the Soviet Union* (1982); Mary Buckley, *Perestroika and Soviet Women* (1992); and Linda Edmondson, *Women and Society in Russia and the Soviet Union* (1992).

Details concerning the health problems in the USSR can be found in Christopher Davis and Murray Feshbach, *Rising Infant Mortality in the USSR in the 1970s* (1980). The revealing comparative figures on infant mortality rates used in this chapter can be found in J. C. Chesnais, *The Demographic Transition* (1992) and *Social Indicators of Development* (1990). A devastating account of environmental and health problems in the former USSR is found in Murray Feshbach and Alfred Friendly, Jr., *Ecocide in the USSR: Health and Nature under Siege* (1992).

Three accounts of Soviet life by journalists are Hedrick Smith, *The Russians* (1976), Robert G. Kaiser, *Russia: The People and the Power* (1976) and David Shipler, *Russia* (1983). All contend that the classless society is a myth in the Soviet Union, that Soviet industry is inefficient, and that the Soviet population is influenced by a pervasive collectivist mentality. Both agree with Inkeles and Bauer that Soviet citizens equate freedom with danger and disorder and believe the state has given them the security they yearn for by providing cheap housing, sufficient food, guaranteed employment, free education and medical care and pensions for the old and disabled. Much good information on living conditions can be found in Abram Bergson and Herbert Levine, eds., *The Soviet Economy: Toward the Year 2000* (1983).

A valuable broad synthesis of politics and society in Eastern Europe is Ghita Ionescu, *The Politics of the European Communist States* (1967). Ionescu argued that the West underestimated the extent of political dissent in Eastern Europe in the sixties. He claimed that the Eastern European countries had an embryonic form of pluralism in the sixties and predicted that they would continue to become more democratic and less communistic. Other studies include Stephen Fischer-Galati, *Eastern Europe in the 1980s* (1982), and Walter D. Connor, *Socialism, Politics, and Equality: Hierarchy and Change in Eastern Europe and the USSR* (1979). A recent comparative study explaining higher education recruitment policies in regards to social class during the first decade of Communist rule is John Connelly, *Captive University: The Sovietization of East German, Czech, and Polish Higher Education, 1945–1956* (2000).

There are many more studies of the Eastern European economies. An important study of the workings of Comecon is Michael Kaser's *Comecon: Integration Problems of the Planned Economies* (1965). There are many studies of the Yugoslav economic system, especially of the Workers' Councils. Competent studies are Jiri Kolaja, *Workers' Councils: The Yugoslav Experience* (1965); M. J. Broekmeyer (ed.), *Yugoslav Workers' Self-management 1947–64* (1968); and Ichak Adizes, *Industrial Democracy: Yugoslav Style* (1971). For a discussion of Yugoslav self-management see Duncan Wilson, *Tito's Yugoslavia* (1979). John Michael Montias, in *Economic Development in Communist Romania* (1967), has detailed Romania's attempts to establish a diversified economy.

The general works listed in the bibliography following Chapter 6 contain information on economics and society in the other East European states. Jean Edward Smith, in *Germany Beyond the Wall* (1967), describes the rapid economic growth in East Germany and the transformation of society. See also A. Zauberman, *Industrial Progress in Poland, Czechoslovakia and East Germany, 1937–1962* (1964); and J. F. Brown, *The New Eastern Europe* (1966) and *Eastern Europe and Communist Rule* (1988). An important collection of essays on the Eastern European worker is Jan F. Triska and Charles Gati, eds., *Blue-Collar Workers in Eastern Europe* (1981) as well as Charles Gati, *The Politics of Modernization in Eastern Europe* (1974). Changes in the Hungarian economy since the economic reforms of 1968 are excellently treated in Paul Hare, Hugo Radice and Nigel Swain, eds., *Hungary: A Decade of Economic Reform* (1981). Finally, Judy Batt, *East Central Europe from reform to Transformation* (1991) emphasizes the politics and economics of the transition period.

See the Further Reading section of Chapter 11 for political studies of events from the 1970s to the 1990s.

10 1968: Year of Crisis and Its Legacies

> To speak of repression in the case of an institution possessing no 'physical' repressive power, such as a university, may seem paradoxical. This repression is part of the very functioning of the institution, its structure, which makes the student passive, because he interiorizes its norms and requirements ... . This passivity kills all real desire and all creative spirit, the expressions of a non-alienated life.
>
> Daniel Cohn–Bendit, in *The Action-Image of Society*, Alfred Willener

> We have introduced the spectre of liquidation of the absolute power of the bureaucratic caste, a caste introduced to the international scene by Stalinist socialism ... . But bureaucracy, even if it has not the dimensions of a class, still shows its characteristics in anything that concerns the exercise of power. It takes preventive measures to defend itself and it will do so to the bitter end ... . We do not endanger socialism: to the contrary. We endanger bureaucracy, which has been slowly but surely burying socialism on a worldwide scale.
>
> 'The Luxury of Illusions,' *Prague Reporter*, 31 July 1968
> The internal hierarchy is to be abolished. Every employee, no matter what his job, will receive the same pay ... .
>
> French workers' pamphlet, Assurance Generale de France, 1968

On its way towards the affluent society, Western Europe was shocked by a series of student-led demonstrations and strikes in 1968 that ultimately brought into question much of what Europe's leaders had been trying to achieve since 1945. Before the riots began, some political scientists had suggested that the relative absence of serious political turmoil could only be explained by an 'end of ideology' brought about by the inappropriateness of radical solutions in the modern welfare state. Both in Europe and in the United States during the 1950s students seemed to have little interest in politics. Although American students became more active in the early 1960s, in response to the civil rights movement and then to the Vietnam War, Europe's students remained quiet. Even if students had been dissatisfied, no one expected that their activities could harm the stable advanced European societies, let alone nearly bring down the government in France.

196

When unrest did erupt, it was not confined to Western Europe as the different opening quotes illustrate. In Czechoslovakia, students and reform-minded Communist party members overthrew an ossified bureaucratic party leadership and blew a breath of fresh air into the party before they themselves fell to Soviet forces in late 1968. Despite the obvious political differences between France and Czechoslovakia, both had come to be perceived by the demonstrators as authoritarian, bureaucratic states that were unresponsive to the needs of the citizenry.

Danger signals, had the political community been alert to them, had already begun to appear in Western Europe in the early 1960s. Dissatisfaction and unrest, first evident in Italy, were directed at the overcrowding in universities, the outdated curriculum and the authoritarian attitude and archaic teaching methods of the professors. The medieval university, where students could select and fire professors, provided a model for students dissatisfied with the overcrowded, bureaucratic Italian universities. In 1967 the ratio of students to professors was 105 to 1, as against 13 to 1 in the United States and 23 to 1 in French universities.

The problem was one not merely of numbers but also of the attitude of European professors. A privileged small professorial elite opposed increasing the number of full professors and making curriculum changes, especially those aimed at instituting new disciplines such as sociology and psychology. Sociology was being taught in faculties of architecture, because of its relevance to urban planning, but professors in general refused to acknowledge sociology as a genuine discipline.

Student Unrest in Italy and Germany

As early as 1965 students rioted at the University of Milan and the University of Trento demanding reforms in the curriculum and a voice in university governance. The most militant students at Milan were those in the faculties of architecture, where courses on sociology were taught. At Trento where the only faculty of sociology existed, students demanded that the university be more closely related to the demands of the modern world. Clearly, the professors had been correct in fearing the consciousness-raising potential of sociology.

After 1967, the students began to incorporate other issues into their protests. In general, there were two orientations to the demands. First, there was an anti-authoritarian discourse; second, a class-conflict discourse. The first was especially strong in the early stages of protest, as it cut across many types of student background. The most widespread tactic of protest from 1967 to 1969 was the university occupation. Despite the common 'enemy' though, the two wings of the student movement occasionally clashed with each other. Gradually, the style of protest changed as the student movement interacted with other groups, such as workers and the New Left. By 1969, the movement had lost momentum, but not before tactics other than occupations and sit-ins, namely political violence, had entered the repertoire.

In West Germany in 1966 the formation of the Grand Coalition, a political partnership between the Christian Democrats and the Social Democrats, ignited the first German student protests. Student leaders of the German Socialist Students' Federation (SDS) felt betrayed by the Social Democrats' actions. They now considered the SPD an integral part of the establishment and therefore uninterested in reform.

The students gave voice to their discontent in widespread protests against the Shah of Iran's repressive regime during his visit to West Berlin in 1967. Underlying this outburst was hostility over German and American support of the shah. The death of one student, Benno Ohnesorg, in the riots steeled the students in their determination to bring down the establishment.

The next target was the conservative newspaper–magazine empire of Axel Springer, whose publications had viciously attacked student leaders such as Rudi Dutschke. When Dutschke was shot by a deranged man, at Easter, 1968, masses of students rose against Springer and succeeded in disrupting the distribution of his newspapers and magazines. In the summer of 1968, in West Berlin, students took part in an organized and violent clash with the police known as the 'Battle of Tegeler Weg'. This event saw the split of the SDS into two factions, one arguing for the legitimate use of violence, the other – the majority – supporting only limited lawbreaking.

Although German students were unable to mount a serious challenge to government policies, they did achieve important changes in the universities. They now have a share in university governance and have impelled most professors to change their teaching methods. As a result of chaotic disturbances in the universities during the height of the turmoil, many professors decided to leave the classrooms for good. And it is now commonplace in German universities to have student-suggested courses in which professors are participants rather than lecturers.

Protest in France

Until 1968, French universities remained so calm that students from Italy and Germany began to doubt the presumed revolutionary mentality of the French. Yet when the explosion came in 1968, it rocked not only the universities but also the Gaullist government. A number of extreme left student groups – Trotskyites, Maoists, and anarchists – had existed since early in the decade. But they could speak for only a minority of the students and had no support at all among the remaining population.

Another surprising thing about the events of 1968 was that they came at a time of unquestioned prosperity and national grandeur. De Gaulle and France played a far greater role in the world than was justified by the nation's resources. Why, then, did the student-led protests in France spread to a much larger segment of the population than elsewhere and lead, despite a resounding election triumph in late 1968, to de Gaulle's resignation?

The immediate causes of protest in France were little different from those in Italy and Germany. For French students the Vietnam War became a symbol of the misplaced priorities of all military-industrial complexes, including the Gaullist regime. Especially annoying to students was de Gaulle's concentration on foreign affairs and his failure to respond to the often deplorable conditions in the universities. Classes at the famed Sorbonne sometimes had nearly 1000 students enrolled; those students who did not arrive early enough had to listen to lectures on closed-circuit television or buy copies of the lectures. The curriculum was filled with obsolete courses. There was little attention to sociology, or modern social problems, or career preparation for those not going on for advanced degrees.

Students directed their dissatisfaction at the French Ministry of National Education and local faculty governing bodies, which, in their opinion, were more interested in training a few researchers than in preparing the mass of students for less exalted careers. In response to student demands for relevance and participation in determining curriculum, the Ministry of Education fell back on tradition and repression. Another major issue grew out of the ministry's attempt to reduce overcrowding in the universities by making examinations more difficult. Therefore, the student demand for an end to examinations was an attempt to prevent the selection of only the gifted few for advanced degrees.

The Events at Nanterre Paradoxically, the protests began at the new university at Nanterre, which had been established to relieve the overcrowding at the Sorbonne. Despite the excellent facilities and lower student–teacher ratio, Nanterre became the centre for student dissatisfaction because it gave students a greater opportunity to question and sometimes embarass their teachers. Classes were interrupted often by questions about the Vietnam War or Franco's Spain. Young instructors and assistant professors, having only recently completed the traditional course of instruction, were hard put to answer these questions. Many of the younger faculty members were won over to the idea of reform of the education system. Moreover, the location of Nanterre near one of the shanty towns housing immigrant labourers promoted debate beyond purely university and academic matters. The contrast between the students' almost entirely middle-class backgrounds, and the living conditions they saw around them convinced many students that the government was impervious not only to the need for change in the university but also to the plight of the poor.

The first incident occurred in November 1967 when sociology students at Nanterre, one of the few universities with a separate sociology faculty, resisted the introduction of a reform plan – called the Fouchet Plan – by the Ministry of Education. Student opposition to the plan foreshadowed the later more violent conflict over the role of the student in university governance. Although the Fouchet Plan responded to some student complaints by providing one course of study for those pursuing the *license* (roughly equivalent to our bachelor's degree) and another for those going on for advanced degrees, the course of study was lengthened by one year for some students. However, it was not merely the Fouchet Plan that aroused dissatisfaction. Both the Ministry of Education and the deans of the faculties refused to let students discuss the changes or participate in the faculty committee governing the school of sociology that debated the plan. This incensed the students and triggered the eruption. The Nanterre protest failed, but it paved the way for the more violent reaction that was to come because it convinced student radicals that a moderate demand for a student voice in university governance was doomed to fail.

During the four months following the initial incident at Nanterre, student radicals (*enragés*) gradually brought together the four major issues of what came to be called the March 22 Movement: opposition to Gaullism; rejection of the organization and structure of the university system; student freedom; and protest against the Vietnam War. While the Maoists and Trotskyites concentrated on the Vietnam issue, Daniel Cohn-Bendit led other students at Nanterre against all forms of administrative, political, intellectual and sexual repression.

Cohn-Bendit's support for sexual freedom was a part of the much larger issue that students should be free to decide their own living conditions on campus. It was also a challenge to the repression that Cohn-Bendit found throughout the society. Cohn-Bendit also struck out at the ossified, bureaucratic French Communist Party that he considered unresponsive to demands for change. His campaign instilled a desire for action into a left that had theretofore limited itself to the discussion of revolutionary objectives.

When the university attempted to expel Cohn-Bendit, the conflict enlarged beyond the revolutionary left. First the sociology department assembly, composed of faculty and students, came out in support of Cohn-Bendit. Gaining confidence as they picked up student and faculty support, student leaders became more outspoken and disruptive. When the Vietnam Committee leaders were arrested on 22 March, students invaded and occupied the administration building at Nanterre.

From this point onward, many rooms at Nanterre became meeting places for student groups engaged in discussing the university structure, Vietnam, and student-worker relations. By April many instructors and assistant professors had joined these discussion groups. This breakdown in the traditional relationships among faculty members unnerved the dean of the faculty of letters. Then student leaders proposed two anti-imperialist days for 2 and 3 May at Nanterre, and a rightist student group began gathering support for an attack on the student radicals. At this point the dean decided to close the university on 2 May. With this decision, Nanterre ceased to be the center of agitation. The supporters of the March 22 Movement then moved to the Sorbonne and the potentially more volatile Latin Quarter.

The Events at the Sorbonne   The protest at the Sorbonne might have been confined to the university community had not the violent reaction of the police enlarged the scope of the 'events of May' to other groups in the society. Cohn-Bendit and other leaders of the March 22 Movement had been notified that they were to face the disciplinary council of the University of Paris on 6 May. More than 400 leftist students, including the March 22 Movement leaders, met at the Sorbonne on 3 May to discuss their course of action at Nanterre. The rector at the Sorbonne, acting on the advice of the Ministry of

Paris demonstration in support of French students, May 13, 1968.
(© Topham Picturepoint)

Education, decided to call in the police in the hope that such a move would break the back of the student protest movement.

The sight of students being thrown into police vans on university grounds spread the protest beyond the original student activists, since a centuries old tradition guaranteed the security of students within university walls, and the police had not entered any university grounds since 1791.

In the Latin Quarter that night, police battled thousands of students who were demanding that the imprisoned students be freed. Three days later, on Bloody Sunday, thousands of students and faculty sympathizers armed with cobblestones battled police around the Sorbonne. Although 435 policemen and an untold number of demonstrators were injured, battles continued day after day in the Latin Quarter.

From 3 May to 13 May the protest movement was predominantly a student struggle, fought out in the streets. As the injury toll mounted, public opinion swung to the students. The police were stymied. The more they attacked, the greater grew the number of demonstrators and the popular support for the insurrection. The government turned a deaf ear to student demands to remove the police, open the faculties at the Sorbonne, and grant an amnesty to the imprisoned demonstrators. The confrontation continued.

Ultimately, on the Night of the Barricades – 10–11 May – students surrounded the Sorbonne and the police with makeshift barricades. The barricades symbolized the students' refusal to abandon the Latin Quarter to the police and provided the psychological boost to keep the protest alive. The police attack on the barricades, followed by beatings of students in the police vans and at police stations, had several repercussions: it launched the general strike of 13 May; it brought on the government's capitulation; it triggered the student occupation of the Sorbonne; and it spread the protest far beyond the original student nucleus.

From Student Protest to General Strike   It was at this point that the French upheaval went beyond the student uprisings elsewhere. Whereas German students had had to face the wrath of workers, French students got their support. This cannot be explained by wages alone since the French workers were not content to accept a wage increase negotiated on 27 May. What is more, neither the Communist party, nor the CGT, usually dominated by it, had approved of the workers' joining the students.

Workers, especially the young ones, were protesting their lack of decision-making power in an ever more complex bureaucratized world. Among other things, they were asking for greater delegation of authority – the right of co-management – just as the students were. French industry, led by the major federation of French employers, the *Conseil National du Patronat Français* (CNPF), resolutely supported its traditional authoritarianism. Most industrialists, with CNPF backing, had refused to set up or empower the factory management-workers councils, *comités d'entreprise*, that had been established under de Gaulle after the war. Although these councils had no real share in management decisions but were limited to overseeing welfare activities and conferring with management, by 1965 only 6000 and 25,000 firms had complied with a 1945 ordinance to establish them. During the demonstrations, the *Confédération Français et Démocratique de Travail* (CFDT), a labour union with strength among both blue- and white-collar workers, made its position plain:

> The student struggle to democratize the university and the workers' struggle to democratize industry are one and the same. The constraints and institutions against which the students are rebelling are paralleled by even more intolerable forms in factories, or worksites, in offices and workshops ... . Industrial and administrative monarchy must be replaced by democratic institutions based on self management.

Some of those who joined in the protest were white-collar workers who also desired a change in the bureaucracies that governed them. Striking workers at the *Assurance Générale de France* (AGF), the second-largest French insurance company, demanded that those in positions of responsibility 'be accountable for their actions to the entire staff', that they be subject to dismissal 'by those who have appointed them', and that AGF property and stock become 'the property of all, managed by all'.

To protesting workers and intellectuals the Gaullist regime seemed the prime example of an overbureaucratized, technocratic, soulless institution. With the Communist party becoming a part of this mammoth bureaucracy, workers saw little hope for change. Workers' slogans during the uprising, such as 'down with alienation', and 'co-management', expressed their sense of estrangement.

The strike of producers and journalists at the nationalized French television stations characterized the rebellion of many, including young physicians and other professionals, and showed that the events of May were not restricted to students and workers. Television producers saw the May riots as their opportunity to end the centralization of programming and to gain a measure of local autonomy. Everywhere it was the same – a reaction against the centralization of authority that had stripped the individual of his right to make decisions. As former premier Pierre Mendès-France explained in 1968:

> The dispute is not simply over personalities or institutions. It also dramatizes the determination of Frenchmen no longer to be considered impotent subjects in a harsh, inhumane, conservative society, but rather to perform their own role freely in a society they can look upon as really their own.

With the power of the workers thrown into the fray, the Gaullist regime was soon on the verge of collapse.

On 13 May a twenty-four-hour labour strike brought Paris to a standstill. Nearly 300,000 people marched in a Paris without transportation, electricity, or postal service. Beginning on 15 May, throughout France workers occupied factories, set up strike committees, even established worker management of factories. Everywhere, the organization and management of the firms were criticized more than the workers' material conditions. Signs appeared proclaiming, 'The boss needs you – you don't need him.' By 17 May nearly 10 million workers were out on strike and hundreds of young workers had joined the demonstrators in the streets. Action committees and student soviets sprang up all over France. The massive worker response finally forced the Communist party to support labour's demands for reforms. Even the Socialist party, led by Mitterrand, joined the protest movement when it appeared that the Gaullist regime could be toppled. Under duress, the government negotiated a settlement with the CGT that increased wages substantially. But when the rank and file refused to accept the agreement, the nation was at a standstill. Mendès-France and Mitterrand offered an alternative government but the Communist party refused to cooperate with them.

De Gaulle's Counterattack Until 30 May, when de Gaulle finally acted, the protestors had good reason to believe that the government would fall. Except for the beleaguered police in the streets, little had been heard from the government. When de Gaulle left Paris on 29 May, many expected him to relinquish power. Only his close associates knew that he had gone to West Germany to assure himself of the support of French troops stationed there.

Some of the causes for the discontent were not clear to the government when de Gaulle began his counterattack. He was inclined to the belief that worker demands for higher wages and student excesses were primary causes of the unrest. In any case, he had no intentions of tolerating what he considered to be anarchy or allowing his plans for French grandeur to be put in jeopardy.

After visiting the commander of French troops in West Germany, de Gaulle returned to Paris and announced new parliamentary elections for June and firm measures to end the anarchy. In a television address on 30 May, in order to rally all anti-communist forces to his side he unjustly accused the Communist party of instigating the outbreaks. Then he presented France with a choice: communism or Gaullism. As the students feared, his pleas were answered with massive support from most of the bourgeoisie and from the provincial areas. Immediately following his speech, one million French, including many from the provinces, staged a mass demonstration in Paris in favor of de Gaulle. This outpouring of support demoralized the rioters. Workers ended their occupation of factories and students left the colleges they had seized. De Gaulle arrested radical leaders and outlawed leftist student groups. The same forces that rallied to de Gaulle, which had been afraid to speak out during the height of the crisis, gave de Gaulle an impressive majority in the June elections; Gaullists increased their representation in the legislature from 200 to 299, while the left's representation dropped from 194 to 100.

De Gaulle's victory was short-lived. Within a year he felt it necessary to resign when his proposed changes to the Senate were rejected in a referendum. The Gaullists remained in power for five years more, losing the presidency in 1974, partly as a result of a changed attitude in France brought about by the events of 1968. Even during the presidency of de Gaulle's successor George Pompidou, national priorities had been moving toward happiness (*bonheur*) and away from grandeur. This in itself meant greater attention to pressing domestic problems and less attention to France's world mission.

For the students and workers, the results of 1968 can be measured with greater accuracy. University students gained many of their demands. Overcrowding in universities was relieved, by increasing the number of universities from twenty-two to sixty-five. Students achieved a measure of joint management in most universities. Greater autonomy, although much less than students fought for, has permitted universities to avoid some of the rigid centralization of instruction under the Ministry of Education. The more radical demands for the abolition of exams and an end to the Ministry of Education itself have not been granted.

Labourers received increased pay following the riots (see Chapter 10), but they were still among the lowest paid in Western Europe. Workers also won the right to be represented through their unions on the governing boards in some enterprises; union representatives were given some free time to carry out union duties during working hours. Although workers did not achieve joint management, which was so important an aspect of their demands in 1968, they did receive flexible hours and a relaxation of the strict factory discipline. French managers, incapable of overcoming their hierarchical conceptions of factory relations, resolutely opposed giving workers a share in factory management.

Unrest in Czechoslovakia: The Prague Spring

Although there are many differences between the unrest in the West and in Czechoslovakia in 1968, there was one major similarity: the revolt against centralized, bureaucratic, authoritarian structures. Under the leadership of Antonin Novotny, Czechoslovakia had instituted rigid centralization by the early 1960s. Even though two Communist parties existed in the country, one in Slovakia and one in the Czech lands, all areas of the country were ruled dictatorially from Prague. Economic growth was slowed by rigid planning and resource allocation. No important decisions of any kind could be made without the approval of the Communist party in Prague.

Novotny was quite popular when he came to power in 1957 because he had rid the party of Stalinists, but his brand of authoritarian national communism soon became as oppressive as the Stalinism before him had been. Changes in Moscow, however, soon weakened his control over the party. The Soviet Union's continued denunciation of Stalin, Khrushchev's desires to decentralize economic decision making at home, and Yugoslav decentralization provided support for Czech reformers. The cultural division of the country into Czech and Slovak segments further weakened centralization.

Soviet denunciations of Stalinism had also encouraged Czech intellectuals to challenge Stalinist dogma at home. Czech Philosophers began to undermine the Stalinist system through the study and discussion of such unorthodox Marxists as Antonio Gramsci and Herbert Marcuse. They turned also to Marx's *Economic and Philosophical Manuscripts* where they found a humanist Marxist alternative to Stalinism. Marxism with a 'human face' began to appeal to Communist leaders wishing to legitimize their party's leadership. Historians began to weaken Stalinism by a frank investigation of the country's recent history. Czech and Slovak writers and film makers managed to conceal clever satires of the Stalinist leadership from censorship. By the time the authorities adopted harsh measures against the Writers' Union in late 1967, it only increased the resentment of reforming party members who had already been influenced by the criticism. This intellectual opposition would combine with desires for economic reforms and decentralization demands to slowly undermine the Stalinist leadership.

Slovak demands for economic decentralization soon received support from some Czech party members who sought to overcome a severe economic crisis that had begun in 1962. Because of the decentralization in the Soviet Union,

Czech and Slovak reformers felt they could try similar reforms at home. The Slovak party ousted its Stalinist leader, Karol Bacilek, in 1963 and replaced him with the reformer Alexander Dubcek. From 1963 until 1968, Novotny and the conservatives fought a losing battle against the reformers.

The conservatives' Achilles' heel proved to be the country's economic weakness. Led by economic expert Dr. Ota Sik, the reformers forced Novotny to accept decentralization of the economy in 1966. The reformers had managed to convince the party members that excessive planning, excessive resource allocation, and inattention to the consumer goods industry were responsible for Czechoslovakia's economic ills.

Novotny had been trying to fulfill Czechoslovakia's assigned role in Comecon as the producer of heavy industrial goods and had neglected to develop light industry. The economy had also suffered from a typical East European economic policy: instead of improving factories to overcome low output, Novotny merely built new factories and thus spread raw materials and labour even thinner. The reformers, following changes already instituted in Yugoslavia and the Soviet Union, succeeded in pushing through a system of profit accountability whereby industrial production could be measured more accurately (see Chapter 9).

In November, 1967 Novotny's position as party chairman received a decisive jolt. His savage suppression of student demonstrators from the Charles University in Prague protesting dormitory living conditions brought widespread sympathy for the students and strengthened the party reformers. The reformers, who joined with the Slovaks to form a majority in the Central Committee of the party, compared Novotny's treatment of the students to his opposition to all reformers within the party. With his base of support eroded, it was a simple matter to replace Novotny as party chairman in December 1967. The selection of an outspoken reformer, Dubcek, as his successor as First Secretary indicated the extent of the reformers' victory. In March 1968 Novotny lost his position as president of Czechoslovakia to a moderate, the military hero General Ludvik Svoboda. The reformers' April 1968 action program was an attempt to legitimize the Communist Party by making it defend its actions in public forums. As Dubcek said 'authority must be renewed, it's never given to anyone once and for all'. The programme guaranteed the freedoms of assembly, organization and movement and the protection of minority rights and personal property. It also intended to open up decision-making outside the party in order to promote initiative at the local level.

With Novotny gone, a relaxed and joyous mood set in throughout the country. By June 1968 the changed attitude was immediately evident. Caught up in the euphoria, Czechs informed visitors that they needed American economic and diplomatic aid, not military help. The press, carried away with its new-found freedom, was given to exaggerating the changes contemplated by the new leadership. There was discussion of a viable political opposition and a political system that, to the rest of the Communist world, smacked of Western parliamentary government.

This euphoria turned out to be one of Dubcek's major problems. Had he tried to prevent such discussion – and he may not have been able to do so – he might have lost the support of his countrymen; but unless he controlled the enthusiasm, he risked losing the support of the Soviet Union. Dubcek was never able to free himself from this problem. To illustrate Dubcek's difficulties, most newspapers published an extremely liberal manifesto, 'The Two Thousand Words', written by the most liberal elements in the country. The manifesto promised military support to Dubcek if other East European countries or the Soviet Union should invade, and it questioned the achievements of communism in Czechoslovakia. When Dubcek did not publicly denounce this manifesto, the other Eastern European states, all of them Warsaw Pact members, assumed that he approved it.

Despite Dubcek's repeated protestations of loyalty to a Communist-dominated state, his actions hardly served to allay fears in other Eastern capitals. In April Dubcek permitted non-communist political groups to form. Although he assured Moscow that these organizations would not become independent political parties but would be a part of the Communist-dominated National Front, it is easy to see why the Soviets would be suspicious. Further, the Communist party promised to bring to trial all those responsible for the Stalinist-inspired political trials in the 1950s, a move that threatened to incriminate Soviet officials. Some papers had in fact demanded an investigation into Soviet involvement in the apparent suicide of Czech Foreign Minister Jan Masaryk during the Communist coup in 1948.

From April until the Soviet invasion on 20 August 1968, the 'Czechoslovak experiment' became hopelessly entangled with Polish and East German fears that a similar 'democratic' contagion might spread to their countries, and with Soviet fears that Dubcek's policies might eventually lead Czechoslovakia out of the Warsaw Pact. As early as March Poland's leader Wladyslaw Gomulka had been upset by students' shouts of 'We want a Polish Dubcek.' But East German party secretary Walter Ulbricht was not merely upset; he feared that his weaker authoritarian regime could be overthrown by similar reformers.

Czech leaders had already established contacts with West Germany in order to open trade relations between the two countries. The Soviet Union was willing to permit more internal liberalization in Czechoslovakia than in East Germany or Poland, but was afraid that Czech reformers might eventually demand an independent foreign policy similar to that of Romania. Soviet hard-liners conjured up visions of an anti-Soviet alliance of Yugoslavia, Romania and Czechoslovakia.

Certainly Soviet military experts had much more to fear from a Czech withdrawal from the Warsaw Pact than they did from Romanian disaffection. Not only did Czechoslovakia border on Western Europe, but its withdrawal from the Warsaw Pact would have cut Eastern Europe in two and would have severely complicated military strategy in case of war with the West. The Czech reform was also ill-timed. Stung by the Soviet humiliation in Cuba in 1962, the Sino – Soviet imbroglio, Albanian support for China, and Romania's withdrawal from the Warsaw Pact, Soviet hard-liners were adamant in their opposition to Czech liberalization and possible loss to the Warsaw Pact countries.

Soviet and East European leaders, with the exception of those of Romania and Czechoslovakia, began their offensive against Dubcek with the Warsaw Letter of 14–16 July, ordering that Czechoslovakia reestablish the dictatorship of the Communist party or face invasion. Dubcek stoutly rejoined that the Communist party was still in control, and he convinced the Soviet leadership. Still, it took a meeting between Dubcek and Soviet leaders at Cierna in Slovakia to avert the intervention of Warsaw Pact armies that just happened to be on maneuvres in Czechoslovakia at the time.

Even though Dubcek convinced the Soviets that the Communist party was still in control and that Czechoslovakia had no intention of pulling out of the Warsaw Pact, East Germany and Poland were not convinced. These two states demanded a meeting of all East European leaders at Bratislava in Slovakia on 3 August. At that meeting Dubcek was forced to sign the Bratislava Declaration promising not to go beyond the Polish reforms instituted by Gomulka in the late 1950s.

Between the Bratislava meeting and the invasion on 20 August, several decisions by Dubcek were seen by other Communist governments to have violated the Cierna and Bratislava agreements. When Tito and Romanian leader Nicolae Ceausescu were given warm receptions in Prague, the action was taken to indicate that Dubcek was not going to adopt the attitude of other East European states toward Yugoslavia and Romania. More damning was a Czech draft of new party statutes permitting the existence of factions within the Communist party. Such actions hardly convinced Ulbricht and Gomulka that Dubcek was opposing ideological heresy even in the Communist party.

However, Soviet leaders may already have decided on intervention as early as the Bratislava meeting. To Soviet leaders, the advantages of an invasion seemed to outweigh the disadvantages. They realized that they would be sharply criticized in the international press for a time, but they were convinced that it would not last much longer than the 1956 outburst following the invasion of Hungary.

Because of the policy of detente with the United States with its recognition of mutual spheres of influence, they did not fear American intervention. On the other hand, the military and political example that Czech disaffection would have established was intolerable to many Soviet leaders.

After Dubcek had been taken into custody by invading Soviet forces, President Ludvik Svoboda refused to appoint as new premier a conservative opponent of Dubcek's and a man already approved by the Soviets, Alois Indra. The adoption of passive resistance by most of the population further frustrated Soviet designs to make the invasion appear to have been no more than a change of government. Some Czechs did throw Molotov cocktails or stones at Soviet tanks, but for the most part they merely tried to place obstacles in the way of the Russian advance. Svoboda's refusal to negotiate with the Soviet Union until Dubcek was released probably saved Dubcek's life, but nothing could be done to save the Czech experiment. Leaders subservient to Moscow were soon installed in office – Gustav Husak as party secretary and Lubomir Strougal as prime minister – press censorship was renewed, and Soviet troops were kept on Czech soil to protect the country against 'imperialism'.

Legacies of 1968: Political Violence

The events in Paris and Prague had their finales. The elections in June defused the threat to the regime in France, and the deposing of Dubcek restored traditional Communist and Soviet control in Czechoslovakia. However, in Italy and West Germany, the student mobilization of the years 1967 to 1969 did not mean the end of continued confrontation with the state. Instead, a minority of those who took part in the intense events of those years maintained their militancy, but in different, and in some cases deadly ways.

Italy From 1970 onwards, mobilization within the universities declined. On the other hand, protest beyond the academic world grew, as many student activists found it difficult to return to normal, everyday life. In particular, left-wing students sought links with workers, hoping to combine their critique of society with class-based organization. In Turin, this meant above all becoming involved in the strike mobilization at Fiat. Clashes with police as well as the radical Right continued, and some groups came to specialize in the use of violence, known as the *servizi d'ordine*. These semi-military groups argued that 'the best form of defence is attack', rather than simply defending themselves during spontaneous actions. The first underground group taking this strategy to the extreme was the Red Brigades (Brigate Rosse), founded in 1969.

The reputed founder of the Red Brigades was Renato Curcio, a left-wing student at the University of Trento. The Red Brigades were initially active in Milan and Turin, where they sabotaged factory equipment and broke into factory offices and trade union headquarters. In 1972, the Red Brigades added kidnapping to their activities. By 1974 the Red Brigades were also active in Rome, Genoa and Venice. Kidnapping prominent industrialists and now attacks on police and security forces increased. From 1976 onwards, attacks and kidnappings included magistrates, in order to pressure juries to dismiss cases against the Red Brigade members captured by the police and put on trial. In 1978, the Red Brigades staged their most spectacular kidnapping and murder. Aldo Moro, a former Italian prime minister from the Christian Democratic party (DC), a pivotal figure in arranging the historic compromise between the Italian Communist Party and the DC-led government, was abducted. After a widespread manhunt, his body was discovered in the trunk of a car. Widespread revulsion at this act, and the all-out assault by the Italian police and security forces over the next two years, spelled the beginning of the end for the Red Brigades, although formally it continued for another twenty years. But its heyday had been the 1970s, when its declared aim of creating a revolutionary state and to separate Italy from the

Former Italian Prime Minister Aldo Moro, murdered by the Red Brigades, who were holding him captive.
(© Mykola Lazarenko/Reuters/Corbis)

Western Alliance, ultimately failed. The Red Brigades were not the only such organization engaged in this type of violence- for example, there was Front Line (Prima Linea), but were the most prominent.

Germany   At the beginning of the 1970s, former SDS members who supported the strategy of violent confrontation with the state – Thirwald Proll, Horst Sohnlein, Gudrun Ensslin, Andreas Baader, and journalist Ulrike

Meinhof – founded the Red Army Fraction (Rote Armee Fraktion, RAF). The group were also known as the Baader-Meinhof Gang. In 1970, after a violent shootout with police, the group went underground to the Middle East for training. When they returned to Germany, they turned to bank robberies to fund their activities, including purchasing explosives, and arson attacks against US military bases, police stations and buildings associated with the Axel Springer press conglomerate.

The leaders of the RAF stood trial in May, 1975, the so-called Stammheim trial (after a district of Stuttgart). The trial lasted two years, and was a tense and politically charged affair. The Bundestag, the German legislature, went so far as to amend the Code of Criminal Procedure in order to exclude attorney's accused of sympathizing with the group. On 9 May 1976, Ulrike Meinhof was found dead in her cell, hanging from a rope made from jail towels. Although an investigation concluded she had hanged herself, other more conspiratorial theories contested this finding, adding to the tense atmosphere of the trial. Finally, in April 1977, the remaining defendants were convicted of several murders and attempted murders, and sentenced to life imprisonment. This, though, was not the end of the RAF, as a 'second' generation had become active. During the so-called 'German Autumn' of 1977, a wave of terrorist attacks occurred. The federal general prosecutor Siegfried Buback and the head of Dresdner Bank, Jurgen Ponto, were assassinated; the president of the Association of German Industrialists, Hanns-Martin Schleyer, was kidnapped and eventuallu murdered; and a Lufthansa airplane was hijacked by Palestinian terrorists who added RAF demands to their own, namely the release of the Stammheim prisoners. In a dramatic rescue operation in an airfield in Mogadishu, Somalia, all of the passengers were freed and the hijackers killed. The day after this successful operation was broadcast in Germany, the Stammheim prisoners were found dead, apparently shot in a collective suicide pact.

The events of 1977 were the culmination of this series of left-wing urban terrorist operations that gripped the headlines and intensified the confrontation between the state and radicals. Although a 'third' generation of RAF members were active in the 1980s and 1990s, the climate of crisis had abated. Later, it was discovered that the RAF had secured financial and logistical support from the Stasi, the security and intelligence organization of Communist East Germany.

Legacies of 1968: Growth of the Green Movement and Parties

The student protesters of 1968 in various European countries generally shared the anti-authoritarian ideology that fed into a fundamental critique of the state, and in some cases, industrial society itself. In an intersecting or overlapping manner, the New Left of the 1960s (small political parties and groups rejecting the bureaucratic and authoritarian profile of most

212 Europe Since 1945: A Concise History

Communist parties, but nevertheless retaining a Marxist orientation) and an environmental consciousness emerged. This radicalized 'green' movement did not just criticize polluters and other harmful residue of industrialization, but called into question the very nature of politics and the organization of society and called for a re-balancing of the economy and personal life. Activists of both a New Left and green perspective colluded in early movements. Protest, though non-violent, was considered an integral part of their strategy. Some of these green movements eventually became political parties, and in some cases joined government coalitions in the 1990s, for example in Belgium, Germany and France. The 'green challenge' to social democratic parties in the 1980s and 1990s were two-fold. First, as left-wing parties, they competed for members and voters. Second, their appeal, especially among younger people, generated a 'greening' of social democracy itself.

Germany The green movement in Germany was particularly strong owing to three main features: the strength of the alternative milieu; the alienation of parts of the middle-class from the SPD in the 1970s; and the strength of green organizations and environmental protest into the 1980s. The alternative milieu was exactly that, areas or 'ghettos' in major cities that were self-sufficient, that is, they did not interact with the wider environment, either in careers or daily life. Anti-nuclear power protests mobilized many of these groups, and eventually some of them led to the formation of the Green party, Die Gruene, in 1980. Many disillusioned younger SPD members left to join the green movement as well, angry at the 'turn to the right' of the party under Helmut Schmidt after 1974. In addition, so-called citizen's initiatives, or Burgerinitiativen (BI's), expanded their activities, namely citizen participation in local issues, from local transport and playgrounds, to environmental issues. A co-ordinating body, the Bundesverband Burgerinitiativen Umveltschutz (BBU), established in 1972, linked 1000 groups (approximately 300,000 members).

The SPD's support in 1976 in favour of nuclear power was a turning point for these groups. The BBU suggested a green electoral list for the European Parliament elections in 1979. Although Die Grunen remained divided between ideological sub-groups, most noteworthy between the fundis (those arguing for an autonomous political strategy) and realos (those in favour of more conventional party politics), it first built support at municipal and state parliaments before finally succeeding in being elected to the Bundestag in 1983. The continuing widespread support for environmental concerns meant that eventually German governments had to engage with these issues. Die Grunen entered national government in 1998 with the SPD in the so-called Red-Green coalition.

France France, like Germany and Italy, also had an alternative milieu that grew out of the events of 1968. However, unlike Germany, it did not achieve the same level of size and self-sufficiency. The first politically symbolic – and environmental – focus from an alternative political movement was the occupation of the site of a proposed extension to the military base at Larzac, in the Midi region, begun in 1971. The twin concerns of the protesters were protection of the rural life-style, and anti-militarism. The first demonstration attracted 5000 people, but by the following year had swollen to 20,000. In the presidential election of 1974, the agronomist Rene Dumont ran and garnered a little over 1 per cent of the vote. Although a small amount, it did much to point ecology activists in an electoral direction. As Dumont espoused concerns that also attracted left-wing interests, his campaign raised the issue of the relationship between environmental politics and the main parties of the Left, mainly the Communists (PCF) and Socialists (PS).

Unlike in Germany, political ecology remained mostly at the fringes of electoral politics and the alternative milieu. There was no equivalent of the BI's, nor sub-national levels of government with real decision-making power to target, owing to the centralized nature of French government. In addition, the re-founded PS, unlike the SPD, was welcoming of various social movement activists, so it blunted in a way the need for a specifically French green party. The election of Mitterrand and his Socialist party in 1981 also removed some of the more high-profile environmental issues from the scene, by cancelling the Larzac project and reviewing the nuclear energy policy. Still, in 1984, a green party was formed, Les Verts. By the mid-1980s disillusionment of left-wing voters with the Socialist government had begun to set in (the PS lost the national parliamentary elections in 1986), and les Verts benefited to a certain extent, gaining 11 per cent of the vote in the 1989 EP elections. By the 1990s, political ecology in France had become mostly an electoral phenomenon, and in 1997 les Verts joined the PS, the PCF and a couple of smaller parties to form the government majority under Prime Minister Jospin (PS). Dominique Voynet, on the green leaders, was named minister for the environment and regional planning. Although they returned to the opposition after the 2002 elections, they remain in both the French legislature and share with Die Grunen a large proportion of members of the Green group in the European parliament.

FURTHER READING

Robert Daniel's *Year of the Heroic Guerrilla: World Revolution and Counterrevolution in 1968* (1989) provides a comparative survey of events during 1968 throughout the world. He contends that an attack on power and a drive for equality (social, national, administrative) united rebellions throughout the world. Rebellions in Eastern and Western Europe found common ground in the attack on hierarchical conservatism. Also useful works include Carole Fink, ed., *1968: the World Transformed* (1999); David Caute, *The Year of the Barricades: A Journey Through 1968* (1990); and Arthur Marwick, *The Sixties Cutural Revolution in Britain, France, Italy and the United States* (1998). Focusing on the role of student movements and political activity is Ronald Fraser et al., *1968: A Student Generation in Revolt* (1988).

Although a large number of works have appeared on the 1968 French upheaval, only a few are of major importance. Probably the best general coverage is in Adrien Dansette's *Mai 1968* (1971). The most complete coverage of the workers' role is provided by Pierre Dubois et al., *Greves Revendicatives ou Greves Politiques* (1971). On the role of the Communist party see Daniel Cohn-Bendit's left-wing denunciation, *Obsolete Communism: The Left-Wing Alternative* (1968); and Richard Johnson's balanced study, *The French Communist Party versus the Students* (1972). General works on the event of May by non-French writers include D. Hanley and A. Kerr, eds., *May '68: Coming of Age* (1989); and Keith Reader, *The May 1968 Events in France* (1993).

A highly critical treatment of the student rioters can be found in Raymond Aron, *The Elusive Revolution* (1968).

Four generally favourable treatments of the actions of the rioters are Daniel Singer, *Prelude to Revolution* (1970); J. J. Servan-Schreiber, *The Spirit of May* (1969); Alain Touraine, *The May Movement: Revolt and Reform* (1971); and Alfred Willener, *The Action-Image of Society* (1970). Singer believes the 1968 upheaval proved that a full-scale Socialist revolution was still possible in the developed Western countries. He maintains that there were valid reasons for the upheaval in France. He unfortunately spends much of his time arguing for revolution and outlining the proper revolutionary strategy to achieve a Socialist society.

J.-J. Servan-Schreiber argues that the upheaval was caused by French cultural and social rigidity. This theme is similar to the one presented by Michael Crozier in *The Stalled Society* (1973). Touraine feels that the upheaval was a legitimate response to the advanced capitalist societies and their managers, who manipulate and control in an authoritarian manner all aspects of society. The events in France were therefore merely one instance of many possible revolts against post-industrial societies. Willener believes that a combination of political and cultural resistance gave the upheaval its intensity. The student demands for a new culture included action, egalitarianism, anti-authoritarianism, self-management and imagination.

The most comprehensive treatment of the Czech upheaval is H. Gordon Skilling, *Czechoslovakia's Interrupted Revolution* (1976). He has also written the forward to a recent collection of works which include Kremlin Politburo documents on the event in Jaromir Navratil et al., eds., *The Prague Spring 1968* (1998). A short treatment by an expert on Czech history is Z. A. B. Zeman, *Prague Spring* (1969). Eyewitness accounts are provided in *A Year Is Eight Months: Czechoslovakia in 1968* (1970); and Zdenek Mlynar, *Nightfrost in Prague: The End of Human Socialism* (1980). William Shawcross has provided some insights into the character and policies of Dubcek in *Dubcek* (1970). Two studies that attempt to place the Czechoslovakian revolt into a broader perspective are Vojtech Mastny, *Czechoslovakia: Crisis in World Communism* (1972); and William 1. Zartman, *Czechoslovakia: Intervention and Impact* (1970). The role of the press can be followed in Frank L. Kaplan, *Winter into Spring: The Czechoslovak Press and the Reform Movement, 1963–68* (1977). Kaplan contends that the press served as one of the primary factors in bringing about Soviet intervention as well as bringing about the reform movement. Milan Simecka's *The Restoration of Order: The Normalization of Czechoslovakia* (1984) is a sound analysis of the period after the uprising. Zdenek Suda provides an excellent history of the Communist Party in *Zealots and Rebels: A History of the Communist Party of Czechoslovakia* (1980).

For the Soviet decision to invade see Jiri Valenta, *Soviet Intervention in Czechoslovakia, 1968: Anatomy of a Decision* (1979); Robin Edmonds, *Soviet Foreign Policy: The Brezhnev Years* (1983); and Karen Dawisha, *The Kremlin and the Praque Spring* (1984).

Regarding the literature on the legacies of 1968, both in terms of political violence into the 1970s and especially the birth of new social movements such as the ecology movement, there is a substantial amount. A comparative overview of the phenomenon of political challenges to the legitimacy of the west European liberal democracies is Russell Dalton and M. Kuechler, eds., *Challenging the Political Order: new social and political movements in Western Democracies* (1990). A comprehensive comparative analysis of the political violence in Italy and Germany in the 1970s is by Donatella Della Porta, *Social Movements, Political Violence, and the State: a comparative analysis of Italy and Germany* (1995). On Italy in particular, see Sidney Tarrow, *Democracy and Disorder: Protest and Politics in Italy, 1965–1975* (1989), and Robert C. Meade, *The Red Brigades: The Story of Italian Terrorism* (1989). For Germany, an interesting comparison between the US underground terrorist group the Weather Underground and the German equivalent is Jeremy Varon, *Bringing the War Home: The Weather Underground, the Red Army Faction, and Revolutionary Violence in the Sixties and Seventies* (2004).

Green, or environmental movements, have a much larger literature and history, but a good introduction into the area is John Dryzek et al., *Green States and Social Movements* (2003), which provides a historical overview beginning in and around 1970. Two more comparative works are Chris Rootes, ed., *Environmental Protest in Western Europe* (2003); and Brian Doherty, *Ideas and Action in the Green Movement* (2001).

11 Eastern Europe and the Soviet Union to the 1970s and Beyond: Decline, Fall and Transition

Today, Eastern Europe is again Central Europe – which it has always been historically, culturally and philosophically.

Zbigniew Brzezinski, 7 March 1990

The Soviet Union and Eastern Europe have experienced four major phases since 1968 with Soviet directives or experiences the predominant influence in the first and third phases and indigenous east European developments decisive in the second stage. The first phase ensued immediately after the suppression of the 1968 Czech uprising when the Soviet Union sought to shore up its Eastern European empire through a carrot and stick approach. Adherence to the Warsaw Pact and Comecon were stressed and any attempts to challenge the supremacy of the Communist Parties or to develop political pluralism were rejected. To make such a policy palatable, the Soviet Union encouraged consumerism through subsidies and Western credits in order to legitimize communist regimes through an improved standard of living and to divert attention from the absence of political freedom. Although these policies succeeded in the early 1970s, the serious worldwide economic downturn after the mid-1970s coupled with the failures of economic planning in the Communist Bloc brought huge debts and economic chaos to Eastern Europe.

The second phase emerged in the late 1970s in Poland and Hungary. The economic downturn and political immobilism of the leadership permitted opposition groups to form openly and challenge the Communist elite and begin the rejection of the Soviet economic model of centralization and one-party dictatorship. A third phase began about 1985 with the coming to power of Mikhail Gorbachev in the Soviet Union; the further development of the Polish Solidarity Movement in the 1980s with its extensive political

216

EASTERN EUROPE
(EAST-CENTRAL EUROPE)

NORWAY
Oslo
Stockholm
Tallinn
ESTONIA
RUSSIA
Moscow
SWEDEN
Riga
LATVIA
Baltic
Sea
LITHUANIA
Vilnius
Minsk
BELARUS
Copenhagen
Berlin
GERMANY
Warsaw
POLAND
Kiev
Prague
CZECH
REPUBLIC
UKRAINE
SLOVAK
REPUBLIC
Bratislava
Vienna
Budapest
MOLDOVA
Chisinau
AUSTRIA
REPUBLIC OF
HUNGARY
ROMANIA
Ljubljana
SLOVENIA
VOJVODINA
Zagreb
CROATIA
Novi Sad
Sava River
Bucharest
BOSNIA AND
HERZEGOVINA
Belgrade
Danube River
Black Sea
Sarajevo
SERBIA
Rome
Adriatic
Sea
MONTENEGRO
BULGARIA
Pristina
KOSOVO
Sofia
Podgorica
Skopje
ITALY
MACEDONIA
Istanbul
Tirane
ALBANIA
GREECE
Aegean
Sea
TURKEY
SICILY
Ionian
Sea
Athens
Valletta
MALTA
CRETE
CYPRUS

KEY
● National Capitals
○ Yugoslav Republic Capitals

0   250   500
Scale of Miles

consequences; and the rejection of Communist Party leadership throughout eastern Europe. The dissolution, finally, of the Soviet Union into its constituent republics, now independent countries, marks the end of this period, with the transition to post-Communist societies heralding a fourth phase. The re-emergence of 'Central Europe', as Brezezinski comments, is part of this last phase. As will be discussed below, these phases have resulted primarily from a long-term social transformation of the elite; the failure of the centralized communist economic-social model with its attendant political consequences; and the emergence of internal opposition movements.

The Brezhnev Years, 1964–82

Although little is known of the party deliberations that gained Leonid Brezhnev leadership of the party after Khrushchev's removal as general secretary, his subsequent activities indicate that he was chosen by the Politburo because he was a good party man who would respect the rights and privileges of party members. This so-called 'respect for Cadres' attitude inhibited reform since it was very difficult to replace ineffective party functionaries with reform-oriented members. Brezhnev immediately ended the division of the party into agricultural and industrial branches thereby restoring authority to local officials. Still, his quest for institutional stability did not exclude economic reform. He continued to stress an increase in the production of consumer goods, a policy some have called 'Goulash Communism', in order to raise living standards and support for the government. However, the lack of political change continued to slow a shift from producer to consumer goods.

Brezhnev was immediately confronted with a growing division in the communist world. China had become an independent centre among communist nations as a result of its struggle with Khrushchev and Albania and Romania had used the Sino–Soviet rift to gain increasing autonomy. But Brezhnev was not prepared to permit an east European country to end the monopoly of a Communist party, as the Warsaw Pact invasion of Czechoslovakia was to show (see Chapter 10). After the crushing of the Czech revolution in 1968, the Soviet Union promulgated the so-called Brezhnev Doctrine. By claiming that the autonomy of any Communist party or state was limited by the interests of 'socialism', the Soviet Union reserved the right to intervene in 'socialist' countries to protect 'socialist' gains. The Soviet Union now had established a principle upon which to base Soviet intervention in Eastern Europe and Brezhnev had secured his position atop the Soviet ruling elite. With Eastern Europe cowed after the Czech invasion, West German recognition of the existing East German borders, and increasing economic and cultural exchanges with the West, Brezhnev was able to concentrate attention on areas other than Eastern Europe in the early seventies.

Brezhnev's greatest legacy would undoubtedly be the enhanced foreign role of the Soviet Union. The enormous increase in military spending, often at the expense of the consumer goods industry, made the Soviet Union a military equal of the United States. The 1972 SALT (Strategic Arms

Limitation Talks) negotiations with the United States on military hardware acknowledged this parity. With their feelings of military inferiority receding and their sphere of influence apparently secured – West German recognition of the East German borders and the crushing of the 1968 Czech uprising – Brezhnev moved towards détente with the West.

From the beginning a misunderstanding existed between the Soviet Union and the United States over détente. While the United States thought it prevented the Soviet Union from challenging it outside its own sphere of influence, the Soviet Union thought it meant seeking a relaxation in relations with the United States and western Europe but continued competition for influence and position throughout the world. The Soviet Union thought the competition, called 'separatism' by some experts on Soviet policy, justified since the United States had frozen the Soviet Union out of Middle East peacemaking efforts and was challenging the Soviet Union in such places as North Vietnam and along the Soviet Union's southern border. In their opinion, Iran, which had been heavily armed by the United States and Afghanistan were within the Soviet sphere of influence. Since the United States could challenge them in these areas, the Soviet Union reasoned that they could challenge the United States in Africa and Latin America. As it became clear to the Soviet Union that the United States perceived separatism to be inconsistent with détente, its advantages began to be outweighed by its disadvantages. Finally, with the American move to befriend China (the Soviet Union hoped détente would isolate China), the American Senate's failure to ratify the SALT II Arms Treaty, the American opposition to Soviet treatment of dissidents and Jews and Brezhnev's failure to obtain the American economic credits and technology he hoped would flow from détente, the Soviet Union lost interest in détente with the United States. However, Brezhnev and the western Europeans continued to pursue détente since the trade ties and technological exchange between them made it almost indispensable (see Chapter 12). With American President Ronald Reagan's attacks on Soviet policy after 1980, the gap between the Soviet Union and the United States widened until Gorbachev came to power in 1985.

The Soviet Union's Eastern European empire became an increasing economic and military burden in the mid-1970s. The 1975 Helsinki Accords, which Brezhnev hoped would confirm Soviet hegemony in Eastern Europe through Western recognition of existing borders, were subsequently used by the West to demand greater autonomy for Eastern Europe. But the biggest shock to Brezhnev and the Politburo was the Polish Solidarity Movement beginning in the late 1970s.

Added to the growing Polish unrest in the early eighties was a continuing Soviet war against Afghan rebels and enormous economic difficulties in every eastern European country. With the Soviet Union's own economy suffering severely (see Chapter 9), the Soviet Union became during Brezhnev's final years – a mighty military empire, threatened increasingly by its economic weaknesses and the continuing dissent and dissatisfaction among its many components.

In the midst of this tumultuous period, Brezhnev died. The political machinations that resulted in bringing Yuri Andropov to the post of party secretary in November 1982 demonstrates the effectiveness of the one major achievement of the party in the post-Stalin period – collective leadership. The choice of Andropov over Brezhnev's long time friend and collaborator Konstantin Chernenko was made possible by political manoeuvring prior to Brezhnev's death. When Andropov was appointed to the Central Committee Secretariat in early 1982, he became one of the four men who held positions in both the Politburo and the party secretariat and was thus in an excellent position to succeed Brezhnev. Andropov's attempts to reform the economy by increasing labour productivity were cut short by his death in February 1984. Although Mikhail Gorbachev had the support of the Andropov faction to succeed Andropov, Gorbachev apparently agreed to let Chernenko take the reins as general secretary in order to avoid a battle in the Central Committee. The Chernenko faction also agreed to continue Andropov's economic reforms. Chernenko, at age 72, became the oldest man to become general secretary, surpassing Andropov's record by four years. His early death prevented him from making any impact on Soviet policy.

The Gorbachev 'Phenomenon'

Chernenko's death on 10 March 1985 brought Gorbachev to power. Gorbachev's policies of 'new thinking' (novoe myshlenie), 'restructuring' (perestroika), and 'candor' (Glasnost) has unleashed forces in the Soviet Union and Eastern Europe that many in the Soviet leadership found intolerable, especially where they challenged Soviet dominance or the Socialist egalitarian model. His 'new thinking' included an openness about internal affairs and efforts to 'democratize' internally when necessary in order to obtain efficiency. He was particularly intent on breaking down the excessive central-ization of economic decision-making and eliminating bureaucratic inertia.

There were long-term precedents for his domestic reform efforts. Khrushchev's failed reforms as well as the limited reform efforts of Brezhnev and Andropov provided earlier attempts at reform that had not been realized due to internal obstacles. As Andropov's second secretary, Gorbachev had been responsible for economic reforms, and it was expected that he would continue such efforts once he took power. Gorbachev benefited from a long-term transformation of Soviet society that provided a growing technical elite impatient with the Soviet Union's technical backwardness.

Gorbachev brought an entirely new tone to international affairs as well. In foreign affairs, his 'new thinking', included removing the nuclear threat, international interdependence and cooperation, and 'reasonable sufficiency' in armaments. These views, articulated at the 27th party conference in 1986, were soon followed by deeds. The past Soviet foreign policy of Stalin and Brezhnev was criticized, Soviet troops were pulled out of Afghanistan, agreements were reached with the West over reducing intermediate-range missiles in Europe, and extensive on-site verification was permitted.

Mikhail S. Gorbachev, the last Soviet Communist Party General Secretary, served from 1985 to 1991.

(© Empics)

Gorbachev instituted his reforms slowly in order not to alienate his conservative opposition. Before the 27th Party Conference, he concentrated on increasing discipline and investment and reducing alcoholism. When he began to restructure economic activity by promoting incentives, he reassured conservatives by promising them that reforms would save *socialism*. Reform was also tied to a more efficient, stronger military. Gorbachev argued that the previous system was undermining Soviet defences.

It was only when Gorbachev's attempts to restructure the Soviet economy encountered political and bureaucratic opposition that he began to stress openness and democracy in order to spread economic decision-making outside the party and bureaucratic elite. Without political reforms, Gorbachev's economic reforms would have failed as those of Khrushchev and Premier Aleksei Kosygin did in the mid-1960s. He announced democratization in early 1987 and claimed, 'It is either democracy, or social inertia and conservatism; there is no other way, comrades.' But attempts to decentralize decision-making and inject profit incentives and wage differentiation into the Soviet economy met opposition from entrenched interests and workers who opposed the growing inequality in a socialist economy. Such opposition drove Gorbachev even further towards political reforms that would make it possible to realize the economic reforms.

The political reforms began in June 1988 when a new Congress of People's Deputies was established to select the members of the Supreme Soviet, which debated issues and vetoed government appointments. This two-stage election process and the fact that only two-thirds of the Congress was elected from candidates previously approved by the party does not make it a democratic body in the Western sense. But the fact that Congress's debates are open to the public and are reported to the public brings many issues into the open that were previously decided exclusively by the party. In May 1989, when the Congress was convened in Moscow, it elected Gorbachev to the new post of executive president of the USSR. Nevertheless, in June 1989, the Supreme Soviet showed some limited authority when it rejected 8 of the 71 party candidates for the ruling Council of Ministers headed by Prime Minister Nikolai I. Ryzhkov. Gorbachev's moves in the early 1990s to strengthen the powers of the presidency indicated that he would utilize this new government structure to circumvent Communist Party conservatives and gain the modernizing elite to institute his programmes. The Party's dramatic renunciation of its monopoly of power in February 1990, in effect a rejection of Lenin's dictatorship of an elite revolutionary leadership, appeared to be another stage in Gorbachev's disassociating himself from a weakened party.

At the same time that Gorbachev was attempting to restructure the government of the USSR, that is, the all-Union institutions, the Republic of Russia itself had been setting about refashioning its governmental politics. In March of 1990, the Russian Congress of People's Deputies held an essentially free and competitive election. Convened in May, it elected Boris Yeltsin chairman of the Supreme Soviet (the power-wielding core of the

Congress). For the next year, Yeltsin used this position to challenge the authority of Gorbachev and the all-Union institutions. In fact, on 12 June 1990, the Russian Congress adopted a declaration of sovereignty, which asserted that the Russian Federation (as it is formally now known) had primacy over all-Union legislation as well as Russian natural resources. Finally, in June 1991, direct elections were held in Russia for the posts of president and vice-president. These elections were won overwhelmingly by Yeltsin, (president) and Aleksandr Rutskoy (vice-president).

Within six months, the Soviet Union ceased to exist as the political entity established by Lenin. On 19 August 1991, one day before a new Union Treaty was due to have been signed, an attempted coup against Gorbachev by conservative Communist politicians took place, with the conspirators seizing power in Moscow. The coup fizzled after only three days, but the damage had been done. Although Gorbachev returned to power, the prestige of Yeltsin soared, as he was seen by many as the hero of the day. Events moved swiftly after that, and on 21 December 1991, the leaders of Russia, Ukraine and Belarus formally established a commonwealth of eleven states (Commonwealth of Independent States-CIS) from the former Soviet Union. On 25 December, Gorbachev resigned as the last President of the USSR.

Russian politics and economics for the remainder of the decade involved a series of zigzags. Throughout the decade Yeltsin's health deteriorated, partially attributed to his alcohol intake and his control over the institutions of the new state were fragile at times. The Communist Party continued in existence, usually in opposition to many of the economic reforms promoted by Yeltsin's first prime minister, Yegor Gaidar. Ultra-nationalist parties also sprang up, contesting what they saw as a weakening of Russian standing in the world order. Probably the most critical showdown between Yeltsin and his opponents occurred in September 1993, when the parliamentary leadership of the Congress of People's Deputies, meeting in emergency session, confirmed the vice-president Aleksandr Rutskoy as president and voted to impeach Yeltsin. On 27 September military units surrounded the legislative building (known as the White House), and after a two-week standoff, tanks shelled the building. In December 1993, a new constitution re-organized executive-legislative relations in favour of a strong president, and was approved in a referendum by 58.4 per cent of Russia's registered voters.

The territorial integrity of the Russian Federation also came into question, with attempts by one of its constituent republics, Chechnya, to break away. The brutality and clumsiness of the Russian Army's suppression of the rebels cast light on the ability of the Russian government to deal with these sorts of instability. After several more years of scandal and erratic policy-making, Yeltsin appointed Vladimir Putin prime minister in August 1999. Putin had had a career in the KGB, having been posted to East Germany in the latter half of the 1990s. His law and order image helped him overcome rivals for the presidency, which he won on 26 March 2000. Putin set out to boost the legitimacy of the President, and in so doing drew attention to a centralizing trend, which some commentators have interpreted as a slide towards authoritarianism.

The Chechnya war erupted again and once again the Russian army used heavy-handed tactics to suppress the rebels, although in the aftermath of the formal fighting, rebels have attacked targets inside Russia itself, most notoriously in the town of Beslan, killing scores of schoolchildren in September 2004. Putin was re-elected president on 14 March, 2004, with about 71 per cent of the vote. Although the Russian economy has begun to improve and Russia's relations with the United States are businesslike (Putin has joined with President George W. Bush in the 'fight against terrorism' after 11 September 2001), the political situation remains fluid in Russia. By law, Putin cannot serve for more than two successive terms as president, and his successor, from whatever party, is not readily identifiable in 2005. Nevertheless, Russia has continued to develop ties with the European Union, and the era of instability under Yeltsin seems to be coming to an end. What Russian-style democracy will eventually resemble after Putin is difficult to foresee, but a return to the Communist past is now unthinkable.

Poland: Solidarity and Beyond

Stemming from worker resentment of a government that brutally put down labour strikes in 1970 and 1976, the Solidarity union movement eventually challenged the Communist party's monopoly of power in Poland and threatened Communist parties elsewhere. The government of Edward Gierek (1970–80), which replaced the Gomulka regime after the 1970 strikes, successfully lulled the population by providing ample consumer goods in the early seventies. Underwritten by Soviet subsidies and Western loans, this consumer policy collapsed in the mid-1970s when Western loans were reduced and Soviet energy prices were increased. When Gierek attempted to cut budget deficits by raising the price of necessities in June 1976, workers' protests forced a rescinding of the price increases the next day. The government's use of force destroyed the support that Gierek had built up by his consumerist policy and began a widespread self-government movement the so-called 'self-organization of Polish society'. This anti-government movement was bolstered by the selection of the archbishop of Kraków, Karol Cardinal Wojtyla, as Pope John Paul II, on 2 October 1978. When the Pope visited Poland in June 1979, the massive outpouring of support for him further stimulated the movement for self-government. The enthusiasm for the Catholic Church and the self-organization movement contrasted sharply with the scorn accorded to the government. The Gierek regime fell when it foolhardily attempted to raise meat prices to overcome rapidly increasing government indebtedness.

The major strikes of August 1980 brought a change in government. Gierek was replaced by Stanislaw Kania; but more important, authority began to shift from the Communist party to a workers organization that had emerged out of the Self-organization of Polish Society movement, Solidarity. At first the Party was forced to make concessions to Solidarity because of the threat of strikes that would cripple an already weak economy. The workers, led by

Lech Walesa, won the unprecedented right in a communist country to strike and organize independent trade unions. The government also agreed to let the state radio broadcast Catholic Sunday Mass along with a series of concessions that opened the government to closer public scrutiny of its activities.

By January 1981, Solidarity had become more than a labour union. With ten million members and National Coordinating Council newly elected by regional councils, Solidarity had become an alternative to the government. Faced with the overwhelming popularity of Solidarity, the Communist party could only delay and make limited concessions that they did not intend to honour. Solidarity was torn between the moderates and radicals, or 'cautious' and 'audacious,' as one commentator (Martin Malia) called them; the moderates sought to gain their ends through negotiation, while the radicals thought only confrontation would be effective. When further agitation forced the Party to recognize Rural Solidarity in March 1981, the regime came near to collapse. Solidarity, led by the moderates around Lech Walesa, called off any action for four months in order to let the Party recover and avoid possible Soviet intervention. Although Soviet efforts to depose Party Secretary Kania failed in June, the threat of intervention prevented radicals from gaining control of the movement. Still, Solidarity's proposal for self-management in heavy industry struck at one of the sources of Party strength by removing the appointment of industrial managers from the Party and putting it in the hands of workers.

In the initial phase of the struggle between the Party and Solidarity from August to December 1981, Solidarity challenged the very basis of Communist authority. With the unprecedented meeting of Solidarity's National Congress in September 1981, it had become a real alternative to the Party and a threat to Communist systems throughout Eastern Europe. From this point on, Solidarity threatened direct appeals to the masses if the Party did not act on such issues as self-management. Solidarity's acceptance of a limited self-management offer led the more radically oriented National Congress to propose that a 'council of economic control' share power with the Party and the Catholic Church. The Party, led after October 1981 by General Wojciech Jaruzelski (Prime Minister between February and October), proposed a 'National Front' that would have reduced Solidarity and the Church to minor partners in a ruling triumvirate. Jaruzelski succeeded in forcing Solidarity into the 'radical' demand for democratic elections in December. Apparently having decided upon the use of military force even before December – the organization of the military takeover required long-range planning as well as Soviet cooperation since the Russians controlled much of Poland's military logistics – Jaruzelski merely needed further evidence of Solidarity's 'radicalism' in order to convince the military to follow him. The Soviet Union obviously pressured Jaruzelski – who was sympathetic to Moscow in any case – to use Polish troops to put down a movement that destroyed Communist authority. Jaruzelski's imposition of martial law and a military dictatorship in December 1981 demonstrated the bankruptcy of Party rule and the widespread support for Solidarity.

Although outlawed, Solidarity survived and grew underground. While Jaruzelski felt strong enough to lift martial law in 1983, he could not obtain the support of the Polish population, despite many concessions, nor solve Poland's burgeoning economic problems. With no means of solving the economic crisis without cooperation from labour and apparently with Gorbachev's approval, Jaruzelski opened talks with Lech Walesa and Solidarity in February 1989. These 'Round Table' talks produced an agreement to set up a new 100-member Senate with veto power over all legislation, to permit 35 per cent of the seats in the lower house (*Sejm*) to go to the opposition, and to establish a new office of president that would be chosen by Parliament. Solidarity granted the Communist Party a majority in return for a promise to move to fully competitive elections in four years and a popularly elected president in 1995. The government calculated that these concessions were necessary to secure economic cooperation from the public and foreign aid. The Communists also calculated that Solidarity would become a junior partner in a Communist-led coalition government and would have to share responsibility for economic reforms that would initially bring unemployment, higher consumer prices and a hold on wage increases.

The government's expectation that Solidarity would not be able to organize an effective campaign in time for the elections proved to be wrong. The June 1989 elections produced a resounding victory for Solidarity: Union-backed candidates won 99 of the 100 seats in the Senate and all of the 161 Sejm seats set aside for the opposition. But an even more humiliating result was that of the 299 Sejm seats allotted to the Communists and their allies, only five party members gained the required 50 per cent of the votes needed, although they were running unopposed. Those failing to gain the required vote included the Prime Minister, Mieczyslaw Rakowski and Interior Minister Czeslaw Kiszczak. In order to save the Round Table agreement, Solidarity and the government coalition reached an agreement to elect the rejected candidates in a runoff election. The government also failed to gain Solidarity's participation in a governing coalition led by the communists that would have made it possible to impose the necessary economic reforms. Although Jaruzelski ultimately obtained sufficient votes for the presidency (all of the required 270), it was only because of Solidarity manoeuvring in order to save the compromise with him.

The most remarkable change came in August 1989 when the Communists, unable to gain a majority in the Sejm, permitted a Solidarity-led cabinet. Although Solidarity leaders would have preferred to wait until they could form a government on their own, they bowed to strong popular sentiment to form a coalition government with the Communists. The Solidarity Prime Minister, Tadeusz Mazowiecki, formed a cabinet with 11 Solidarity, 4 communists, 4 Peasant Party and 3 Democratic Party members. Mazowiecki had extreme difficulty in solving Poland's economic problems. Although Poland obtained some loans and technical assistance from the West, the attempt to establish free market mechanisms brought about extreme hardship before they became effective. Solidarity itself

Table 11–1   Polish ownership of consumer durables (per 100 households)

	1985	1990	1993	1999
Cars	27.2	33.2	37.6	NA
Colour televisions	23.1	67.1	77.8	98.9
Video-cassette recorders	NA	20.1	44.1	56.6

Source: Central Statistical Office, London. *The Economist*, 16 April 1994. 1993 and 1999 figures taken from the Polish Agency for Foreign Investment (www.paiz.gov.pl).

experienced a multi-faceted division, including a traditional Roman Catholic branch and a secular liberal branch. In order to gain some legitimacy, the Communist Party changed its name to Social Democrats in late January 1990. The Solidarity-led government's economic plan to save the Polish economy divided Solidarity members. Solidarity had in fact been tied to the large unproductive industries such as coal mining and ship building and therefore it was not too surprising that it split over reforms that required eliminating inefficient industries.

What perhaps couldn't have been predicted in early 1989 was that within four years the Communists would be back as the driving force of the Polish government. How did this occur? As we shall see below, Poland is not the only East European country to have voted *back* into office its former, now reformed, Communist parties. By 'reformed' we mean that the parties have accepted without reservation the civil and political rights understood to be an fundamental part of western democracy, for example freedom of the press, freedom of speech, etc. In addition, they have accepted the workings of a market economy. In Poland's case, the decision to pursue an economic shock therapy produced an economic downturn in the short-term, industrial unrest, and also raised the profile of haves and have-nots in Polish society. This, together with governmental instability during the first few years, no doubt made the now reformed Communists, the Social Democrats, look like a more fair and stabilizing force.

The period from 1990 to the fall elections of 1993, which brought the Social Democrats back into government, witnessed not only the schism within Solidarity, but the first post-Communist woman prime minister in all of eastern Europe, Hanna Suchocka; the beginnings of an upturn in the economy; and a reform of the electoral laws (in the elections to the Sejm in October 1991, 29 parties won representation, with no single party securing a decisive mandate). By 1993, though most Poles were materially better off than they were under Communism, their sense of well-being had not improved in step. According to *The Economist*, a survey in 1993 by the University of Warsaw and the Polish Academy of Sciences found that 48 per cent of Poles thought that economic transformation left them 'at a loss' or narrowed their opportunities. Only 10 per cent said the changes had expanded opportunities; 36 per cent said little had changed. Still, as Table 11–1 shows, Poles have become western- style consumers.

The Polish experience of governmental instability, the development of a growing gulf between a *nouveau riche* and poorer Poles (set against a 45 year official ideology of equality) and political schisms, was one not limited to just Poland, as we shall see below. The issue of abortion in Poland, which mobilized the Catholic Church to bring great pressure upon legislators, was specific to Poland. But the other factors we noted above were present in many East European nations undergoing the transition from a planned economy and Communist political system towards a western-style economy and parliamentary system.

Hungary

Party secretary János Kádár's transition from villain to father figure continued in Hungary with the New Economic Mechanism (NEM) after 1968. Although Kádár had crushed the opposition to the Communist dictatorship after the 1956 rising, he began to relax the heavy hand of authoritarianism before 1968 with a relatively liberal travel policy, increasing economic freedoms, and public discussion of issues. Peasants, given freedom to till private plots and sell the products, made many forget the brutal reimposition of collectivization between 1959 and 1962. Both Khrushchev's de-Stalinization and the economic reforms continued by Brezhnev supported Kádár's relaxation. But it was the NEM, with its transfer of much decision making from centralized agencies to the factories, local self-management of the collective farms, and a partially free market, that brought a greater measure of well being to Hungary. At the time, Hungary was better off than other eastern European countries, and greater popular support for the Communist party than anywhere else in Eastern Europe (see Chapter 9 for details). The reforms in Hungary during the 1960s became a model for some of Gorbachev's post-1985 reforms.

As it turned out, the time was not yet ripe for such innovative changes in Eastern Europe. Pressure from the Soviet Union and from Hungarian workers who did not approve of the wage differentiation introduced by the NEM brought about the suspension of much of NEM policies between 1972 and 1978. Against the economic logic of the NEM, workers' wages were raised by the Party Central Committee, and 50 large enterprises were put under the direct administration of the Council of Ministers. Some of those responsible for the NEM lost their places in the party leadership. When the worldwide oil crisis brought higher energy prices and the Western recession reduced orders for Hungarian products, the Hungarian economy went into a tailspin. By 1988, Hungary's foreign debt increased to $20 billion from only $1 billion in 1970, or $1500 per capita. Budapest's image as a showplace of the East suffered a corresponding collapse. When these economic difficulties continued in the early 1980s, Kádár lost the admiration that he had built up with such difficulty after 1956, and the Communist party lost its claim to legitimacy that it had gained in the 1960s.

The worsening economic situation apparently convinced party officials and the Soviet Union to permit Hungary to renew its economic reforms after 1978. Party reformers such as Karoly Nemeth, Ferenc Havasi, Miklos Nemeth and Imre Pozsgay took over important functions within the party. The reformers argued that economic advance needed political freedoms to free up decision-making. These reformers pushed through many reforms in the early 1980s as Kádár's health slipped. Society and even the Communist party fragmented in the mid-1980s as economic difficulties multiplied and as reformers and conservatives clashed. Many of the economic reforms, with their emphasis on increasing output and profits, caused economic dislocation and unemployment. Attempts to decrease the foreign debt led to import restrictions, consumer goods shortages, and a dimming of Hungary's image.

Supported by Gorbachev's reforms in the Soviet Union and his oft-repeated emphasis on letting Eastern Europe find its own way to socialism, the Hungarian reformers slowly gained control of the government. In May 1988, Kádár relinquished his post as first secretary to Karoly Grosz, and two leading reformers, Rezso Nyers and Imre Pozsgay, were promoted to the ruling Politburo. But Grosz's ineffectiveness led to the naming of Miklos Nemeth as premier in early 1989, with Grosz retaining the party leadership. Grosz's position was further weakened in June 1989 when a four-member presidium – including Grosz, Nyers, Pozsgay and Nemeth – took over party leadership. When the reformist majority changed the name of the party to Socialist in October 1989, a small right-wing broke away and renamed itself the János Kádár Society. Pushed by reformers, the Parliament changed the name of the country to the Republic of Hungary, dropping the word 'People's', and voted 333 to 5 to adopt the 'values of both bourgeois democracy and democratic socialism.'

In mid-October, the National Assembly approved fundamental amendments to the Constitution, including the removal of the clause guaranteeing one-party rule. With many non-communist political groups emerging and repeated calls for political pluralism, Hungary appeared headed for the first completely non-Communist government. Although the Hungarian Communists were responsible for instituting many reforms, they were expected to gain only about ten per cent of the vote. The Communists had also split into the Hungarian Socialist Party (HSP) and the more hard line Hungarian Socialist Workers Party (HSWP). As it turned out, the elections, held in two rounds on 25 March and 8 April 1990, were contested by over twenty parties and groups. The Hungarian Democratic Forum (HDF) received 42.7 per cent of the votes for 165 of the 386 seats in the National Assembly. The Independent Smallholders' Party (ISP) and the Christian Democratic People's Party (CDPP), both of which contested the second round of the elections with the HDF, secured 43 and 21 seats, respectively. The liberal Alliance of Free Democrats (AFD) won the second largest proportion of the vote at 23.8 per cent for 92 seats. The HSP won 8.5 per cent of the vote for 33 seats. The hard line HSWP failed to secure more than 4 per cent of the vote necessary for representation.

The new government coalition of the HDF and the junior ISP and CDPP moved quickly to introduce a western-style market system. Sharp increases in the rates of inflation and unemployment ensued, although by 1992 inflation began to decline, from 35 per cent in 1991 to 23 per cent in 1992. In December 1992 12.2 per cent of the labour force were unemployed. In addition to the problems associated with the transition to a market economy, Hungary returned to the 1956 uprising in order to decriminalize what most Hungarians had felt to have been a popular uprising against authoritarian government. At first, the new Constitutional Court ruled in March 1992, that retroactive legislation against individuals responsible for the crimes of the former Communist regime was inadmissible. By late September 1993, however, the Constitutional Court announced that the events of the 1956 uprising were to be considered as having occurred under a state of 'war', thereby allowing the trial of persons accused of 'crimes against humanity' as defined in the Geneva Convention.

The government coalition led by prime minister Antall of the HDF, although persevering in the task of building a market economy, experienced continued government instability, e.g., individual ministerial resignations, coalition party threats to withdraw, and disagreements between the prime minister and the president, over a host of non-economic problems. One of the most noteworthy, in that public protests were generated, had to do with the media. In mid-June 1992, the government ordered the dismissal of the presidents of the state radio and television corporations, but was blocked by the opposition of the president, Arpad Goncz. The Court allowed the government six months to come up with new legislation regulating broadcasting to replace Communist-era statutes that had allowed government supervision of the media. The government failed, however, to pass the necessary legislation in December 1992, which required a two-thirds majority, since opposition parties felt that the government would still retain too much control and interference. The two state radio and television corporation presidents resigned in January 1993, claiming that they could no longer promise broadcasters impartiality. In September 1993, senior television staff, on the *Est Egyenleg* evening news programme were suspended by the government, thus signaling the end of politically independent news coverage on Hungarian television. Later in the month a journalist from a far right-wing publication was appointed president of the state radio, thereby exacerbating the situation. In late October, 10,000 people demonstrated in Budapest to demand press freedom. In January of 1994, the government proceeded nevertheless with further dismissals of senior radio staff.

The media freedom issue, the perception among the public of a rise in extreme right-wing sentiment (in September 1992, 50,000 people staged a demonstration in Budapest against such developments within the HDF), and a financial scandal in 1993, led to increased public support for the HSP, the reformed former Communist party. Finally, in May 1994, parliamentary elections were held, again in two rounds. The HSP, predicted to do well, captured even a higher percentage of the vote than expected, thereby allowing it to form the new government, which it did in June along with the AFD. The HSP secured 209 seats in the 386-seat Parliament. The AFD came in far behind with 70 seats, and the HDF had a humiliating 37 seats. Hungary had now joined Poland as nations that, after experiencing a bumpy transition to capitalism and parliamentary government, now turned to their refurbished Communists to bring stability into political affairs. Coincidentally, both the Polish and Hungarian former Communist parties pledged to continue the process of market development, although with some priority given to the social ramifications of the transition.

East Germany: From Communist Orthodoxy to 'Unification'

After losing three million people to the West between 1945 and 1961, the building of the Berlin wall permitted East Germany to halt the immigration of its skilled work force and achieve by far the best economic performance in the Eastern Bloc in the 1960s. This so-called economic 'miracle' (see Chapter 9) was overshadowed however by the West German economic resurgence that continued to undermine the leadership of hard-line party secretary Walter Ulbricht. But Ulbricht's New Economic System for Planning and Management (NES) gained the support of many through its decentralization of economic decision making. Ulbricht's opposition to increased contacts with West Germany during the early stages of détente and Willy Brandt's Eastern Policy (Ostpolitik) led the Soviet Union to demand and obtain his replacement in May 1971.

East Germany's international isolation ended in September 1971 with the Berlin Accords, signed by Berlin's occupying powers and not by East Germany. These accords forced East Germany to increase contacts with West Germany and permitted West Berliners to make regular visits to East Germany. Forced to deal with the West Germans, East Germany then made its own agreement, the Basic Treaty of November 1972, with West Germany. The GDR gained West German de facto recognition, something it had always sought, and in 1973 admission to the United Nations.

The new first secretary, Erich Honecker, took a more pragmatic, technocratic approach to policy than Ulbricht. But he tried to limit the impact West German tourists, television and trade would have on his regime by limiting contacts as much as possible. In order to counteract the West German's land-of-plenty image, Honecker concentrated on raising living standards, increasing the supply of consumer goods, improving housing and enhancing the East German image through athletic excellence. At the same time there was an increased stress on preserving the Communist monopoly of political power through enhanced ideological training, the suppression of dissent and criticism of Western materialism. Despite some economic success, Honecker's restriction of intellectual freedoms limited his regime's popular acceptance.

*The Berlin Wall served as a symbol of the Cold War and, later, of East German economic
and political failure. It was opened in November 1989.*

(© Magnum Photos)

With few natural resources, East Germany was hit hard by the worldwide
energy crisis in the 1970s. West German tourist money and economic subsidies helped counteract some of the consequences of high energy costs and
convinced Honecker that the West German contacts were worth continuing
when détente waned in the late 1970s after the Soviet invasion of Afghanistan.

Gorbachev's drive for reform in the Soviet Union and the messages he
relayed to The East German leadership during his visit to commemorate the
40th anniversary of the German Democratic Republic proved to be instrumental in the massive peaceful protests that forced Honecker to resign in
October 1989. Gorbachev message to Honecker that the Soviet troops in East
Germany would not take part in any suppression of popular discontent was
leaked to the public. He also encouraged reform-minded Communists to oust
Honecker. The leadership was therefore in a weakened position in late 1989
and feared its own troops would join the protesters. Gorbachev's encouragement to the reformers joined with the internal opposition that had been
building since early in the year. Honecker later admitted that he was responsible for rigging May 1989 local elections that covered up a large protest
vote against his regime and initially led to extreme frustration and desperate
attempts by East Germans to leave the country. The pent up anger against the
Communists and the lure of a better life in West Germany led to a massive
flight to the West through Hungary and a rapidly deteriorating economy. The
Honecker government used police force against the demonstrators until,
9 October when it suddenly stopped. Why force was no longer used is not

clear. But it is doubtful that any force would have succeeded against the massive number of demonstrators and Russian opposition to the use of force. On 18 October Honecker resigned.

In November 1989, an interim Communist government opened the Berlin Wall in the hope that it would stem the exodus of its population to the West. But as the exodus continued at the rate of about 2000 a day and the economy continued to deteriorate, East German leaders were forced to turn to West Germany for aid. These contacts received support from continuous demonstrations of East Germans for unification with West Germany. In order to distance itself from past policies, the Communists changed their name to the Party of Democratic Socialism and admitted opposition groups to the government. The emergence of indigenous reform parties such as New Forum quickly lost out to the East German branches of the West German Social Democrats and Christian Democrats. Although opinion polls predicted that the Social Democrats would win the March 1990 elections in East Germany because of the greater support for their social policies, the Christian Democrats and the two small parties won 48 per cent and the Social Democrats only 22 per cent of the vote.

The Christian Democrats' emphasis on national unification appealed to a private East German yearning for German national greatness that was never eradicated from individual consciousness by the Communists. Even so, all parties campaigned with unification as a basic policy; the differences arose in the proposed timing. In this sense, the Christian Democrats' insistence upon rapid unification, rather than the suggested go-slow approach of the Social Democrats and New Forum, seems to have been the special factor that attracted East Germans. An additional issue, though perhaps of a technical matter to most voters, was the exact unification process. Would it be carried out as quickly as possible in accordance with article 23 of the West German Basic Law, that is, with East Germany re-constituted as federal states simply linking up to the West German states, as favoured by the Christian Democrats? Or, through the slower and more politicized convocation of a constitutional convention (article 146), which could presumably have addressed other issues concerning West Germany as well as the East. In the end, the Christian Democrats formed a coalition government with the Social Democrats and the Liberals in April 1990 in order to negotiate a union with West Germany based upon article 23. Financial integration started in July 1990 when East Germany accepted the West German mark as their official currency. Formal political union took place on 3 October 1990, with the first all-German parliamentary elections scheduled later in December 1990.

Czechoslovakia: From 'Velvet Revolution' to 'Velvet Divorce'

The suppression of the Czechoslovak reform movement in 1968, the so-called Prague Spring, produced the most dejected, sullen population in Eastern

Europe. Gustav Husák, placed in power in April 1969 by the Soviet Union, purged those who had not already fled and stripped the population of all political responsibility. In order to gain some meager legitimacy, Husak instituted a policy of consumerism to divert attention from the loss of political freedoms. With aid from the Soviet Union the government directed funds towards improving the material condition of the population. Those owning cars increased from 1 in 17 in 1971 to 1 of 8 in 1979. The number of weekend homes, dachas, increased from 128,000 in 1969 to 225,000 in 1981. Government officials overlooked a large illegal or second economy that provided the population with additional goods and income. Much of the population sullenly accepted a materially improved but depoliticized life style. As a young construction worker remarked, 'We don't look forward to much, and we don't trust anyone' (*Time*, 18 April 18 1988).

Only in the mid-1970s did the Husák regime begin to experience any concerted opposition. A parallel or alternative culture led by two group of intellectuals, Charter 77 and VONS (the committee for the Defence of the Unjustly Persecuted), kept up a discussion of public issues despite persecution. Many dissidents, such as Vaclav Havel, published their criticisms from prison while others, Milan Kundera and Josef Skvorecky being the most famous, criticized the regime from exile. By avoiding any direct denunciation of the regime and publishing their thoughts in the underground press, these intellectuals provided an alternative culture to the official one.

Beginning in the mid-1970s the Czechoslovakian economy began to suffer severely because of high energy costs and shortages. The situation worsened in the late 1970s due to failed investment policies that left 30,000 industrial projects uncompleted in 1981. Severe shortages of consumer goods forced the government to divert funds from investment in order to prevent inflation and stem social unrest. Husák's failed policies finally led to his downfall in 1987. His successor as General Secretary, Miloš Jakeš, promised 'restructuring' but instituted no meaningful reforms.

Popular opposition to the Communist regime jelled on 17 November 1989, when a student-organized demonstration in Prague was brutally broken up by riot police in Wenceslas Square. Students had been actively organizing opposition for over a year in youth clubs, in underground publications, in discussion clubs and together with intellectuals in literary magazines. The police action ignited strikes at Charles University and among actors supporting Vaclav Havel. Havel and his supporters in Charter 77 joined on 20 November with other opposition groups, including members of the People's and Socialist parties, to form Civic Forum, the later governing movement. When the enormous demonstrations beginning on Monday, 21 November, came off without government intervention, the right of the popular masses to organize and voice their complaints had been established. The government was probably unsure of the loyalty of its armed forces. But more important, obtaining even a Communist majority ready to defend the failed system with force would have been difficult. The Civic Forum, involved in the most open discussions imaginable in the Magic Lantern theatre, used the support of the demonstrations (they often chanted 'Long live the Forum') to force a meeting with the government on 23 November. The Forum leadership was also aware that Gorbachev had been pressing the Czech leadership to implement reforms. Forum received further support through the daily press conferences that were broadcast worldwide to admiring audiences.

On Friday, 24 November, Forum's image was further enhanced when Alexander Dubcek, the leader of the 1968 Prague Spring, joined the revolutionary forces. Immediately after Dubcek's address to the crowd on Wenceslaw Square, Jakeš and the entire Communist Politburo resigned. The final blow to the Communist leadership came on 27 November, with a successful general strike and an agreement by the government to negotiate with Forum. These negotiations led to the Communist government's agreement to delete the leading role of the Communist Party from the constitution, remove Marxist-Leninism as the basis of education and form a coalition government with Civic Forum. After 29 November, the Slovak liberation movement Public Against Violence (PAV) joined with Civic Forum. Round table discussions between Forum, PAV and the Communist Party led to a Communist-led coalition government (only 8 of the 21 ministers were Communists) and the resignation of President Husák on 10 December. Havel's election as president on 29 December capped off the meteoric rise of Civic Forum. As an umbrella protest organization, Forum now had the task of making the transition from movement to political party. In the June 1990 elections, Civic Forum won 53 per cent of the vote for the Czech legislature (House of the People) and its Slovak counterpart, Public Against Violence (PAV) won 32.5 per cent of the Slovakian legislative vote. The Communists won only 13.6 per cent of the vote in the Czech lands and 13.8 in Slovakia. The mostly peaceful nature of this transition from Communist to democratic rule was dubbed the 'velvet revolution'.

As we pointed out above in the cases of Poland and Hungary, each East European nation emerging from Communist rule had one or more issues particular to their political situation. The role of the Catholic Church in Poland was highlighted over the abortion issue; the reaction against right-wing sentiment together with the heavy-handed government policy towards the media in Hungary; and in Czechoslovakia tension in the Czech-Slovak relationship quickly emerged. Even before the June 1990 legislative elections, the Federal Assembly had voted to rename the country the Czech and Slovak Federative Republic (CSFR). The decision followed Slovak demands that the new title should reflect the equal status of Slovakia within the federation. This was only the beginning of a swift, yet peaceful, process that ultimately led to the formal division of the country into two, the Czech Republic and the Slovak Republic. Apart from nationalist sentiments on the part of Slovak political leaders (polls showed that a majority of Czechs and Slovaks were opposed to the country's division right up to the end), an added strain on the Czech-Slovak relationship came from the economic reforms pursued by the government, which hurt Slovakia more so than the Czech lands.

In March 1991, Vladimir Meciar, the Slovak prime minister and a founding member of PAV, formed the Movement for a Democratic Slovakia (MDS), later established as a political party. The economic policies promoting a transition to a market economy also took their toll on the Civic Forum. Two groups emerged in February 1991 – the conservative Civic Democratic Party (CDP), led by Vaclav Klaus, and the liberal Civic Movement (CM), led by Jiri Dienstbier. Klaus and the CDP argued for a more rapid pace towards a market economy with the CM invoking the social and political effects of such a policy. The economically poorer half of the country, Slovakia, consequently suffered disproportionately from the direction of economic management, thus fuelling resentment tapped into by nationalist politicians, especially Meciar.

The results of the legislative elections of June 1992 proved to be decisive for the country's eventual dissolution. The MDS, led by Meciar, emerged as the dominant force in Slovakia with 34 per cent of the total Slovak vote. As expected, the CDP led by Klaus (in coalition with the Christian Democratic Party), won the largest share in the Czech lands, about 34 per cent, thus setting the stage for the division of the country by the two political leaders holding opposite views on economic policy. On 25 November 1992 the Federal Assembly adopted legislation providing for the constitutional disbanding of the federation. A general ratio of 2 to 1 was used for the dividing of the country's assets and liabilities as well as its armed forces, based on the relative size of the Czech and Slovak populations. At midnight on 31 December all federal structures were dissolved and the Czech Republic and the Slovak Republic came into being. Like the 'velvet revolution', the political parting of the way between Czechs and Slovaks might be termed a 'velvet divorce'.

The Czech Republic was probably the best positioned of all the east-central European countries to solve its economic problems. It did not have a huge foreign debt (see Table 9–2) and had started to move away from rigid central planning before the November upheaval and slowly but deliberately set about moving towards a free market economy. The capital, Prague, has become a mecca for entrepreneurs and foreign investment by Americans and Germans. On the other hand, the Slovak Republic – now simply called Slovakia – inherited the old-time Communist industrial infrastructure, which provided for a good portion of employment. Consequently, the drive towards privatization has been slower owing to the higher political costs of aggravating unemployment in a rapid fashion. Meciar, who became the new Slovak Republic prime minister, also proved to be politically divisive, thus rendering the political and economic situation less conducive to outside investment.

Bulgaria: The Dutiful Ally

Bulgaria has been the only east European country not to oppose Soviet hegemony in any way. Bulgarian loyalty resulted from a friendship reaching back into the nineteenth century (see Chapter 6), and complementary economic interests. Bulgarian concentration on light industry, agriculture, agricultural industry, electronics and tourism fit in well with the Soviet economic plans for Eastern Europe. The Soviet Union supplied Bulgaria with heavy industrial goods, oil and investment funds.

Politically, Bulgarian developments mirrored those in the Soviet Union. Both Communist party leaders Georgi Dimitrov and Vulko Chervenkov dutifully followed the Stalinist nationalization and collectivization of industry and agriculture under a strict communist party rule. When Khrushchev called for an Eastern European division of labour in the 1960s, Bulgaria, under its new party head, Tudor Zhivkov, obligingly complied. Zhivkov also used Khrushchev's denunciation of Stalin in 1961 to eliminate the Stalinists such as Chervenko from party offices. Zhivkov rule of over 35 years (1954–89) was characterized by what Joseph Rothschild describes as 'autocratic yet accessible and with a common touch' that suits the Bulgarian egalitarian social tradition. Although the Bulgarian economy experienced steady longterm growth, it began to encounter serious energy and technological obsolescence problems in the 1980s. Soviet oil supplies and investment funds also dried up, as the Soviet Union had to seek funds externally for its own reforms. Bulgaria's attempts to Bulgarize all its minorities, especially the forced emigration of many ethnic Turks, produced international opposition to Zhivkov's regime.

In response to change throughout the Soviet Bloc, the Bulgarian Communists appear to have made only a minimal amount of change in order to prevent the rise of any popular opposition. The removal of Zhivkov from power on 10 November 1989 and his subsequent indictment for inciting ethnic hostilities and for corruption and mismanagement permitted his successors to blame him for all Bulgaria's ills. The party's surrender of its legal monopoly of power in January 1990 was another move by the new party leader, Alexander Lilov, and head of state, Petar Mladenov, to establish party legitimacy. The party's attempt to bring opposition groups into the government in February 1990, failed when they all refused to join a Communist-led coalition government. The opposition groups realize that they could only lose by joining a coalition: any government successes would be claimed by the Communist majority and any failures would have to be shared by all coalition partners. The lack of a democratic tradition in Bulgaria and the weakness of the opposition groups such as the Agrarian Party (BAPU) and the Union of Democratic Forces (UDF) led to a Communist, now renamed Socialist (BSP), party victory in the June elections. In the 400-seat Parliament, the Socialists won 211 seats, the Union of Democratic Forces won 144 seats, and the Movement for Rights and Freedoms (MRF) secured 23 seats. The MRF was established in early 1990 to represent the country's Muslim minority (mostly ethnic Turks).

Bulgaria breaks the pattern we have seen so far of ruling Communist parties losing their country's first democratic election, as was the case in Poland, Hungary and Czechoslovakia. In the Bulgarian case, the BSP secured an absolute majority in the legislature, though failed in obtaining the required two-thirds majority necessary for approval of constitutional reforms. Further breaking the pattern of Communist parties championing a go-slow approach to economic liberalization, it was the BSP government that attempted to 'show good faith by implementing IMF economic reform programmes before the IMF required them'. The resulting price increases and immediate economic deterioration boosted the political support for the opposition UDF, which called for a vote of no-confidence in the government. Although the government survived the vote, a large-scale four-day strike organized by the Podkrepa Trade Union Confederation finally led to the resignation of the government and a government of 'national consensus' comprising members of the BSP, the UDF, BAPU and four independents. This government, surprisingly, continued with IMF-determined policies such as abolishing price controls in February 1991. New elections were finally held to the reformed legislature (a new constitution was adopted in July 1991), and the UDF emerged with the largest share of the vote, 34.4 per cent and 110 seats. Yet the BSP obtained 106 seats, while the MRF secured 24 seats, thus holding the balance of power in the 240-seat National Assembly.

Bulgaria continued along the road of economic liberalization all the while experiencing turnover in the post of prime minister. Two issues stand out in the Bulgarian situation. The first was the very desperate economic situation. All of the east European states under Communist rule (except Romania, see Chapter 6) concentrated on trading within the Soviet bloc, and in particular with the Soviet Union. With the collapse of the Soviet economy, and with it, the coordinating organization COMECON, the trade patterns built up over the past 45 years disintegrated, obviously hurting those nations with the most integrated economies. Such an economy was Bulgaria, where, for instance, 85 per cent of exports went to COMECON members (63 per cent went to the Soviet Union alone). In contrast, one-quarter of Polish exports went to the Soviet Union and 19 per cent to other COMECON members in 1987, and 20 per cent of Hungary's exports went to the Soviet Union and 27 per cent to other COMECON in 1988. The blow to the Bulgarian economy was then far more severe compared with other COMECON nations, for instance in spare parts for machinery, brand new currency regulations, etc. To top it off, Bulgaria was the most dependent upon energy imports from the Soviet Union, which now had to be paid for in hard currency.

Finally, the minority question in Bulgaria flared throughout the late 1980s and early 1990s, to a great extent as a consequence of Communist legislation beginning in 1984. The Turkish minority in Bulgaria, which comprises approximately ten per cent of the population, was forced to adopt Slavic names in advance of the 1985 census, part of a 'Bulgarization' campaign by the Zhivkov regime. They were also banned from practicing Islamic religious rites. The next several years witnessed police repression of ethnic Turk demonstrators and their forced expulsion numbering in the thousands. Amnesty International also reported numerous arrests and imprisonments for refusal to accept new identity cards and forced resettlement in other parts of the country. Beginning in 1990, the new government began to move away from these practices, for instance permitting ethnic Turks to use their original Islamic names. In late 1991 the government decreed that Turkish be taught as an optional subject four times weekly in the regions concerned. By 1994 it seemed that although ethnic tensions still remained, the Communist-era 'Bulgarization' campaign was a thing of the past.

By 1994, the UDF-led coalition government was immobilized by internal bickering and appeared to have lost the will for more reform. Progress on privatization of the economy had slowed, and the promise of material improvement faded for many. Like Hungary and Poland before it, the December 1994 elections returned the former Communists, the BSP, back to power. The BSP won an outright majority of seats, 124 out of 240, with 43.5 per cent of the vote.

Romania: The Collapse of the last Stalinist Bastian

Romanian opposition to Soviet hegemony began in the 1960s during the last years of Gheorghiu-dej's leadership and continued under his successor, Nicolae Ceaucescu (1965–89). Khrushchev's desire for a division of labour among Comecon countries relegated Romania to that of raw materials supplier and light industry manufacturing rather than full economic development. Popular support for the Communist party's drive for a fuller economic development produced government legitimacy seldom obtained among East-Bloc governments. Romania's independent course received further support from the Sino-Soviet split. Not only were China and Romania still following a Stalinist course, but China also opposed Soviet interference in the affairs of other Communist countries. Romania also did not provide Soviet leaders with sufficient reason for a military intervention. Although Romania refused to cooperate fully economically, it maintained strict one-party rule, thus providing no ideological heresy, and did not withdraw from the Warsaw Pact but only refused to participate in manoeuvre. Romania's finest hour came when it refused to participate in the invasion of Czechoslovakia in 1968. Although Ceaucescu despised the direction the Czech reforms were taking, he wanted to uphold the rights of Communist countries to develop as they saw fit. The rapid economic development in the 1960s and growing contacts with the West, for economic reasons, brought Romania and Ceaucescu international acceptance.

The 1970s and 1980s were to produce another image of Romania. Ceaucescu's Stalinist attitudes and growing megalomania led to the loss of popular legitimacy and international respect. As the Soviet Union developed more reformist practices with a relaxation in the Communist domination of power, Ceaucescu became even more despotic in order to maintain power. Ultimately, he came to trust only family members whom he placed in important government positions. Rothschild has described his rule as 'dynastic socialism' to distinguish it from that of other Communist countries.

Any legitimacy Ceaucescu's regime possessed turned sour in the late 1970s, when energy and capital shortages led to a ruthless austerity programme. Rationing of energy was enforced by secret police squads sent out to enforce compliance. Naturally, the Soviet Union was not inclined to offer extensive aid to save such a maverick. Ceaucescu turned to draconian measures to halt the decline. In order to increase Romania's traditionally low agricultural productivity, Ceaucescu attempted to replace all small farming plots and some 8000 small villages with huge agro-industrial centres where production would presumably be more efficient. They were also intended to eliminate ethnic-cultural differences such as the Hungarian and German settlements in Transylvania. He also attempted to proletarianize cities such as Bucharest by destroying the old bourgeois quarters and replacing them with huge socialist housing developments with no private bathrooms or kitchens. In order to increase the population, Ceaucescu forbade all forms of contraception. Medical units were stationed in factories to detect pregnant women and penalize them if no birth occurred. Women who did not conceive by age 25 had to pay an addition tax of between 10 to 15 per cent of their salary. These policies increasingly isolated his regime from society, from the West and from the Gorbachev regime. Ceaucescu reduced the foreign debt to a low $50 per capita by 1988 by exporting almost everything that was not tied down but it also caused mass misery by producing many shortages.

Such conditions produced a reaction like no other in Eastern Europe, and has continued to influence the post-revolutionary situation. Instead of large peaceful demonstrations and limited violence by the Communist regimes typical elsewhere, Romania experienced savage government reaction. The revolutionary period began when government troops and security agents, the Securitate, massacred hundreds of demonstrators in Timisoara on 17 December 1989. The demonstrators had protested the treatment of a minister and police brutality against a small group of people who tried to protect the minister. The crowd eventually marched to Communist party headquarters where they were ruthlessly broken up by the Securiate and police. Ceaucescu apparently wished to avoid the fate of other East European regimes and chose to follow the Chinese policy of massive repression. That the regime lasted only four days longer, however, apparently resulted from the extremely hostile popular resentment of his rule. After returning from a scheduled trip to Iran, Ceaucescu delivered an arrogant radio and television speech on 18 December in which he took responsibility for the government action against those he termed 'hooligans' and 'fascists.'

His speech on 21 December in Bucharest, to a crowd that he had packed with his supporters, revealed to him the popular hostility to his regime and steeled the resolve of all those who opposed him. After some preliminary favourable responses from his supporters, student led chants of 'Ceaucescu the dictator' were spontaneously picked up by most of the crowd. Ceaucescu fled the scene but was captured by the military. Four days later, on 25 December Ceaucescu was executed by forces of the Council of National Salvation. Violent confrontations then took place between the army and the hated Securiate until the latter were either killed or driven into hiding. This Council later set up a 253-member provisional Council for National Unity to act as a parliament until national elections in May 1990. These elections gave the National Front 80 per cent of the vote. Ion Iliescu was elected president with 85 per cent of the votes cast. Although the Council of National Salvation contended that it had been established six months before Ceaucescu's down-fall, it appeared to many Romanians that this may have been only a ploy to reestablish the legitimacy of the Communists who make up its membership. Despite the fact that the Communist party relinquished its legal monopoly of power, the continued dominance of the Council of National Salvation brought about frustration and attacks by those who wanted the immediate establish-ment of more democratic forces. Since the Communist dominated Council of National Salvation controls the media, oppositions groups did not get ade-quate national exposure. Many Romanians felt that their revolution was derailed and prevented from reaching a true anti-Communist resolution.

Throughout the rest of 1990 and into 1991, unrest marked by large demonstrations against the government and its economic policies continued. In November 1990, 100,000 marched through Bucharest to protest the deteriorating economic situation. The march was organized by the Civic Alliance, a newly-founded opposition grouping. Finally, in September 1991, in reaction to violent clashes in Bucharest between miners and the security forces, during which the legislature was sacked and the television headquar-ters besieged, the government resigned. A coalition government was put together in October and in November, acting as a constituent assembly, the legislature approved a new Constitution, enshrining a multi-party system, guarantees of human rights and a free-market economy. Against this background, new legislative and presidential elections took place on 27 September 1992 (local elections in April of that year confirmed the decline in support of the NSF). The pro-Iliescu NSF, now known as the Democratic National Salvation Front (DNSF) managed to get 117 of the 328 seats in the Assembly of Deputies, still the largest single amount for any party. The main opposition party, the Democratic Convention of Romania (DCR) Alliance, grouping six parties, won 82 seats. Iliescu was re-elected president on the second round with 61.43 per cent of the vote.

Yugoslavia: From Tito to Turmoil and then Disintegration

Although the growing fragmentation that engulfed Yugoslavia in the 1980s appears on the surface to be primarily the result of Marshall Tito's death in

1980, it had its origins as far back as the 1950s and Tito is partially responsible for it. The self-management system, instituted in 1952, increased local authority by decreasing centralized economic decision-making. Since the 1950s, a battle between reformers and conservatives has become entangled with ethnic-provincial allegiances: in broad terms the reformers have sought decentralized decision making and are associated with the more economically advanced northern regions of Slovenia and Croatia and the conservative centralizers have found their main strength in Serbia.

Since the self-management system was originally conceived as an ideological counter to Soviet pressures in the period 1948–52 and continued to serve as a justification for the Yugoslav system, it cannot be lightly discarded, no matter how poorly the economy performs. Its justification was that it brought the worker to the centre of economic-political decision making and was, therefore, a much more advanced form of socialism than the Soviet system. The League of Communists took on the role of guide and teacher rather than undisputed decision-maker.

Several decisive battles were decided in favour of the reformers in the 1960s, while the economy improved steadily and provided Yugoslavia, predominantly Croatia and Slovenia, with the highest standard of living in Eastern Europe. A new 1963 constitution gave increased autonomy to local enterprises and administrative units (communes) at the expense of federal, central authority. It paved the way for major reforms, known as 'The Reform' by Yugoslavs, in 1965. The Reform introduced mainly market mechanisms for the economy, cut out government subsidies for weak enterprises, and moved to integrate the Yugoslav economy into the world market. The immediate economic dislocation caused by the reform led to a massive migration of Yugoslav workers to Western Europe and to their enrichment in comparison with those who stayed at home. Conservative opposition to these reforms was dealt a severe blow when the centralist Serbian-oriented Vice President Rankovic fell from power in 1966. His fall gave the reformist forces renewed momentum and further restricted federal power. However, the reformist forces' aggressive promotion of efficiency (Croatia, Slovenia) versus equality (southern Yugoslavia) and local autonomy, led Tito to purge them in 1971. He was later to remark that he should have used this occasion to tame the 'eight little autarchies.' But the constitution had just been amended, in 1970, to give prime authority to the six republics and two autonomous provinces. The federal government retained authority over foreign policy, defence and some financial and monetary policy. Decentralization was expanded even further with the 1974 constitution that reduced the federal government's domestic duties to primarily that of arbitrator among the republics and provinces and gave Kosovo and the Vojvodina veto rights over federal decision-making.

A change in the self-management system, in 1966, with the aim of bringing workers into the decision making process and of reducing the managerial-technocratic monopoly of local power vis-à-vis local party officials added to the decentralization of power. Tito apparently believed that self-management so designed would reduce ethnic particularism by breaking up the solidarity of ethnic blocs. The result of this reform was ineffective, inexperienced work councils that had to depend on the technocratic-managerial elite. When the economy turned down in the late 1970s and 1980s, self-management began to be viewed as a sham.

The mid-1980s brought a renewed debate between reformers and conservatives with the economic decline. With local enterprises enabled to negotiate loans, Yugoslavia's indebtedness increased rapidly to over \$20 billion. These loans were in many cases ineffective since there was no centralized Yugoslav market and local enterprises often lacked the capability to compete internationally.

The solution worked out for Tito's successor contributed to the decline of the centre. Unable to groom a true 'Yugoslav' successor and aware that a Serb or Croat would not be acceptable as a long-term leader, Tito promulgated the 'standing rules' for collective leadership in October 1978. Leadership was to be rotated: the presidency of Yugoslavia and party were to be rotated annually on an ethnic basis and prime ministers every four years. The lack of continuity in leadership coupled with strong powers of the republic areas limited the effectiveness of the central government. As the government immobility worsened and the economic problems grew, the decentralization achieved earlier came increasingly into question. Some demanded re-centralization while others are demanding even more free market mechanisms and greater provincial autonomy. Changes in 1988 increased the amount of land an individual could hold privately from 10 to 30 hectares, granted the right to strike, and increased private enterprise. But the economic problems increased nationalism and enhanced the possibility of a conservative solution. A strong national Serb leader, Slobodan Milošević, encouraged Serbs to dream of a greater Serbia by limiting the autonomy of Kosovo and the Vojvodina. At the same time, the reformist provinces of Croatia and Slovenia began to move towards an even freer economy and greater independence from the centre. After the Yugoslav League of Communists voted to permit a multi-party system on 22 January 1990, the Slovenian Communist party broke away from the national party on 4 February and renamed its party the Party for Democratic Renewal. Despite this Communist transformation, the Slovenian multi-party elections in April 1990 produced a separatist majority and a decisive defeat for the Communists. A coalition of six parties, called EMOS, won 55 per cent of the vote for the social-political chamber. The Communist party finished third, behind the Liberal Party, with only 20 per cent of the vote. Two weeks later, a centre-right Croatian Democratic Alliance, advocating autonomy for Croatia, won 70 per cent of the vote for Croatia's social-political chamber. The Democratic Alliance's stress on Croatian nationalism appeared to have been the decisive issue, since the Communists also advocated a democratic system and autonomy for Croatia.

The federal prime minister at this time, Ante Markovic, tried to rapidly modernize Yugoslavia's economy. He moved to gain international convertibility for the dinar on 1 January 1990 by tying it to the West German mark. He also attempted to open the country to heavy foreign investment by permitting 100 per cent foreign ownership of business and 99 per cent ownership of banks. However, Yugoslavia was pulled apart by its ethnic differences before his reforms could take effect. In fact, the wide gulf in economic indices such as per capita income and living standards between the north – Slovenia and Croatia – and the south – Macedonia and Kosovo – added to the centrifugal forces pulling apart the Yugoslav state.

The events signalling the unravelling of the Yugoslav state, accompanied by civil war inflamed by nationalist passions, occurred in rapid succession between 1990 and 1992. In July 1990, the Serbian Republic legislature suspended the government of the autonomous region of Kosovo, populated overwhelmingly by ethnic Albanians. This occurred after the Kosovo legislature declared itself a separate territory within the Yugoslav federation. In November and December of 1990, the first free legislative elections were held in Macedonia, Bosnia and Herzegovenia and Serbia. By March of 1992, whether through popular referenda or legislative acts, proclamations of independence, not simply autonomy, were announced by Slovenia, Croatia, Macedonia and Bosnia. The Republics of Serbia and Montenegro announced on 27 April 1992 that they composed a new Yugoslavia (Milošević of Serbia had already exploited Serbian nationalist pressures to install more subservient leaders in Montenegro a couple of years earlier).

Unfortunately, the proclamations of sovereignty and statehood by the various Yugoslav republics were accompanied by violent reactions and the mobilization of local militias, newly created national armies and the involvement of the old Yugoslavian federal army, now inherited mostly by Serbia. Although Slovenia escaped by and large from armed conflict, the presence of a sizable number of ethnic Serbs in portions of Croatia sparked the first large-scale military operations in the Balkans. A UN-sponsored cease-fire was finally implemented in 1992 after Serbs had captured large parts of Croatia. Bosnia was the next scene of military confrontation. Despite numerous UN-sponsored cease-fires, conflict continued well into 1995, including the involvement of NATO aircraft. Territorial partition plans were offered as the only solution to the problems experienced by this extremely multi-ethnic former Yugoslav republic, but the civil war continued. During this conflict, the worse massacre in Europe since the Second World War, took place in the Bosnian town of Srebrenica. Protected by Dutch UN peacekeepers, who were ultimately unable to defend the population, the Serb army under the command of Ratko Mladic, segregated the civilian population into groups of males – young and old – and women. Most of the males were shot, their bodies buried in mass unmarked graves. For this crime, Mladic, still on the run by the time of writing, was indicted for war crimes by the International Tribunal in the Hague. A peace agreement was finally achieved in the American city of Dayton, on 21 November 1995. Events continued, this time within Serbia, or the rump Yugoslavia, involving the region of Kosovo. This long-simmering conflict, aggravated by the nationalist actions of Milošević, came to a head with outright war-fare, including civilian massacres and ethnic cleansing. In the end, NATO aerial bombing of sites in Sderbia, including the capital, Belgrade, brought Milošević to the negotiating table. Milošević himself was arrested on 1 April, 2001, on charges of abuse of power, and on 28 June was handed over to the UN International Criminal Tribunal for the Former Yugoslavia, where he stands indicted for war crimes stemming from the numerous con-flicts described above.

How does one explain, briefly, the rapid descent of Yugoslavia into the nightmare of savage fighting and "ethnic cleansing" (the forcible removal of an ethnic group by another in order to 'purify' ethnic representation in an area through intimidation and murder)? No single factor can explain this interethnic violence. Internally, the Serbian reaction (led by Milošević) to Slovene and Croatian calls for even greater decentralization by mobilizing Serbian nationalism as a means for asserting greater central control undermined any continuing Communist cohesion between the republics. The economic situation already mentioned, the Yugoslav north-south division, and its worsening throughout the late 1980s, spurred the better off republics – Slovenia and Croatia – to leave the federation. Finally, the use of nationalist appeals by various political leaders other than Milošević, especially those of the Croatian leader Tjudman, rekindled hostilities that had developed during the Second World War between Serbs and Croatians. Externally, other actors such as the United Nations, the European Union, NATO and the United States, delayed until well into the conflict attempts to find solutions to the escalating fighting. The focus upon the US-led Gulf War against Iraq together with a belief that however unfortunate, the Balkans, in a post-Cold War era, were no longer strategically significant to warrant major outside involvement. A book published in 1991, *Securing Europe* by Richard Ullman, maintained that the unfolding Yugoslavian tragedy would no doubt stay 'contained', unlike the earlier Balkans crisis that led to the First World War. Consequently, the belated entry of UN-peacekeepers and threats of NATO air strikes could only lead to solutions legitimizing *de facto* territorial aggrandizement through ethnic cleansing.

While the overthrow of authoritarian regimes in 1989 was aided by Gorbachev's policies and his sometime timely interventions, the main impe-tus for change came from within these countries. All the upheavals except that in Romania were marked by massive peaceful demonstrations against the leadership. The widespread opposition to the communist leadership had long existed. For instance, Vaclav Havel wrote of the double life character-ized by a public support but private disdain for the regimes. Once the populations perceived that some possibility existed to overthrow the regimes, the private side was given vent in the massive demonstrations. The fact that no counter-revolution occurred, except in Romania, can be attributed to the communist hierarchy's loss of faith in their right to rule. They no longer thought the system worth defending. Communist central planning and thought control contained the seeds of its own destruction.

McDonald's in St. Petersburg
(Photo: Dirk Ingo Franke. This image is licensed under the "http://www.gnu.org/copyleft/fdl.html" GNU Free
Documentation License)

In all of the former Communist states, including the former Soviet Union
and the post-Soviet states that emerged, any illusions that western prosperity
would rapidly accompany the democratization of these regimes were ended
within a few short and tumultuous years. The return of reformed Communist
parties (almost all of them now called Socialist) to government through free
elections in Poland, Hungary and Bulgaria, the halting steps toward market
economies in Romania and Russia, etc., demonstrated that the transition
from centrally controlled and planned economies to the Western model
would be long and difficult.

The Transition

Although we can precisely date the fall of the Communist regimes, it is more
difficult to pinpoint a particular date upon which we can say these countries
were in transition to western liberal democracy and market capitalism. As we
have seen above, the first few years after the fall of Communist rule were
full of uncertainty in matters related to the economy – how to 'switch' from
command control to market mechanisms with as little social disruption as
possible – and politics – distrust of 'party', the reawakening of old ethnic and
nationalist attitudes, and so on. However, by the late 1990s, certain patterns
began to emerge. Eastern Europe, now more commonly (and accurately)

referred to as the Baltic states and east-central Europe, had appeared to make the transition to political stability. Even Slovakia, which until 1998 was almost a pariah state owing to the authoritarian and nationalist presence of Meciar, returned to the path of moderate politics. Secondly, after a variety of different experiments in instituting market economic principles and dynamics – from Polish shock therapy to a more gradual Czech process, all of these countries began to enjoy high and sustained economic growth by the end of the decade.

If a single factor is to be isolated in the transition period it is the role played by the European Union. In March 1998 the EU formally invited Latvia, Lithuania, Estonia, Poland, Hungary, Czech Republic, Slovakia and Slovenia to begin accession negotiations leading to membership. The formal set of requirements for membership, known as the Copenhagen conditions (after a 1993 EU summit hosted by Denmark), state that an applicant country must (a) be democratic, with respect for human rights and the rule of law, (b) have a functioning free-market economy and the capacity to cope with the competitive pressures of capitalism, and (c) be able to take on the obligations of the *acquis communitaire* (the body of laws and policies already adopted by the EU). The attraction of membership – free access to the markets of the EU countries as well as development aid from the EU's Cohesion policy – provided a great mobilization for governments both centre-left as well as centre-right. By May 2004, when these countries formally joined the EU, they were experiencing greater economic growth

Orange revolution demonstration in Kiev, Ukraine.
(© Mykola Lazarenko/Reuters/ Corbis)

than many of the older and larger EU member states. They had quickly become magnets for foreign investment for both West European and North American companies. The educated, skilled and yet comparatively lower paid workforce made their products extremely competitive with west European products. According to a 2005 study by Mercer Human Resources Consulting, the world's largest employee benefits consultancy, labour costs in the new member states are, on average, less than a quarter of the level of the older member states. This is quite a contrast. The study found that the highest annual employment costs were in Belgium, Sweden and Germany where the total financial package of employing a worker, including benefit costs, was more than 50,000 euros ($58,000) a year. This is compared with 4752 euros in Latvia; 5649 euros in Lithuania; 8257 euros in Poland and 9540 euros in the Czech Republic. We can assume that even with rising wages over time, these countries are going to be prime areas of European economic growth for some time.

Two countries that have not followed the pattern of east-central Europe or the Baltic states are Belarus and Ukraine. As we mentioned above, with the fall of the Soviet Union, three of its component parts, the Russian Federation, Belarus and Ukraine, formed the Commonwealth of Independent States, or CIS. Belarus has remained essentially a dictatorship, moving from a Communist party dominated political system to one of autocracy. The current president, Aleksandr Lukashenko, was elected president in 1994. Having won 45 per cent of the vote in the first round, he went on to win in the run-off with 80 per cent. After a 1996 referendum that extended his term in office until 2001, he ran for re-election in 2001 and won with a self-declared landslide. The OSCE stated that the conditions of this election 'fail[ed] to meet international standards'. In late 2004, Lukashenko used another referendum to eliminate any term limits for president, a referendum his government claimed was approved by 79.42 per cent. He has used censorship and other aspects of state intervention to maintain his power, and Belarus remains the only European country without full membership in the Council of Europe, due to its undemocratic nature.

As for Ukraine, neither a east-central European 'velvet' transition nor a Belarus-style authoritarianism took place, but perhaps we could label its post-Soviet evolution as somewhere in between those two experiences. After a period of re-writing the constitution and treading carefully with Russia over the fate of Crimea (where the Russian Navy has a port), former Prime Minister Leonid Kuchma became president in 1994 (he was re-elected once). His period in office became characterized as somewhat erratic in economic policy which prevented Ukraine from attracting much foreign investment, mired in scandals – one in which it was claimed he was connected with the murder of a journalist, and restrictions on press freedoms. However, in the election to choose his successor, fought between incumbent Prime Minister Viktor Yanukovych and former Prime Minister Viktor Yushchenko, and series of protests took place in response to allegations of massive corruption in the counting of the votes in a run-off, allegedly robbing Yushchenko of victory. What became labelled the Orange Revolution – orange was adopted as the official colour of the movement – helped force a second run-off and Yushchenko was elected. Calling for closer relations with the EU – and in fact future membership, he was seen as being more openly pro-western than his competitor – who was favoured by Putin in Russia. It is too early to say definitively, but Ukraine may finally join other east European states for which the economic benefits expected from adopting western market policies are now beginning to be felt.

FURTHER READING

For the Gorbachev period, see Richard Sakwa, *Gorbachev and his Reforms, 1985–1990* (1990), Archie Brown, *The Gorbachev Factor* (1996). Michael McFaul analyses the difficulties in establishing stable political institutions under Gorbachev and then Yeltsin's first term in *Russia's Unfinished Revolution: Political Change from Gorbachev to Putin* (2001). Some authors foresaw the collapse of the Soviet Union, such as Zbigniew Brzezinski in *The Failure of Communism* (1988); and Judy Shelton in *The Coming Clash* (1989). Shelton argued that the Soviet leadership was losing its ideological hold and that it could not produce economic improvement soon enough to legitimize itself.

As for the 'new' Russia, Richard Sakwa gives a comprehensive and readable evaluation of Putin's first term as president in *Putin: Russia's Choice* (2004). Martin McCauley gives an informative (and entertaining) account of the economic transition during the Yeltsin years, giving in-depth scrutiny to many of the 'oligarchs' that made millions of dollars from the privatization of the Russian economy, in *Bandits, Gangsters and The Mafia: Russia, The Baltic States and the CIS since 1992* (2001).

Social and economic changes are examined further in David Lane and Cameron Ross, *The Transition from Communism to Capitalism: ruling elites from Gorbachev to Yeltsin* (1999); Peter Rutland, *Business and the State in Contemporary Russia* (2000); David Lane, *Russia in Flux: The Political and Social Consequences of Reform* (1992); James Millar and Sharon Wolchik, *The Social Legacy of Communism* (1994); and Andrei Shleifer and Daniel Triesman, *Without a Map: political tactics and economic reform in Russia* (2000). For a general account of Russian foreign policy, see Michael Bowker and Cameron Ross, *Russia After the Cold War* (2000). For a more detailed account, see Ted Hopf, ed., *Understandings of Russian Foreign Policy* (1999); and Michael Mandelbaum, ed., *The New Russian Foreign Policy* (1998). On relations with NATO, see J. L. Black, *Russia Faces NATO Expansion: bearing gifts or bearing arms?* (2000). The interplay between domestic and international factors is examined in Malcolm *et al.*, *Internal Factors in Russian Foreign Policy* (1996); and Celeste Wallander, *The Sources of Russian Foreign Policy after the Cold War* (1996). The Chechen conflict continues to impact both Chechnya and beyond, and is analyzed by John Dunlop, *Russia Confronts Chechnya: Roots of a Separatist Conflict* (1998); and Robert Seely, *Russo-Chechen Conflict, 1800–2000* (2001). Both authors trace the origins of Chechen-Russian conflict back many centuries.

Anatol Lieven gives a very engaging, frontline perspective in *Chechnya: Tombstone of Russian Power* (1999). Finally, contemporary analyses can be found in recent editions of *Developments in Russian Politics*, edited by Stephen White, Alex Pravda and Zvi Gitelman.

A comprehensive and readable account of the events of 1989 is Gale Stokes, *The Walls Came Tumbling Down: Collapse of Communism in Eastern Europe* (1993). Two excellent studies that have provided much information and insight in this chapter include Joseph Rothschild, *Return to Diversity: A Political History of East Central Europe since World War II*, 2nd edition (1993); and J. F. Brown, *Eastern Europe and Communist Rule* (1988). Another general work is Roger East and Jolyon Pontin, *Revolution and Change in Central and Eastern Europe* (1997), which provides superb background on individual countries. On the Balkans in particular, see R. J. Crampton, *The Balkans since the Second World War* (2002); Karen Dawisha and Bruce Parrott, eds., *Politics, power and the struggle for democracy in Southeast Europe* (1997); and Dennis Hupchick, *The Balkans: From Constantinople to Communism* (2001). See also Sten Berglund *et al.*, eds., *The Handbook of Political Change in Eastern Europe* (2nd ed. 2004), as well as the most recent edition of *Developments in Central and East European Politics 3* (2003), edited by Stephen White, Judy Batt, and Paul G. Lewis. For a specific analysis of organized labour in post-communist countries, see Stephen Crowley and David Ost, eds, *Workers After Workers' States: Unions and Politics in Eastern Europe Since the Fall of Communism* (2001).

As for individual countries, there are many works from which to choose, and individual country chapters are available in both Berglund *et al.* and White *et al*, mentioned above. An indicative list would include, for Ukraine, Sarah Whitmore, *State Building in Ukraine* (2004); Roman Wolczuk, *Ukraine's Foreign and Security Policy, 1991–2000* (2002), which traces the efforts to re-orient Ukraine's perspective from east to west and Marta Byzcok, *Ukraine: Movement without Change* (2000), which would give a useful background to the unanticipated events of the orange movement cited above. For Poland, see works cited in Chapter 9 for coverage during the early Communist period. Timothy Garton Ash explores the Solidarity experience in *The Polish Revolution: Solidarity* (1985) and the events of 1989 in Poland and elsewhere in *The Magic Lantern: The Revolutions of 1989 Witnessed in Berlin, Prague, Budapest and Warsaw* (1990). See also H. Tworzecki, *Parties and Politics in Post-1989 Poland* (1996); I. Prizel, *National Identity and Foreign Policy: Nationalism and Leadership in Poland* (1998); and Marjorie Castle and Ray Taras, *Democracy in Poland* (2002). For Hungary, see A. Bozoki *et al.*, *Post-Communist Transition: Emerging Pluralism in Hungary* (1992); T. Cox and A. Furlong, *Hungary: The Politics of Transition* (1995); and Rudolf Andorka *et al.*, *A Society Transformed: Hungary in Time-Space Perspective* (1999). For the former East Germany, see Mary Fulbrook, *Anatomy of a Dictatorship: Inside the GDR, 1949–1989* (1995); and Charles Maier, *Dissolution: The Crisis of Communism and the End of East Germany* (1997). For Czechoslovakia, see Sharon Wolchik, *Czechoslovakia in Transition* (1991); Bernard Wheaton and Zdenek Kavan, *The Velvet Revolution in Czechoslovakia, 1988–1991* (1992); and Steven Saxonberg, *The Fall: A Comparative Study of the End of Communism in Czechoslovakia, East Germany, Hungary, and Poland* (2004). For Bulgaria, see Robert McIntyre, *Bulgaria: Politics, Economics and Society* (1988); and J. D. Bell, ed., *Bulgaria in*

Transition: Politics, Economics, Society and Culture after Communism (1998). For Romania, see Michael Shafir, *Romania: Politics, Economics, and Society* (1985); and Tom Gallagher, *Romania after Ceausescu* (1995). For Yugoslavia, one can begin with the break-up itself by reading Misha Glenny's *The Fall of Yugoslavia* (1992). For the period after the break-up, see J. B. Allcock *et al.*, *Conflict in the Former Yugoslavia* (1998); S. L. Burg and P. S. Shoup, *The War in Bosnia-Herzegovina: Ethnic Conflict and International Intervention* (1999); and Sabrina Ramet, *Balkan Babel: The Disintegration of Yugoslavia from the Death of Tito to the War for Kosovo* (1999).

12 Political and Economic Trends Since the 1960s in Western Europe

> It's not worth beating one's head against the wall because there are more Germans than French.
>
> – President François Mitterrand, TV interview, 14 July 1994

European economic and social renewal in the sixties provided strong support for the political status quo. Conservatives in Western Europe and socialists in Scandinavia continued their decades-long rule during this long period of economic resurgence. But the economic downturn that began in the early 1970s, described below, helped unseat incumbent political parties throughout Europe as electorates voted for change. A leftward trend that had begun in Western Europe in the 1960s as a result of relaxed East-West tensions and a growing socialist political moderation accelerated rapidly in the 1970s. The apparent moderation and national-centered policies of some Western European Communist parties, or 'Euro-communists' as they were called for a brief period in the 1970s, gained them some additional support. Europeans no longer thought that a vote for a Communist candidate was necessarily a vote for Moscow. The continued relaxation of tensions between East and West and Europe's desire to pursue an independent foreign policy had promoted a policy of détente, or increased understanding and contacts, between Western Europe and the Communist world. The deepening of the Franco-German rapprochement also contributed to stability, as the Mitterrand quite suggests. These contacts, especially the economic ones, were maintained or even enhanced despite the United States–Soviet animosity in the early 1980s. Gorbachev's assumption of power again relaxed East-West tensions and permitted a resumption of contacts. By the 2004, many of the former Communist states of Eastern Europe had joined NATO, and Russia had even signed up to an arrangement with NATO, the Partnership for Peace.

As a Western European economic crisis deepened in the late 1970s, incumbent political parties either lost office or had their majorities sharply reduced. In Great Britain, West Germany, Norway, Sweden for a time and the Benelux countries, parties on the left either lost power or influence. In

France, Italy, Spain and Greece the moderate socialist left gained power or reduced the conservative hold on political office. In all Western European countries the Communist parties lost support beginning in the late seventies due to Soviet actions in Afghanistan and Poland, competition from Socialist parties, and a popular rejection of a radical state-oriented transformation of society. Political changes in the major Western European countries are described more fully below.

End of Authoritarian Government in Southern Europe

The fall of three authoritarian governments in the 1970s – Portugal, Spain, and Greece – had broad significance for both the inhabitants of those countries and for Europe as a whole. Their membership in the European Community, beginning with Greece in 1981 and Spain and Portugal in 1986, also facilitated their economic integration with the rest of Western Europe.

Portugal   Most remarkable was the overthrow in Portugal. In 1974 the seemingly impregnable rightist dictatorship of Premier Marcelo Caetano, successor to Antonio Salazar, was suddenly overthrown in a coup d'etat carried out by junior army officers and a few sympathetic generals. These officers had been forced to serve repeated tours of duty in Portugal's African colonies of Angola, Guinea-Bissau and Mozambique; they had received low pay and few promotions; and they had been given inferior equipment with which to fight Soviet-armed guerrillas.

To make matters worse, a new government policy permitted university students to obtain second-lieutenant bars after undergoing a short course at the military academy. This debasement of their stature was what drove the officers to form the Movimento des Forces Armades (MFA), or Armed Forces Movement, which was responsible for toppling the Caetano regime.

The political views of these young officers had been shaped by constant contact with disgruntled Portuguese university students who had been compelled to serve in Portugal's African territories, and by captured African guerrilla leaders who convinced many of the officers that they were no less manipulated and suppressed than the native Africans. The students and captured guerrilla leaders, many of them Communists, persuaded these junior officers that only a thoroughgoing change in Portuguese society and leadership would improve the position of the military. This explains the strong socialist-communist sympathies of the original military leadership.

These captains and majors became convinced that they could not win the colonial wars and that they were going to be blamed for the defeat in Africa, as they had been blamed for the loss of Goa to India in 1961. At that point they began to question their support for what they believed to be a corrupt, inefficient, reactionary government in Lisbon that was prepared to sacrifice the army in order to save itself.

The revolt in April 1974, euphorically dubbed the 'Carnation Revolution' because the revolutionaries put carnations into the barrels of their rifles (symbolizing a peaceful revolution), brought to power General Antonio de

Spinola. He had recently been dismissed from his post as the army's deputy chief of staff because he had openly urged the democratization of Portugal and an end to the costly colonial wars in Africa. Because of Spinola's widespread popularity among the Portuguese population, the MFA threw its support to him in order to achieve some respectability for the military junta.

Spinola lost the first round when the MFA forced him to accept a member of the Coordinating Committee sympathetic to the Communists, Vasco Goncalves, as prime minister. When the MFA and the Communist party forced Spinola to cancel a rally of his supporters in September 1974 – considered a coup attempt by the MFA – Spinola resigned the presidency.

Portugal's military leaders were guided by their conviction that a powerful parliament, dominated by the Socialists and parties to their right, would halt the military's policy of nationalization and impede the movement towards greater equalization of wealth. But the Communist party had supported the military's economic and social program, and it therefore exerted a major influence on the military leadership until November 1975. At that time the removal of the Communist-backed Goncalves because of Western pressure, coupled with the opposition of more conservative military leaders, led military units sympathetic to the Communists to attempt a coup. Its failure reduced Communist influence among military leaders and in the country as a whole.

Nationalization of the Communist-dominated television and radio stations and reorganization of the Communist-influenced, state-owned press severely weakened the Communists. The now-moderate Council of the Revolution, the executive authority led by General Francesco Costa de Gomes, acted rapidly to remove leftist military officers from the armed forces.

The authority of the military declined as a result of the ideological differences among military leaders and the parliamentary election victories of the Socialist party (led by Mario Soares), and the bourgeois parties. The Socialist victory in the April 1976 parliamentary elections and the demand for a return of parliamentary government put the Socialist party in a dominant position in the newly formed legislature. The Socialists shared power with the newly elected President Antonio Ramalho Eanes, the army chief of staff, who won 61 per cent of the presidential vote in the June 1976 elections. Before the 1982 constitution, the government was responsible to the president.

The results of the 1976 election showed how far the political leadership had moved to the right since the revolution. A once-popular leftist military leader, Major Otelo Saraiva de Carvalho, received only 16 per cent of the presidential vote, whereas Eanes, who was responsible for crushing the rebellion of leftist military units, won easily. The original revolutionaries, whose goal was a complete revamping of society, were now disillusioned and powerless.

Power began to shift towards the right after 1976. But a series of minority governments between 1976 and 1987 produced weak administrations and caretaker governments. The 1987 elections provided a dramatic change when Anibal Cavaco e Silva's center-right Social Democratic Party (PSD) gained an absolute majority of the votes and seats in the legislature. Cavaco, who had headed a minority government since 1985, was aided by the disunity of the left, a rapidly improving economy, and low energy prices. The Communist party faded to only 12 per cent of the vote in 1987. A two party system may be forming as the Socialist Party gained 22 per cent of the vote in 1987 and almost 30 per cent in 1991. However, the Portuguese dual executive relationship (president and prime minister) took on a new twist when former Socialist Prime minister Soares was elected president in 1986 and actively used his office to blunt certain policy initiatives by the PSD government. Despite the tensions caused by this state of affairs, on 13 January 1991, President Soares was reelected with more than 70 per cent of the votes cast. Legislative elections were held on 6 October 1991, and the PSD, running on its economic management record, received an absolute majority in the Assembly, 50.4 per cent of the votes for 135 of the 230 seats. The Socialists took 29.3 per cent of the votes for 72 of the seats.

The Socialists were returned to power in 1995 under the leadership of Antonio Guterres, just missing an absolute majority by four seats. Again, in 1999, Guterres led the Socialists to re-election, this time missing the historic majority by just one seat. By the end of the decade, Portugal had begun to feel the benefits of European integration, especially through the acquisition of development funds for new infrastructure and urban and rural development projects. Tourism grew as another source of income, and in 2000 Guterres hosted an EU summit in Lisbon which launched an ambitious drive to overtake the United States as a world leader in high-tech jobs and economic growthy. Big losses in municipal elections in 2001 led Guterres to resign, and new elections were called, with the PSD returning to power, but in a coalition with the right-wing People's Party. José Manuel Barroso became Prime minister, leaving in 2004 to become president of the European Commission. In the 2005 elections, the Socialists returned to power, joined by the former mayor of Lisbon, Jorge Sampaio, who was re-elected president in 2001. The return of the Socialists occurred at a time of fiscal distress, as Portugal was in breach of EU guidelines on budgetary deficits. The new Prime minister, Jose Socrates, unveiled a program of stiff economic medicine. It is too early to tell if this new policy will work, but although Portugal remains one of the poorest countries in Western Europe, it has certainly ended its marginal existence at the geographic fringes of Europe.

Spain   In terms of its size (38 million inhabitants) and ultimate importance in any possible European union, democracy's gain in Spain was the most significant south European transition. General Francisco Franco, supported by the Catholic Church, the army and the fascistic Falange movement, made only enough concessions in his decades-long authoritarian government to avert rebellion. Many liberals were appeased in the 1960s by the relaxation of press censorship, the abolition of military courts, rapid economic advances and the election of an opposition comprising one-sixth of the parliament. Even before Franco's death in 1975, reform movements among more progressive members of his regime, younger army officers and the Catholic Opus Dei movement supported a relaxation of authoritarianism. Through a long process of negotiation with opponents of Franco, these more moderate supporters of Franco prepared the way for a surprisingly smooth transition to democratic government under Franco's handpicked successor, King Juan Carlos and his prime minister, Adolfo Suarez. Elections in 1977 gave power to a Union of the Democratic Center (UDC), with Suarez as prime minister. The Socialists (PSOE), perceived as moderate by most voters, received a very substantial 28.5 per cent of the vote. The Communists (PCE) received only 9.3 per cent of the vote.

Spanish reverses resulting from the economic slump that began in Europe in the mid-1970s, temporarily undermined some of the popular support for democratic rule. Some Spaniards looked back nostalgically at Franco's last years which had seen rapid economic growth. The economic problems, combined with Basque separatist terrorism and increased crime, gave the army sufficient excuse to attempt two coups to 'restore order'. The last one, in February 1981, was beaten back only by Juan Carlos's stout defense of democracy and his prestige among military leaders. Another result of the economic slump and political turmoil was the discrediting of the ruling UDC. In the October 1982 elections, the Socialists under the leadership of Felipe Gonzalez won decisively. With 46 per cent of the vote and 202 of 350 seats in the legislature, the Socialists promised to modernize and democratize Spain. The election itself represented the surmounting of another hurdle on the way to true democratic government. There was fear worldwide that the military would not permit the socialists to take power. But the Socialists' moderate program combined with the devastating Communist defeat – they dropped from 11 to 4 per cent of the vote – apparently persuaded the military to give the Socialists a chance. In fact, 22 per cent of the military in Madrid voted Socialists. Another factor was the strength of the rightist Popular Alliance (AP) party that gained 107 seats in the new legislature (and 105 and 107, respectively, in the 1986 and 1989 legislative elections). The military undoubtedly thought that the AP would serve as a brake on any possible Socialist excesses. The Socialist's continued moderation and the almost total collapse of the Communist Party (the United Left received only seven seats in 1986) brought about political calm, which some refer to as a trivialization of politics, similar to political life in much of Western Europe.

Few expected that the socialists would still be ruling in the 1990s. But favourable international economic trends, especially a lowering of oil prices and a reviving worldwide economy and the disunity of parties on the right, led to a long tenure for the Gonzalez's Socialists. The Socialists lost a few seats in every subsequent election (in 1986 from 201 to 184; in 1989 to 176; and in 1993 to 159) due to their austerity program to stem a too-rapid economic growth and corruption scandals in 1992 and 1993. The government formed after the 1993 elections produced a coalition, as the Socialists were unable to acquire an outright majority. They were supported by votes from a small Catalan nationalist party, Convergence and Union (CiU), with its 17 seats. This party, conservative in its economic outlook, prevented the Socialists from turning to their left in order to revive their fortunes. In one sense, the big winner of this election was the PP, or Partido Popular, the successor to the AP, which for the first time nearly pulled even with the Socialists, after languishing with roughly the same amount of seats since the 1982 election. This time it obtained an impressive 141 seats.

Gonzalez also proved to be a moderate in foreign policy. Although public opinion polls indicated that Spaniards were opposed to membership in NATO and the Socialists had opposed Spain's entry in 1982, Gonzalez convinced Spaniards to approve Spain's membership in 1986. Gonzalez calculated that NATO would help modernize his military forces and speed Spain's integration in the EC. He gained approval by getting NATO to agree not to store nuclear weapons in Spain and by convincing the United States to reduce its military presence in Spain. The separatist movements continue to trouble Spain. Although Catalonia, the Basque country and other regions were granted autonomy in 1980, Basque terrorism for complete independence has continued. While Spanish democracy is therefore still under some stress, Spain appears to be in the democratic camp to stay.

In 1996, the PP, under its leader Jose Maria Aznar, won the parliamentary elections, signaling the return of conservative rule in Spain. The PP went on the win an outright majority of seats in the 2000 election, albeit with 45 per cent of the vote. During the period of PP rule, the Socialists entered a post-Gonzales phase, as it tried to find the right formula and leader to challenge Aznar's PP. Spain continued during this time to experience high economic growth, with the construction and the tourist industry leading the way. Aznar also forged close relations with the United States, becoming one of President George W. Bush's staunchest allies post-9/11. Aznar kept a tight grip on the PP, and opposed calls for a further devolution or regionalization of Spain. However, Spanish regional identity continued to grow, and not just in Catalonia, where the Catalan language is the official language of the regional government, nor in the Basque region. On 14 March 2004, the elections – surprisingly to some – returned the Socialists to power, under a new and young leader, Jose Luis Zapatero. He campaigned on bringing Spanish troops home from Iraq, and in the wake of the al-Qaeda train bombings in Madrid, ousted Aznar from power. This result obviously changed Spain's relations with the United States, and Zapatero has made a point of improving relations with France and Germany.

Greece   Greece might well have followed the Western European political pattern had it not been for a military coup in 1967. Prior to the military takeover, a center-right coalition under Constantine Karamanlis had given way to George Papandreou's Progressive Center Union (EPEK) in 1964. Papandreou could have formed a coalition government with the EDA, a Communist-front organization, but chose instead to call an election in which he gained a majority for the EPEK. The army, sensing in Papandreou's victory a challenge to its authority, took a stand in opposition to the EPEK. When it became clear that the EPEK would win the 1967 elections, the army carried out a coup d'etat and set up a right-wing military dictatorship. Papandreou and other center-left politicians were forced to flee the country.

Despite worldwide criticism, often led by Greeks in exile, the military maintained its dictatorial rule. An abortive attempt by the deposed King Constantine to overthrow the military junta ended with his flight into exile. During its years of authoritarian rule, the military junta tried to establish Greek suzerainty over Cyprus to satisfy the Greek majority on the island and the Greek nationalists at home. When its attempt to oust the ruler of Cyprus, Archbishop Makarios, brought Greece close to war with Turkey and close to civil war, the junta was forced to recall Karamanlis in 1974. Karamanlis's center cabinet, which restored the 1952 constitution, won victory in the 1975 elections. Since a 1974 plebiscite had abolished the monarchy, Greece was prepared for a full-scale return to democracy. The government of Karamanlis, fraught with continuing economic problems, quickly lost the parliamentary majority it had enjoyed in 1974–75. Karamanlis's one major achievement was arranging Greece's membership in the EC in 1981. After years of political fragmentation and weak coalition government, Andreas Papandreou's Panhellenic Socialist Movement (PASOK) won a decisive victory behind an anti-NATO, anti-EC, nationalist, socialist program in 1981. As in the major European countries, much of his support came from those who desired change rather than from those attached to any specific program. With 172 of the 300 seats in parliament, PASOK had the necessary majority to implement its program. However, the enormity of Greece's economic difficulties forced Papandreou to go slowly with his socialization programs. After some initial wage and welfare increases that only added to Greece's high inflation, he adopted a pragmatic economic program that emphasized economic recovery rather than social welfare. His threats to pull out of NATO were not carried out primarily because the United States would have found it necessary to strengthen Greece's major opponent, Turkey, in NATO if Greece left. This would threaten the Greeks in Cyprus where 20,000 Turkish troops are stationed to protect the Turkish-controlled area of the island.

PASOK won the 1985 parliamentary elections but with a reduced majority of 22 seats. Severe economic problems forced Papandreou to impose austerity measures and limit his anti-American, anti-EC policies in order to obtain economic aid. These measures produced popular dissatisfaction and reduced PASOK's popularity. The Papandreou government fell in 1989 after party members were implicated in a series of financial scandals. The June 1989 elections produced a coalition government of center-right New Democracy and the communist-dominated Alliance of the Left and Progress. Once this coalition finished its investigation of the corruption charges against the Papandreou government, it called a new election for November. Though indicted for its role in the corruption, PASOK gained three seats in the legislature (from 125 to 128) as did New Democracy (145 to 148). The Communist led Alliance, however, dropped from 28 to 21 seats as a result of their co-operation with the right. New Democracy would have won a majority except for a change in the electoral system in June 1989 that made it more difficult for any party to win a clear majority. Another election was avoided only by the formation of an all-party government on 21 November. Elections in April 1990 gave New Democracy 150 of the 300 seats in Parliament and Papandreou's Socialists 123 seats. With the support of one independent (who later joined New Democracy in June), New Democracy formed the first single-party government since 1981.

Although many supposed that this would be the end of the Papandreou era, the unpopularity of the economic programs of the government kept the hopes of the Socialists alive. Massive strikes and industrial unrest in 1992 and 1993 signaled opposition to the government's privatization program of parts of the public sector. In September 1993, two New Democracy MPs withdrew their support, and with the government's majority gone, it was obliged to resign and call for new elections. The election, on 10 October, produced a political comeback for Papandreou. Leading PASOK into the campaign, the party won 46.9 per cent of the votes, securing 170 seats, while New Democracy obtained 41 per cent of the vote and 111 seats. Though many in the business community feared a rollback of the economic measures of the New Democracy governments, especially the privatizations, the PASOK government acted in a fairly restrained manner.

In 1996, due to ill health, Costas Simitis was appointed to succeed Papandreou. Following Papandreou's death in June 1996, Simitis was elected PASOK leader. Simitis moved PASOK to the political center, softening much of the radical nationalist rhetoric of the Papandreou years. Instead, Simitis positioned PASOK in the mainstream of Western European social democratic parties. His two major achievements were to lead Greece into the eurozone in 2002, and to launch the beginning of a rapprochment with Turkey. Simitis led PASOK to victory in the 2000 elections, but in 2004, New Democracy, led by the nephew of Constantin Karamanlis, Costas Karamanlis, won the election. Greece, while still a relatively poor country by Western European standards, has, like Portugal and Spain, benefited from EU development aid, and under Simitis and his successor, become a more mainstream government in foreign relations and economic policy.

Foreign Policy Independence

The independent foreign policy initiatives begun by Gaullist France in the 1960s accelerated in the 1970s as United States' policy vacillated, as European contacts with the Soviet Union and Eastern Europe increased and as Europeans sought to reduce their economic and diplomatic dependence on the United States. The end of the Cold War, marked by the collapse of the Soviet Union, the dismantling of the Warsaw Pact, and finally membership by many of these countries in NATO, testified to the fundamental change in the political and security landscape in Europe. While foreign policy measures will be discussed in further detail in the sections on each country, the general outline can be summarized here.

A strong initial impetus for a lessening of tensions or détente with the Soviet Union came from the United States-Soviet confrontation in Cuba in 1961–62. When Khrushchev was forced to withdraw Soviet missiles from Cuba by an American blockade in 1962, the way was prepared for an understanding. Having come so near to war, both sides moved towards reducing the tensions that had brought them to the brink. Only one year after the crisis, they agreed to ban the testing of nuclear weapons in the atmosphere, sea, and outer space. Moreover, the emergence of China as a new superpower in the 1960s demanded that the two superpowers bury their differences to meet this new challenge.

There were also compelling domestic reasons for the Soviet move towards detente. In order to develop their economy fully, Soviet leaders wanted to reduce defense spending – possible only if an understanding with the United States could be reached – and to obtain financial and technical aid from both the United States and Europe. Commitments in Vietnam made the United States desirous of achieving a *modus vivendi* with the Soviet Union. Events after the Czech invasion in 1968 – which proved to be only a mild setback to the policy of detente – indicated that the Soviet Union had become a status quo power.

In addition to a multitude of cultural and economic agreements with the West, the Soviet Union became one of President Richard Nixon's staunchest supporters during his unsuccessful attempt to escape the consequences of the Watergate scandal. Afraid that a new president might reverse the Nixon policy of detente, the Soviets charged that anti-Soviet forces in the United States were hoping to use the scandal to change American foreign policy. In the 1974 national elections in France, the Soviet Union favoured the ultimately victorious Liberal party candidate, Valery Giscard d'Estaing, over the candidate of the Left coalition, Francois Mitterrand, on the ground that Mitterrand's election might lead to turmoil in France and thus upset the many economic and diplomatic arrangements between the two countries.

Western Europe's foreign policy also reflected the relaxation in international tensions. As the apparent need for American military protection lessened and contacts with the East increased, Western European countries began to shape their own foreign policy. De Gaulle pulled France out of NATO and West Germany formulated its own *Ostpolitik* (Eastern foreign policy). Europe's tendency to pursue a more independent policy was promoted in the 1970s by economic exchanges with the East, the hope that increased contacts would modify Soviet behaviour, the United States military and foreign policy failures (Vietnam and Iran) and continuing economic weaknesses. When the new United States president, Ronald Reagan, attempted to return to a policy of confrontation with the Soviet Union after 1980, he encountered the stiff resistance of much of Europe. In 1982, the refusal of France, Italy, Britain and West Germany to stop the shipment of high-technology goods to the Soviet Union to build a gas pipeline to Europe forced the Reagan administration to drop its opposition to the shipments. An embargo on such goods to the Soviet Union would have affected 96 per cent of West German exports to the Soviet Union but only 18 percent of American

German army jeeps participating in French national day parade in Paris.
(© Corbis)

exports. Obviously, Western Europe had much more invested in detente than the United States. Not even the Soviet invasion of Afghanistan in 1979 and Soviet-backed suppression of the Polish Solidarity Movement in December 1981 altered seriously what Europeans considered to be an essential understanding with the Soviet Union.

Gorbachev's initiatives, (described in Chapter 11), further reduced East-West tension and led to a weakening of both the Warsaw Pact and NATO. The United States and the Soviet Union began a gradual scaling down of their military weaponry after 1985 as the economic burden of keeping up the arms race and modernizing the Soviet economy proved to be too much for the Soviet economy. Once arms reductions began, Western European countries pushed for even greater reductions in order to reduce tensions and the possibility their countries might become future battlegrounds. Increasing economic ties, especially between West Germany and Eastern Europe, also reduced tensions. By the mid-1990s, former Warsaw Pact countries had entered into a relationship with NATO that began their military integration into the North Atlantic Alliance. The reduced version of membership that the Partnership for Peace (signed in January 1994) represented nevertheless stated that full membership was the ultimate goal.

The end of the Cold War and demise of the Soviet Union raised new issues for NATO and national military missions. Without an enemy to defend *against*, NATO was confronted with the task of re-defining its existence and military strategy. From its involvement in the Yugoslav tragedy, especially in Bosnia, it seems that peacekeeping, with its attendant development of an integrated rapid

Table 12–1   Declining numbers in uniform

	1985	1994	2005
Germany	478,000	408,000	284,000
France	476,600	431,700	259,000
Italy	385,100	325,000	200,000
United Kingdom	327,100	293,500	155,600 (2003)
Spain	320,000	201,000	166,000 (2000)

Sources: The European, 22–28 July 1994. Reprinted by permission of The European, London, England. 2005 figures taken from GlobalSecurity.org, 'Active Duty Uniformed Troop Strength' (http://www.globalsecurity.org/military/world/active-force.htm); UK statistics taken from National Statistics Online (http://www.statistics.gov.uk); Spain figures taken from nationmaster.com.

deployment force, is the direction NATO is evolving. This new direction must also be placed in the context of declining military budgets and demographic changes necessitating smaller armies, as shown in Table 12–1. On 29 March 2004, seven former Communist-run countries formally joined NATO: Bulgaria, Estonia, Latvia, Lithuania, Romania, Slovakia and Slovenia (the Czech Republic, Hungary and Poland had joined in 1999). With NATO now bordering Russia (and Ukraine has expressed an interest in joining NATO after its Orange Revolution), the strategic concept of NATO as solely a European peacekeeper, is now finished, as seen by its involvement in Afghanistan.

European Problems: The End of Rapid Economic Growth

Europe's major problem has been the economic slump and its consequences that began in 1973. After two decades of rapid economic growth, Europe faced an economic crisis that no longer responded to Keynesian economic measures (see Chapter 4). Almost every European nation described itself as being particularly susceptible to this tenacious economic malady: Englanditis, the Dutch disease, le mal Belge. But there were common causes for the slump. The recession resulted from high energy costs that began with the quadrupling of oil prices between 1973 and 1975, increased competition from low-cost, high-technology countries, popular economic and social expectations, and governments' bungled attempts to overcome the crisis.

Although high energy costs have often been singled out as the major cause of the European crisis, the British and Dutch experiences indicate that it may not have been the major cause. British North Sea oil and Dutch North Sea gas have made them self-sufficient and even net exporters of energy. Still, they suffered as much as the other European countries from the crisis. Also, in the first years of the oil price increases, the West Germans were able to overcome high energy costs by an aggressive export policy to the OPEC countries. Moreover, the Japanese, with almost no domestic energy sources, overcame the high costs of energy through conservation and increased exports. The answer then is much more complex than excessive energy costs.

A more important factor may be Europe's decline in productivity and loss of technical superiority in comparison with newly industrialized states. The once clear superiority of European automobiles, steel and capital goods products no longer exists. Sweden, which held 7.5 per cent of world export markets in 1961 primarily due to its high-quality products, saw its share slip to 3 per cent in 1976. Higher cost Volvo and Saab automobiles no longer had a clear superiority over Japanese cars that they once had. Only West Germany's huge favourable balance of trade (a $81 billion surplus in 1989) provided the EC countries with a favourable balance of trade. After only a 3 billion dollar deficit in 1978, the EC had a combined 28.5 billion dollar deficit in 1979 before recovering to a near balance in 1987.

In order to come to grips with the economic consequences of the slump, governments often exacerbated the problems. To meet the social problems caused by the crisis, many governments ran huge budgetary deficits that fueled inflation. To keep living standards from falling, governments continued to support wage and benefit increases with extensive borrowing. Such borrowing increased inflation by bidding-up the price of capital and reducing the amount of money available for industrial investment. Reduced investment – it dropped from 4 percent of national income in 1970 to 2 per cent in 1982 – reduced the West's technological superiority over Japan, South Korea, Brazil and other developing countries. It became almost impossible to stop the economic slide since the economic alternative seemed to offer only economic suffering and political disaster for incumbent parties. But continuing economic problems eventually led to a change in attitude among electorates. They began to vote incumbents out of power if they failed to balance budgets and bring inflation under control. Beginning in the late 1970s, European governments began to impose austerity measures – price and wage controls, higher taxes and interest rates, curbs on government spending – in order to bring down inflation. Even the new Socialist government in France, after an initial period of deficit spending, followed Great Britain, Italy, Holland and Belgium in imposing austerity measures. Unfortunately, the short-term consequences of such measures are higher unemployment and reduced government investment in industry. Ultimately, austerity measures are intended to bring down inflation, reduce manufacturing costs by holding down wages, and therefore increase exports. Such policies were not able to increase exports sufficiently due to the continuing competition from the much lower cost, high-technology countries. This fact, together with an ideological predisposition to favour market forces, led conservative governments in the late 1980s and 1990s to begin massive privatization programs. Even social democratic governments such as the French Socialists did not rule out nor reverse previous privatizations.

It was in this climate of sluggish or no-growth that the proposal to pool resources and re-launch European integration, beginning with the Single Market program aimed at completion by the end of 1992, took place. By the end of the 1990s, the recession had been overcome, and unemployment figures had begun to drop. However, in some countries such as France, an economic recovery on company's accounts was not generating equivalent jobs. This 'jobless recovery' was a phenomenon also witnessed the United States. The German economy, still burdened with restructuring the eastern Germany, and Italy, continued with very slow economic growth well into the 2000s. The picture in 2005 is of a dynamic eastern European economy, and a sluggish western European one, or at least the large countries. The British economy seems to be the exception, as the upturn in its economy that began at the end of the Major years has continued throughout New Labour's tenure in office.

If the 1970s and 1980s were characterized by the first substantial and wide-spread economic downturn since the Great Depression of the 1970s, by the end of the 1990s some of the indicators demonstrated a victory of sorts. Rampant double-digit inflation was firmly under control, no more than between 3 and 4 per cent in most EU member states. The period of stagflation had also ended, as most countries rarely sustain at least modest economic growth rates, though the German and Italian economies in the early 2000s have slowed. France and Germany continue, though, to experience high unemployment, especially among the young, and as far as one can ascertain from the 2005 French EU referendum 'No', the further liberalization of services is not what many view as the answer. Other constraints – at least viewed by some as such – on the flexibility of governments to manage or steer their economies, is the EU's Stability and Growth Pact. This is an agreement made in the mid-1990s to insure financial discipline by those countries adopting the euro. Promulgated by the conservative German finance minister Theo Waigel, it states, among other things, that annual budget deficits must not exceed 3 per cent. This has proven to be a straitjacket for some governments who struggle in the early 2000s to meet this condition, in particular large countries such as Germany, France and Italy, and others such as Portugal. French and German breaches of the 3 per cent limit in 2003 and 2004 led in 2005 to a loosening of some of the Pact's conditions. It is too early to tell if this will alter these governments policy behaviour.

Germany: From Western Ally to European Power

West Germany provides one of the earliest examples of the political transition outlined in the introduction to this chapter. After reconstruction and the development of the social market and welfare system in the 1950s and 1960s, West Germany, beginning in the 1970s sought the legitimacy and normalcy of a mature democratic European state, albeit still within the framework of the Cold War division. The same trends that removed incumbent parties from office following the economic downturn in the 1970s affected West Germany, as well as other cross-national issues discussed below. The unification of West and East Germany in 1990, and the dynamics associated with melding two different social, political and economic systems presented Germans with a daunting task, especially as this

Table 12–2 *Bundestag* seats and votes (in percentages)

Party		1957	1961	1965	1969	1972	1976	1980	1983	1987	1990	1994	1998	2002
CDU-CSU	Seats	270	242	245	242	225	243	226	244	223	319	294	245	248
	Votes	50.2	45.3	47.6	46.1	44.9	48.6	44.5	48.8	44.3	43.8	41.4	35.2	38.5
SPD	Seats	169	190	202	224	230	214	218	193	186	239	252	298	251
	Votes	31.8	36.2	39.3	42.7	45.8	42.6	42.9	38.2	37.0	33.5	36.4	40.9	38.5
FDP	Seats	41	67	49	30	41	39	52	34	46	79	47	43	47
	Votes	7.7	12.8	9.5	5.8	8.4	7.9	10.6	7.0	9.1	11.0	6.9	6.2	7.4
Greens	Seats								27	42	8	49	47	55
	Votes							1.5	5.6	8.3	5.0	7.3	6.7	8.6
PDS	Seats										17	30	36	2
	Votes										2.4	4.4	5.1	4.0
Others	Seats	17												
	Votes	10.7	5.7	3.6	5.4	1.0	0.9	0.4	0.4	1.5	4.1	3.6	5.9	3.0

occurred at approximately the same time as European integration was accelerating.

Before Unification After the German Social Democratic party (SPD) dropped its revolutionary program in 1959 at its Bad Godesberg conference, it slowly increased its representation in the Bundestag, as Table 12–2 shows, first at the expense of the Christian Democratic party (CDU) and its Bavarian affiliate the Christian Social Union (CSU) and later of the Free Democratic party (FDP). The election gains in the 1960s show clearly the result of the SPD's adoption of a reform rather than a revolutionary program.

The SPD first gained a share of power in 1966 as a part of a so-called Grand Coalition put together by CDU Chancellor Kurt Georg Kiesinger. It was Kiesinger who wanted the SPD in the coalition because the FDP would be unwilling to support the strong economic measures he considered necessary to bring Germany out of a recession. Also, he did not want the CDU to shoulder all the blame for the unpopular tax increase he was going to institute. The coalition solved the economic problems by raising taxes, cutting military spending and encouraging investment.

An unfortunate aspect of the economic crisis and the coalition was the growth of right-wing radical groups. An extreme nationalist group, the National Democratic party (NPD), with many former Nazis as members, won 48 seats in provincial elections in 1967. Although it won another 12 seats in 1968 by playing on the fears of those who had been upset by the student demonstrations, the return of economic stability soon halted the NPD growth. Moreover, once the CDU was in opposition after 1969, voters registered their complaints by voting for the CDU rather than for the NPD.

In foreign policy, West Germany began to break away from American tutelage under Kiesinger. With Willy Brandt as foreign secretary, the first steps were taken to establish normal diplomatic relations with the East. But it was not until Brandt became chancellor in a coalition with the FDP in 1969 that

West Germany's *Ostpolitik* (Eastern policy) began in earnest. Brandt's policy went beyond the reopening of diplomatic relations with East European states to the recognition of East Germany and an acceptance of the boundaries set up between Poland and East Germany after Second World War.

This recognition, vehemently opposed by German conservatives and never even contemplated by earlier Christian Democrats, convinced most East Europeans that Brandt was sincere in his efforts to normalize relations with the East. The possibility that his *Ostpolitik* might ultimately lead to a reunification of Germany was looked upon with considerable trepidation by other Western European countries.

Brandt remained in power until 1974, when he stepped down because of his disappointment with the failure of European unification, the slow pace of social reform, and the discovery of an East German spy among his advisers. His successor, Helmut Schmidt, representing the technocratic element in the SPD, was ideologically far from the postwar revolutionaries' brand of socialism or even Brandt's dedication to the concept of social improvement. Brandt told the German people to prepare for long-term social reforms that he was contemplating, whereas Schmidt spoke only about the solution of present problems. Schmidt claimed, 'I'm not a visionary and I'm skeptical of all the visionaries. Germans have an enormous capacity for idealism and the perversion of it.' One of his first moves was to drop several of Brandt's reform proposals, but in an effort to satisfy the left wing of the party, he decided to push Brandt's proposals for giving workers a say in the management of large businesses.

Schmidt's concentration on resolving economic problems produced immediate dividends in overcoming an economic slowdown brought on by the shortages and high cost of oil from 1973 to 1975. Germany overcame the shortages and trade imbalance by cutting its oil use 20 per cent and by increasing exports to the OPEC countries sufficiently to wipe out a ten billion mark deficit in three years. Germany was not to suffer serious economic difficulties again until 1979.

The economic slump did influence the 1976 elections. Before the extent of Germany's recovery became apparent, the voters returned the CDU/CSU to its legislative levels of the 1960s and reduced the SPD-FDP coalition to only a ten seat majority in the lower house. Although the governing coalition recovered in the 1980 elections to a 44-seat majority, divisions between the coalition partners and within the SPD curtailed the SPD's room for manoeuvre and increased the FDP's influence far beyond its parliamentary numbers.

The political differences within the parties and between them reflect the social transformations at work in German society since the sixties. The SPD became deeply divided between an increasingly influential left wing and a traditional moderate right wing. Schmidt, who leaned more towards the right, had to relinquish party leadership to the only person able to pacify both wings, former chancellor Willy Brandt. The left, primarily an outgrowth of the New Left movement of the 1960s, opposed nuclear energy and weapons, NATO and industrial society. Since the right wing of the SPD and it's perennial coalition partner, the FDP, supported all these things, the government often found it either impossible to act or had to make short-term compromises on many important issues. While Schmidt walked a tightrope between these two factions, the SPD began losing support on both the left and the right. When Schmidt had to compromise on social welfare to satisfy the FDP, the SPD lost labour and left wing supporters. His inability to stop the growth of unemployment – 7.5 per cent in 1982 – resulted from the SPD right and FDP pressure to keep down expenditure and inflation. In June 1982 the SPD had to cut back government borrowing, an anti-inflationary action, in order to satisfy the FDP. Strong pressure from the public and the CDU/CSU to stem radicalism was considered undemocratic by the left wing of the SPD.

The FDP, the so-called dog-wagging tail of West-German politics, was in coalition with the SPD from 1969 to 1982. The more strongly free-market FDP blocked an extension of welfare, growth of the national debt and any extension of a labour voice that went beyond the co-determination practice in industrial management. Of course, much of the SPD right, as well as Schmidt, were happy with these 'compromises'. But increasing disagreements over the means to deal with an economic slump, led the FDP to leave the governing coalition in October 1982. When the FDP's demand for reduced welfare expenditure was rejected by the SPD, the governing coalition became deadlocked. When Schmidt demanded that the FDP acquiesce, they left the coalition and joined with Helmut Kohl's CDU/CSU bloc to form a new majority in the *Bundestag*. A number of local election losses had also convinced many FDP deputies that the German public was moving to the right and a coalition with the CDU would be in their own best interest.

The SPD had long profited from the lack of unified opposition from the CDU/CSU. Both the heads of the CDU, Helmut Kohl, and of the CSU, Franz Josef Strauss, lacked Schmidt's popularity and had strong opposition within their own parties. CDU/CSU losses in the 1980 elections were a rejection of the CDU/CSU's authoritarian chancellor candidate Strauss and his policies. With Strauss no longer the chancellor designate, however, the CDU/CSU presented a more united front in the 1983 elections and under Kohl's leadership increased their seats in the legislature from 226 to 244.

A new political group that changed the direction of West German politics in the 1980s was the ecologist or 'Greens' (*Die Grünen*). Originally an environmental group, the ecologists attracted members of the peace movement of the early 1980s as well as activists from the citizen's movement, or *Burgerinitiativen*, of the 1970s (see Chapter 10). They are closer to the left of the SPD in that they oppose economic growth, nuclear energy and nuclear weapons and parts of the Atlantic Alliance with the United States. Their similarity to the left of the SPD has cost the SPD political support. But divisions within the 'Greens', has limited their development into a rival to the two main parties. They are divided between those who wish to take government positions (realists) and those who wish to remain an opposition party (fundamentalists), who believe that any political participation would compromise the movement's principles. This divide was more or less overcome by the late 1990. The 1983 elections brought about the first political representation for the Greens at the national level, 27 seats, and confirmed the new CDU/FDP coalition in office.

Parliamentary elections in January 1987 reconfirmed the shift to the CDU/FDP coalition. As Table 12–2 indicates, the elections further showed a continued decline for the SPD. The SPD's traditional labor constituency continues to decline as a portion of the population. Since the SPD moved more towards the political centre, most left-leaning youth have supported the Greens. An even larger number of youth have become conservative CDU voters. There was a general feeling that the CDU/FDP could better manage the economy in difficult economic times. The CDU also profited from the increased economic-cultural ties with Eastern Europe since 1985.

United Germany The incorporation of East Germany into a united Germany came as a surprise to just about everyone. At first, many thought that it would probably result in greater support for the Socialists due to East Germans presumed desire to keep as socialistic as possible their welfare system. Yet the March 1990 elections in East Germany demonstrated that nationalist and economic motives to join the west overrode most other considerations for a large proportion of East Germans. This was borne out in the December 1990 all-German elections. Kohl succeeded in his quest to become the 'unification' chancellor, at least for the initial phase. Those opposed or expressing reticence about a quick unification suffered at the polls, with the West German Greens failing to gain a seat when they were unable to muster enough votes to reach the 5 per cent threshold. The East Germans appeared to support the SPD's greater commitment to social welfare but the nationalist euphoria resulting from unification under the CDU increased the latter's support. Kohl also campaigned on a general 'quick and painless' image of the unification process.

Germany inherited economic problems from the 1980s that were less a result of internal policies and more a result of foreign competition. In 1982 the Japanese controlled 95 per cent of the once strong German photography market, 11–12 per cent of the automobile sales, and were making strong inroads in many other areas. The smooth sailing with high economic growth rates and low unemployment that Germans had come to expect in the 1950s and 1960s is no longer possible. Germany faces a problem common to advanced industrial societies in competition with countries with high technology but lower labour costs. Still, Germany remains the leading exporting nation by a large margin. In 1987 West Germany exported $294 billion worth of goods compared to $250 for the United States and $231 for Japan. As previously noted their 1989 trade surplus of $80 billion topped all countries. German unification, although causing substantial revisions in terms of how soon the east would be rebuilt and standards of living catch up with the west, has not hurt German exporting as much as the recession among its trading partners in the EU and elsewhere. Ironically, the high interest rates set by the German Bundesbank in the early 1990s to pay for unification helped prolong the regional recession by keeping other national rates high and thus making borrowing for new plant and machinery (and jobs) prohibitive.

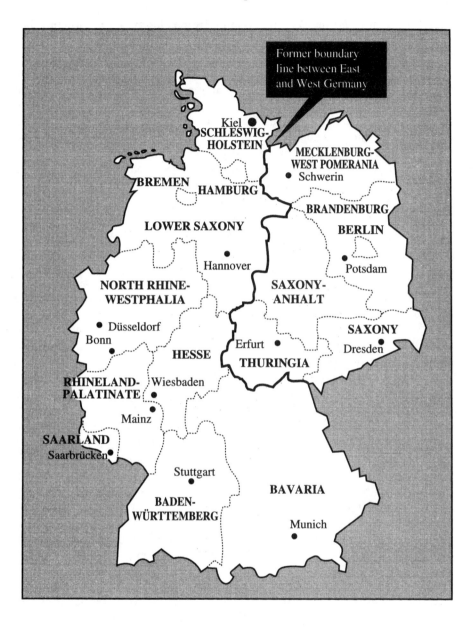

Former boundary line between East and West Germany

Kiel
SCHLESWIG-HOLSTEIN

MECKLENBURG-WEST POMERANIA
Schwerin

BREMEN
HAMBURG

BRANDENBURG

LOWER SAXONY

BERLIN

Hannover

Potsdam

NORTH RHINE-WESTPHALIA

SAXONY-ANHALT

Düsseldorf
Bonn

SAXONY

Erfurt
Dresden

HESSE

THURINGIA

RHINELAND-PALATINATE
Wiesbaden

Mainz

SAARLAND
Saarbrücken

Stuttgart

BAVARIA

BADEN-WÜRTTEMBERG

Munich

Unification spawned many other problems during the first several years. What should first be realized is that the euphoria experienced by west and east Germans following the opening of the Berlin Wall in November 1989 began to rapidly evaporate in late 1990, though not so soon as to prevent the re-election of Kohl and his CDU/CSU-FDP government. The monetary union that began on 1 July 1990, with a one to one exchange rate between the West and East mark almost overnight undermined the industrial and exporting sectors of the eastern economy by placing eastern German products too high on world markets. Very quickly, western analysts discovered that the much-vaunted East German economy (considered for a long time the 'jewel in the crown' of Eastern European Communist economies) was in a deep state of decay and inefficiency far more severe than expected. In most sectors it was uncompetitive with western economies, themselves refitting and readjusting for the intense competition from low-wage high-tech economies in the developing world. Thus the early hopes of many East Germans that they would soon be living at a level commensurate with their fellow citizens in the western part of the country had ended by 1991, as unemployment began to soar. By July 1991, overall industrial production in the east was down by a staggering 70 per cent, and unemployment had risen to 3.5 million out of a work force of 8.5 million.

Another phenomenon, a cultural one so to speak, was the development of an 'us' and 'them' mentality between citizens of the east and west, or 'ossies' and 'wessies', respectively. Again, after the euphoria of unification wore off, and the economic adjustment began to raise unemployment rates in the east and taxes in the west, a perceptible nostalgia for certain aspects of the old GDR and negative attitudes towards the westerners developed (by 1994 old East German brand names were making a comeback, with items such as beer and cigarettes). Some have argued that beyond the economic disparity between the two halves of Germany, another division has been erected, a 'wall in the mind' (*Mauer im Kopf*). The 'wall in the mind' metaphor assumes that for many eastern Germans, a romanticized view of the past has added to their souring on the benefits of unification. These attitudes, it is suggested, add to the difficulty of eastern Germans to fully adapt to the requisites of a capitalist democracy. For instance, writing in the January 1994 issue of the *Journal of Democracy*, Klingemann and Hofferbert point to a survey taken in late 1993 that showed majorities ranging from 56 to 96 per cent believing that the former GDR 'was stronger than West Germany in such policy domains as security of employment, child care, protection against criminals, social security, education, equal rights for men and women, human relations and social justice. West Germany, on the other hand, is seen by the Easterners as being stronger in economic prosperity, political freedom and environmental protection.' On the other side of the mental 'wall,' as financial aid from western Germany in the form of transfer payments has risen (an amount equal to 5 per cent of the west German GDP for 1993 alone), many west Germans refer to themselves as 'victims of unification'. In terms of electoral politics, the former East German Communist party, now known as the Party of Democratic Socialism (PDS), had some modest electoral advances in local and regional elections in eastern Germany in 1993 and 1994. This may reflect some of the lingering support for aspects of the East German welfare state as well as the difficulty of the main west German parties in establishing roots in the east. Political scientists also point to the long-term process of re-socialization of newly elected politicians from the east, for whom the give-and-take of parliamentary democracy can be disconcerting.

In October 1994, Germany went to the polls again, and once more Chancellor Kohl and his coalition partner the FDP were returned to power. But as Table 12–2 demonstrates, this was a much smaller majority. The FDP itself just managed to make it over the 5 per cent hurdle for representation, and the SPD increased its majority in the upper house, the Bundesrat. Even without the special dispensation in the electoral rules for the 1990 election, the PDS managed to win four seats in the Bundestag, although they did it by virtue of winning specific districts in Berlin.

The economic slowdown that began in 1992 continued, sapping support for Kohl's government. Since reunification in 1990, Germany has experienced annual average real growth of only about 1.5 per cent, along with persistent high unemployment. Weak domestic demand, coupled with the costs of unification, contributed to this state of affairs. Bert Rürup, head of Germany's Council of Economic Advisors, estimates reunification accounts for two-thirds of Germany's growth lag compared to its EU neighbours. Furthermore, the success of the West German economy was also very much due to the thriving small to medium-sized company sector, and this is something that, understandably, eastern Germany lacks.

In 1998, Kohl lost the elections to the Bundestag. Instead, the first national so-called 'Red-Green' coalition came to power. The SPD, led by chancellor-candidate Gerhard Schröder, together with the Greens, represented by Joschka Fischer, won 298 and 47 seats, respectively. Fischer became Foreign Minister and for much of the following years in power, was the single most popular politician in Germany. The PDS also did well in this election, returning 36 deputies to the Bundestag, as they were just able to surmount the 5 per cent electoral threshold. The CDU entered a period of turmoil. Kohl and his deputy Wolfgang Schäuble, were implicated in a party financing scandal and Kohl was replaced in 2000 as chair of the party by an eastern German politician Angela Merkel. Kohl's disgrace led him to retire from politics and for the next several years the CDU lacked a strong figure to challenge the government. The economic situation in Germany did not dramatically improve under Schröder, though the best economic growth rate – 3 per cent – was registered in 2000. Domestically, one Red-Green success was the liberalizing of nationality laws, which enabled many Turkish immigrants' offspring to acquire citizenship. In foreign relations, Germany began to assert itself in EU inter-governmental bargaining. The economic situation though, remained the single biggest problem, and many believed that the 2002 Bundestag elections would be won by the CDU/CSU, led by the Bavarian CSU politician Edmund Stoiber. However, terrible flooding in the south of the country just prior to the elections boosted the personal standing of Schröder, who appeared to take personal charge of the rescue and clean-up operation. The Red-Green coalition was returned to power, but the SPD had lost 47 seats.

This second Red-Green government experienced a rough time, as unemployment continued to grow, domestic demand remained stagnant, and the upper house, the Bundesrat, representing the länder that were increasingly coming under control of the opposition, was unsympathetic to a good portion of government legislation. In this virtual stalemate, Schröder attempted to implement structural changes in the German economy, particularly in the labour market, which many economists blamed for the lack of business dynamism. Calling it Agenda 2010, the government attempted to legislate a reform package aimed at making labour more flexible, making adjustments to the unemployment compensation programs – basically trying to amend them in the direction of American and British reforms by reducing or ending benefits sooner, and giving tax incentive to companies to hire workers. This attempt, to essentially reform the German welfare state or portions of it, was not popular among SPD supporters and demonstrations against the legislation occurred sporadically in 2004 and 2005. Their unpopularity was also reflected in a series of SPD losses at länder or regional elections. Finally, in a dramatic gesture, Schröder called an early election after the SPD suffered an historic defeat in May 2005 in the land of North Rhine Westphalia, were it had governed for generations. Elections were not due until September 2006, and bringing them forward by a year disconcerted many SPD supporters, especially members of the Bundestag, many of whom expected to lose their seats. The CDU, having named Angela Merkel as their chancellor candidate, won the election, but was forced into a 'grand coalition with the SPD.

French Political Transition

In France the establishment of the Fifth Republic under the powerful presidency of de Gaulle upset the traditional political balance between right and left. By the 1970s a bi-polar party system had emerged, with the Socialist party supplanting the Communist as the dominant party on the left. The election of the Left in 1981 heralded what many called the normalization of French politics, and the age-old drama between Left and Right seemed to have settled during the 1980s and 1990s into a more conventional competition rather than a contest with revolutionary overtones.

De Gaulle's new Republic and his own stature were strengthened early on by the introduction of a directly elected president, confirmed in a 1962 referendum. Both the fortuitous economic situation and de Gaulle's adept handling of the Algerian rebellion swung support to the right during the 1960s. During the 1965 presidential elections, de Gaulle alone received 44 per cent of the vote on the first round, whereas the Left Federation of Communists and Socialists, headed by François Mitterrand, got only 32 per cent of the vote.

The elections began to shift towards the left after 1965, as Table 12–3 indicates. In the 1967 parliamentary elections, the Gaullists' vote declined from over 50 per cent in 1962 to 38 per cent of the total. The overwhelming Gaullist victory in 1968 following the student-worker riots proved a temporary response, reflecting the belief of many voters that their only choice was between Gaullism and communism. The election victory only temporarily overshadowed the shortcomings of de Gaulle's regime. With his policies often verging on megalomania – for example, his disregard of his own ministers – many of the French breathed a sigh of relief when he departed

Table 12–3 Seats and votes (in percentages) in the National Assembly throughout the Fifth Republic

Party		1958	1962	1967	1968	1973	1978	1981	1986	1988	1993	1997	2002
PC	Seats	10	41	73	34	73	86	44	35	27	24	38	21
	Votes	19.2	21.7	22.5	20.0	21.4	20.6	16.2	9.8	11.3	9.2	9.9	4.8
PS-MRG	Seats	76	105	116	57	114	114	279	206	269	60	253	147
	Votes	24.0	20.4	19.0	16.5	22.6	24.8	37.5	31.2	37.0	18.5	24.9	25.6
Centre and right	Seats	190	90	86	94	119	112	53	127	129	213	108	29
Gaullists	Seats	199	233	200	293	183	153	88	150	126	247	134	357
	Votes	19.5	31.9	32.5	37.0	28.9	23.0	21.2	27.0	19.2	20.4	15.7	33.7
FN	Seats								34	1		1	
	Votes						0.8	0.2	9.9	9.8	12.4	14.9	11.3
Greens	Seats											7	3
	Votes						2.1	1.1	1.2	0.4	7.6	6.8	4.5
Others	Seats		13	12	3		26	27	24	23	34	36	20
	Votes	3.3	11.0	7.5	7.5	6.6	4.7	2.1	5.4	3.8	12.8	13.6	15.3

the political scene in 1969. He retired when his referendum on limiting the Senate's power and composition and granting regional governments more authority was defeated. While De Gaulle expected that the decentralization proposal would be sufficiently popular to help overcome opposition to reducing the senate's power, he interpreted the referendum's defeat as a rejection of his own authority.

De Gaulle's successor, Georges Pompidou, continued many Gaullist policies but stripped them of their authoritarian character. He was not too proud, as de Gaulle had been, to devalue the franc and thereby increase French exports. He also gained popularity by dropping French opposition to British entry into the EC. But Pompidou's policies, after this promising start, lost momentum. French political theorists, such as Michel Crozier, began to write about France's 'blocked' or 'stalled' society. They contended that France's social-political structure – many conservative small farmers and shopkeepers and a politically dominant and inflexible bourgeoisie – blocked any significant reform. Adding to Pompidou's woes were a deteriorating economy, the Arab oil embargo and failing health. After his death in 1974, the possibility for a United Left – Communist and Socialist parties – election victory appeared likely because of the unpopularity of the Gaullists. However, the French still remained true to that old stereotype that their heart is on the left but their checkbook is on the right by electing as their next president Valery Giscard d'Estaing, the technocratic Liberal party candidate of the centre-right. The youthful-looking Giscard had run a Kennedy-style campaign. Although more elitist than de Gaulle, he ran his campaign as a man of the common people. Still, his margin of victory over the United Left candidate, the socialist Mitterrand, was only 1.2 per cent of the popular vote.

Giscard d'Estaing's presidency began with much promise. Operating under his slogan 'change without risk', he pushed through many liberal reforms with the support of the left; he lowered the voting age to 18, reduced state control over the media, imposed a capital gains tax on the rich and liberalized divorce and abortion laws. Still, France's tax system remained one of the more unfair in Europe with excessive indirect taxation. Giscard continued an independent foreign policy as had his two predecessors but was less opposed to the United States than de Gaulle had been and was more committed to Europe. It was Giscard, in fact, who helped to launch the G-7 (Group of Seven rich industrial democracies) annual meetings by hosting the first one in 1975. Giscard admired the openness of American society and hoped to move France in that direction.

Because of a worsening economic situation and the growing popularity of the left at the departmental and municipal levels, a victory for the United Left appeared imminent in the 1978 legislative elections. But a split in the left brought about by the Communist party's fear of aiding a rapidly growing Socialist party under Mitterrand – the Socialists out-polled the Communists for the first time in the 1978 election – weakened them on the eve of the elections. In addition, the old fear of the left, nurtured by Giscard during the election campaign, helped give the right 51.5 per cent of the vote and a legislative majority of 89 seats. After Giscard's triumph, he began to lose popularity due to inattention to needed domestic reforms and a turn from his earlier populist style to an almost de Gaulle-like regal style. But the economic problems – energy shortages, high inflation, and unemployment – were even more decisive in reducing Giscard's popularity.

The stage was set for one of the most remarkable political turnabouts in postwar France. Starting with a new Socialist party in 1971 – the old SFIO disbanded in 1969 – Mitterrand's socialists became the dominant party on the left in 1978 and in the National Assembly in 1981. Mitterrand's election to the presidency in 1981 by a 51.8 to 48.2 per cent margin over Giscard was as much a rejection of Giscard as an endorsement of the left, in that many French were merely voting for a change. Certainly the Gaullists lukewarm support of Giscard was an important factor. Instead of uniting against the left on the first presidential ballot, the Gaullists ran their own candidate, Jacques Chirac. Giscard's 28 per cent of the vote rather than the predicted 36 per cent in the first round did not provide him with a sufficient springboard for the second round. But Mitterrand's victory also resulted from changes in French society and a transformation of the French left. The social groups who have traditionally supported the right – farmers, small shopkeepers, the wealthy bourgeoisie and non-working women – have declined relatively in comparison with those who tend to support the left – salaried workers and wage-earning women. Even more important has been the shift from the Communists to the Socialists. In the National Assembly elections, the Socialist party's vote jumped from 16.5 per cent of the popular vote in 1968 (the SFIO) to a commanding 37.5 per cent in 1981. The Communists slipped from 20 per cent in 1968 to only 16.2 per cent in 1981. Some of this resulted from the Communists' abandonment of the United Left. About one-quarter of the traditional Communist voters who still believed in a united left switched to Mitterrand in the 1981 elections. Also, the Communists' return to a more hard-line, pro-Moscow position – leader Georges Marchais refused to condemn Soviet actions in Afghanistan – cost the Communists support. French voters were also less fearful of the left once they realized that a smaller Communist party would have limited influence over the decisions of any left-of-centre government.

National Assembly elections, brought about by Mitterrand's dissolution of the conservative dominated assembly, resulted in an absolute majority for the socialists; 288 of the 491 seats. The Socialists' majority in the National Assembly would have permitted the Socialist prime minister, Pierre Mauroy, to govern without the Communists. However, Mauroy included them in his government, four of forty-four cabinet posts, in order not to appear to be the one responsible for the break-up of the united Left and also to keep the support of many blue-collar workers who were members of Communist-dominated trade unions.

Mitterrand began his first term of office in traditional socialist fashion; he increased the minimum wage, expanded social benefits, added a mandatory fifth week of paid vacation for salaried workers, reduced the work-week to 39 hours, imposed higher taxes on the rich, and nationalized the major banks. While these policies were popular among all but the rich, they exacerbated the economic difficulties. The fact that most of France's trading partners were pursuing at this time deflationary policies made France's exports fall and dramatically increased its trade deficit. Mitterrand had come to power at the same time that British prime minister Thatcher and U.S. president Reagan were extolling the virtues of monetary policy, not the active type of Keynesian, government-interventionist policy that the Left in France were ambitiously launching.

In 1983, Mitterrand switched to an austerity program in order to reduce the huge budget deficit and high inflation. Emphasis was now placed on modernization rather than socialization, encouraging new private enterprises and reducing public expenditures. Especially alarming to the left wing of the Socialists was the breaking of the indexing of wages to rising prices. While these policies began to lower the inflation rate, they increased the unemployment rate as firms reduced work forces and government support dwindled. Unable to support such a free-market program, the Communist ministers left the government in 1984.

Since these economic policies had stirred up some resentment, the Socialists lost the 1986 parliamentary elections to a center-right coalition. With 31 per cent of the vote and 215 seats, however, the Socialists remained the largest party in the assembly. For the first time the Fifth Republic had a president who did not represent the majority in the National Assembly. Mitterrand still had two years left of his seven-year term and he refused to resign. Mitterrand's appointee as prime minister, the neo-Gaullist (and mayor of Paris) Jacques Chirac, pursued economic policies not too different from those of the previous administration. He speeded up the economic modernization of French industry through more rapid privatization, and reduced government expenditures. But he differed from Mitterrand in limiting immigration, increasing police powers and reducing the wealth tax introduced by the Mauroy government. This period of cohabitation, a president and prime minister from different sides of the political spectrum, came to an end in 1988 when Chirac lost to Mitterrand in the presidential elections. Mitterrand had gained much support by appearing to stand above politics while Chirac had alienated many in the day-to-day running of the government.

The June 1988 parliamentary elections increased the Socialist assembly seats to 276 and reduced the center-right to 258. Some of this slim majority was due to Mitterrand's public plea not to give the Socialists an overwhelming majority, since it might strengthen the more left-wing forces too much and threaten his programs. The Communists won only 27 seats and became even more marginalized in French politics. The extreme right-wing National Front of Jean LePen dropped from 33 seats to one due to a change in the electoral system away from proportional representation and back to the system used since 1958, a majoritarian, single member district, two round ballot.

The Socialist minority government lasted until the March 1993 legislative elections. It was a minority in the sense that without an outright majority it depended upon support from the Communists on certain bills, or their abstention, and divisions within the conservative opposition in order to put together ad hoc coalitions on certain bills the Communists opposed. During this period, three Socialist prime ministers served. Michel Rocard, a long-time rival of Mitterrand's within the Socialist Party took the first crack at running the government. He pursued policies that differed little from those of Chirac, although notably he created a minimum income policy, known as the *revenue minimum d'insertion*, or simply RMI. The center-right favoured more privatization than the Socialists but they were one in their modernizing, deflationary policies. The center-right also approved more restrictive policies concerning immigration, civil rights and the freedom of information. Following Rocard's departure from office, the first woman prime minister in French history was appointed, Edith Cresson. More of a protegé of Mitterrand, she had a brief, but volatile time in office, serving about one year. Finally, the Finance minister, Pierre Bérégovoy, was appointed, and served until the next set of elections. Continuity in economic policy and tight relations with Germany characterized the three successive governments from 1988 to 1993.

The 1993 legislative elections spelled the definitive end of the Socialist experiment. As Table 12–3 clearly demonstrates, the Socialist Party, the single largest party in seats and proportion of the vote, was almost wiped out. From 276 seats to 57, the Socialists were reduced to legislative impotence in the new parliament. Former Prime minister Rocard himself was unable to retain his seat. The causes of this electoral debacle are many, but a few factors stand out. First, a series of corruption scandals involving shady dealings with big business eroded what moral standing the government had as the defender of the 'little guy'. Second, the austerity policies pursued by the government, although bringing inflation down to all-time lows, were ineffective against the relentless upward creep of unemployment, hitting 11 per cent by 1993. Third, the leftist vote for the Socialists abandoned them, as they themselves admitted to lacking a clear vision for the future. The abstention rate for this election was also high, 33 per cent. The new cohabitation government, led by Prime minister Eduard Balladur of the RPR, continued with the economic policies of the Socialists, hoping for a regional upturn in the European economy out of recession in order to help the fortunes of the government as it prepared itself for the next presidential elections 1995.

1995 spelled the end of the Mitterrand era. He had already declined in health over the preceding year, and although not constitutionally prevented from doing so, was too old and sick to try for another term of office. His legacy in domestic terms has several aspects. First, he presided over an orderly alternance of power, from the right to the left. Second, he championed European integration, being one of the key players in the Maastricht Treaty. Third, his governments advanced the social liberalizing of French society, begun under Giscard's presidency. Finally, he re-fashioned the Socialist Party into an electoral machine, capable of winning elections. In foreign affairs, Mitterrand took a tough stand against Soviet actions in Afghanistan and Poland and pledged to support the Atlantic Alliance politically although not participate militarily in NATO. With the end of the Cold War, the foreign policy position of France – to serve as a middle power in between the U.S. and the Soviet Union – disappeared. In this new context, the primary focus of France under Mitterrand – and his successor – seems to be a greater focus on European security issues, with a French-German tandem the driving force of the EU's ambition to create a common foreign and security policy. Its relations with developing countries, especially in Africa, where France remains the dominant European military power, were only slightly scaled back to the extent the United Nations can step into the breach, especially in humanitarian matters. Nevertheless, as the tragedy in Rwanda attests, France remains committed to active intervention in African affairs, both in military as well as in economic matters. France's primary foreign policy problem will be to adjust her vision of grandeur with her declining ability to cut an independent path in international affairs.

RPR leader Jacques Chirac won the 1995 presidential election, although Balladur did challenge him in the first round. The Socialist candidate was former party first secretary and Education minister Lionel Jospin. Jospin's respectable showing against Chirac earned a stature in the PS that allowed him to exercise real party leadership. Chirac named Bordeaux mayor and right-hand man Alain Juppé Prime Minister. Juppé's task was to rein in France's budget deficit, as part of the overall strategy to qualify for membership in the single currency, envisaged to begin in 1999. However, massive public sector strikes opposing cuts in parts of the French welfare state, led him to back off, and this signaled a reinvigoration of opposition parties and interests groups such as trade unions. Chirac, in a grand miscalculation, called for parliamentary elections in 1997, one year early, ostensibly to renew his parliamentary majority before even further difficult economic medicine was to be administered. Instead, a majority of left parties won the election, and a so-called plural left (*la gauché plurielle*) coalition composed of the Socialists, the Communists, the Greens (*les Verts*) and a couple of minor parties, with Jospin as Prime Minister, formed the government, working in cohabitation with president Chirac.

Jospin's government, which served its full five-year term until 2002, was notable for several things. In order to combat persistent high unemployment, his government introduced legislation bringing about a 35-hour workweek (with no reduction in pay), and created 350,000 government paid jobs. Social legislation extended equality for women and same-sex couples and in economic and financial policy presided over the introduction of the euro. In EU affairs, Jospin took the first tentative steps in joining with Britain to develop a common defense policy, the agreement between the two countries known as the St Malo Agreement, signed in a summit in December 1998. Jospin did represent, in terms of political symbolism, one side of the social democratic spectrum, that is, the more state-centered approach to policy-making (as the employment policies demonstrated). He often was characterized as representing the opposite of British Labour party leader and Prime Minister Tony Blair, who was much more market-friendly in his ideological outlook.

2002 became another in a series of remarkable elections in the Fifth Republic. Most people assumed that the presidential election would come down to a second-ballot run-off between incumbent president Chirac and Jospin. Instead, due to the disunity of the various parties on the left, which fragmented the votes, Jospin emerged third in the first round, and was therefore eliminated from the second round. This became a contest between Chirac and the leader of the far-right National Front, Jean Marie LePen. Chirac won handily, with 80 per cent of the vote. Nevertheless, it was the first time since 1969 that a candidate from the left had not made it to the second round of presidential elections. The parliamentary elections that occurred soon thereafter were also a blow to the Socialists, as a newly configured party on the right, consisting of the RPR and most of the UDF, joined together to form the pro-Chirac Union for a Popular Majority (UMP), and won a large majority. Chirac appointed a little known regional politician, Jean-Pierre Raffarin Prime minister. The French economy had begun to slow in 2002, and unemployment, which had dropped down to around 8 per cent, was creeping back upwards. Raffarin's policies did not appear to remedy the situation much, and together with the dubious legitimacy of Chirac, who was under indictment for past years party financing corruption, and the fact that he won in a virtual one-sided contest in 2002, meant that the UMP lost the regional elections – giving the Socialists control over 21 out of 22 regions, and European elections in 2004, where the Socialists registered their best ever number of members to the European Parliament. The defeat of the EU constitutional referendum in May 2005 – which Chirac publicly supported – only adds to the government's woes.

Italian Political Transition

After decades of political muddling through and corruption, the 45-year political dominance of the Christian Democrats (DC) came crashing to an end in the 1990s due to public outrage at DC corruption and distrust of politics in general. The political consequences of this transformation have produced brand new parties and a different party system. The political logic that kept the largest party of the left out of power since WWII disappeared, and there is now a more conventional bi-polar competitive party system.

The growing importance of the left in the 1960s and 1970s was nowhere more apparent than in Italy, even though ideological divisions hindered its progress. The Socialists (PSI) and Communists (PCI) refused to cooperate on the national level, although they cooperatively ruled many regional and local areas in popular front governments, thereby preventing the left from exercising an effect on politics and society commensurate with its popularity. The non-Communist left, although sharing in center-left coalition governments between 1963 and 1969 – the Christian Democrats' (DC) 'opening to the left' – never had the strength to alter the policies of the ruling DC majority significantly.

The center-left coalition failed to meet the expectations of the public. In five years it had done little to modernize Italy's schools, hospitals or law courts. The public, primarily the lower classes, suffered from poor public transportation, inadequate housing, and the lowest wages in the developed European countries. The nationalization of electricity, a major achievement of the coalition, aided the former owners and only burdened the government. A plan to decentralize administration by setting up regional administrators did not become effective until the early 1970s. Nor had Italy yet begun to profit from two agreements Fiat made to build car factories in the Soviet Union and Poland.

Unfortunately for the Socialists, only the DC gained political favour from the coalition. In the 1968 elections, the United Socialist Party (PSU) – formed when the PSI and the Social Democrats (PSDI) merged in 1966 – lost twenty-nine seats. As Table 12–4 shows, twenty-three seats were won by the Socialist Party of Proletarian Unity, the former left wing of the PSI which broke away in protest against PSI leader Nenni's co-operation with the DC. These changes and a Communist party gain indicated that the trend to the left had not ended. The losses led the PSU to break-up in 1969; in protest against the coalition, the PSU split into the former PSI and PSDI factions. Although a majority of the PSI remained loyal to the new DC premier, Mariano Rumor, his unwillingness to meet their demands reduced the coalition to a policy of muddling through. In 1972 the center-left coalition collapsed.

The political fortunes of the PCI improved remarkably in the 1970s, especially on the local level. Local election victories increased the PCI's control from the so-called 'Red Belt' of Emilia-Romagna, Tuscany, and Umbria in 1970 to six of Italy's 20 semi-autonomous regions and most of the major cities from Naples northward. The lack of corruption among Communist officials, the support of young voters, an increasingly more moderate program and the continued immobility and corruption in the DC-dominated national government were primarily responsible for the Communist gains.

During the 1960s and 1970s, the Communist leadership under Palmiro Togliatti and Enrico Berlinguer emphasized a Euro-communist position with the expectation that it might gain them a share of power – that much

Table 12–4   Seats and votes (in percentages) in the Italian Chamber of Deputies

Party		1958	1963	1968	1972	1976	1979	1983	1987	1992	1994	1996	2001
Communist	Seats	140	166	171	171	227	201	198	177	107	115	172	136
Party[a]	Votes	22.7	25.3	26.9	27.1	34.4	30.4	29.9	26.6	16.1	20.4	21.1	16.6
Refounded	Seats									35	40	35	11
Communists	Votes									5.6	6.0	8.6	5.0
La Rete	Seats									12	9		
	Votes									1.9	1.9		
Social Democrats	Seats	22	33		29	15	20	23	17	16			
(PSDI)	Votes	4.6	6.1	91	5.1	3.4	3.8	4.1	2.9	2.7			
Socialists (PSI /	Seats	84	87	14.5	61	57	62	73	94	92	15	–	
SDI)	Votes		13.8		9.6	9.6	9.8	11.4	14.3	13.6	2.2	0.4	8
Greens	Seats								13	16	11	21	2.2
	Votes									2.5	2.8	2.7	2.5
Radicals	Seats					4	18	11	13	7	6		
	Votes					1.1	3.5	2.2	2.6	1.2	3.5	1.9	2.3
Socialist Party of	Seats			23	0	6	6	7	8				
Proletarian Unity[b]	Votes			4.4	1.9	1.5	1.4	1.5	1.7				
Republicans	Seats	6	6	9	15	14	16	29	21	27			
	Votes	1.4	1.4	2.0	2.9	3.1	3.0	5.1	3.7	4.4			
Christian	Seats	273	260	265	265	263	262	225	234	206	33	80	83
Democrats[c]	Votes	42.3	38.3	39.1	38.7	38.7	38.3	32.9	34.3	29.7	11.1	6.8	14.5
Liberals	Seats	17	39	31	20	5	9	16	11	17			
	Votes	3.5	7.0	5.8	3.9	1.3	1.9	2.9	2.1	2.9			
Forza Italia	Seats										113	123	178
	Votes										21.0	20.6	29.4
Northern League	Seats								1	55	117	59	30
	Votes								1.3	8.6	8.4	10.1	3.9
Neo-Fascists[d]	Seats	24	27	24	56	35	30	42	35	34	109	93	99
	Votes	4.8	5.1	4.5	8.7	6.1	5.3	6.8	5.9	5.4	13.5	15.7	12.0
Monarchists	Seats	28	8	6									
	Votes	4.8	1.7	1.3									
Others	Seats	5	4		8	4	12	6	6	27	5	2	15
	Votes	4.1	1.3	1.5	2.1	0.8	2.6	2.9	1.9	7.0	6.6	6.5	9.2

Notes: [a]1963–1987: PCI, 1992, 1994: PDS, 1996, 2001: DS
[b]1968, 1972: PSIUP, 1979: PDUP, 1976, 1983, 1987: DP
[c]1958–1992: DC, 1994: PPI, 2001: La Margherita
[d]1958–1992: MSI, 1994–2001: AN

discussed 'historic compromise' – with the DC. Euro-communists stressed a peaceful path to socialism rather than a Leninist seizure of power. They also sought to distance themselves from Moscow, especially after the 1968 crushing of the Prague Spring, by emphasizing their national roots. Throughout the 1970s Communist parties attempted to join with other left or center parties to gain a share of power. The PCI even dropped its opposition to NATO and the Catholic Church. Although the PCI never gained the historic compromise, despite gaining 34.7 per cent of the popular vote in the 1976 parliamentary elections, they did co-operate with DC-led governments from 1976 to 1979 by supporting them, or at least not opposing them, in the legislature. When the PCI's demand for cabinet positions from the DC for their continued support was rejected in 1979, the PCI withdrew their support from the government and it collapsed.

Since 1979 the PCI has fared less well. It lost 4 per cent of its popular vote in the 1979 elections because some on the left thought it had moved too far towards the center, while some on the right were not convinced that it genuinely supported democratic government. Also the PCI lost votes to the more aggressive and less ideologically narrow Socialists (PSI) and Radicals (PR). The PCI's shift in 1979 to a possible 'left alternative' government – PCI and PSI – was rejected by a PSI leadership that had visions of replacing the PCI as the power on the left.

The PSI resurgence was one of the most notable political occurrences in the 1980s. After the failure of the political alliance with the PSDI in the late 1960s, the PSI remained in the shadow of the PCI until the late 1970s. It often cooperated in center-left governments with the DC and as the weak partner in popular front governments with the PCI on the local and regional level. But a more pragmatic, reformist leadership under Bettino Craxi gave the PSI greater popularity and more political clout. Beginning in 1979 the PSI became the DC's major coalition partner and the PCI's main nemesis. The PSI challenged the PCI's stated allegiance to democracy and the western alliance by constantly challenging them to clarify their objectives. They also became more attractive to a less ideologically inclined electorate by rejecting further nationalization of property, a centralized direction of the economy, and labour demands for increased wages and benefits.

It was the Craxi-led government from 1983 to 1987 that abolished the *scala mobile* (wages tied to inflation), reduced spending on health and social security, and increased utility costs, transportation fares and luxury taxes. While unpopular to most labourers, these changes were supported by most voters.

As Italian society became more secularized (passage of the divorce and abortion bills) and less polarized socially and politically (breakdown of political subcultures and decline in party identification), more flexible, broadly based parties profited at the polls. These changes also accounted for the growth of the PSI and the Radical Party with its left libertarian program of unilateral disarmament, legalization of drugs, women's liberation and anti-nuclear arms policy.

While these transformations were reshaping the left, the ruling DC party was weakened by Italy's economic weaknesses and political unrest. It was held responsible for not preventing the economic and social conflicts in the 1970s that led *La Stampa* of Turin – one of Italy's leading newspapers – to declare in 1974, 'Italy is shaken by turbid ferment; it runs the risk of becoming a country on the outskirts of civilization and reason.' As Italy was shaken by strikes, student unrest, violence from left and right fringe groups, corruption, high inflation and energy shortages, the DC governed – some would say muddled through – with minority governments and shaky majority coalitions that fell in rapid succession. The DC's monopoly of grass-roots patronage and power and a strong economy in the 1950s and 1960s had diverted attention from the internecine battles between left and right within the party and the political shortcomings of DC leadership. But the enormous difficulties, beginning with student riots and the general strike in the late 1960s, exposed the near political paralysis of the DC. The DC's ineffective and sometimes corrupt rule – the revelation of United States financing of the DC in the 1960s and the Lockheed Aircraft Corporation's bribes to DC politicians in 1970, to name a few – contributed to the political and social turmoil since corrective action could not be taken. Extreme rightist (the neo-fascist Black Order, Third Position and Armed Revolutionary Nuclei) and leftist (Red Brigades, Front Line and others) groups struck with increasing ferocity at Italy's leaders and against each other with little fear of reprisal. The most sensational case was the kidnapping and execution of former premier Aldo Moro in 1978 by the Red Brigades (see Chapter 10). DC leaders, often very capable parliamentary managers such as Giulio Andreotti, Mariano Rumor and Aldo Moro, put together short-term, primarily left-center governments in the 1970s that managed to provide some order but little direction. Their perennial problem has been the formation of political programs that exclude the PCI, always the second largest party in parliament, but have sufficient strength to make and execute policy in the face of PCI opposition.

Economic and political changes decreased social and political unrest in the 1980s. A growing materialism reduced leftist radicalism. A continuing decline of the industrial working class reduced the PCI's normal constituency while the growth of the service class increased support for center and right parties. The PCI loss of 26 parliamentary seats in the 1979 elections, another three in the 1983 elections and another 21 in 1987 reduced their effectiveness and made them more willing to compromise. But a number of factors continued to lead away from the DC monopoly of power. Although the number of DC parliamentary seats declined only slightly from 1979 until 1993, they had lost much of their power and patronage at the local and provincial level to the PCI and PSI. In addition, one of the pillars of DC power, the Roman Catholic Church, began to lose influence in Italy. In an overwhelmingly Catholic country, the Church was unable to prevent the passage of laws permitting divorce (1970) and abortion (1978) or a revision of the 55-year old concordat that ended Roman Catholicism's status as the state religion (1985).

After 1979, Italy was ruled by coalitions comprising the DC, PSI, PSDI, Liberals and Republicans (PRI). With the Prime minister always coming from one of these five parties, Italy had in some respects obtained a relative continuity. For example, Giulio Andreotti, who formed a DC-led cabinet in July 1989, was prime minister five times and held senior cabinet posts in 27 of the 45 post-war governments. These parties combined in the mid-1980s to reduce the Communists' control of local government: the PCI lost almost all mayoralties except that of Bologna. But these five parties were unable to forge a government sufficiently strong to resolve the problem of political instability and immobility.

In 1991, Mario Segni, a well-respected member of the DC, launched the idea of a referendum on reforming the electoral system of Italy, a system many felt contributed not only to the stalemate of ineffective coalition governments but the very partisan control of the economic as well as the political system, what Italians refer to as *partitocrazia*. In June 1991, 95.6 per cent voted for electoral reform in the so-called 'Segni referendum'.

Events unfolded rapidly from this point onwards. In April 1992, new legislative elections were held, though still with the old electoral system. Even so, the traditional parties, especially the Communists (now called the Democratic Party of the Left-PDS) witnessed clear reverses (see Table 12–4). Around this same time, in early 1992, a corruption scandal, involving business payoffs to political parties in Milan quickly took on national dimensions, implicating the governing parties (and later charges against the PDS). Led by the prosecutor Antonio Di Pietro, the *Mani Pulite* (Clean Hands) investigation not only turned him into a national hero, but the very depths of political corruption in Italy began to come to light, and in some cases, charges of Mafia involvement at the prime ministerial level were made. After a national outcry over attempts by the government early in 1993 to pass a decree decriminalizing political kickbacks if the recipients returned the funds, a referendum was called in order to finally introduce a new electoral system. On 18 April 1993, 82 per cent of the electorate voted for a new system that switched from proportional representation to a majority system. (This system resembles the British system in which a single representative with the most votes is chosen – a plurality is good enough. Seventy-five per cent of the seats are chosen in this fashion, with the remaining 25 per cent utilizing proportional representation). Finally, on 27 and 28 March 1994, using the new electoral rules, Italians swept away the old political order.

Before the elections actually took place, changes in the party landscape had already begun. As Table 12–4 shows, the Northern League, a coalition of smaller regional organizations in northern Italy, particularly strong in Lombardy and led by Umberto Bossi, leapt from one to fifty-five seats in the 1992 election. This automatically made it a major political player among the traditional parties, outdistancing all but the top three. Next, business magnate Silvio Berlusconi launched a new political movement that later organized as a party, Forza Italia, during the first half of the year. Finally, the MSI, the neo-Facsist party, attempted to broaden its appeal and in so doing was able to attract just enough other small groups to rename the party the National Alliance. Former Facsist dictator Benito Mussolini's granddaughter, Alessandra, campaigned in local and national elections in Naples under this banner. Finally, the Christian Democrats, the party along with the Socialists most implicated in the corruption scandal, divided into at least three separate groups: a small group of conservative Catholics (CCD) gravitated towards Berlusconi's Forza Italia; another group follwed Segni; and the rest reconstituted the party as the Italian People's Party (PPI). The PSI also suffered major losses, and its leader Craxi fled into exile in Tunisia to avoid prosecution for corruption.

The results of the election were staggering. Running as three separate electoral alliances – the Progressive Alliance made up primarily of the PDS and its breakaway party, Reconstructed Communism, and the Greens and La Rete; the Pact for Italy, composed of the PPI and the Segni Pact; and the Alliance for Freedom bringing together Forza Italia, the Northern League and the National Alliance – over 70 per cent of the new legislature were made up of brand new representatives. The old political elite, either chose not to run or were in jail, or lost. Even more remarkable, the Alliance for Freedom, led by Forza Italia (established only months earlier), swept the elections, securing 366 of the 630 seats in the Chamber of Deputies. The Progressive Alliance led by the PDS, although predicted to win by public opinion polls during the preceding months, managed only 213 seats. The Pact for Italy came in far behind with 46 seats. Thus a new electoral system ushered in a new political class, the old tainted by the scandals pushed into obscurity or the courtroom.

The free-market orientation of Berlusconi, the new prime minister, proved more difficult to carry out than he planned. There was no love lost between the other two parties in the government coalition, as the Northern League rode an anti-Southern Italy sentiment to power and the National Alliance is implanted strongest in the South (Mezzogiorno). Calls by the Northern League for a more federalized territorial division for the country run counter to the National Alliance's desire for strengthened central government. Thus instability was built into the new government. What many Italians hoped would be the beginning of a Second Republic seemed to have really marked instead a prolonged transition. After only eight months in office, the government fell on 21 December when Berlusconi resigned rather than submit to a vote of no-confidence, precipitated by the resignation of four government ministers from the Northern League. The inability of Berlusconi to settle his business dealings so as to avoid a conflict of interest (he owned four of Italy's commercial television stations, viewed by three quaters of Italians) and continued sniping by Bossi came to a head when the Milan magistrates investigating corruption subpoenaed the prime minister.

A former finance minister from a small center party, Lamberto Dini, led a so-called technocratic government until the next elections, which took place in 1996. This election proved to be a watershed in Italian politics, as for the first time the left-of-center coalition, called the Olive Tree, managed to win power. A former economics professor and head of the large state-owned holding company INI (Institute for Industrial Reconstruction), Romano Prodi, became Prime minister, presiding over a somewhat volatile group of parties in which the former Communist party, fully converted to a social democratic identity and now called Democrats of the Left (*Democratici di Sinistra*), were the single largest component. One of the major tasks of the Prodi government was to make sure Italy qualified for membership in the eurozone, and so priority was given to bringing Italy's finances in order. One attempt to reduce deficits was a Europe tax, which the government promised to be temporary. In 1999, Prodi left Rome to assume the presidency of the European Commission in Brussels, where he stayed until 2004, biding his time before he could re-enter Italian politics. In his absence, the leader of the

Democrats of the Left, Massimo D'Alema, a lifelong Communist, became Prime minister. This fact demonstrates how far the former Italian Communist party (apart from a small group still committed to Communism, called the Party of Refounded Communism, *Rifondazione comunista*) had come in Italian political life. No longer shunned by all other parties, its representative had reached the prime ministership and no crisis reaction ensued. D'Alema's government continued with Prodi's economic direction, and Italy did join the eurozone at its launch. Apart from financial prudence, the Olive Tree coalition was notable for advancing labour relations, in which it was able to compensate to some degree the abolition of the *scala mobile* by extending a formal tripartite consultation among labour, management and the state first initiated in 1993.

The fractious nature of the coalition saw D'Alema quit as Prime minister in 2000, handing over the job to Giuliano Amato, a respected politician orphaned somewhat by the collapse of the PSI during the corruption scandals several years earlier. In the parliamentary elections of 2001, Berlusconi led his coalition, named the Freedom Pole, to victory over the Olive Tree. The National Alliance leader, Gianfranco Fini, had gone someway to present his party as a post-facsist party, in fact comparing its present orientation to the Gaullist party in France, that is, conservative and nationalist, but not anti-democratic. After a while, Berlusconi rewarded Fini for his loyalty by naming him Italy's foreign minister, in addition to deputy prime minister. Bossi of the Northern League, given the ministerial portfolio of devolution, continued with his style of brinksmanship politics by threatening every so often to withdraw his party from the government coalition unless his demands were met. Unlike the turbulent Olive Tree government, which did manage to accomplish certain policy challenges while in office, Berlusconi presided over a slowdown in economic growth and a worsening of the state's debt. Although he did manage to get legislation through the Chamber of Deputies and the Senate, where his coalition enjoy comfortable majorities, to strengthen the post of prime minister and continue with the process of devolution (to placate Bossi), his government became increasingly unpopular as the years went by, eventually seeing the electoral tide begin to turn away from the Freedom Pole in regional election in 2005 that were won overwhelming by a convalescing Olive Tree (now led by Prodi who had completed his stint as EU Commission president in 2004). During Berlusconi's time in office, his controversial grip on Italy's media did not recede. Through his company Mediaset, Berlusconi owned the largest private TV stations and through government regulations, also was in a position to influence its competitor, the state-owned channel RAI. This apparent conflict of interest, denounced by the left, was never resolved, and Berlusconi himself did not demonstrate any particular concern. In foreign affairs, Berlusconi supported the United States in the Iraq war, sending Italian troops to Iraq, although this was widely unpopular in domestic public opinion. The 2006 elections brought Prodi's coalition to power, but with the slimmest of majorities. In a referendum held soon after the elections, to ratify Berlusconi's legistation regarding the powers of the prime minister and devolution. The Italian public rejected the changes, thereby strengthening Prodi who campaigned against them.

The Vatican

While Italy has suffered from the lack of decisive leadership in the postwar period, the Vatican has been blessed with strong leadership. The most momentous pontificate was undoubtedly that of Pope John XXIII (1958–63), who brought about one of the most dramatic departures from Roman Catholic tradition. Pope John's policy of updating (*aggiornamento*) the church to bring it into step with twentieth century developments has been correctly called the 'Johnnine Revolution'. While it responded to some Catholics' call for a modernization of the church, it alienated many Catholic conservatives who thought the changes too far-reaching. His 1959 call for an ecumenical council to promote Christian unity was unexpected. Many thought his pontificate would be short and uneventful due to his advanced age when selected (77). Protestants were receptive to the ecumenical movement because of Pope John's engaging personality and sincerity and his sending of observers to the World Council of Churches meeting in 1961. In addition, the fact that the Vatican Council which first met in autumn, 1962 contained a large majority of clergy in favour of ecumenism did not escape the attention of other Christian denominations. Delegates rejected many of the proposals that had been prepared by the Curia due to their more conservative nature. Finally, Pope John's encyclicals captured worldwide attention and widespread approval among all Christians. *Mater et Magistra* (Mother and Teacher) issued in July 1961, expressed deep concern for social and material welfare, peace, international reconciliation and political rights. His next encyclical *Pacem in Terris* (Peace on Earth), covered much of the same ground as *Mater et Magistra* but it was addressed not just to Catholics but to 'all men of good will'. It supported the United Nations, upheld political independence, and called on the rich countries to aid the poor ones. He lifted the ban on co-operation with unbelievers whose objectives might be beneficial to mankind. Thus, he removed the ban on Catholic support for the Left. In practice, he did not oppose the Italian "opening to the Left" that brought Socialists into the government in the 1960s.

Pope John's death in 1963 did not stop the ecumenical movement or reforms in the church. His successor, Pope Paul VI (1963–78) supported ecumenism by seeking reconciliation with other Christians: his visits to leaders of the Eastern Christian churches in Constantinople and Jerusalem brought a new spirit of co-operation among them. He also pushed through many reforms initiated by his predecessor: the Papacy would share more power with bishops, the authority of the Curia was reduced, and the mass would be celebrated in the vernacular. But the liberals did not get all that they wanted. Pope Paul's 1987 support for the practice of clerical celibacy led manyh clergy to leave the priesthood. In *Humanae Vitae* (Human Life), a year later, Pope Paul ruled against the use of contraception.

After the 34-day reign of Pope John Paul, the College of Cardinals in 1978 shocked the world by choosing a non-Italian as Pope. Pope John Paul II, formerly Archbishop of Cracow, attracted great attention due to his own charisma and his support for the Polish Solidarity Movement. His policies tended to be more conservative than those of Pope John XXIII and Pope Paul VI. He supported traditional practices for the clergy and laity, stressed Papal authority in doctrinal matters and restricted liturgical experimentation. But his involvement in world affairs has been more like that of Pope John XXIII and Pope Paul VI. He traveled extensively and exhibited a common touch similar to that of Pope John XXIII. His social-political policies have been rather ambivalent. On the one hand, he has supported social justice but on the other he has restricted the social and political activities of the clergy. He was perhaps concerned that the clergy would become too concerned with worldly issues to the detriment of their religious duties.

In Italy, the Vatican lost some ground partially due to John Paul II's more limited interest in domestic politics. In 1985 the new concordat with the Italian government accepted the civil court's right to adjudicate marital annulments, and agreed that classes in religious doctrine would no longer be obligatory in the schools. In practice, one hour of religious instruction or an alternative hour of instruction in some other area became the rule. Although only 25 per cent of Italian Catholics attend Sunday mass, the Church still wields major influence in their lives. All major occasions, such as baptism, marriage and burial take place in the Church. But a growing secularism tied to modernization is robbing most of the Church functions of their original significance.

John Paul II died in 2005 after a long reign in which he was credited with expanding the Church in Third World countries, particularly in Africa, and

President Clinton points out people in the crowd to Pope John Paul II upon his arrival in Denver, Colorado, in August 1993.

(© Empics)

playing a crucial part in Poland's path to democracy. After a funeral attended by many world leaders and unprecedented media coverage, the College of Cardinals chose another non-Italian as pope, the German-born Cardinal Ratzinger, who chose the name Benedict XVI. Having presided over the Catholic Church's agency for doctrinal matters, he is expected to continue emphasizing more traditional and conservative policies, such as opposition to contraception. The first entry of the new pope into Italian social-political affairs occurred in June 2005, when the Church actively campaigned against an Italian referendum to liberalize laws regulating fertility treatment, specifically dealing with research on embryos. The Church argued for a boycott, since the referendum required at least a 50 per cent turnout to succeed. In the end, the proposals were defeated because turnout failed to reach the 50 per cent threshold (it reached only 24 per cent). Whether or not the Church was fully responsible for the defeat, the new Pope claimed a victory early in his time in office.

British Political Transition

Britain experienced one of the most remarkable political transitions in its history after 1965. After about 34 years of general agreement concerning welfare state policies, the Conservatives under Margaret Thatcher turned radically to an individual-centered, anti-welfare position after 1979. Although the Conservatives left office in 1997, the legacy of Thatcher's years in power are evident in some of the policy positions of the Labour government of Tony Blair.

In the 1960s Britain experienced a slight shift to the left. Conservative party supporters soon discovered that they had little to fear from the Labour party and Prime Minister Harold Wilson, elected in October 1964. Wilson, a former Oxford economics don, represented the right reformist wing of the Labour party. Its left wing, desiring a fully socialized economy with the nationalization of all industry, was in the minority.

Wilson chose to fight the economic problems through the traditionally conservative policies of cutting back on government spending and increasing taxes. After he received a larger majority in the 1966 parliamentary elections, Wilson reduced government spending on both military and welfare programs. Both the increased social security payments and the freezing of prices and wages angered workers and the left wing of the party. Labour's popularity declined even further when Wilson was forced to devalue the pound 14 per cent to raise British exports and reduce imports; devaluation raised the price of such necessities as bread.

By 1969, devaluation had started to have the desired effect: instead of deficits, the economy now had a sizable surplus. But when Wilson called an election in an attempt to take advantage of the improved economic conditions, the attempt failed. The Conservatives, led by Edward Heath, won a thirty-seat majority in 1970. Perhaps the economic improvement was not as apparent to an electorate that had suffered through the economic emergencies and devaluation.

For the next four years the Conservatives tried to end inflation and put the economy on a healthy footing. Instead, Prime Minister Heath had to declare a state of emergency five times in less than four years in office. Moreover, the confrontations between Heath and the coal miners brought serious disruption to Britain's economy and a loss of support for the Conservatives. Labour, under Wilson, returned to power in February 1974. With only a small majority, Wilson was not able to act decisively to overcome the economic problems. He resisted the left wing's demands for more nationalization by pointing out the precariousness of Labour's majority.

While Labour ruled in Britain from 1974 to 1979, the party underwent a political transformation that seriously reduced its effectiveness. The left wing of the party grew in strength as the labour unions, becoming more militant in the face of economic adversity, threw their support to a more radical political program. Contending that private industry had failed to make adequate capital investments, the left wing led by the Labour Industry Manager, later Energy Minister, Tony Benn, planned for massive nationalizations of Britain's largest companies. Heath derisively referred to Benn as 'Commissar Benn' and to his department as the 'Gosplan Department' in an obvious reference to the Soviet planning procedures. But the left did not stop with Benn's program. It moved on to a more radical position, a 'socialist transformation' of society that included the nationalization of Britain's 200 largest corporations, the abolition of all elite institutions – including private schools and the House of Lords, withdrawal from NATO and the EC, and unilateral disarmament. As Labour moved in this leftist direction after 1974, a moderate right wing first lost influence within the party and eventually left the party in 1981 to form the new Social Democratic party. Wilson was one of the first victims of this party turmoil. Unable to forestall this widening gap in Labour, Wilson resigned as party leader and prime minister in 1975. His successor, James Callaghan, was equally unsuccessful in overcoming this division in the party.

While these battles were going on within the ruling party, Britain continued to experience serious economic problems, growing separatist movements in Scotland and Wales, and violence between Catholics and Protestants in Northern Ireland. Crippled by the internal divisions, Labour could only muddle through. In fact, one of Britain's most decisive acts, the positive referendum (67 per cent) on British participation in the EC in 1975, came about because of Wilson's desire to forestall a split in the Labour Party by removing the EEC decision from the badly divided party. Meanwhile, Britain's economy continued to stagnate. In June 1976 the pound's value dropped to $1.71 on its way down to nearly $1.00 as worldwide confidence in the pound declined. Inflation twice topped 20 percent and unemployment passed the one million mark by the mid-1970s. Even more humiliating was the necessity in 1974 to borrow massively from the International Monetary Fund to meet government expenditures.

With the separatist movements in Scotland and Wales and Catholic-Protestant violence in Northern Ireland added to the dismal economic outlook, many began to speak of 'Englanditis' to describe Britain's unique problem. After winning nine parliamentary seats in 1974, Scottish nationalists, who were convinced North Sea oil would permit them to do better on their own, forced the Labour government to consider some form of autonomy, since Labour needed their votes in parliament. British unity was preserved when referenda on 1 March 1979 in Scotland and Wales on the question of devolution failed due to a turnout below the necessary 40 per cent threshold required.

In 1979 the British electorate gave the Conservatives a comfortable 43-seat parliamentary majority and brought the first female prime minister, Margaret Thatcher, to power (see Table 12–5). One must bear in mind, though, that the British electoral system is based on plurality, and so this election demonstrated more a shift or swing in particular districts than a giant repudiation of Labour. The Conservatives captured about 44 per cent of the vote, an increase of around 8 per cent from 1974. Labour's vote decreased by only 2 per cent, and the Liberals lost 4 per cent. Nevertheless, the election can be viewed as both a reaction against Labour's ineffectiveness and the power of labour unions and a vote for change. Thatcher, or, as she was often called, 'the Iron Lady', offered law and order, lower taxes, less government, less welfare and an end to inflation through control of the money supply. Her election signaled a major change in direction for Britain. Until 1979, both Labour and the Conservatives had accepted the welfare state and public ownership that had been ushered in after the war. The consensus on welfare-state policies had become known as Butskellism after the Conservative R.A. Butler and Hugh Gaitskell, the Labour leader. Butskellism aimed at reducing inequalities in income, education, housing and health care. But rapidly rising inflation, continued strikes and industrial uncompetitiveness gradually undermined the consensus. The year of the elections was particularly bleak: popularly known as the 'winter of discontent', 'Englanditis' was exaggerated by numerous strikes that paralyzed the country. Thatcher was also aided by a steadily decreasing percentage of laborers in the voting population who tend to support Labour and a left-right division in the Labour Party that reduced its effectiveness.

The unemployment and cuts in services introduced by Thatcher's budget-cutting monetarist policies (high interest rates to reduce inflation and decreased government expenditures) reduced her popularity during her first three years in office. When it appeared that she might lose the next election to Labour, her policies finally began to work. The inflation rate began to drop and North Sea oil began to bring much needed capital to the British treasury. But it was Thatcher's dramatic recapture of the Falkland Islands from Argentina that restored British pride and permitted her to call and win election again in 1983. Thatcher claimed the Falklands victory put the Great back in Britain. The plurality or 'first-past-the-post' election procedure gave the Conservatives 61.1 per cent of the seats but only 42.4 per cent of the popular vote, Labour 32.2 per cent of the seats but only 27.6 per cent of the vote and The Liberal-Social Democratic Alliance only 3.5 per cent of the seats but 25.4 per cent of the vote (The Alliance ran second to the Conservatives

Table 12–5 Seats and votes (in percentages) in the House of Commons since 1945

Party		1945	1951	1955	1959	1964	1966	1970	1974	1974	1979	1983	1987	1992	1997	2001
Conservative	Seats	213	321	345	365	304	253	330	296	276	339	397	375	336	165	166
	Votes	39.8	48.0	49.7	49.4	43.3	41.9	46.4	37.8	35.8	43.9	42.4	42.3	41.9	30.6	31.7
Labour	Seats	393	295	277	258	317	363	287	301	319	268	209	229	271	419	413
	Votes	47.8	48.8	46.4	43.8	44.1	47.9	43.0	37.1	39.2	37.0	27.6	30.8	34.4	43.2	40.7
Liberal*	Seats	12	6	6	6	9	12	6	14	13	11	23	22	20	46	52
	Votes	9.0	2.5	2.7	5.9	11.2	8.5	7.5	19.3	18.3	13.8	25.4	22.6	17.8	16.7	18.3
Others	Seats	22	3	2	1	0	2	7	24	27	17	21	24	24	29	28
	Votes	2.4	0.7	1.2	0.9	1.3	1.2	3.2	5.7	6.7	5.4	4.6	4.3	5.9	9.5	9.3

* The Alliance in 1983 and 1987.

in 256 constituencies). So, again, the popular vote gives a better indication of Conservative popularity.

With an enhanced Commons majority, Thatcher could now forge ahead with her self-help, anti-welfare state policies. She lowered taxes on wealth and property, stepped-up the privatization of industry, sold municipal housing units to former renters, cut subsidies to inefficient industries, continued her attacks on labour unions and brought down inflation from nearly 20 per cent to about 3 per cent in 1986 with her monetarist policies. Unemployment rose from 4.2 per cent in 1979 to 13.3 per cent in 1983 after which it leveled off to between 9 and 11 per cent as many inefficient factories went out of business. Thatcher can point to many economic successes. British Steel, for example, moved from a $3.3 billion loss in 1980 to a $758.5 million profit in the fiscal year ending in 1988 by reducing the number of factories and jobs and adding performance bonuses. As a whole the British economy grew at about 3 per cent in the 1980s or a rate better than other industrialized countries.

Thatcher became the first prime minister in modern British history to win a third consecutive term with the Conservative victory in 1987. The Conservatives won 43 per cent of the votes (376 seats) against a divided opposition. Labour, weakened by internal divisions and its unilateral disarmament position, gained 32 per cent of the votes but 208 seats because of the concentration of its votes in certain constituencies. The Liberal-Social Democratic Alliance obtained only 22 per cent of the votes (22 seats) because of internal divisions and the resultant lack of a coherent program. Voting reflected the division in Britain between the poor industrial North, where Labour dominated, and the rich commercial South, where the Conservatives won decisively.

Thatcher's revolution extended beyond the destruction of Butskellism. She also undermined the power of the labour unions in Britain and even restricted union's right to strike. She strengthened national against local government and reduced the autonomy of universities and local school authorities. Her stress on self-reliance and the individual severely weakened the decades old British devotion to equality and the community as a whole. While some believe she went too far in her denigration of dependency, even some in her own party, there are many who profited from the economic revival. Two-thirds of Britons owned their own homes in 1988 compared to one-half in 1979, and voter's real income was up by 25 per cent over 1979. Thatcher's economic success led Labour under Neil Kinnock to accept much of the Conservative economic philosophy, reflecting the revolution that Thatcher brought about in the British economy and consciousness.

Thatcher's popularity began to fade in 1990 as the inflation rate rose to about 7.5 per cent. Although respected Thatcher was not loved by the public. Thatcher added to her unpopularity by her arrogant treatment of her associates. In the fall of 1990, the government's popularity plummeted due to Thatcher's insistence on pushing through what came to be known as the 'poll tax'. This was an attempt to shift local government revenue collection to a broader base of people, including renters. Many viewed it as inherently unfair and led to large protests. Fearing for their re-election chances, the Conservative Party turned on Thatcher at their biennial party congress that fall, replacing her with John Major. So ended the tenure in office of the longest serving British prime minister in modern times.

Major was expected to continue Thatcher's policies (except the poll tax) but offer a more congenial image to the public. Throughout the following several years, despite maintaining the Thatcher economic legacy – closing unprofitable coal mines, privatizing the railway system, etc. – Major never seemed to be in firm control of the party. Although winning election in 1992, his troubles with Conservative critics gave his government an image of 'being in Government, but not in power'. His greatest challenge came from a number of Conservative critics of the European Union (dubbed Euro-sceptics by the press), who opposed British ratification of the Maastricht Treaty in 1992 and 1993 (see Chapter 7). Although his government enjoyed a majority in the Commons, in the summer of 1993 Major was forced to use the threat of calling a general election in order to enforce voting discipline among the Euro-sceptics.

The legacy of eleven years of Thatcherism can be seen on the Labour Party as well. After suffering defeat in 1992, Neil Kinnock resigned, and one of his lieutenants, John Smith, became Labour Party leader. Smith sought to continue Kinnock's attempts at 'modernizing' the party, and to this end he engineered a new relationship between the party and the trade unions. The block votes that unions wielded at Labour party congresses was ended and individual votes by union members was instead instituted, diluting the power of union leaders over party policy. An effective orator, Smith was considered to have the best chance in a decade to finally unseat the Conservatives at the next election. But Smith died of a heart attack in the spring of 1994. His replacement, forty-one year old Tony Blair, represented an even more straightforward break with Labour's past. Burying one part of Labour's past was the elimination of what was termed Clause 4 from the party's constitution. This 1918 commitment to the nationalization of the economy, or the 'means of production, distribution and exchange', which in fact had been something Labour leaders did not seriously contemplate enacting once in power, was replaced in 1995 with more anodyne language about working for 'enterprise of the market', etc. This was a glimpse of what was to come when Blair spoke of the modernization of the party and country.

In the 1997 parliamentary election, the Labour Party (now referred to as 'New Labour') won with a 179-seat majority (see Table 12–5). John Major resigned as Conservative Party leader and was replaced by William Hague. With his overwhelming majority, Blair set about an ambitious program of political, institutional, economic and social reform. Blair's government was lucky enough to inherit a growing economy, signs of which were becoming apparent too late to save John Major's government from defeat. Gordon Brown was appointed Chancellor of the Exchequer (finance minister) and maintained for the first two years the spending targets of Major's government. Proclaiming that he was led by 'prudence' in spending matters, Brown tried to show that New Labour was a responsible financial and economic manager, an

British Prime Minister Tony Blair.

(© Empics)

attempt to dispel Labour's association with the problems of the 1970s 'winter of discontent.' Through to 2005, the British economy did in fact maintain annual rates of respectable growth, with high levels of employment and low inflation, a contributing factor to Labour's re-election in 2001 and 2005.

Other matters regarding state intervention, especially public services, proved to be more controversial. Blair, along with sympathetic scholars such as the sociologist Anthony Giddens, tried to articulate a new vision for centre-left politics, dubbing it 'the Third Way'. One feature of the Third Way was to introduce the competitive nature of market dynamics into state or public enterprises. As Thatcher and Major had privatized most state-owned companies such as the airline, steel, the railroads, utilities such as water, gas and electricity, etc., this left the big spending areas of health and education. In health matters, the pride of the British welfare state, the National Health Service (NHS) came under pressure to introduce internal competition, even allowing for private providers to take over certain activities. Self-managing (financially) hospitals called foundation hospitals were introduced. Many traditional Labour supporters, not to mention doctors and nurses, objected to what they perceived was 'privatization through the back door', and the government was constrained from more wholesale transformation. The same Third Way logic was introduced into education, were a more varied landscape for primary and secondary schooling was promoted. Certain schools called 'city academies', essentially privately owned and run schools, were actually encouraged by Blair, much to the annoyance of the teachers unions. Free, university education was replaced by fees, and the ending of maintenance grants, thereby seeing American-style student debt make its appearance in Britain.

One of the most significant and far-reaching changes was the implementation of devolution, a campaign promise in 1997. Government legislation in 1998 saw the creation and elections to a Scottish Parliament and Welsh Assembly in May 1999. The nationalist parties in Scotland and Wales, the SNP and Plaid Cymru respectively, made respectable debuts in these elections and those held thereafter. In Scotland, the regional party system produced a coalition government between the Scottish Labour Party and the Liberal Democrats, something not repeated at Westminster. Although the Scottish Parliament has more legislative power than the Welsh Assembly, both have contributed to a rejuvenation of regional identity. Another constitutional reform involved the House of Lords. Blair had promised to do away with the hereditary system in the Lords, and in 1999 introduced legislation that eliminated all but ninety-two hereditary peers. A second stage in the Lords reform has been delayed due to the lack of consensus over exactly what role the House of Lords should ultimately play in the legislative process and what type of electoral procedure should be used.

Finally, in foreign policy the Blair government has been very active, if not interventionist, as well as controversial. The first foreign secretary, Robin Cook, proclaimed that New Labour would aspire to an 'ethical foreign policy', for example preventing the sale of arms to regimes with bad human rights records. Although this language was not supported by all of his colleagues, Blair himself condoned interventions for human rights preservation, as in the civil war in Sierra Leone in May 2000. The single largest British intervention abroad, and the most controversial in terms of British public opinion, was in Iraq, where Blair stood shoulder-to-shoulder with US President George W. Bush in the coalition sent to overthrow the regime of Saddam Hussein. When it became apparent that the basis on which Blair convinced Parliament – and the public – that Hussein posed a security risk to Britain was not in fact as rock-solid as he made it appear at the time, his

Sinn Fein leader Gerry Adams (left) attending a peace rally in Belfast, Northern Ireland, in September 1994.

(© Empics)

popularity plummeted, and was no doubt a contributing reason for his declaration that he would not lead the party into the next parliamentary elections scheduled for no later than 2010. As regards British relations with the European Union, Blair did manage to repair Britain's reputation after it had sunk to low depths under John Major. Through bi-lateral relations with Italy's Berlusconi and Spain's Aznar, Blair was able to interject more market-oriented reforms in the EU, though at times the Franco-German alliance opposed him. Blair's legacy will be one in which the economic landscape brought about by Thatcher was not undone, but rather only changed at the margins. The modernization of his party and the country, although controversial in parts, will be his main contribution.

The Conflict in Northern Ireland

From the late 1960s until the mid-1990s, Northern Ireland witnessed a resurgence – or second phase – of violence that came to be known as the Troubles. The historic first phase of the Troubles coincided with the Anglo-Irish battles that eventually led to the creation of the modern Irish state. Northern Ireland comprises the six counties of Ireland which became part of the United Kingdom after the partition of the island, leaving the south independent, the Irish Free State in 1922 (later named the Republic of Ireland in 1949). The term Ulster technically refers to a historic groups of provinces of Ireland, a portion of which became part of Northern Ireland. Today, Ulster is a politicized term in Northern Ireland, invoked by Protestant groups, which use it as part of asserting their identity.

The contemporary Troubles date from the late 1960s, involving sporadic communal violence, the police and paramilitary organizations. Animosity grew as the Catholic minority in Northern Ireland complained of political and economic discrimination. A civil rights movement modelled somewhat on the civil rights experiences of Martin Luther King and others in the United States, became active in the debates between the two communities. The growing conflict resulted in 1969 with the arrival of British troops. In response to a campaign of bombing, internment without trial was introduced in August 1971. Violence continued to grow, and a particularly violent episode occurred in Londonderry on 30 January 1972, in which 13 civil rights protesters were killed by British paratroopers, came to be known as *Bloody Sunday*. In March the British government suspended the Northern Ireland parliament, the Stormont, and direct rule from London ensued.

The following 20 years of the Troubles saw the Irish Republican Army (IRA) take its violent campaign to remove British troops from Northern Ireland and detach it from the United Kingdom to the streets of London and other big cities in Britain, such as Birmingham and Manchester. So-called Protestant Loyalist paramilitaries – such as the Ulster Defence Force (UDF) – responded in kind in Catholic areas of Belfast and elsewhere in Northern Ireland. Direct rule was not sustainable over the long-term, and the British government sought ways out of the impasse. One was an Anglo-Irish

Agreement in 1985 that led the Republic of Ireland become part of the process leading to peace by institutionalizing an intergovernmental conference. In 1993 John Major and his Irish counterpart, Albert Reynolds, issued a Downing Street Declaration that recognized the right to 'selfdetermination' by the Irish people. On 31 August, 1994 the IRA announced a 'complete cessation of military operations'. Although there was a resumption of IRA 'operations' two years later with a bombing in London, in 1997 the IRA again announced a cease-fire, and the following year a historic agreement was reached, called the Good Friday Agreement. Ratified in both the Republic as well as Northern Ireland in May 1998, it brought about the resumption of Stormont, the release of political prisoners, the reform of the Northern Ireland police force, changing its name from the Royal Ulster Constabulary to the Police Service of Northern Ireland, and the end of bombing by the main protagonists (a breakaway group from the IRA, calling themselves the Real IRA, exploded a car-bomb in the town of Omagh in Northern Ireland killing 28 people, the single largest amount of casualties during the modern Troubles.

The party-political landscape of Northern Ireland has changed over the past thirty years. The largest parties are Sinn Fein, the political wing of the IRA, the Social Democratic and Labour Party (SDLP), both of these parties drawing primarily from the Catholic community, and the Ulster Unionist Party (UUP) and the Democratic Unionist Party (DUP), both representing Protestant political views. Other parties have tried to break the hold of these four, but all have remained quite small. The issue of evidence of IRA decommissioning of its weapons to the satisfaction of the leader of the DUP, Ian Paisley, has prevented the Stormont from pursuing its business since 2004. Still, although low-level violence continues in Northern Ireland – for example, so-called punishment beatings – the days of widespread bombings, assassinations, etc., appear to be over.

Political Transition in the Smaller Countries

Among the smaller European countries, a political shift towards the left occurred in the 1960s. But in the 1970s, a turn back towards the centre began as electorates expressed their displeasure with the economic slump, higher taxes, and the possibility of more extensive welfare measures from Communist or far-left socialist parties. The moderate socialist parties became an oft-chosen coalition partner as they became more reform oriented.

Belgium, Luxembourg and the Netherlands In Luxembourg, three parties, the Christian-Social People's Party, the Socialist Worker's Party, and the Democratic or Liberal party have dominated the political coalitions. Although the Christian Social and Liberal parties tend to support a free-market economy more than the Socialists, all three support the social welfare measures introduced since the war. The Communist party experienced a two-decades decline primarily because it did not adopt a more moderate Euro-communist position. Major socio-economic conflicts have been avoided through the cooperation of the labour unions, business and government. Although Luxembourg has not experienced the severe economic problems of the other Benelux countries, it adopted austerity measures and cut taxes in the mid-eighties in order to control inflation and unemployment and keep the economy strong. By the mid-1990s, the same parties were continuing in power, although the prime minister since the late 1980s, Jacques Santer, left in 1994 to succeed Jacques Delors as the new president of the European Commission in Brussels. His successor Jean-Claude Juncker, served as prime minister for at least the next ten years. In 2004, Juncker became the semi-permanent President of the group of finance ministers from the 12 EU countries that comprise the eurozone. Over the past few decades, Luxembourg diversified its economy, and its banking sector now accounts for a good portion of its economy. Luxembourg has close trade and financial ties with Belgium and the Netherlands, the three countries often referred to as the BeNeLux countries. As noted in Chapter 8 Luxembourg has the highest GDP per capita in Europe. As with other Western European countries, Luxembourg now has a Green Party, and in the 2004 parliamentary elections, gained seven members, an increase of two seats.

After heading several center-left coalition governments since 1979, Belgium's Prime Minister, Wilfrid Martens formed a center-right coalition in 1982. His Christian Democratic-dominated government imposed an austerity program in order to deal with the economic slump. Government subsidies to industry and wages were cut, the Belgian franc devalued, consumer prices frozen, and tax incentives for industrial investment raised. With inflation decreasing and trade back in balance by 1984, Martens returned to office after the 1985 and 1987 elections. Although the 1987 elections produced a Christian Democratic-Socialist-Flemish Nationalist coalition, economic retrenchment continued. In fact, the Socialists stressed the ethnic issue rather than traditional economic-social issues. The Belgian Communist party's stubborn adherence to an orthodox Leninist position led to its decline and virtual disappearance from parliament after 1985. Continued austerity measures reduced the inflation rate below 2 per cent in 1989 and brought an economic growth rate of about 3 per cent. But Belgians had to accept increased unemployment as inefficient firms failed and successful ones became leaner. Belgian's other major challenge was linguistic politics, primarily the Flemish-Walloon (French-speakers) split. In 1970 a constitutional revision declared that Belgium consisted of three economic regions – Flanders, Wallonia and Brussels, and in 1980 a devolution bill established cultural as well as economic powers to these regions. Most Belgians had hoped that this granting of further local autonomy would make it possible for the Dutch and French speaking inhabitants to live together in one state. Further devolution and then outright federalization of the country in 1993 saw the central government's jurisdiction include only foreign affairs, defense, justice, social security and monetary policy. Despite these changes, a Flemish right-wing (neo-facsist according to some) separatist party, Vlaams Blok, has succeeded in gaining regional and municipal representation in Flanders, where it became the single-largest party in Antwerp. In 2004, the party was declared illegal on the grounds that it was a racsist party. It dissolved itself and was immediately reconstituted as Vlaams Belang (Flemish Interest). Legal questions over whether or not it was the same party – and therefore still illegal – were debated and it was found to be essentially the same party. Yet it continues to exist.

In the Netherlands, moderate centre-right or centre-left governments alternated in power during the 1980s. When Labour withdrew from the centre-left government in 1982 due to their refusal to support cuts in public spending, an interim government headed by the Christian Democrats was formed. A centre-right government of Christian Democrats and Liberals took power after elections in September 1982 and implemented cuts in government spending, taxes, and government employees and ended the indexing of wages and welfare benefits. Although these austerity measures were painful, the public returned this center-right government of Ruud Lubbers to office in 1986. But the Lubbers government fell in May 1989 when it failed to respond energetically to environmental issues. The September 1989 elections returned a Labour led centre-left government. Elections in 1994 produced the first notable changes in government coalition members since the Second World War. For the first time, the Christian Democrats were not part of the government. Instead, a progressive liberal party, D-66, together with Labour and the (conservative) Liberals (VVD) formed the new government, with Labour leader Wim Kok as prime minister.

The Kok government presided over the Netherlands entry into the eurozone, as well as hosting one of the crucial EU summits that provided for treaty amendments, the Amsterdam Treaty. Wim Kok was himself a popular politician, and he led his government into a second term after elections in 1998. This second term of government turned out to be much more difficult. The economy began to slow (although it would be 2003 before the country actually experienced its first recession since 1993), and even more distressing, a UN report on the massacre at Srebrinica (see Chapter 11) implicated the Dutch peacekeepers, a finding that led Wim Kok to resign. The 2002 election turned out to be anything but normal for Dutch politics. An independent politician by the name of Pim Fortuyn came to prominence on a platform that sounded racsist to many people, although he refused to be compared to far-right politicians such as LePen in France or Haider in Austria. His controversial views on Islam and his anti-immigration positions gained him widespread attention in the run-up to the elections. On 6 May 2002, just nine days before the election he was assassinated by an animal-rights activist, the first political assassination since WWII. Whether in sympathy or not, his party, known as the Pim Fortuyn List (*Lijst Pim Fortuyn*), won 26 seats, which represented 17 per cent of the seats in parliament. Without his leadership, the List MPs quickly lost any cohesiveness, and their disintegration prompted new elections one year later, in which the Christian Democrats lead a center-right government.

Scandinavia   In Scandinavia, popular dissatisfaction with the costly social welfare programs, high taxes and government spending swept the Social Democrats from power in Sweden from 1976 to 1982, in Norway from 1981 to 1986 and in Denmark after 1982. Although there was widespread satisfaction with Scandinavia's high standard of living, the taxation rates of near 70 per cent of income that were needed to support the costly social-welfare programs spread dissatisfaction, as did the general European economic downturn.

From the late 1970s, Danish voters shifted their ballots towards parties in the middle of the political spectrum rather than the left, producing a political standoff between right and left. The result was a series of minority governments in the 1980s. The radical Communist and left-socialist parties lost all political representation in the 1980s. From 1982 until 1993, Poul Schluter from the Conservative People's Party served as the first non-socialist prime minister since the interwar period. But his centre-right coalition government ruled as a minority government. Political dissatisfaction was been expressed in the increased representation for the anti-tax Progress Party. It gained 16 seats in the 1988 elections on a programme of reduced taxes, government spending and bureaucracy. But its extreme anti-war, anti-immigrant positions kept it from any government coalition. In 1992, the Danes rejected the EU Maastricht Treaty in a referendum. Although they later voted again, and this time supported it, their opt-outs regarding monetary union meant that Denmark did not join the eurozone at the end of the decade. In elections held in 1993, Schluter finally lost his post as prime minister, and was replaced by a new coalition header by the Social Democrats, led by Poul Nyrup Rasmussen. Rasmussen asked the Danes again if they would join the euro, but in a 2000 referendum they again said No. After a snap election in the wake of the 9/11 attacks in the United States, the Social Democrats lost power. A centre-right coalition took over, led by Prime Minister Anders Fogh Rasmussen, leader of the Liberal Party (*Venstre*). This government promised tighter immigration controls, and although not formally part of the government, the far-right Danish People's Party wielded some influence on the government's policies in this area. In elections held in 2005, Rasmussen's coalition was returned to power.

In Sweden, where the Social Democrats lost power in 1976 (the first time since the 1930s) but remained the largest party, squabbling among the three non-socialist parties gave the Social Democrats an opportunity to return to power in 1982. But it is not the same Social Democratic Party that held power before 1976. The party moderated its views in order to accommodate the new public consensus. The late party leader and prime minister Olaf Palme led the party towards moderate wage agreements, reduced taxes and a postponement of a proposed wage earners' fund proposal (the Meidner plan) that probably cost the Social Democrats victory in the 1976 and 1979 elections. In a country that has had what most Swedes consider to be a healthy mix of social welfare and private enterprise, the wage earners' fund proposal seemed to threaten a system that works well in spite of economic reverses in the 1980s. After Palme's assassination in 1986, Ingvar Carlsson headed up a Social Democratic coalition with the moderate, former Communist party, renamed the Left Party. In the 1988 parliamentary elections, the Social Democrats slipped from 159 to 156 seats and the Left Party rose from 19 to 21 seats. The three main non-socialist opposition parties lost 19 seats (171 to 152). Carlsson's promise to lower income-tax rates and provide a sixth week of paid annual vacation was more appealing than the opposition's tax cut proposals. Sweden's high standard of living, second only to that of Japan, and low unemployment rate – 1.7 per cent in 1988 – may have been other important factors in Carlsson's success. The election of 20 Greens to the parliament (Riksdag) marked the advent of environmental issues as an important consideration in future elections.

In the 1990s, Sweden faced increasing economic difficulties as a result of its full-employment policy, extensive welfare system and labour attitudes. Although Swedish workers work an average of only 31 hours a week, their absentee rate is the highest in Western Europe. Sweden's share of the world market has declined 4 per cent a year beginning in 1988. The remedies for Sweden's economic ills were unpopular. Carlson's government fell in February 1990 when his austerity package failed to win approval. Labour refused to agree to a wage freeze. An income-tax reduction to 50 per cent did pass in 1989 but indirect taxes were raised to maintain revenue. This backing away from the egalitarian society many Swedes cherish met stiff resistance. Nevertheless, elections in 1991 brought a four-party conservative coalition to power led by Conservative party leader Carl Bildt. The main political theme throughout Bildt's term in office was the serious state of the economy, manifested in several ways: rising unemployment; rising national debt; and intense speculation against the Swedish currency, the krona. A reduction in the numbers of public employees, one third of the work force, to obtain a more market-oriented economy, was unpopular. Nevertheless, Sweden signaled its desire to join the European Union, and in late 1994, following scheduled legislative elections in October, Swedes voted in a referendum on EU membership. Resistance emanated from farmers and other groups who believe a certain distinctiveness of life may be lost due to what they see as the homogenizing effects of integration. Most of the major political parties, however, favoured admission. The success of the Social Democrats at the October elections substantially added to the odds of a 'Yes' victory, achieved with 52 per cent. Although Sweden was now part of the European Union, it was clear that a good portion of Social democratic voters and members remained opposed, again on grounds of diluting Sweden's welfare state. This point was made in a September 2003 referendum, when voters rejected by a comfortable margin joining the eurozone. The Prime minister, Goran Persson, gambled that he could persuade enough Swedes to follow him, and scheduled the referendum one year after his Social Democrats were returned to power in September 2002. Drama also ensued during the campaign for the euro referendum when the popular (and pro-euro) foreign minister, Anna Lindh, was murdered just days before the vote.

Norway's disunited Labour Party lost power in the 1981 elections to a coalition of Conservative, Christian People's, and Centre parties. The electorate apparently tired of high taxes, excessive public spending and declining industrial efficiency. After five years of conservative rule, Labour returned under the popular leadership of Gro Harlem Brundtland. Labour, though divided over Norway's relationship with the EU and NATO, continued to rule until September 1989. Brundtlund promoted the progressive image of Scandinavia by choosing eight female cabinet members. Women also comprise a substantial portion of seats in the legislature (see Chapter 8). The Labour Party requires that 40 per cent of its candidates for public office be women. The 1989 elections produced an increased vote for the tax-cutting, welfare-reducing Progress Party and prevented either Labour or the three non-socialist moderate parties from obtaining a majority. Since neither Labour nor the moderate conservatives wished to cooperate with the Progress Party, government instability existed until the next elections in 1991, when Labour formed another minority government.

Relations with the EU were also put somewhat into doubt when Norwegians voted against membership (the second time in a little over 20 years) on 28 November 1994. Although Prime Minister Brundtland personally campaigned for a 'Yes' vote, the result was 53 per cent against, 47 per cent for. Norway's rejection of the EU has not harmed its economy. It has continued to experience respectable rates of growth, and its trade with EU countries is assured by its participation in the European Economic Area (EEA), basically membership in the EU's Single Market but without the political presence and input in its institutions. In 1997, a conservative coalition took power, led by Kjell Magne Bondevik of the Christian people's Party (Bondevik is himself a Lutheran priest). Re-elected in 2001, in which Labour suffered its worst election result in 90 years, he has maintained Norway's tradition of including 40 per cent of women in government.

Austria   In the midst of all of this political fragmentation and governmental instability in Western Europe, Austria was been a model of stability for several decades. Until 1966, Austria was ruled by two main parties, the People's Party and the Socialist Party under a system called *Proporz* that alternated members of these parties in various bureaucratic posts and in the cabinet. This style of consensual collaboration is called consociationalism, a form of governance usually associated with divided societies, Belgium and the Netherlands are also examples. After a brief period in opposition (1966–69), the Socialists, led by Chancellor Bruno Kreisky until 1983, ruled alone until 1986. Both Austria's avoidance of the worst aspects of the post-1972 economic slump and the flexible 'catch-all nature' of her political parties led to the political stability. Neither party adheres strongly to an unbending ideological position. Since Austrian labour held down its wage demands because of a system that permits labour to arbitrate wages and prices cooperatively with government and industry – the so-called social partnership – Austria's labour market was extremely calm. In addition, the Socialists concentrated on establishing a modern industrial state as much as on social welfare. The party's fear that higher taxes would reduce economic investment made it refuse to shift ever more of the tax burden onto the wealthy.

Austria's long-running success story was interrupted in the 1980s by the election of Kurt Waldheim to the presidency in 1986 and by increasing economic problems. Waldheim, the former Secretary general of the United Nations, doggedly clung to the presidency despite intense international and internal pressure that he resign after it was disclosed that he had concealed his role as an SS officer in the Second World War. This controversy led to Waldheim's isolation and instigated a national soul-searching concerning Austria's role in the National Socialist era. Added to Austria's woes was an economy that had turned flat because of overemployment, excessive bureaucracy and technological obsolescence. Franz Vranitsky, the reformist Socialist chancellor in a coalition government with the People's Party beginning in 1986, moved to modernize outdated industries and reduce government expenditures. In doing so, Austria's social partnership began to wane and was slowly replaced by a more competitive pattern of interest group relations. Thus, some of the stability, security and consensus for which Austria was known increasingly gave way to competition and conflict. The public reacted by supporting the Freedom Party, a right-wing populist party led by Jörg Haider. In the elections of 1994, the Freedom Party won an astonishing 22.5 per cent of the vote. Later that year, on 12 June, Austrians voted in a referendum on the question of joining the European Union. The high turn-out rate produced a strong show of support for membership, 67 per cent voting yes, and Austria joined the EU in 1995 (along with Sweden and Finland).

Austria's political woes had yet to end however. In the 1999 elections, the Freedom party increased its share of the vote to about 27 per cent. Even though it came a close third, The People's Party leader, Wolfgang Schüssel, formed a coalition with the Freedom Party in early 2000. This resulted in the EU imposing (symbolic) sanctions on Austria, which were revoked six months later. The presence of Haider's Freedom Party was the reason, as Haider's comments over the years regarding the Nazi era seemed to make him appear to be an apologist for some of the crimes during that period. Haider himself did not take part in the government, but was elected governor of one of Austria's provinces, Carinthia. In 2002, the government coalition was re-elected, but this time Haider's party declined to only 10 per cent of the vote. In 2005, he left his party, and those following him hope to set up a newly revitalized party, as the Freedom Party had entered a steep decline in its popularity.

FURTHER READING

There are many country and area as well as subject specific periodicals one can consult in addition to the books listed below. For example, *West European Politics, Southern European Politics and Society, Journal of Southern Europe and the Balkans, Modern & Contemporary France, French Politics, German Politics, Parliamentary Affairs*, and *Scandinavian Political Studies*, just to name a few. On-line resources from the OECD, ILO, UNESCO, World Bank and IMF are easily accessible and provide good comparative studies. Newspapers that provide good coverage of daily European political news include the *Financial Times* and the *International Herald Tribune*.

The focus of the readings here are from the 1970s onwards. Earlier postwar selections are found in the Further Reading section of Chapter 4.

Authoritarian governments fell in Spain, Portugal and Greece in the 1970s. Literature on this phenomenon includes comparative as well as single country studies. Comparative studies include Guillermo O'Donnell, Philippe Schmitter and L. Whitehead, *Transition from Authoritarian Rule* (1986), Geoffrey Pridham, ed., *The New Mediterranean Democracies: Regime Transition in Spain, Greece and Portugal* (1984); and *Securing Democracy: Political parties and Democratic Consolidation in Southern Europe* (1990). For Spain, see D. Gilmour, *The Transformation of Spain* (1985); and Paul Preston, *The Triumph of Democracy in Spain* (1986). For Greece see C. M. Woodhouse, *The Rise and Fall of the Greek Colonels* (1985) and Kevin Featherstone, ed., *Political Change in Greece: Before and After the Colonels* (1987). For Portugal see Hugo Gil Ferreira and Michael W. Marshall, *Portugal's Revolution: Ten Years On* (1986); and M. Kayman, *Revolution and Counter-Revolution in Portugal* (1987). A good overview of southern European politics is provided by Giulio Sapelli *Southern Europe: Politics, Society and Economics Since 1945* (1995).

Foreign policy initiatives and changes during the period covering the end of the Cold War and after are explored in many works. On the Cold war period, see Dana H. Allin, *Cold War Illusions: America, Europe and Soviet Power, 1969–89* (1995); and S. J. Ball, *The Cold war: An International History, 1947–1991* (1998). Michael Kort, *The Columbia Guide to the Cold war* (1998) is also useful. As for the ending of the Cold war in particular, see Michael R. Beschloss and Strobe Talbott, *At the Highest Levels: The Inside Story of the End of the Cold War* (1993), Robert L. Hutchings, *American Policy and the End of the Cold War: An Insider's Account of US Policy in Europe, 1989–1992* (1997); and Michael Hogan, *The End of the Cold War: Its Meaning and Implications* (1992). The post-Cold War era is explored in David C. Gompert and F. Stephen Larrabee, *America and Europe: A Partnership for a New Era* (1999); and Michael Cox, Ken Booth and Tim Dunne, *The Interregnum: Controversies in World Politics, 1989–1999* (2000). A good introduction to the more specific issues of security in Europe, see W. Park and G. Wyn Rees, *Rethinking Security in Post-Cold War Europe* (1998); and James H. Wyllie, *European Security in the New Political Environment* (1997). The country at the centre of the Cold War in Europe, Germany, and its part of the relationship, is admirably explored and analysed by Wolfram Hanrieder, *Germany, America, Europe: Forty Years of German Foreign Policy* (1989) and Peter Alter, *The German Question and Europe* (2000).

The years after the end of the long post-war economic boom is explored by a number of authors, some focussing on the political decisions and others on economic trends. A good introduction into the broader context of economic changes is Philip Armstrong, Andrew Glyn and John Harrison, *Capitalism Since World War II: The Making and Breakup of the Great Boom* (1984). Also useful is Andrea Boltho, ed., *The European Economy: Growth and Crisis* (1982). The social implications of slow economic growth and the impact on the welfare state, is explored and readings listed in Chapter 8.

The following list of books are concerned with individual countries. Students may also wish to consult the 'Developments in ...' series by Palgrave for more up-to-date information. There are recent editions of *Developments in French Politics, Developments in German Politics, Developments in British Politics*, and *Developments in West European Politics*. Richard Sakwa and Anne Stevens, *Contemporary Europe* (2000, 2006) is also useful for a general background.

For a general introduction to both West Germany and the unified Germany, see Peter Pulzer, *German Politics, 1945–1995* (1995), Geoffrey Roberts, *German Politics Today* (2000) and David Conradt and Thomas Cronin, *The German Polity* (2004). On relations between the two Germanys, see A. J. McAdams, *Germany Divided* (1993). On the place of the new Germany in Europe, see Peter Katzenstein, *Tamed Power: Germany in Europe* (1997). On specifically German-EU relations, see Kenneth Dyson and Klaus H. Goetz, eds, *Germany and Europe: A Europeanizaed Germany?* (2003). On electoral patterns in unified Germany, see Christopher Anderson and Karsten Zelle, eds, *Stability and Change in German Elections: How Electorates Merge, Converge, or Collide* (1998). On the events and politics of the unification of the two Germanies, see Peter Merkl, *German Unification in the European Context* (1993), Micheal G. Huelshoff et al., eds., *From Bundesrepublik to Deutschland* (1993) and M. Donald Hancock and Helga Welch, eds., *German Unification: Process and Outcome* (1994). On the economic issues arising from unification, see Gerlinde *Sinn* and hans-Werner Sinn, *Jumpstart: The Economic Unification of Germany (1992)*. Social issues are surveyed by, among others, Eva Kolinsky, *Women in Contemporary Germany* (1993) and Kathleen Thelen, *Union in Parts: Labor Politics in Postwar Germany* (1991).

Like Germany, there is a large literature in English on recent French politics. A good introduction would be Alistair Cole, *French Politics and Society* (2nd edition, 2005). Socio-economic change up to the 1990s, is covered by Henri Mendras and Alistair Cole, *Social Change in the Fifth Republic* (1991). On politics during the Mitterrand years, see Anthony Daley, ed., *The Mitterrand Era: Policy Alternatives and political Mobilization in France* (1996). On the relationship between France and the export of American commercial culture, see Richard Kuisel, *Seducing the French: The Dilemma of Americanization* (1993). On French EU relations, see Alain Guyomarch et al., *France in the European Union* (1998) and G. Hendriks, *The Franco-German Axis in European Integration* (2000). Recent French party politics is competently analyzed by Jocelyn Evans, ed., *The French Party System* (2003). Chirac became president in 1995, and many issues in France that faced him are covered in John Keeler and Martin Schain, *Chirac's Challenge: Liberation, Europeanization, and Malaise in France* (1996). Organized labour and its attendant politics is explored in Herrick Chapman, Mark Kesselman and Martin Schain, eds., *A Century of Organized Labor in France* (1998). Immigration and national identity are analyzed in Gerard Noiriel, *The French Melting Pot: Immigration, Citizenship, and National Identity* (1996). Women and French state reforms are presented by Amy Mazur, *Gender Bias and the State: Symbolic Reform at Work in Fifth Republic France* (1996).

Italian politics has experienced a major shift in the 1990s, and this is reflected in recent literature. Up to the sea-change in Italian politics in the mid-1990s, a good reference is Donald Sassoon, *Contemporary Italy: Politics, Economy & Society since 1945* (1986), and Frederic Spotts and Theodor Wieser, *Italy: A*

Difficult Democracy (1986). David Hine, *Governing Italy* (1993) is the best work treating Italian politics right up to the spectacular upheaval in the party system. On the political changes, see Stephen Grundle and Simon Parker, eds., *The New Italain republic: From the Fall of the Berlin wall to Berlusconi* (1996); and Patrick McCarthy, *The Crisis of the Italian State* (1997). Subsequent political events and issues are covered in Martin Bull and Martin Rhodes, eds., *Crisis and Transition in Italian Politics* (1998) and Vittorio Bufacchi and Simon Burgess, *Italy Since 1989: Events and Interpretations* (1998). *Italian Politics: A Review*, published since 1986 (by different subsequent publishers) is excellent in finding more recent material. Economic and social issues are treated by, among others, Richard Locke, *Remaking the Italian Economy* (1995), Judith Adler Hellman, *Journeys Among Women: Feminism in Five Italian Cities* (1987), and peter lange and Marino regini, eds., *State, Market, and Socia regulation: New Perspectives on Italy* (1989).

The literature on British politics from the 1970s onwards concerns itself quite often with Thatcher and Blair. On a more general level though, in addition to the *Developments in British Politics* series, also useful is the series *Britain at the Polls*, covering individual elections. Additionally, see Pippa Norris and Geoffrey Norris, eds., *Critical Elections: British Parties and Voters in Long-Term Perspective* (1999). On specifically the British party system, see Paul Webb, *The Modern British Party System* (2000). For a good overview of the workings of British government, see Bill Coxall et al., *Contemporary British Politics* (2003, 4th ed.). Andrew Gamble, in *Britain in Decline* (1989) gives a sober analysis of the direction of British politics in the 1970s and 1980s. On the constitutional changes and devolution, see Vernon Bogdanor, *Devolution in the United Kingdom* (2001). On the Thatcher years, see Peter Jenkins, *Mrs. Thatcher's Revolution: The Ending of the Socialist Era* (1988) and Dennis Kavanaugh, *Thatcherism and British Politics: The End of Consensus* (1987). For an excellent comparative study, see Paul Pierson, *Dismantling the Welfare State?: Reagan, Thatcher, and the Politics of Retrenchment* (1994). On British social issues and welfare state, see Bhiku Parekh, *The Future of Multi-Ethnic Britain: The Parekh Report* (2000), Paul Gilroy, *"There Ain't No Black in the Union Jack": The Cultural Politics of Race and Nation* (1991), John Brown, *The British Welfare State: A Critical History* (1995) and Alison Park, ed., *British Social Attitudes: The 20th Report* (2003). On Labour under Blair, see Stephen Driver and Luke Martell, *New Labour Politics after Thatcherism* (1998) and Anthony Seldon, *The Blair Effect* (2001).

Recent publications on the politics of Northern Ireland that provide background in general, and specific attention to the Good Friday Agreement, are David McKittrick and David McVea, *Making Sense of the Troubles* (2001); and Michael Cox, Adroan Guelke and Fiona Stephen, *A Farewell to Arms? Beyond the Good Friday Agreement* (2005).

Most of our attention has centered on the 'big' countries of Western Europe and those making the transition from authoritarian rule. The smaller countries and Scandinavia also deserve some attention, and the following is an indicative list. Up-to-date coverage of Spanish politics is made by Richard Gunther, J. Montero and J. Botella, *Democracy in Modern Spain* (2004). A recent work covering all southern European political systems is Kostas Lavdas and Jose Magone, *Politics and Governance in Southern Europe: The Political Systems of Italy, Greece, Spain and*

Portugal (1997). The politics of Belgian federalization is ably presented by Liesbet Hooghe in *Leap in the Dark: Nationalist Conflict and Federal Reform in Belgium* (1991). For the Netherlands see Rudy Andeweg and Galen Irwin, *Governance and politics of the Netherlands* (2005, 2nd ed.). Kurt Richard Luther and Peter Pulzer cover Austria over the entire postwar period in *Austria, 1945–1995* (1998), and a more political focus is given in Luther and Wolfgang Muller in *Politics in Austria* (1992). The Nordic political model is analyzed up to the last set of elections in the 1990s by David Arter, *Scandinavian Politics Today* (1999).

13 Thought and Culture Since 1945

Is it not barbarous to write poems after Auschwitz?

Theodore Adorno

After the experiences of Second World War – the mass exterminations, the bombing of civilian centres, the atomic bombing of Japan – a pervasive cultural pessimism settled over continental Europe in the immediate post-war period, reflected in Adorno's statements. For if the land of Goethe and Bach could carry out the atrocities of Auschwitz, what hope was there for mankind in general? Only after extensive soul searching could Europeans, especially the Germans, begin to seek answers to this paradox. Except for those who remained loyal to some form of Marxism, Europe's intellectuals first turned against all ideological systems, all attempts at understanding the whole, to a distrust of all 'facts' and 'knowledge.' This existential attitude was most evident immediately after the war in philosophy and literature.

A broader cultural-intellectual influence that transcended the war experience continued to transform cultural endeavour, particularly the arts, in the post-war period. This so-called Modernist movement was a search for novelty and a rejection of the cultural forms that had dominated the nineteenth century. Building on the late-nineteenth century rejection of Enlightenment rationalism, a Modernist avant-garde revolted against realism and figuration in art, against story and representation in literature, and against ornament in architecture. Some of the artistic elite rejected the modern industrialized, bourgeois, world. An iconoclastic avant-garde (Dadaists, Surrealists, etc.) purposely produced works that upset or could not be enjoyed by the bourgeoisie. The result was a distancing of the artistic elite from society and a division between high and popular culture.

By the 1960s a post-modern attitude began to supplant the Modernist perspective. But it was not a complete break with Modernism as can be borne out by its affinity with certain giants of the Modernist period such as Sigmund Freud, Friedrich Nietzsche, James Joyce, Pablo Picasso, Arnold Schoenberg, Samuel Beckett, Anton von Webern, Jorge Luis Borges and the Surrealists. This post-modern impetus was to take many forms as it was to a large extent a reaction against individual Modernists; against the International

Style in architecture (Le Courbusier, Mies van der Rohe), against abstract expressionism in art, against any philosophical attempts to seek unity or wholeness. The post-modernist turn to popular culture (Pop art, Op art, etc.) multiplied the forms and made it difficult to distinguish high art from kitsch. The post-modernists, to an exaggerated degree, believe that they are constricted by existing cultural patterns, by history, and therefore their attempt to escape them goads them on to even greater breaks with the past.

These culturally innovative trends have revolutionized art and music but captured only a small avant-garde in literature. While a literary avant-garde experimented with language forms in order to break previously accepted modes of communication, the mainstream continued to be concerned about plot and the narrative. The constant search for novelty, or free invention as its practitioners termed it, produced many new styles in rapid succession and ultimately fragmentation. Emerging out of this artistic morass in the 1970s was a trend back to representation, story and history. A closer study of philosophy and the various arts will reveal these dominant trends.

Philosophy

Existentialism   Existentialism was an appropriate response to the war and post-war pessimism. Although existentialism had been formulated long before the war in the works of Soren Kierkegaard, Friedrich Nietzsche, Martin Heidegger, Edmund Husserl, Karl Jaspers and others, it gained broad intellectual acceptance only in the post-war period due to the widespread skepticism and disenchantment among intellectuals on the Continent. To these intellectuals, the Second World War seriously undermined any rational attempts to understand the world. The existentialist rejected all systems based upon a mechanistic understanding of the universe such as rationalism and positivism. In this absurd, incomprehensible world only an ultimately skeptical philosophy such as existentialism could give meaning to existence. If, as the existentialist claimed, all facts were suspect, all knowledge relative, the individual was alone and isolated in a world without meaning. Existential man, according to its most outstanding post-war exponents, John Paul Sartre and Maurice Merleau-Ponty, must find his own meaning in this meaningless world. Sartre's major work, *Being and Nothingness*, maintained that with God and reason both dead, the only course left open to man was an individual adjustment to an absurd existence. To free oneself from such a meaningless existence, one must make choices and act on them. Acting creates values, or, as Sartre explained, essence. Man is essentially what he makes of himself. Existence is given meaning through commitment, and for Sartre this commitment was to Communism. Sartre had by this choice given the very individualistic philosophy of existentialism a broader social base. Even when he became aware of the shortcomings of Communist regimes – the Stalinist concentration camps, the suppression of the 1956 Hungarian Revolution, etc. – he maintained his allegiance, since in his opinion Communism was ultimately superior to capitalism. Sartre's adamant defence of Communism eventually weakened existentialism, since many of his followers, including Merleau–Ponty, who had once defended Stalin's Moscow Trials of political opponents, could no longer accept his position. Sartre's close associate Albert Camus broke with him over his commitment to Communism. Camus retained the existential distrust of abstract ideas and ideologies that, in his opinion, produced hatred and suffering. Camus moved, however, from the absurdity of existence concept, best argued in *The Stranger*, to an exaltation of the everyday pleasures in life. But by the 1950s the lack of effective action by the existentialists, their internal haggling and rapid economic advance in France had reduced the support for such a 'meaningless' philosophy. Many intellectuals were no longer able to accept Sartre's gloomy view of existence, his extreme rejection of bourgeois society, and his doctrinaire commitment to Communism. The legacy of existentialism is, on the one hand, a healthy skepticism, and on the other, cynicism, defeatism and apathy.

In the Anglo–Saxon world an Analytical school, influenced by Ludwig Wittgenstein, mounted a similar assault on understanding the whole in the 1950s. Since the world of language is divorced from world of fact, any attempt to understand the world is folly. One can only make up myths. The best one can do is to minutely examine phenomena in order to get rid of error, purge ambiguity, clarify and define.

Structuralism Once existentialism was undermined, no major movement emerged to replace it for over a decade. Only in the 1960s, did another notable philosophic movement, some say only a method or viewpoint, emerge. Called structuralism, it differed from existentialism in that it viewed man less as a free agent. Structuralists maintained that man's choices were determined by the existing structure of the basic units in a society. By understanding the relationship of the various units rather than by understanding the content of phenomena, truth would emerge. Claude Levi–Strauss, the anthropologist and father of structuralism, held that all societies have similar underlying mental structures – apparent in their myths – that guide them. Phenomena could be analyzed, he maintained, by reducing them to their simplest components. He rejected the view that some societies are more advanced than others, since all can be reduced to these essential structures. He thus rejected the idea of historical progress from primitive to advanced stages of civilization. Although the key that would unlock these essential components of all societies has not yet been found, Levi–Strauss influenced scholars in many fields to search for underlying structures. The psychologist Louis Lacan sought to unravel the unconscious as one would a text, since the key to both is the structure of language. We can, according to Lacan, understand Freud's meanings more clearly by studying his use of language. Even many who refuse the structuralist label approach their work from a structuralist point of view. The Marxist Louis Althusser attempted to uncover economic structures, class situations, and polarization in the societies he studied.

In language studies, structural analysis had preceded Levi–Strauss by many decades. Before the First World War, the Swiss linguist, Ferdinand de

Saussure, had begun to experiment with a science of language, and his work served as the groundwork for the modern study of structural linguistics. Building on Saussure's pioneering work, post-war linguistic structuralists – Roland Barthes, Noam Chomsky, etc. – posited that language is composed of elements that logically relate to each other. Since this relationship orders one's thoughts and therefore determines one's ideas, what one says or writes determines what one thinks rather than the opposite. Here again, one's thoughts are ordered by these underlying relationships, which are not consciously perceived. Language leads to classification and classification is oppressive. One can achieve understanding only by uncovering these internal relationships. While the structuralists hoped to impose order on what they considered to be the anarchy in thought brought on by existentialism and its demise, they frightened away many intellectuals who viewed structuralism as imposing a deterministic order on reality. Moreover, Levi–Strauss's failure to find those 'universal mental structures' diminished the appeal of structuralism.

In the subsequent 'postmodernist' era, philosophy has become exceedingly fragmented and specialized although tending to focus on linguistic and conceptual analysis. The postmodernists typically venture beyond structuralism to a critique of language, history, truth, time, space and existence that breaks existing boundaries even more than structuralism had done. They reject attempts to understand anything in its entirety. Therefore, most oppose any totalizing view of history, such as Marxism, or any search for coherent patterns, such as the structuralists search for a common code underlying all languages. Jacques Derrida, a French philosopher of language, attempted to achieve an original structuralist aim, the complete destructuring of language. He read important philosophical texts of his contemporaries and 'deconstructed' many of their basic assumptions. Derrida, Foucault and Barthes were all poststructuralist to the extent that they did not believe in universal, timeless mental structures as Levi–Strauss did but contended that thought patterns change over time. Foucault, for example, argued that societies' codes of knowledge are constantly being transformed. Most poststructuralists have undermined the original structuralist search for universal structures by giving thought and language a historical dimension. Levi–Strauss called them ministructuralists. On the other hand, Derrida contended that Levi–Strauss did not go far enough in his study of myths, since he did not attempt to find out if all myths are equivalent. Derrida, as well as other poststructuralists, believed that many of the basic tenants of Modernism were already outmoded and therefore not 'modern' when first presented. In other words, Modernism preserved much that was traditional, according to the poststructuralists. Therefore, they want to examine all the underlying assumptions of Modernism in order to get at reality.

Marxism In the period of intellectual fragmentation after 1960, Marxism experienced a revival. Marxism in its totalitarian, Stalinist form was rejected and replaced by a Western liberating, emancipatory Marxism – the humanistic Marx of the early manuscripts rather than the economic determinist of

Das Kapital. The Frankfurt School of social theorists led by Theodor Adorno, Max Horkheimer and Herbert Marcuse, joined with the followers of the Italian Antonio Gramsci and the Hungarian Georg Lukács in emphasizing Marx's cultural message. Marx, in his early writings, they maintained, had pointed out that capitalism had not only alienated man from his work through mass production techniques but had also undermined his cultural values. Marcuse extended Marx's theories to modern society, where he held capitalism had created materialistic automatons or one-dimensional cultural philistines. Marcuse's quest to free man from both political and sexual oppression and thereby restore his true nature was especially attractive to the New Left. These 'humanistic Marxists' tended to downplay revolution in favour of gradualism. Gramsci had stressed that the first stage should be an alternative to the hegemonic capitalist culture and only later an alteration of politics. Some Marxists rejected this stress on the young Marx. Louis Althusser argued that revolution would not just come about gradually but had to be prepared for and organized. To Althusser the real Marx was the Marx of *Das Kapital*. By the 1970s, Marxism had become hopelessly splintered as intellectuals and the New Left fashioned their own Marxism to fit their specific situation.

One notable attempt to save Marxism in the face of the poststructuralist onslaught on any unifying theory has been that of Jurgen Habermas. Against the poststructuralists rejection of all attempts to find any coherent patterns in history, to understand the whole, Jurgen Habermas sought to restore a Marxist holistic view of history. Habermas feared that much of post-structuralist thought, especially that of Foucault and Derrida, threatens to undermine political democracy through its rejection of enlightenment rationalism. Despite Habermas' efforts, the philosophical avant-garde continued to be dominated by a neo-Nietzscheanism, poststructuralist attack on any attempts to find wholeness. Beginning with André Glucksmann's *The Master Thinkers* (1977) and Bernard–Henri Levy's *Barbarism with a Human Face* (1977), French thinkers began an attack on Marxist and post-structuralist modes of thought. These so-called new philosophers were reacting to Alexander Solzhenitsyn's *Gulag Archipelago*, the Cambodian massacres under Pol Pot, and the rise of Solidarity in Poland. This rejection of Marxist and structuralist dogmas ushered in a new 'liberal' rationalist perspective. Alain Finkelkraut emerged as a leading opponent of the post-war French left's antirational thought. In *The Defeat of the Mind* (1987), Finkelkraut defended the rational universalism of the Enlightenment. He rejected the post-structural and Marxist view that a single truth is an ideological cover for invisible structures and power. He maintained that ideas of equality and diversity pertain to individuals, not groups, and that the Enlightenment championed them in order to protect individuals from groups. Group thinking, he insisted, leads to cultural relativism and ultimately servitude. People immerse themselves in group thinking since it frees them from making difficult individual moral judgments.

Literature

Although no new literary genre arose in the immediate post-war period to challenge such Modernist giants as James Joyce, Thomas Mann and André Gide, two trends or moods became widespread. Immediately after the war, a common theme among writers was a disgust, a repugnance, with European civilization brought on by fascism and the war and by the economic and moral poverty of the pre-war period. These essentially existentialist writers concentrated on the meaningless, bleaker aspects of life. Novels dwelt on such themes as crime, inhumanity, poverty, despair and cultural pessimism. Although this trend never vanished completely, another mood became dominant in the late 1950s. It rejected the values and attitudes associated with the affluent society, mass consumerism and complacency that became typical in Europe in the 1960s. By the 1970s, literature began a retreat from social concerns towards private individual themes. These directions in literature were overshadowed in some countries, France in particular, by the post-structural critique of language that raised questions of form and structure above questions of content. This movement's emphasis on difference and hostility to any coherent view of phenomena promotes the present extreme fragmentation in literary modes.

The immediate post-war period produced an outpouring of socially committed 'engaged' writers. In the first post-war decade the message of most was an existential one. In France Albert Camus, Sartre and Simone de Beauvoir searched for meaning in what they regarded as an absurd, incomprehensible world. They passionately attacked the bourgeoisie, whom they held responsible for all the world's ills, by writing novels they would not understand or enjoy. They tended to emulate the unconventional Surrealist novelists of the interwar period. Although these existentialists failed to transform radically the form or language of the novel, they did alter the content away from the traditional entertaining plots and character portrayal to what they considered to be a realistic depiction of man's sorry condition. However, Sartre and de Beauvoir soon turned away from the novel, since they did not believe that form was effectively imparting their message. Sartre turned to the theatre and de Beauvoir more to scientific investigations of the human condition (*The Second Sex*) and direct attacks on the new Fifth Republic of de Gaulle.

German writers such as Günter Grass, Heinrich Böll and Wolfgang Borchert described the moral and political bankruptcy of Germany by bringing Germans face-to-face with the excesses of the Nazi period and the war. Borchert described the despair and loneliness of a soldier returning home after the war in *The Man Outside*. In the *Tin Drum*, Grass has a dwarf tell about the moral inadequacies of the middle class before and during the war. Both in the *Tin Drum* and in *Dog Years*, Grass demythologized the Nazi period by showing how vulgar and ludicrous the Nazi officials and sympathizers had been. Grass also became actively involved in political and social causes and thereby rejected the traditional German separation of the artistic and political communities. Boll concentrated at first on the physical and psychological toll wrought by Nazism and the war in *Acquainted with the Night* and *House without Keeper*. But he soon turned his pen against bourgeois social climbing and what he perceived as a crude materialism in *Billiards at Half-Past Nine* and *The Clown*. His *Group Portrait with Woman* described how a woman's life was destroyed because of bureaucratic insensitivity and concentration on power and money.

The most outstanding German dramatist, Carl Zuckmayer, described anti-Nazi resistance in *The Devil's General* and *Chorus in the Pyre*. The two other most noted playwrights writing in German were Swiss, Max Frisch and Friedrich Durrenmatt. Frisch's and Durrenmatt's themes included man's failings after the war; in their many plays, inhumanity, greed, complacency, cowardice and weakness are ever recurring themes.

In Italy, Alberto Moravia, Cesare Pavese, Carlo Levi, Elio Vittorini, Vasco Pratolini and others adopted a stark neo-realism to depict the moral, political and social shortcomings of Italy before and during the Fascist period. Levi's *Christ Stopped at Eboli* revealed the economic and social problems of southern Italy. A Fascist opponent exiled to Eboli experiences the grinding poverty that is endemic in the South. Many, Elio Vittorini and Vasco Pratolini among them, adopted a Communist perspective in their novels about the economic and social problems of the working class. In *Hero of our Time*, Vittorini's main character's murder of his mistress is depicted as a logical outcome of his bourgeois social–political upbringing. Existentialism had little influence in post-war Italian literature. Perhaps their greater optimism shielded them from the existential despair felt by their French counterparts. The post-modern aesthetic had also influenced Italian literature. Italo Calvino's *If on a Winter's Night a Traveler* directly implicates the reader by introducing the character of the Other Reader into the plot. By far the most popular writer worldwide, beginning with his *The Name of the Rose* is Umberto Eco, also a professor of semiotics. Setting a detective story in a medieval monastery, the novel is a murder mystery, a presentation of high politics during religious persecution, etc. This style continued with subsequent novels, such as *Foucault's Pendulum*, which combined conspiracy theories with Jewish mysticism/Kabbalah, among other items.

In the first post-war decade, Great Britain produced no new literary movement of note. The major writers – George Orwell, Graham Greene, Evelyn Waugh, T. S. Eliot and E. M. Forster – were very individualistic and therefore not part of any school. Communism was not only not a major influence as it had been on the Continent, but it was attacked by George Orwell in *Animal Farm* and *Nineteen Eighty-four*. Perhaps the absence of past social and political problems on the scale of those on the Continent, and the post-war welfare state reforms of the Labour government limited the despair or need for action felt by many continental intellectuals. These factors, combined with a British dislike of abstract philosophical speculation, could also be the reason for the lack of an existential literary movement with its rejection of past values and experiences.

In the late 1950s, a notable group of British writers joined in the criticism of the affluent society. A group identified as the 'angry young men' or 'kitchen-sink school,' alienated by the developing consumerism and continuing class distinctions, lashed out at the type of society the welfare state was producing. Still, most confined their anger to what they viewed as the shortcomings of the welfare state, without calling for its overthrow. While writers such as Kingsley Amis poked fun at class pretensions in *Lucky Jim*, Alan Sillitoe in *Saturday Night and Sunday Morning* and John Osborne in *Look Back in Anger* went beyond criticism of class barriers to depict a working class world devoid of real meaning.

In the 1960s, a new generation dissatisfied with the reforms of the welfare state and distraught over the spread of nuclear weapons and the widening Vietnam War turned to a more radical opposition to the government. Repelled by this New Left onslaught some turned in the other direction. In *Lucky Jim's Politics*, Kingsley Amis rejected his former anti-government position and attacked political socialism. Doris Lessing expressed her disenchantment with Communism in her cycle of novels, *Children of Violence*, and in her celebrated exploration of the political, psychological and sexual revolutions of our time, *The Golden Notebook*. The impact of the Thatcher years on social relations and the increasingly multi-cultural character of Britain in the 1980s and 1990s produced new literary voices, very much concerned with contemporary identity issues. Probably the most (in)famous writer was Salmon Rushdie, whose *The Satanic Verses*, published in 1988, provoked a 'fatwa' or death sentence from the Islamic republic of Iran for allegedly blaspheming against the Prophet Mohammed, forcing Rushdie into hiding. Issues of racial, sexual and ethnic identity were explored by writers in addition to Rushdie, for instance by Monica Ali in *Brick Lane*, Arundhati Roy, *The God of Small Things* and Alan Hollinghurst, *The Line of Beauty*.

Literature experienced a major change in the 1950s when a French avant-garde began to experiment as James Joyce and Borges had done earlier with the form, writing and theory of the novel. These 'new novelists', Alain Robbe–Grillet, Michel Butor, Claude Simon and Nathalie Sarraute, disengaged the novel from its previous attempt to understand the past or present. Writers now sought to describe things as they appeared and not seek a deeper underlying meaning or try to influence their audience to act. For these writers literature was anti-intellectual, anti-ideological. Robbe–Grillet spoke for them all when he stated, 'We no longer believe in depth.' To these writers the search for meaning in life served no purpose and should be abandoned.

Robbe–Grillet was the most influential of these novelists. The content in his works exists merely to draw attention to their form and procedures. His repetition of key sentences, with slight variation, in such works as *Project for a Revolution in New York*, is intended to deaden any emotional response from the reader. In *Project*, the continued repetition of a torture eventually robs it of its tragic nature. Such an approach, from Robbe–Grillet's point of view, liberates the writer from traditional sentimentality and ultimately deadening bourgeois assumptions. If a text could not be interpreted in any one way, Robbe Grillet reasoned that it would demand a freer participation by the reader much as in post-modernist art.

Jean Ricardous aimed to destroy (deconstruct) the traditional novel by concentrating on the relationship between language and consciousness. In order to undermine traditional reading habits, Ricardous' work *La Prise de Constantinople* does not number pages or chapters, has no main characters, no narrator and no point of view. The structure of the fiction is supposed to serve as a plot.

These new post-modern writers were trying to transform literary form in the same way that music and art forms had been revolutionized previously. One gets the impression that they were envious of the bold experimentation in music and art. Indeed, some of their experiments with language looked towards music and poetry. Butor's *Mobile* has been praised for its 'rhetoric or modulation.'

With plays by Sartre, Jean Genet, Samuel Beckett and Eugene Ionesco, the theatre also broke sharply with traditional form. Driven by the demise of ideology and the problem of communicating, their plays relentlessly attacked man's absurd condition. But the form in which they chose to display this absurdity drove most people away from the theatre. Beckett's *Waiting for Godot* (1952) brought James Joyce's stream of consciousness to the stage. In *Waiting for Godot*, two tramps await the arrival of M. Godot who never appears. They ultimately continue the vigil for its own sake, according to Beckett, as people waste their lives awaiting better times.

The Mitterrand years of the 1980s and early 1990s, which at first raised the hopes of many on the left for profound social and political change, and then dashed them as economic reversals and corruption marked this period, also affected literature. The themes, though, differed from those of the 1950s and 1960s in that new voices from France's immigrant communities raised new issues in addition to critiques of the new global order. Of the latter, Michel Houellebecq, whose *Atomised* stirred up controversy by examining the central character's nihilistic routines, in particular sex tourism in south-east Asia. Writers from France's north African or Caribbean communities include Patrick Chamoiseau, *Écrire en pays dominé* and Assia Djebar, *Women of Algiers in their Apartment*.

In the 1960s a small German avant-garde began to move towards the post-modern negation of literary form and story telling. Ernst Jandl, Arno Schmidt, Herbert Achternbusch and many others began to subvert existing literary forms. Jandl wrote poems that were merely a series of sounds. Arno Schmidt experimented with phonetic transcriptions of spoken language. All attacked existing grammar rules and literary form as inhibiting and authoritarian. A comparable Austrian group led by Oswald Wiener and Peter Handke concentrated upon language and its authoritarian hold over them.

Following the 1970s, the literary elite returned to novels that are concerned with character development and story telling, a mode that the popular writers had never abandoned. Chief among them are Michel Tournier, Jean-Marie-Gustave Le Clezio and Marguerite Yourcenar. While these novelists returned to earlier literary forms, they did not revert to the earlier French tradition of the novelist as social critic. There are, of course, some exceptions. Clezio's *Le Deluge*, an early work, is critical of modern urban existence. Tournier's *The Ogre* explores individual attachment and restores humane values to literary endeavour. In the *Ogre* (Erl-King), the hero gives up his life to save a Jewish child.

With no comparable post-industrial, post-modern society to spread dissatisfaction with materialism and a censorship that demanded adherence to the dictates of Socialist realism, Soviet literature had quite different battles to fight. Among other things Socialist Realism stressed Russian chauvinism, hatred of foreigners, praise of the new Soviet man and glorification of Stalin. Those who would not bow were destined for a Soviet labour camp and possible death. From the death of Stalin to Khrushchev's fall from power in 1964, Soviet writers were permitted a greater latitude in what they could write. But writers were still not free to write as they wished. An early work that broke sharply with Socialist Realism, Boris Pasternak's *Doctor Zhivago*, showed the limits of the relaxation or thaw under Khrushchev. Zhivago's apolitical nature was viewed as inconsistent with the Soviet Union's commitment to socialism and, as a result, Pasternak was refused permission to accept the Nobel Prize in 1958. But Khrushchev's continuing need to fight off his Stalinist opponents led him to denounce Stalin at the 20th Party Congress in 1956 and to support literary works that exposed the horrors of Stalin's past. As a result he approved the publication in 1962 of Alexander Solzhenitsyn's *One Day in the Life of Ivan Denisovich* that not only exposed the evils of Stalinism but also brought to light the skills of one of the most gifted literary figures in post-war Russia. This and subsequent works, *The First Circle, Cancer Ward, The Gulag Archipelego* and *August 1914* established his name as one of the great novelists of the post-war period. Many lesser lights such as Ilya Ehrenburg in *The Thaw*, joined Solzhenitsyn in denouncing Stalin. Another means whereby serious literature gained exposure was through *Samizdat*, underground literature that circulated among intellectuals. When the forum provided by Khrushchev proved to be still too limited for the expression of ideas, writers turned to the *Samizdat*.

Poetry also broke with Socialist Realism during the thaw. Evgeny Yevtushenko, a popular poet of occasional inspiration, criticized the Stalin period with the approval of Khrushchev. Another officially sanctioned popular poet was the balladeer, Bulat Okudzhava. His use of the popular ballad is deeply rooted in the Russian tradition, not in Socialist Realism. The most significant poet is Joseph Brodsky, who is in the tradition of the great Russian poets, Pushkin and Anna Akhmatova. His poetry has ties to European poetry as well and is therefore not insular as is that of many of his contemporaries. His poetry, dealing with eternal questions such as death, loneliness and suffering, has no utilitarian purpose and was therefore not looked upon favourably by Soviet officials.

The Brezhnev era brought a renewed repression of Soviet artists. Both Yuli Daniel and Andrei Sinyavsky were sent to forced labour camps for publishing outside the Soviet Union and Brodsky was sent to Siberia for 'parasitism' – living without a permanent job. Despite this more repressive environment, a number of important works were published. Andrei Sakharov criticized the Stalinist excesses from a democratic-reformist perspective. Roy Medvedev produced a classic of historical scholarship in his criticism of the Stalin period, *Let History Judge*. From the mid-1970s, two brilliant satirists emerged at the top of the literary heap. Vladimir Voinovich, with a keen eye for the comic and absurd, pointed out the gap between the real and the ideal in Soviet society. One of his best works, *The Life and Extraordinary Adventures of Private Ivan Chonkin* describes the inauthentic existence forced upon Soviet citizens by the system of authority and ideology. The other satirist is Alexander Zinoviev, who in his *The Yawning Heights* and *The Radiant Future* was critical of utopian schemes and the intelligentsia. Both Voinovich and Zinoviev, as well as most other literary greats, were forced into exile by the KGB in the 1970s.

The post-Soviet era, though not that long in relative terms, has not yet produced writers with international appeal. Vasily Aksyonov, *Generations of Winter*, a story about three generations of a family living under Stalin, has had some appeal in English translation. Tatyana Tolstaya's *Kys* (recently translated into English as *The Slynx*) is a dystopian novel set in the future, but could also be read as a commentary on present-day conditions in Russia.

In the 1970s and 1980s much literary effort involved opposition to the Communist regimes. Milan Kundera's *The Book of Laughter and Forgetting* (1979) and *The Unbearable Lightness of Being* (1984) emphasized the importance of remembering the oppressive nature of the Communist dictatorships when it was easy to forget or repress the memories. The East German writer Christa Wolf pursued such Western themes as individuality and the search for self–identity in *The Quest for Christa T.* (1970), which brought her into disfavour with the regime. Still, she remained in the country and was criticized after the regime fell for her failure to strongly oppose the regime and for her acceptance of the privileges given to notable individuals. Others, such as Stefan Heym, *The King David Report*, were exiled. This did not deter those who stayed, such as Christoph Hein, *The Alien Friend/Dragon's Blood*, from attacking the darker side of Communist society. In the post-unification period, Peter Schneider's *The Wall Jumper* (1990) explored the mental wall that divides 'Easterners' and 'Westerners'. In *The German Comedy* (1991), he examined the absurdities of life in Germany without the wall. Older writers such as Günter Grass returned to Germany's immediate post-war history – and discussed the suppressed memories of victimhood – in *Crabwalk* (2004).

Making sense of the post-communist transition in east–central European countries has been a theme of the literature appearing since the 1980s. Andrzej Stasiuk's *White Raven* recounts the experiences of growing up and travelling throughout Poland. Herta Müller's *Land of Green Plums* is a story about a Romanian village caught between the legacies of the Ceauşescu era and the lure of the West. Jachym Topol explores the 'everything goes' urban culture of Prague in *City, Sister, Silver*.

Cinema

For the masses and many intellectuals, the post-war cinema replaced literature and the stage as their main source of drama. Many European intellectuals chose the cinema because they wished to reach a wider audience and believed that the creative possibilities were greater in the cinema than in the theatre. Although there are many exceptions, the post-war cinema can be divided into several phases: the Italian neo–realist ascendancy immediately after the war, the French 'new-wave' predominance beginning in the mid-1950s, a broader phase led by the dynamic new German film makers in the 1970s and in the 1990s the entry of films from post-Communist Eastern Europe.

Neorealism From the end of the war until the mid-1950s, the Italian neo–realist school had no equal in Europe. Led by Luchino Visconti, Roberto Rossellini and Vittorio De Sica, the Italians revealed the poverty, political corruption and moral inadequacies of past and contemporary Italy. Rossellini's *Rome Open City* (1945) and *Paisa* (1946) graphically depicted Italy's suffering under German occupation in 1943–44. The object was not to entertain the audience but to shock them. A favourite method employed by the Italian neo–realists to make their films more realistic and to overcome the high costs of film making was to shoot the films on location and use local and often untrained actors who were down and out themselves. De Sica followed Rossellini with *Shoeshine* (1946) and *The Bicycle Thief* (1948). In *Shoeshine*, De Sica depicts society's inhumane treatment of two boys caught up in the post-war black market. The *Bicycle Thieves* concerns a man's attempts to recover a stolen bicycle that he needs in order to take a job as a bill-poster and society's insensitivity to his plight. In Visconti's *The Earth Trembles* (1947), the over-population and resultant poverty and violence of rural Italy is depicted. Influenced by the Marxist Gramsci, Visconti deals with the class divisions that subvert the poor's attempts to escape their condition.

By the late 1950s Italy's growing affluence had led the cinema-going public to a reduced interest in films that concentrated on only the negative aspects of life. But by this time a new group of directors had turned away from neorealism to an imaginative investigation of sensations and personal relationships. Federico Fellini pursued the sensual and the spiritual in films such as *Juliet of the Spirits* and *Satyricon*. Michelangelo Antonioni's films investigated the emotional tensions, human alienation and the failure to communicate. *L'Avventura*, his best film, depicts human weaknesses in the form of many betrayals as it moves towards a final understanding and reconciliation between the main protagonists.

The New Wave Traditionally, French cinema had dominated European film making. Directors such as Clair, Carne and Renoir had overshadowed their European counterparts in the 1930s. But in the first post-war decade, French cinema had declined despite the existence of thousands of cine-clubs and the French preference for the cinema rather than the stage. Then in the 1950s a group of former film critics turned to film-making and the French cinema once again became dominant. A group of young film-makers were often lumped together as the 'new wave', because the directors were given extensive freedom to fashion their films, a freedom that became known as the auteur theory of film making. Roger Vadim's film about a sensual, emancipated young woman, *And God Created Women* (1956), starring his wife Brigitte Bardot, was the first commercial success of the new wave films.

Soon, however, a number of new film-makers including Alain Resnais, Jean Luc Godard, Claude Chabrol, Louis Malle and François Truffaut became internationally acclaimed for their films. In their hands, the film became an intensely creative process with the director being more important than the stars. Some went beyond the Italians in this regard, in that they became primarily concerned with film-for-film's sake rather than making any social or political statement. Truffaut, with the exception of his four semi-autobiographical films (*The 400 Blows, Stolen Kisses, Bed and Board, Love on the Run*) that deal with social roles, was not concerned with a social or political message. He has concentrated on human relationships and the theme of love. Malle concentrated on controversial topics such as incest, prostitution, poverty and suicide. His study of how a French boy came to join the Nazi occupation forces, *Lacombe Lucien*, expertly captured how many apolitical persons became Nazis.

With Jean-Luc Godard, however, we see a member of the new wave who became intensely ideological. He also broke more sharply with the traditional narrative form and plot of the cinema by concentrating on a social or political message. His attacks came from the left against what he considered to be a dehumanizing, mechanized modern world. In *Alphaville* (1964) he attacked mechanization, in *Weekend* (1967) the meaninglessness and materialism of bourgeois existence, and in *Every Man for Himself* (1980) and *Slow Motion* (1980) sexual degradation and economic exploitation. Some of these French films became so experimental, so much a personal creation, that they were viewed by only a few avid cinema fans. In the 1980s and 1990s French filmmakers emphasized more pure entertainment and the larger television audiences. In order to attract a larger audience, they concentrated on love (*Lovers on the Bridge*) and violence in the American style (*La Femme Nikita*). But French filmmakers also produced widely popular sentimental comedies such as Amélie and *Jean de Florette* and its sequel *Manon of the Springs*, all finding an international audience. Smaller or more select audiences continued to be treated to the more intimate works of Claire Denis's *Chocolat* and Régis Wargnier's *Une Femme Française*.

German Filmmakers Most noteworthy since 1965 was the renaissance of the German cinema. After two decades of producing escapist, imitative films, Germans such as Volker Schlondorff, Rainer Werner Fassbinder, Werner Herzog, Wim Winders and Margaretta von Trotta, began to produce imaginative, unconventional works in which directors worked out their own personal style in the French *Auteur* manner. Schlondorff's *Young Torless* (1966) and the *Tin Drum* (1979) received international acclaim. The former, an adaptation of Robert Musil's novel, juxtaposes the psychological strains of life in a boys' school and life in Nazi Germany. The *Tin Drum*, an adaptation of Grass's novel, shared the Grand Prix prize at Cannes in 1979. His films have intricate political and social themes. His *The Lost Honor of Katharina Blum* (1975), based upon a Heinrich Böll novel, studies the destructive effect the press can have on individuals.

Fassbinder's films had an equally strong social message. They normally dealt with the downtrodden, the underdog and the oppressed. *Katzelmacher* (1969) and *Ali: Fear Eats the Soul* (1973) treat foreign workers in Germany. Perhaps to exorcise the domination-dependence relationship among homosexuals, he treated homosexuality in a number of films (*The Bitter Tears of Petra von Kant*, 1972; *Fox and His Friends*, 1975; *In a Year of 13 Moons*, 1979). Shortly before his death from drugs in 1982, he finished *Lili Marleen* (1981) and *Lola*. One of his commercially most successful films, *The Marriage of Maria Braun* (1979), suggested that Germany had to prostitute itself morally to achieve economic recovery in the post-war period.

Concerned with human failings, Herzog dramatized our unquestioning adoration of technology and rationalism. His *Stroszek* (1977) dealt with what he regarded as the plastic cheapness of much of American culture. Wim Wenders's films such as *Paris, Texas* and *Wings of Desire* deal with the male wanderer who is always under way, employing the American road-movie genre.

Bergman and Buñuel While this national approach to the post-war cinema has exposed its major trends, it has omitted several giants of the screen, Ingmar Bergman and Luis Bunuel. Although Bergman's very individualistic style makes his work difficult to categorize, his themes of interpersonal relationships, evil, suffering, death and the meaning of existence have raised the cinema to new heights. In one of his greatest movies, *The Seventh Seal* (1956), a medieval knight gambles with Death in order to have time to consider the value of living. Organized religion is relentlessly attacked as an instigator of death – the Crusades, the Inquisition, etc. In *Wild Strawberries* (1957), the main character, an old doctor, is also facing death and tries to determine if his life has been of any use. Some of his later films, such as *Cries and Whispers* (1973) returned to the theme of death and reassessment of life. *The Virgin Spring* (1959) treated the subjects of youthful innocence, evil and retribution. A daughter's rape and murder are avenged by her father in a must brutal manner. Some of his later films were masterful studies of interpersonal relationships. In *Persona* (1967), Bergman deals with the relationship between a nurse and a mentally disturbed actress who has refused to speak for years, since she believes that existence is meaningless.

Excessively pessimistic about humanity, Bunuel was a constant critic of the Catholic Church and social institutions. In *Belle de Jour* (1967), a brothel is depicted as a place of genuine passion in contrast to marriage where passion is artificial. In *Viridiana* (1961), he pointed out the uselessness of faith and charity. In *The Discreet Charm of the Bourgeoisie* (1973), he poked fun at bourgeois pretentions and objectives.

East European Filmmaking There was also a great outpouring of imaginative cinema in Eastern Europe since Stalin's death. Although nationalized, the film industry served as a forum for social criticism and ideological exchange during periods of de-Stalinization. The Polish, Czech and Hungarian cinemas experienced unusually productive and creative periods during political thaws in the 1950s and 1960s. In Poland, Andrzej Wajda's neo-realist films – *A Generation*, 1954; *Canal*, 1956; *Ashes and Diamonds*, 1958 – established his reputation as one of Europe's major directors. A number of major directors emerged in the 1960s and 1970s but were forced out of Poland by re-Stalinization (Roman Polanski, Jerzy Skolinowski, etc.). Some, such as Polanski went on to establish and develop their reputations abroad, but without turning to political issues. Others, such as Wajda, in his film *Danton*, produced an explicitly political film, even though it was ostensibly about the French Revolution, though it was easily seen as a film about Solidarity and the Polish Communist state.

Even more impressive was the profusion of world-renowned, innovative Czech films and directors. Building upon a strong pre-war film tradition and profiting from the liberalization of the mid-1960s, a Czech new wave produced such award winning films as Elmar Klos and Jan Kadar's *Shop on Main Street* (1965) and Kiri Menzel's *Closely Watched Trains* (1966). Mensel's film combined humour and tragedy in the coming of age of a boy both politically and sexually in Nazi-occupied Czechoslovakia. Klos and Kadar's *Shop on Main Street* also mixed humour and seriousness. The main character, a Chaplinesque figure, shuns work and respectability during the Nazi occupation. As an Aryan controller in Jewish widow's button shop he is ultimately forced to decide whether he will protect the old woman from being sent to a concentration camp or protect himself. His vacillation ultimately leads him to unintentionally murder the woman and then hang himself out of guilt. The political crackdown after 1968 forced Kadar, Jasny, Forman and others to flee the country and thus stifled much of the creativity of the Czech cinema.

Hungary's major contribution to the cinema came during the political thaw from 1953 to 1956 and during the unexpectedly relaxed rule of Janos Kadar after 1956. As in Czechoslovakia, the Hungarian directors, especially Andras Kovacs and Miklos Jancso, were extremely innovative in form and technique. Both attacked the debilitating influence of authoritarianism, political terror and bureaucracy on creativity: Kovacs, in *Difficult People* (1964) and *The Stud Farm* (1979); Jancso, in *The Round Up* (1965), *Silence and Cry* (1968) and *Red Psalm* (1972).

Only Yugoslavia, of the other East European countries, produced films that compared with the creative cinema of Western Europe. Severely limited by censorship, Soviet filmmaking did not measure up to that in other East European countries, though an exception was Andrei Tarkovsky's *Solaris* (1972), an examination of human perceptions and failings.

The post-communist era for cinema is complicated by the privatization trends running throughout formerly state-supported enterprises. Despite these obstacles, there have been some stunning films produced, such as Krzysztof Kieslovski trilogy based on the French tricolore, *Blue, White* and *Red*.

Postmodernist Filmmaking Although many film modes exist side-by-side since the 1980s, an international Post-Modernist genre has emerged with the films of Hans–Jurgen Syberberg, Jean–Jacques Beineix and Hugh Hudson. These films employ what Andreas Huyssens describes as double-coding – the mixing of highcultural and popular cultural modes and the past with the present. Syberberg's *Parsifal* (1984) attempted, according to Jim Collins, to 'interconnect simultaneously' many German cultural traditions. He juxtaposed Richard Wagner's opera Parsifal, a high-cultural mode situated in Germany's mythic past, with the contemporary experience. The nineteenth century opera is tied to the medieval Parsifal myth and the myths surrounding Nazi Germany. Beineix's *Diva* (1981) mixed the mass cultural detective mode with the elitist opera mode in order to demonstrate how different discourses shape reality. The intertwining of the two modes culminates in the final scene when opera star and male 'commoner' embrace on stage. These Post-Modernist directors view such mode-mixing as necessary to make sense of today's fragmented discourses.

Other national cinemas experienced a re-birth in the 1980s, especially those which had experienced right-wing authoritarian regimes for decades. Spanish cinema is a very good example of the liberalizing of a culture after the downfall of such a regime. Probably no film director embodied this sense of Spanish culture in the 1980s better than Pedro Almodóvar, in films such as *Women on the Verge of a Nervous Breakdown*, a comedy displaying a Spanish culture defying the dictates of ultra-conservative Catholicism and Francoist censorship.

Art and Architecture

Art Art and architecture followed somewhat the same path as the cinema. Immediately after the war a neo-realist, engaged art was dominant. Artists such as Bernard Buffet, Bernard Lorjou and Claude Venard depicted the human condition in a realistic manner. However, the neo-realist goal of describing the human condition was soon overcome by an avant-gardé, non-figurative, abstract, art for art's sake movement that resembled in many ways the 'imaginative' cinema that emerged in France and spread throughout Europe.

Post-war abstractionism rejected those abstract artists schooled in the prewar period – Picasso, Braque, Chagall and the sculptors Giacometti and Brancusi – who still worked with figures or images even though they might be greatly distorted. Art was to create a new reality through the use of materials, colours and form. No former aesthetic or social guidelines were to deter the artist from creative expression. The American Abstract Expressionism of Jackson Pollock and Willem de Kooning, in which the artist sought existential self-realization through action – by throwing or frantically brushing paint on a canvas – was very influential in Europe. The European Art Informel or Tachiste group led by Jean Fautrier, Georges Mathieu, Pierre Soulages, Nicholas de Stael and Karel Appel strove for self-definition in the non-representational use of colour and form. Meaning or images would appear on the canvas without any premeditated image in mind. The canvas became a space in which to act rather than to compose. Some rejected imagery completely in an attempt to divorce art from subject matter or the artist's feelings. Such paintings – those of the Frenchman Yves Klein are a good example – might be one solid colour. A similar Minimalist movement in sculpture reduced objects to their simplest minimal shapes. The British minimalist sculptors, Anthony Cato and Philip King, reduced everything to geometric forms.

But even greater attacks on traditional conceptions of art were to emerge in the 1960s. Popular (Pop) Art, begun as an attack on the products of mass culture by some and an open acceptance by others, rejected existing aesthetic standards by depicting common objects such as beer cans, cereal boxes, and many other objects from popular culture. To many it symbolized the bankruptcy of modern art. It was also rejected by a group of Optical (Op) artists who disliked any social commentary in art. Led initially by Victor Vasarely in France and by Bridget Riley in Britain, the Op artists explored optical reactions and movement by employing colour shadings and geometric patterns repeatedly. Many Op artists, especially those with strong science backgrounds, were interested in the application of science and technology to art. While many could accept Op and Pop art as legitimate artistic movements, they could not accept such art movements as Earth Art that involved moving huge amounts of dirt in remote areas or wrapping buildings in plastic as serious art. Nor was Conceptual Art – staged events or happenings rather than a physical object – accepted by most of the public as art, no matter how creative.

In reaction to these experimental forms in post-war art, the 1970s produced super-realism and neo-expressionism, which returned to some of the major concerns of nineteenth century figurative painters such as representational forms, light and the mixing of colours. But contemporary painters in these genres differ from their predecessors in that they use excessive amounts and kinds of colour; thus they are often called violent figurative painters. The Italians Sandro Chia, Enzo Cucci and Francesco Clemente and the Germans A. R. Penck, Rainer Fetting, Markus Lupertz and George Baselitz are a few of the leading super-realist and neo-expressionist artists. While a few Americans are painting in these styles, they have generated a greater response in Europe. They may have ended New York's domination of avant-gardé painting. Although it is impossible to determine if any style is dominant at this time, it is clear those who paint in a representational mode, are no longer ostracized by the artistic community, as they were in the 1950s and 1960s. In some regards, painting has returned to a form of art that the public never deserted. The most popular artists of the post-war period continued to be the giants of the interwar period such as Picasso and Chagall.

Architecture The dominant architectural style of the immediate post-war period harkened back to the early twentieth century views of such architects as Walter Gropius and Mies van der Rohe concerning free-standing crystalline

Bridget Riley, Current, *1964. Collection, the Museum of Modern Art, New York. Philip Johnson fund.*
(© 2005 Digital Image, the Museum of Modern Art, New York/Scala, Florence)

shafts. Termed International Style or Functional, these Modernist glass skyscrapers were constructed throughout the industrial world. All aspects of the buildings were to conform to its essential function, which meant that structures were to be simple and unadorned. Hans Scharoun's Philharmonic Concert Hall in Berlin concentrated all building materials on achieving perfect acoustics. Skyscrapers were normally unadorned, glass structures with no decoration.

In the early 1950s a new style, New Brutalism or Monumental Formalism, began to overcome the International Style. It rejected the customary sleek glass wall of the International Style for a rough, sculpted appearance, usually in concrete, and exposed structural components. Le Corbusier, the world-renowned architect working primarily in France, had already experimented with sculpted components on some of his essentially International Style structures. But in the 1950s he created some of the most impressive examples of this new style. His church Notre Dame-du-Haut at Ronchamp, France, is a good example of the sculpted, rough look of Monumental Formalism. Other

The Guggenheim Museum, Bilbao.

Europeans – Eugene Beandouin, Marcel Lods, Pier Luigi Nervi, Joern Utzon, Viljo Revell, Eduardo Torroja, Felik Candela, among others – soon took up this new style. Torroja and Candela erected large sculpted umbrella roofs with cavernous interiors that could be infinitely divided.

In the 1970s a post-modern style began to replace Modernism. The post-modern continued Modernism in its use of modern building techniques and materials but it added decorative ornament and historical symbolism. Charles Jenks describes it as 'double coding', or the combination of elite/ popular and new/old. These postmodernists argued that the Modernist style did not communicate effectively with the public and was, therefore, alienating. Some observers date the death of the Modernist style with the rejection of cheap fabrication typical of many of the alienating functionalist housing blocs of the sixties. One of the best European examples of the post-modern is the Guggenheim Museum in Bilbao, Spain. A few architects have turned to a Late–Modernist style, epitomized in the Pompidou Centre in Paris that is still dedicated totally to the new.

In residential areas, attention concentrated on the site and the use of natural materials. City architects have attempted to separate motor traffic, shopping and residential areas. In business areas, more attention was paid to relieving the austerity created by numerous glass skyscrapers. This was achieved by building parks, garden atriums in large buildings and breaking up the flat glass facades with concrete or steel geometric forms.

Music

As with painting, post-war serious music must be divided between that which is in most demand by the public – Romantic, Classical – and that being written by postwar composers – total serialism, electronic music or *musique concrete*, and aleatory or chance composition.

Although the music of the post-war avant-gardé was not well received by a more tradition-bound public, it did have strong ties to the past. Total serialism is a logical outgrowth of the serial (twelve-tonal) compositions of the interwar Vienna School – Arnold Schoenberg, Anton von Webern and Alban Berg. Total serialists viewed themselves as architects or engineers of sound who were bringing structure and organization to music. Schoenberg had first hit upon the concept of serialism in the 1920s in order to bring system to a triumphant, intuitive atonality. He attempted to arrange the 12 notes of the chromatic scale in a fixed order. The 12 tonal serialism employed by such composers as Pierre Boulez, Olivier Messaien, Rene Leibowitz and Karlheinz Stockhausen was in some regards a way to bring back order as well. Messaien established scales of pitch, duration and loudness in his composition, *Mode of durations and intensities*. In 1948, Pierre Schaeffer adapted electronic music to natural sounds to produce what has been termed *musique concrete*. Karlheint Stockhausen carried such experimentation a step further to electronic sound synthesis. Stockhausen and Boulez in Europe and the American John Cage soon jettisoned the order so sought after following the war when they began to compose chance or choice compositions. Since little order was provided for sounds and music in their compositions, music was what happened to occur at each performance. In one of Cage's works, *Silent Sonata*, no sounds are made. In Europe, Stockhausen and Boulez composed similar chance or aleatory works that left a great deal up to the individual musician, or freed him, as they would have it, to be creative. A musician could choose his own tempo, measure or pauses, etc. In Stockhausen's *From the Seven Days* (1968), each score is a prose poem that provides only general instructions for the musicians.

While the 1950s experienced a continuation of serialism, the expansion of electronic music and the beginnings of chance or aleatory music, the 1960s produced such a multiplicity of musical forms that it is virtually impossible to isolate any dominant trends. There are those who have gone back to the diatonic harmony of the Romantic and Classical periods (Samuel Barber, Michael Tippett) those who are still experimenting with electronic aleatory music (Boulez, Stockhausen), serialism (Milton Babbitt), Chance (Cage) and revolutionary socialist music (Hans Werner Henze, Luigi Nono). Sampling, a fomat used in popular music by combining scraps of music and lyrics from an assortment of music and blended into a new product, was used in the 1970s by Luciano Berio. The future seems to promise diversity rather than integration.

Culture and the Popular Media

Contemporary popular culture, not to be confused with folk culture, emerged out of the 1950s in the United States and Western Europe on a combined wave of youth culture, new technological media of communication and transmission, notably transistor radios and television, and corporate commercial interests.

A worldwide youth culture began to emerge in the 1960s characterized by the various forms of rock music, television, blue jeans, mass consumerism and hedonism. What is often termed 'Americanization' is more aptly understood as an extension of the post-modern condition throughout the economically advanced world. The multiplication and commodification of cultural forms is now a worldwide phenomenon. An influential youth culture first emerged in the United States but has since spread to Europe and other economically advanced areas. This youth culture, exemplified in the 1960s by such rock groups as the Beatles, the Who and the Rolling Stones spread even beyond economically advanced areas as youth culture was spread by the media and increased travel. In the 1960s and 1970s an anti-authoritarian, anti-military and anti-hierarchical youth culture emerged. It sanctioned drug use, sexual liberation, and poked fun at bourgeois materialism and conformism. This cultural milieu was stronger in countries like England and the United States where the generational gap was more pronounced than on the continent. With the development of punk rock in the late 1970s, the early rock groups now appear tame. In fact much of the support for early forms of rock music now comes from the middle-aged who look back nostalgically to those years of protest against racism, the Vietnam War and 'Establishments' everywhere. Pop music, more generally, became 'big business', with record (the cd) sales in the tens of millions of dollars. Still, rock musicians became involved in global projects. The British rock musician Bob Geldorf organized a massive charity concert in aid of Ethiopian drought victims in 1985, called Live Aid. So-called world music also influenced pop and rock music in Europe from the 1980s onwards, brought to the attention of the public by immigrants from Africa in France and the Caribbean in Britain.

Television occupies an increasingly greater number of viewing hours. Recent popular TV shows quickly spawn imitators in other countries. A 1999 Dutch TV show in which a variety of individuals are holed up in a residence, and are one by one dismissed until the final remaining contestant wins the prize, and all of this watched by an Orwellian 'big brother', was taken up in France – Loft Story – and Britain – Big Brother – and eventually the United States and other countries around the world.

Understanding popular culture in Europe also requires mentioning sport. Although Europe is not alone in this activity, the place of football in popular culture has acquired an elevated, if not exaggerated, place. Major European teams such as Manchester United or AC Milan are not confined to players from their own country, but are very often multinational. Huge salaries have spawned a celebrity status for some players, and the European Cup, played every 4 years, becomes a national focus in many countries.

Summary

The present proliferation of cultural modes and discourses has brought dismay to cultural conservatives such as Adorno, Lyotard and Baudrillard. Such conservatives believe the absence of a dominant Zeitgeist means cultural chaos and the loss of belief and authentic social relationships. But post-Modernists believe that this plethora of cultural modes has not led to a decline in belief or in social relationships. They contend that the existence of many beliefs does not mean that people do not believe. The recent resurgence in religious belief seems to support their position. They also differ on the mass media. The critics contend that the mass media has led to the decline of narrative but the post-Modernists find mini-narrative even in rock music videos and in the television serial. Essentially the conservatives yearn for a dominant cultural ethos while the post-Modernists relish what they consider to be the richness of cultural heterogeneity.

FURTHER READING

Few comprehensive surveys of thought and culture since 1945 exist. The most complete is Roland N. Stromberg, *After Everything: Western Intellectual History Since 1945* (1975). A good background for the period is provided by H. Stuart Hughes' *The Sea Change: The Migration of Social Thought, 1930–1965* (1975). The chapter on culture in Mary Fulbrook, ed., *Europe Since 1945* (2001), from the Short Oxford History of Europe series is very helpful.

Modernism and Post-Modernism can best be studied in Stromberg, Andreas Huyssen, *After the Grat Divide: Modernism, Mass Culture, Postmodernism* (1986); Christopher Butler, *After the Wake: An essay on the contemporary avant-garde* (1980); Hal Foster, (ed.) *The Anti-Aesthetic: Essays on Postmodern Culture* (1983); Jim Collins, *Uncommon Cultures: Popular Culture and Post-Modernism* (1989); and Charles Jencks, *What is Postmoderism?* (1987).

Numerous studies of specific philosophical movements exist. Those which I found helpful were Mary Warnock, *Existentialism* (1970); Walter Kaufman, *Existentialism from Dostoevsky to Sartre*; and Vincent Descombes, *Modern French Philosophy* (1980); Howard Gardner, *The Quest for Mind: Piaget, Levi-Strauss, and the Structuralist Movement* (Second edition, 1981); John Sturrock, (ed.), *Structuralism and Since: From Levi-Strauss to Derrida* (1979); Edith Kruzweil, *The Age of Structuralism* (1980); Jean Piaget, *Structuralism* (1970); and Claude Levi-Strauss, *Structural Anthropology* (1963). For Marxism in the post-war period 1 would recommend Raymond Aron, *Marxism and the Existentialists* (1967); Mark Poster, *Existential Marxism in Postwar France* (1975); and Maurice Cranston, *et al.*, *The New Left* (1971). Tony Judt's *Past Imperfect: French Intellectuals, 1944–1956* (1992) criticizes French intellectuals for their failure to oppose Stalinism. For French intellectual activity see Mark Lilla, ed., *New French Thought: Political Philosophy* (1994). A good example of the neo-rationalist critique of structuralism is Alain Finlelkraut, *The Defeat of the Mind* (1994).

The most up-to-date interpretations of literary trends can be found in the periodicals *Boundary 2, New Literary History*, and *Diacritics*. More comprehensive surveys include Gerald Graff, *Literature Against Itself: Literary Ideas in Modern Society* (1979); Leon S. Roudiez, *French Fiction Today: A New Direction* (1972); John Gatt–Rutter, *Writers and Politics in Modern Italy* (1979); Peter Demetz, *Post-war German Literature* (1970); Geoffrey Hoskins, *Beyond Socialist Realism: Soviet Fiction Since Ivan Denisovich* (1980); Deming Brown, *Soviet Russian*

Literature Since Stalin (1978); and Nicholas Rzhevsky, ed., *Cambridge Companion to Modern Russian Culture* (1998).

Good surveys of music are Paul Griffith, *Modern Music: The avant-gardé since 1945* (1981); Arnold Whittall, *Music Since the First World War* (1977); and Nicholas Cook and Anthony pople, eds, *The Cambridge History of Twentieth-Century Music* (2004).

There are a large number of cinema studies. Five surveys that are instructive are David A. Cook, *A History of Narrative Film* (1981); Gerald Mast, *A Short History of the Movies* (Third edition, 1981); William Jinks, *The Celluloid Literature* (1971); Eric Rhode, *A History of the Cinema: From its Origins to 1970* (1976); Roy Armes, *The Ambiguous Image: Narrative Style in Modern European Cinema* (1976); and *French Cinema* (1985); James Monaco, *The New Wave* (1976); and Pierre Leprohon, *The Italian Cinema* (1972). More recent works include Alan Williams, *Republic of Images: A History of French Filmmaking* (1992); Robert Phillip Kolker and Peter Beiken, *The Films of Wim Wenders* (1993); Pierre Sorlin, *European Cinemas, European Societies: 1939–1990* (1991); Dimitris Eleftheriotis, *Popular Cinemas of Europe: Studies of Texts, Contexts and Frameworks* (2001); and Barry Jordan and Rikki Morgan-Tamosunas, *Contemporary Spanish Cinema* (1998), which covers the post-Franco era.

For art and architecture I would recommend Gerald Woods, *Art Without Boundaries, 1950–1970* (1972); Edward Lucie–Smith, *Movements in Art Since 1945* (1969); Hilton Kramer, *The Age of the avant-gardé* (1973); Norbert Lynton, *The Story of Modern Art* (1980); and Michael Archer, *Art Since 1960* (1997).

Works on national cultures include Paul Julian Smith, *Contemporary Spanish Culture* (2003) and as references, the series of encyclopdedias published by Routledge such as *Encyclopedia of Contemporary French Culture* (2001); *Encyclopedia of Contemporary German Culture* (2001); and *Encyclopedia of Contemporary Italian Culture* (2002).

Popular culture and cultural studies is fast growing. A good introduction for students to this area is Dominic Strinati, *Understanding Popular Culture* (2004), which covers theory and various aspects of popular culture. For music in particular, see Ray Shuker, *Understanding Popular Music* (2001).

14 Europe Enters the Twenty-first Century

> Th[e] intellectual and spiritual basis of European civilization is the the product of thousands of years of history, of the intermingling of many traditions and of vast historical experience, both good and bad. The fall of communism has presented our continent with a unique opportunity to unite on that foundation and to become – for the first time in a very long time, if not in history – a stabilizing force in the world today.
>
> Václav Havel, address to the General Assembly of the Council of Europe in Vienna, 9 October 1993.

By the beginning of the twenty-first century Europeans could point with pride to many post-war achievements: the re-emergence of Europe as a powerful economic and cultural force, the growth of affluence, the rejection of authoritarian government in the South, greater independence in foreign affairs and the end of European overseas colonialism. But most important was the end of the Cold War and division of Europe. With the demise of Stalinism and Leninism and the end of Soviet rule, Eastern Europe and the successor states of the Soviet Union appeared headed for some more democratic form of government and a closer association with Western Europe.

Despite these obvious advances, Europeans had to face up to many enduring and new challenges: an increase in nationalist violence and cultural disillusionment that Vaclav Havel refers to as 'the post-Communist nightmare' the slow political and financial integration of Europe, a continuing inequality for women despite improvements, a need to better integrate ethnic minority groups, ecological threats to the environment and the fading of a distinctively European culture.

1989 and After

The massive popular upheavals of 1989 and Gorbachev's initiatives made it possible to begin the democratization of the former Eastern Bloc countries and to anticipate a long-term development of a 'common house of Europe', as Gorbachev termed it. Gorbachev claimed, 'Europe is indeed a common home where geography and history have closely interwoven the destinies of dozens of countries and nations.' Both for economic and political reasons, Gorbachev had hoped to tie the Soviet Union more closely to Western

Europe and weaken Europe's ties to the United States. Close co-operation with Western Europe might have provided the Soviet Union with the needed economic aid and technical expertise it required to modernize its economy and satisfy a historical Russian yearning to be a part of the European milieu. The once subjugated eastern European states openly rejected their former association with the Soviet Union. Instead, most of the former Comecon states joined either NATO or the European Union, in most cases, both.

Nationalism

Has there, in fact, been a resurgence of nationalism in Europe and thus a decline in the support for a united Europe? Some singled out the strengths of neo-fascist parties in the 1960s, the NPD in West Germany and the MSI in Italy, as proof of rising nationalism. However, the experience of the NPD suggests that its growth was transitory. After winning a number of local elections in West Germany in the 1960s, the NPD quickly lost most of its support. Despite predictions of continued victories, these extremists were never able to win a single seat in the West German parliament. The NPD appears at this writing to be no more significant than the traditional extreme rightist fringe represented by the German Party of the Right from 1946 to 1949 and by the Reich Social party. It seemed at one point in the mid-1990s that former East Germany might provide a future source of nationalism. A rather strident German nationalism appeared in the east as soon as the Communist dictatorship waned. But such nationalist sentiments passed, once eastern Germans began to feel the benefits of German unification and once the cultural-social gaps brought about by division began to diminish. In the early 1990s, the Italian neo-fascist MSI, which had languished for most of the post-war period with 6 or 7 per cent of the vote, experienced an increase in strength as witnessed by the 1994 elections. Echoes of Mussolini's strident nationalism could be heard in the rhetoric of some party leaders despite their claims of reform and commitment to democracy. Ten years later, the renamed National Alliance has been in government since 2001, and their behaviour has not matched earlier rhetoric.

It seems more accurate to say that nationalism in the West has not regained strength but has never been totally eliminated. The support for and opposition to a united Europe, though, does seem to have changed after 30 years of passive acceptance. Ever since the ratification of the Maastricht Treaties in the early 1990, it is probably more accurate to say that public opinion is developing a more complex identification with European integration as opposed to a simple 'for' or 'against'. Although de Gaulle never favoured a truly united Europe except insofar as it enhanced French prestige and power, other French leaders such as Monnet and Delors have been major architects of European unity. The British have always opposed a political unification but have sought further expansion of the Single Market.

The declining support for European unification in the 1970s was more closely tied to economic phenomena. The energy crisis brought about by the cutback in Arab oil production led each country to seek its own solution to the shortages. Countries also had specific concerns concerning a 'deepening' of the economic contacts. Italy was unsure of its industry's ability to compete with those of Germany and France in a customs-free European community, and many British leaders still were anxious about a complete economic integration in the European Commission. Many French farmers opposed Spanish entry, since lower-cost Spanish agricultural products threatened heavily subsidized French agriculture.

In the 1980s and 1990s, increasing foreign competition and the imaginative policies of Delors, the president of the European Commission of the EU, overcame much of the opposition to further integration. In the early years of the new century, however, the dominance of the Franco–German tandem had ebbed. A new generation of political leaders in the west, bereft of the experiences that led to initial support for European integration, have publicly professed a more self-interested policy towards the European integration process, most vividly expressed in the Brussels summit of June 2005. Some of the new Eastern European leaders see this as a national egotism.

In Eastern Europe, nationalism was only temporarily silenced by Soviet might. It appears that eastern Europeans publicly acknowledged the brotherhood of all Communist states but privately harboured many pre-Second World War attitudes. Once the Soviet lid was lifted, earlier nationalistic and anti-semitic attitudes reemerged, most virulently in the former Yugoslavia. These accentuated attitudes may result from a long suppressed population's desire to express its individuality and to reject all those who appear to limit or reject a new-found patriotism. As Vaclav Havel wrote 'nations are now remembering their ancient achievements and their ancient suffering, their ancient suppressors and their allies, their ancient statehood and their former borders, their traditional animosities and affinities – in short, they are suddenly recalling a history that, until recently, had been carefully concealed or misrepresented.'

Loss of European Distinctiveness

The unprecedented material rewards of the new Europe have undermined unique European life-styles. Some Europeans speak of a decline of French-ness, or German-ness, and a rise of materialism they equate with the American way of life. Increasingly, Europeans have discussed measures to preserve the European quality of life. At the same time, other Europeans recommend that Europe adopt many American economic and business practices in order to be able to compete with American companies. One example of remaking European economies to more resemble the American has been the selling off of state-owned industries to private shareholders. The Competition Policy of the EU is premised on the principles of reining in state aid for industries.

Even a casual observer can note the American influence on Europe's languages in newspapers and on television. But, there is a distinct difference from country to country in the extent of the use of English. As might be expected,

McDonald's restaurant in the Champs-Élysées, Paris.
(© Empics)

in France the inroads are relatively slight. An attempt was even made in 1994 by the conservative French culture minister to ban English from all commercial broadcasting, though this was eventually found to be unconstitutional. European elites also oppose the overwhelming influence of American films: 88 per cent of the world's most attended films in 1993 were American. It is going to be difficult for Europeans to avoid the cultural homogeneity that is a byproduct of economic affluence and the close economic ties among European nations and between Europe and the United States. Europeans now have their own fast-food cafes – McDonald's restaurants are a common sight – and European youth are not only attracted by American music, films, TV shows and fashions but have developed their own Euro-versions. The presence of Euro–Disney near Paris only reinforces the symbolic presence of American commercial entertainment culture in Europe. Alain Finkelkraut commented that Euro–Disney was 'A terrifying giant step toward world homogenization.' But Richard Kuisel has suggested in *Seducing the French: The Dilemma of Americanization* (1993) that Europeans are really reacting to the inevitable consequences of their own post-war cultural-social revolution. The noted French philosopher Jean Baudrillard observed that 'America is the original version of modernity. We are the dubbed or subtitled version.'

The loss of distinctiveness may be manifesting itself in other forms, though. Immigration has become an issue, and not only a mobilizing theme for far-right parties. Asylum seekers, refugees, economic migrants, all of these terms have become politically charged since the late 1990s. Here is where common policies agreed at the European level can go quite a way towards making sure that more extreme national policies do not result in a Fortress Europe. Immigrants from Muslim countries, many of whom have lived in France, or Britain, or Spain for decades, now feel as if they are again strangers. Certainly the bombing of the World Trade Towers in September 2001, the Madrid trains of 2003 or London Tube in 2005 goes some way to understanding these sentiments.

On the other hand, Europeans no longer feel inferior, as they did in the 1950s, when American economic and technical superiority was unquestioned. Now Europeans believe they have caught-up if not surpassed the United States in technology and economic well-being. Europeans pointed to the technical inferiority of some American products in the 1980s, especially automobiles, with undisguised pride. As a Frenchman told Anthony Sampson in 1983, 'I remember when I first went to America 30 years ago. Everything looked bigger, newer, faster. Now, everything looks shabbier and older than here.' This new-found pride should also lead Europeans to be less dependent on the United States as is already evident in many European economic and foreign policy initiatives. The new, unified Germany had undoubtedly begun to play an important role in this development of Europe's place in the world as it mediates the fusion of both halves of Europe. It is perhaps now more proper to view both Europe and America as in the forefront of the Westernization of the world. Many of those in the forefront of change in Eastern Europe wish to obtain the benefits of Western economic advances. Opinion polls throughout Eastern Europe shortly before the fall of Communism found that West Germany was the most popular economic model rather than more socially egalitarian Sweden.

Looking to the Future

The end of the Cold War has reduced Europeans fear of war, especially a nuclear war, and opened the way for Europe to reallocate its resources to deal with many pressing domestic problems. For example, resources could be shifted to ecological problems. Since the 1980s elections throughout Europe have brought an increase in the Green or ecological representation in legislatures. Environment ministries are now common in most European states, and recent scientific warnings concerning global warming and a looming oil scarcity means more governmental effort towards environmental issues. Another important issue will be achieving economic equality and greater political representation for women. The advances made by women in Scandinavian countries, provides a model for the rest of Europe and the world. The forging of European integration in the social dimension makes it possible to attack ecological, gender, and other problems on an all-European scale. Still, integration brings constraints on the freedom of governments to respond to national problems, especially in the area of economic policy as the Maastricht Treaties imposed limits on public debt. The European integration process itself is in doubt, both in terms of deepening – due to the-crisis over the European Constitution – and widening – although Turkey has now opened accession negotiation, its potential membership remains a contested issue in many European capitals. The modern welfare state, one of Western Europe's greatest achievements, also seems sure to be rethought as Europe opens up more and more to global trends and competition. A good portion of the anti-globalization movement's critique rests on the perceived threat by liberalization to the high standards in social protection and public services that the welfare state maintains.

Barring a return to authoritarian governments in Russia, Europe's future, though more complex due to new issues and challenges, continues to remain bright. The apparent success of the Orange Revolution in Ukraine, and the Rose Revolution in Georgia, suggest that the last big hold-out in terms of political democracy – Belarus – should have its days numbered.

Index

acquis communitaire, 137
African independence movement, 93–8
 and French territories, 97–8
 Nigerian nationalist movement, 96
 Tanzania state, formation of, 97
Algerian independence, 69, 95
Amsterdam Treaty, 135
Anglo-American zones, 19
Anglo-Soviet Treaty of Alliance, of May 1942, 5
Anti-Comintern Pact, of 1939, 39
Austria, post-war period
 industrial planning, 52
 political affairs, 75
automobile industry, post-war period
 in Europe, 49
 in Germany, 56
 in Great Britain, 57
 in Italy, 58
average wages, in countries, 143

Bad Godesberg party conference, in 1959, 65
Basic Treaty of November 1972, 231
Battle of Tegeler Weg, 198
Benelux countries, post-war period political
 affairs, 74–5
Berlin blockade, 17–19
Beveridge report, 28
Bidonvilles, 149
Big Three meetings, 6–11
Bloody Sunday, 297
Bolshevik Revolution, of 1917, 80
Boxer Rebellion, in 1900, 84
British foreign policy, 3
British massacre, of Indians in 1919, 83
British ruling class education, 164–5
British working class families, 160
Bulgarization campaign, 238–9
Bulletin of Labour Statistics of the International
 Labour Office, report of, 152
Burgerinitiativen, 212

Campaign for Nuclear Disarmament, 72
'Carnation Revolution', 253

'Celtic tiger', 142
Chechnya war, see Soviet Union, phase changes
 since 1968, Gorbachev phenomenon
Christian Democratic parties, 28
Churchill, Winston, 5, 7, 10, 13, 28, 31, 71,
 83, 121
 –Stalin agreements, on Greece, 42
'city academies', 295
CLN, see Committee for National Liberation
CLNAI, see Committee for National Liberation for
 Northern Italy
CND, see Campaign for Nuclear Disarmament
Coal and Steel Community, the, 47
Cold War, 21–2, 35, 123, 259
Comecon, 178, 216, see polycentrism
Committee for National Liberation, 36
 for Northern Italy, 36
Common Agricultural Policy, the, 47, 128
Common Foreign and Security Policy, 133
Common Market, 47, 53–4, 129
Commonwealth Immigrants Act, of 1962, 99
Communist Information Bureau, 15
Communist International, 15
communist party, post-war period, see also Eastern
 Europe, post-war period
 during Chinese nationalist movement, 84–6
 in Italy, 61–3
 Polish anti movement, 107–8
 in Romania, 114–15
 under Stalin, 103
 during Vietnamese independence movement,
 86–8
 in West Germany, 63–6
Constitutional Treaty, 137
culturally innovative trends, post-world war
 art and architecture, 324–7
 cinema, 320–4
 literature, 314–19
 music, 327–8
 philosophy, 310–13
 popular culture and media, 328–9
'Czechoslovak experiment', 207
Czechoslovakia, unrest in, 205–9

Eastern Europe, phase changes since 1968, 216–18
  Bulgaria, 236–9
  Czechoslovakia, 233–6
  East Germany, 231–3
  Hungary, 228–31
  Poland, 224–8
  Romania, 239–241
  transition of, 246–9
  Yugoslavia, 241–6
Eastern Europe, post-war period
  agricultural production, 182–3
  changes in education, 189–190
  and elite class, 190–1
  pluralist societies, 191–3
  social structure, 188–9
  standard of living, 186–7
  status of women, 187–8
  worker status, 187
Eastern Europe economic modernization, 177–181
East European filmmaking, 322–3
East-West relations, during second world war, 5–6
economic 'miracle,' 231
elite class, post-war period, *see* European society,
    post-war period
embourgeoisement, 158, 160
EMOS, 243
EPU, *see* European Payments Union
Europe, post-war period
  1989 and after, 332–3
  and automobile industry, 49
  demographic changes, 48–9
  economic recovery, characteristics of, 45–6
  European life-styles, 334–6
  future of, 336–7
  nationalism, 333–4
  post-war development patterns, 58–9
European Coal and Steel community, *see*
    European integration process
European countries, political transition in
  Austria, 303–4
  Belgium, 298–300
  Luxembourg, 298–300
  the Netherlands, 298–300
  Scandanavia, 301–3
European Defence Community, *see* European
    integration process
European Economic Community, *see* agricultural
    production, 182–3
European Free Trade Association, 73, 126
European Industrial Relations Observatory, 155
European integration process
  beginnings of unity, 121–2
  council of Europe, 122–3
  defense community, 124–5
  economic community, 125–132

expansion of European union, 134–7
re-launch of European union, 132–4
steel community, 123–4
'European model of society', 139
European Payments Union, 47, 123
European society, post-war period
  class structure, 140–2
  elite class, 161–2
  elite education, 164–7
  labour strikes, 154–7
  plutocrats, 167–9
  political attitudes and social class, 169–71
  social levelling, 158–61
  standard of living, 150–2
  status of immigrant labourers, 148–150
  status of women, 144–8
  wage structure, 142–4
  working conditions, 152–4
existentialism, 310–11

'fifth columns', 13
Fouchet Plan of 1961, 131, 199
foundation hospitals, 295
France, post-war period, 31–6
  demographic changes, 48–9
  economic development, 54–5
  industrial planning, 52
  national independence movement, 98–9
  political affairs, 66–71
  political transitions, 272–8
  student unrest (*see* student riots, in France)
Franco, 39
freedom fighters
  Gandhi, Mahatma, 82–3
  Ho Chi Minh, 82
  Mao Zedong, 82, 84–6
  Nehru, Jawaharlal, 81–2, 84
  Nkrumah, Kwame, 81–2, 95–6
  Sukarno, Achmed, 82, 88–9
Free French movement, 31
French Communist party, 34
French elections, 1945–46, 34
French politics, normalization of, 272
French ruling class education, 165–6

Gasperi, De, 37–8, 121
Gaulle, General Charles de, 31–3, 36, 55, 68–71,
    97, 126–8, 272–4, *see also* France, post-war
    period, political transitions
  and general strike in France, *see* student riots,
    in France
  veto of British entry, into Common
    Market, 72
G-7 countries, 274
German 'Autumn' of 1977, 211

German centre, collapse of, 1
German filmmakers, 321–2
German occupation (1941–44), 42
German reparations, post war, 8–11
German ruling class education, 166–7
Germany, industrial production of, 11–12
  and German Banks, 55–6
Germany, post-war period
  and automobile industry, 56
  demographic changes, 48–9
  economic planning, 51
  foreign trade, 47
  legacies of 1968, 210–11
  before unification, 265–8
  united Germany, 268–272
Glasnost, 220
Gorbachev phenomenon, *see* Soviet Union, phase
  changes since 1968
Goulash Communism', 218
Government of India Act, 83
Great Britain, post-war period
  and automobile industry, 57
  conservative party, defeat of, 28–9
  economic decline, 56–7
  economic planning, 51
  economic recovery, 30–1
  Labour program, economic and political
    programs of, 29
  National Health Service Act, 30
  national independence movement, 98–9
  National Insurance Act, 29–30
  and Nationalization, 57
  and Parliament Act of 1911, 29
  political affairs, 71–3
  political transitions, 288–297
Greece, post-war period, 42, *see also*
  Southern Europe and authoritarian
  government
Greek Civil War, in 1944, 7
green movement
  in France, 212–13
  in Germany, 212
gross domestic products
  of countries during 1949–63, 47
  of countries during 2005, 142
gross national product, of countries, 180
guerrilla warfare, 42

hard-currency debt
  of East European states, 179
  of Soviet Union, 179
Hitler, Adolf, 2, 12, 39, 121
Housing Act of 1950, 55
Hungarian revolution, 108–11

ideological contamination, 4
immigrant labourers, in Europe post-war period,
  see European society, post-war period
India Independence Bill, 84
Indochina war, 35
industrial production, during interwar years
  in Europe, 2
  in US, 2
Investment Aid Act, 55
iron curtain, fall of, 12–5
Italy, post-war period, 36–9
  and automobile industry, 58
  economic development, 58
  foreign trade, 47
  industrial planning, 52
  legacies of 1968, 210
  political affairs in, 61–3
  political transitions, 278–86

Jewish immigration, 90
Johnnine revolution, 286

Kennedy Round of tariff negotiations, 127
Keynesian economics and economic
  planning, 50
Khrushchev
  decentralization policy of, 174–5
  fall from power, 115–17
  leadership of, 106
Kuomintang, 85

labour strikes, *see also* European society, post-war
  period
  in France, 202–4
League of Communists, 106
left popularity
  in Austria, 43
  in Belgium, 42
  in Denmark, 42
  in Greece, 42
  in Luxembourg, 43
  in Netherlands, 43
  in Norway, 43
  in Sweden, 43
  in Switzerland, 43
living standard, in Europe post-war period, *see*
  European society, post-war period
London Six-Power Conference, 17

Maastricht Treaty, 134
Marshall Plan, 12–17, 36, 41–3, 122
  recovery aid, to Western Europe, 46–7
Marxism, 312–13
Mater et Magistra, 286

Middle East, national independence movements in
Arab-Israeli conflict, 90–1
Suez crisis, 91–3
modern capitalism, 50
Monnet Plan, 51
Morgenthau Plan, 9
Morroco, independence of, *see* African
independence movement
Mouvement Republicain Populaire, 33
MRP, *see* Mouvement Republicain Populaire

Nanterre protests, *see* student riots, in France
national independence movements
in Africa, 93–8
in Britain, 98–9
in China, 84–6
France, 98–9
in India, 82–4
in Indonesian, 88–9
in Middle East, 89–93
stages in, 81–2
in Vietnam, 86–8
National Syndicalists, 40
NATO, *see* North Atlantic Treaty Organization
Nazi–Soviet Non-aggression pact, 5
neo-capitalism, *see* modern capitalism
neorealism, 320
Netherlands, post-war period
foreign trade, 47
New west German State, 19
Nice summit, 135–6
Nice Treaty, 136
North Atlantic Treaty Organization, 19
Northern Alliance Treaty Organization,
259–62, 277
Northern Ireland, conflict in, 297–8, *see also* Great
Britain, post-war period, political transition
novoe myshlenie, 220

OEEC, *see* Organization for European Economic
Co-operation
Organization for European Economic
Co-operation, 21, 122
Ostpolitik, 129

Pact for Italy, 284
partitocrazia, 283
PCF, *see* French Communist party
perestroika, 220
Petöfi Circle, 109–110
Pim Fortuyn List, 300
PME, 54
Poland, post-war period, *see* Eastern Europe,
post-war period

Polish–German border issues, 10
Polish October, 106–8
political affairs, post-war period
in Austria, 75
in Benelux countries, 74–5
economic factors, role of, 76–7
in France, 66–71
in Great Britain, 71–3
in Italy, 61–3
legacies of 1968, 210–13
in Scandinavian countries, 73–4
in Southern Europe, 75–6
in West Germany, 63–6
'poll tax', 292
polycentrism
and Council for Mutual Economic Assistance
and Economic Nationalism, 115
dogmatism in China, 113–14
national communism in Romania, 114–15
revisionism in Yugoslavia, 112–13
Portugal, post-war period, 40–1, *see also*
Southern Europe and authoritarian
government
post-modernist filmmaking, 324
post second world war developments
allied ostracism, 39
and Big Three meetings, 6–11
Cold War, 15–21
development patterns, in Europe, 58–9
east–west relations, 5–6
end of war, 21–2
and German economy, 11–12
and Great Britain, 3
iron curtain, fall of, 12–15
Soviet union, domination of, 3–5
superpower, emergence of, 1–3
Potsdam conference, *see* Big Three meetings
Poujadist movement, 54
Prague Spring, 233, *see also* Czechoslovakia,
unrest in
Proporz, 303

Quebec Conference, in September 1944, 8–9
Quit India Resolution, in India, 84

Rally of the French People, 36
Red Belt' of Emilia-Romagna, 279
Red-Green coalition, 212, 271
Reparations Commissions, *see* Yalta declaration
revenue minimum d'insertion, 276
Rome Treaties, of 1957, 126
Roosevelt, Franklin D., 5, 8, 10, 31
RPF, *see* Rally of the French People
Russo-Japanese War, of 1905, 80

Salazar, Antonio de Oliveira, 40
Scandinavia, post-war period political affairs, 73–4
Scandinavian ruling class education, 167
Schengen Agreement of 1990, 149
secret police (NKVD), 103
'Segni referendum', 283
servizi d'ordine, 210
Single European Act, 132
small European countries, post-war period
  Austria, 41
  Belgium, 41
  Finland, 41
  Holland, 41
  Norway, 41
  Sweden, 41
Solidarity union movement, *see* Eastern Europe, phase changes since 1968, Poland
Sorbonne protests, *see* student riots, in France
Southern Europe, post-war period political affairs, 75–6
Southern Europe and authoritarian government
  Greece, 257–9
  Portugal, 253–5
  Spain, 255–7
Soviet Union, phase changes since 1968, 216–18
  Brezhnev years, 218–20
  Gorbachev phenomenon, 220–4
Soviet Union, post-war period
  agricultural problems, 181–2
  economic policy of Gorbazhev, 175–7
  economic policy of Kosygin and Brezhnev, 175–7
  economy, 104, 174
  society, 103–4
  standard of living, 184–6
Soviet Union, post-world war, 3–4
Soviet Union control, of Eastern Europe, 6
Sovnarkhozy, 111
Spain, post-war period, 39–40, *see also* Southern Europe and authoritarian government
  post-war allied ostracism, 39
Spanish Civil War, in 1939, 39–40
Stalin, Josef, 3–5, 7–8, 17, 42
  post-war Soviet Union economy under, 104
  post-war Soviet Union society under, 103–4
  and Soviet Union control, of Eastern Europe, 6–7
  successor of, 104–6
Stalinism, 4, *see* Stalin, Josef
Stalin–Tito rift, in 1948, 42
Stammheim trial, 211
St Malo Agreement, 278

Strategic Arms Limitation Talks, 218–19
structuralism, 311–12
student riots
  in France, *see* student riots, in France
  in Germany, 197–8
  in Italy, 197–8
student riots, in France
  de Gaulle's counterattack, 204–5
  events at Nanterre, 199–200
  events at Sorbonne, 200–2
  general strike, 202–4
Suez crisis, 91–3, 125
superpowers, emergence of, 1–3
Sweden, post-war period economic planning, 51

Teheran conference, *See* Big Three meetings
the 'Iron Lady', 290
The Two Thousand Words' manifesto, 207
Tripartism, 35–6
Truman Doctrine, 12–17, 30, 42

United States
  aid to Europe, 46–7
  challenges to, post-world war, 21–2
  emergence as super power, 1–3
  industrial production, in interwar years, 2
  military dominance in Europe, 19–21
  policy of containment of communism, 4, 11

Vatican, 286–8, *see also* Italy, post-war period, political transitions
velvet divorce, *see* Eastern Europe, phase changes since 1968, Czechoslovakia
velvet resolution, *see* Eastern Europe, phase changes since 1968, Czechoslovakia
Vichy collaborators, purge of, 31
'victims of unification', 270

Warsaw Pact, 207, 216, 218, 239, 259
Western Europe, economic recovery of
  agricultural developments, 52–3
  characteristics of, 45–6
  and demographic changes, 48–9
  foreign trade stimulus, 47–8
  industrial concentration, 51–2
  by Marshall plan, 46–7
  and nationalization, 51–2
  and new capitalism, 49–51
Western Europe, since 1960
  end of authoritarian government, 253–9
  European problem, 262–4
  foreign policy independence, 259–62
West Germany, 264–72

West Germany, post-war period
  economic development of, 55–6
  political affairs, 63–6
women
  earnings percentage, 146
  labour force share, 145
  percentage of legislative seats, 147
  status in government office, 147
working population, 140–1

Yalta decisions, *see* Big Three meetings
Yalta declaration, 7–9
Yugoslavia, *see also* Eastern Europe, post-war
      period
  ostracism in, 4
  revisionism in, 112–13
  self-management system of, 178, 242–3

Zhdanov era, 103